New developments in applied general equilibrium analysis

New developments in
applied general equilibrium analysis

Edited by

JOHN PIGGOTT
Australian National University

and

JOHN WHALLEY
University of Western Ontario

CAMBRIDGE UNIVERSITY PRESS

Cambridge

London   New York   New Rochelle

Melbourne   Sydney

CAMBRIDGE UNIVERSITY PRESS
Cambridge, New York, Melbourne, Madrid, Cape Town, Singapore, São Paulo

Cambridge University Press
The Edinburgh.Building, Cambridge CB2 8RU, UK

Published in the United States of America by Cambridge University Press, New York

www.cambridge.org
Information on this title: www.cambridge.org/9780521309295

© Cambridge University Press 1985

First published 1985
This digitally printed version 2008

A catalogue record for this publication is available from the British Library

Library of Congress Cataloguing in Publication data
Main entry under title:
New developments in applied general equilibrium
analysis.
Based on a conference on numerical micro-models,
held Aug. 1983 at the Australian National University,
Canberra.
1. Equilibrium (Economics)—Congresses.   I. Piggott,
John.   II. Whalley, John.
HB145.N46   1985   339.5   85-11300

ISBN 978-0-521-30929-5 hardback
ISBN 978-0-521-07468-1 paperback

TABLE OF CONTENTS

Tax Applications (continued)

Preface and Acknowledgements

This collection of papers had its origins in a conference on numerical micro-models which was held in August 1983 at the Australian National University, Canberra. It comprises a selection of the papers presented there, together with a number of additional contributions which were solicited or offered later. One of the aims of the conference was to bring together individuals with a diversity of views who had worked on a wide range of applications, and this orientation is reflected in the range of the papers appearing here. As a whole they represent important recent advances in applied general equilibrium, broadly defined.

Our biggest debt is to Adrian Pagan who supported the idea of the conference from its inception in 1981. He was active in helping to organize the conference and offered much valuable advice and many useful suggestions. We would also like to thank Cathy Baird of the Centre for Economic Policy Research, Australian National University, for her enthusiastic and able administration and Barb Ross, of the University of Western Ontario, for her organisational support. Financial support was forthcoming from the Centre for Economic Policy Research and the faculty of Economics, Australian National University; the Industries Assistance Commission, Canberra; the Reserve Bank of Australia; and the IMPACT Project, Melbourne. We are grateful to the individuals in these organisations who supported the conference in such an essential way. A number of people, some of whom did not participate in the conference, agreed to referee papers for the volume, and we are indebted to them.

In producing this book, a serious attempt has been made to minimise delay in making the contributions collected here generally available. By and large, the papers in the volume report research commenced since the beginning of 1983 and in some cases first drafts were not available until mid-1984. Finally, therefore, we would like to thank Colin Day and Cambridge University Press for expediting the publication process.

John Piggott

John Whalley

December 1984

Mathew BUTLIN, Australian Treasury, Canberra

Rob BUTTERWORTH, Industries Assistance Commission, Canberra

Tony CHISHOLM, Australian National University

Ken CLEMENTS, University of Western Australia

Larry COOK, Monash University

Russel COOPER, Macquarie University

Richard CORNES, Australian National University

Erwin DIEWERT, University of British Columbia

Richard FILMER, Industries Assistance Commission, Canberra

Larry GOULDER, Harvard University

Paul GRETTON, Industries Assistance Commission, Canberra

Phil HAGEN, Industries Assistance Commission, Canberra

Glenn HARRISON, University of Western Ontario

Hasan IMAM, Wilfrid Laurier University

John JAMES, University of Virginia

Dale JORGENSON, Harvard University

Larry KIMBELL, University of California

Nico KLIJN, Industries Assistance Commission, Canberra

Peter LLOYD, Australian National University

George MAILATH, Reserve Bank of Australia

Keith MCLAREN, Monash University

Will MARTIN, Bureau of Agricultural Economics, Canberra

Tony MEAGHER, La Trobe University

Frank MILNE, Australian National University

Knud MUNK, Aarhus University

Brian PARMENTER, La Trobe University

Adrian PAGAN, Australian National University

John PIGGOTT, Australian National University

Jonathan PINCUS, Australian National University and Monash University

Alan POWELL, University of Melbourne

Albert SCHWEINBERGER, Australian National University

Joel SLEMROD, University of Minnesota

John SPENCER, New University of Ulster

John SUTTON, Industries Assistance Commission, Canberra

Ron TILLACK, Industries Assistance Commission, Canberra

Rodney TYERS, Australian National University

David VINCENT, Industries Assistance Commission, Canberra

Alan WOODLAND, University of Sydney

INTRODUCTION

John R. Piggott
The Australian National University

Background to the Field

Over the last 10 years, applied general equilibrium (AGE) modelling has become a rapidly expanding field of research. Its focus is to develop techniques to facilitate economy wide quantitative assessment of allocative and distributional policy issues. AGE models do not claim a forecasting role, but they do aim to provide numerical guidance to policy makers on the economic impacts of alternative policy options. In this broad sense research on AGE models may be seen as complementary and analogous to the development of macro econometric models to investigate questions of stabilisation policy. AGE modelling is now being undertaken by applied economists in government and semi-public organisations, and more and more academic economists are being drawn into various aspects of the research field.

The scene had been set for this explosion of activity by the seminal research of Scarf, Shoven and Whalley. Scarf's discovery of numerical solution techniques for Walrasian models[1] provided the basis for constructing the first AGE models in the early 70s. Early methodological issues raised in applying these techniques to policy issues were addressed by Shoven and Whalley in a series of papers,[2] and by the mid 70s output from early economy-wide models (eg. Whalley (1975), Miller and Spencer (1977)) were beginning to appear. At this stage feasibility of construction and solution had been demonstrated, at least for relatively small scale models.

Over the following few years, there was a rapid spread of applications of these "first generation" AGE models with a steady increase in sophistication. The early efforts mentioned above were soon joined by models of the EEC (Whalley, 1976), the UK (Piggott and Whalley, 1977), the US (Fullerton et al., 1978), Australia (Piggott, 1980), and Mexico

1

(Serra-Puche, 1981).

Research on economy wide multi-sectoral models was being
carried out by other groups as well. In Australia, the ORANI model (Dixon
et al, 1982) was being developed with the co-operation of a number of
government agencies with the explicit intention of application to policy
reform proposals. At the World Bank, AGE models were also being developed
(see Dervis et al, 1982). These models shared with the Scarf-Shoven-
Whalley tradition the same concern to quantitatively address microeconomic
policy issues on an economy wide basis. Their theoretical basis, however,
was somewhat different. Models of the Scraf-Shoven-Whalley type were
"strictly" Walrasian. In contrast, for example, the ORANI model (represented in this volume) separates demand from income in its typical mode.
This treatment allows macroeconomic issues to be addressed (through the
exogenous adjustment of aggregate demand) in the context of a model with
many production sectors, but quite explicitly abandons any notion of an
Arrow-Debreu theoretical underpinning. Broadly, these various research
programmes and the individuals identified with them combined to give the
field of AGE modelling the critical mass necessary for its continued
expansion.

A further important factor in accounting for the scale of
research activity in AGE modelling is that microeconomic policy issues
began to receive an increasing amount of attention in the 70s. Since
many of these issues - for example, trade policy and tax policy - are
quite widespread in their impact on the economy, AGE models were seen as
especially appropriate for investigating the effects of reform proposals.
This led to the adoption and development of AGE models by government
bureaucracies and international organisations. In addition to the World
Bank research mentioned above, the GEMTAP model of the US economy was
developed in association with the US Treasury, and ORANI was completely
integrated with various Australian government departments. The
integration of AGE models into policy environments was also facilitated
by the discovery of a variety of reliable short-cut solution algorithms.

At the beginning of the 80s, then, AGE models had been
developed to the point where, for the analysis of tax and trade issues,
they were being used as an input into the policy formulation process.
Research had also begun to extend to applications beyond these two areas
of policy intervention: price rigidities and the incorporation of public
goods were two new areas where computational feasibility had been

demonstrated. This picture of the state of the art is captured in a
previous volume of conference papers on this topic edited by Scarf and
Shoven.[3] The 1981 NBER San Diego conference on which that book is based
could be characterised as establishing that AGE models had come of age;
they were feasible to construct and use, and there was a solid core of
researchers engaged in the task of building and analysing them.

NEW DEVELOPMENTS IN THE 80s

As the titles of the papers in this volume indicate, the major
focus of research has moved on from the preoccupation with feasibility
which was evident at the San Diego conference. As with that conference,
papers in this volume reflect the great variety of problems that are
being approached using AGE analysis and the equally varied levels of
rigour and sophistication used by different practitioners. But now that
feasibility is no longer in dispute, attention is being paid to methodological and interpretative problems, as well as to some of the less
tractable forms of micro-policy intervention. The papers in the volume
reflect this. They are arranged in groups which reflect their areas of
application with some papers included in the first "methodology" section.

Recent developments in AGE modelling can be divided into two
categories. Firstly, much effort has been directed at a more satisfactory
modelling of a wider range of policy issues. The analysis of policies in
the context of multiple jurisdictions has been greatly expanded - every
trade application in the volume examines customs union type issues in one
way or another. Even more notable is the effort that has been devoted to
the modelling of price rigidities.

Secondly, some of the methodological and interpretative
problems which have been raised (and in some degree finessed) in earlier
applications are now receiving explicit attention. The impact of
alternative model closures on the results of policy application is an
important problem area of this type. A number of the papers address
various aspects of this issue. Problems associated with specification
and parameterisation procedures typically used in the empirical implementation of AGE models also receive attention from a number of authors.
Finally, the interpretation of results from models is treated in detail
in two of the papers.

1. Methodological Issues

John Whalley's paper on "Methodological Challenges" may be
thought of as the second part of the introduction, and will therefore not
be discussed here at any length. Briefly, the paper relates some of the
major themes of the AGE literature to the development of the discipline
generally. Whalley links some of the more recent modelling literature
with the 1930s debate on central planning associated with Hayek, Robbins
and Lange. He points out that central planning and AGE type policy
evaluation in modern mixed economies are closely related activities, and
draws parallels between the doubts expressed by Robbins about the feasibility of centralised calculations of Pareto optimal calculations for planning, and specification problems arising with modern AGE analysis. Finally
he stresses the contribution AGE models can make by analysing the
perceptions which underlie and drive much policy, while noting the
subjective judgment inherent in the construction and use of AGE models.

The second paper under "Methodology" is Erwin Diewert's study
of the measurement of waste and welfare in AGE models. For many uses of
these models, their major results are estimates of welfare cost. Until
now, however, no paper was available which treated the waste measurement
literature with AGE applications in mind. The paper uses a model of the
small open economy to illustrate alternative measurement concepts.

Diewert identifies two types of measures. In Sections 3-5,
he focuses on a quantity oriented approach to the measurement of waste in
the tradition of Debreu's (1951) coefficient of resource utilisation.
Diewert defines the Allais-Debreu (AD) measure, provides a second-order
approximation and derives an analytical approach to sensitivity testing.
Section 6 sets out the alternative price oriented measure of Hicks and
Boiteux (HB). This is the same as the sum of the Hicksian equivalent
variations, calculated from a comparison of the tax distorted equilibrium
and an arbitrary reference Pareto optimal equilibrium, at Pareto prices.
The problem that the HB approach naturally poses is the selection of the
reference Pareto equilibrium. In Section 7, Diewert appeals to the
literature on fair and equitable allocations to suggest an answer to this
question.

The HB measure (the sum of equivalent variations) can be
thought of as the difference between the values of a utilitarian social
welfare function in the two equilibria being compared. This observation
motivates Sections 8 and 9, which examine the properties of various social

welfare functions. Section 10 offers a means of decomposing social
welfare losses into "efficiency" and "equity" components. Finally in
Section 11, the possibility of non-uniqueness among "fair" Pareto optimal
allocations is considered.

Diewert emphasises the element of arbitrariness in both
approaches, and that these loss measures are unlikely to give the same
answer under normal circumstances. He concludes by noting that the AD
measure has the advantage that it is a pure efficiency measure and that
it does not require a selection of the economy's best allocation.

The paper by Adrian Pagan and John Shannon provides the first
systematic theoretical treatment of sensitivity analysis used by AGE
modellers. They point out that over the last decade or so, AGE models
have reached a stage where they are receiving considerable attention from
policy makers. This has motivated increasing concern about the question
of sensitivity, and in particular, the criticism that AGE models have
embodied in them particular values for various key elasticity parameters.
Thus far, researchers have attempted to deal with this problem by using
recalibration strategies, such as changing parameters thought on some
a priori basis to be especially important for the problem at hand. Pagan
and Shannon argue that such recalibration strategies can only provide a
very partial account of sensitivity. Users can neither be sure that the
parameters selected are the important ones nor that the combination of
values considered are not biassed towards a particular outcome. They
suggest that a much more comprehensive approach to sensitivity analysis
is needed, and their paper is designed to provide such an approach.

The substantive part of their paper begins by pointing out
that the approach to sensitivity should vary with the requirements of
individual researchers and the available information. They suggest two
approaches to "overall sensitivity": a mean-variance approach and an
extreme-bounds approach.

It is easiest to understand their analysis by assuming a
model which can be written as $z = z(\theta)$, where θ is a vector of unknown
parameters, estimated by a vector $\hat{\theta}$. The most important conclusion of
the mean-variance approach is that the expected value of z need not
equal the value of z implied by the expected value of θ. This result,
which has not been generally appreciated until very recently in the AGE
literature, is also emphasised by Harrison and Kimbell in their paper
later in this volume. We will return to this point there.

An alternative approach suggested by Pagan and Shannon is to apply sensitivity analysis to the determination of extreme bounds for z. In this formulation, the problem is to find the maximal variation in z given that the parameters θ are constrained to be selected from a given confidence interval, assuming that $\hat{\theta}$ is distributed normally. They show that for simple cases, the variations in θ required to establish this maximal variation for a high confidence interval (say 95%) can be very dramatic unless the t-statistics on the estimated parameters are very high.

Pagan and Shannon then turn their attention to the selection of individual parameters in the model. Using the extreme bounds approach, they show, not surprisingly, that sensitivity depends on the size of the elasticity of z with respect of Θ. Their analysis in the context of individual parameters reinforces their earlier suggestion that to achieve acceptable confidence levels, variations in Θ may often have to be large. In the case where Θ is a single coefficient, estimated with a t-statistic of 2, a 100% variation in Θ is required for a confidence interval of 95%. While variations of this order of magnitude have in fact been carried out in AGE policy applications, the results of such exercises have been widely interpreted as overstating the variation in the exogenous variables. The Pagan-Shannon analysis shows that it may be necessary to reassess this interpretation.

All the alternatives to systematic sensitivity analysis proposed by Pagan and Shannon depend upon various derivatives of z. With linearised AGE models, the value of such derivatives are easy to calculate. The authors show, both analytically and with a numerical example, that

(a) elasticities will vary with the experiment: it is never possible to conclude that a coefficient is always a crucial one, only that it is crucial for a particular policy change in a particular structural frame-work;

(b) the difference between the expected value of z and the value of z implied by the expected value of θ can be large;

(c) combinations of two parameter changes can compound non-linearly in their effect on the range of change in z; and

(d) the elasticities used depend critically upon the particular policy configuration.

The authors conclude by pointing out that their approaches can in principle be extended to non-linear models by use of numerical differentiation. However, they warn that this may be a complicated procedure and that its feasibility would need to be examined much more thoroughly before any of their results could be extended to this more general case.

2. Trade Applications

Next in the volume comes a group of papers which have as their primary policy focus applications to trade policy issues of various kinds. All the papers examine some form of multiple tier trade policy structure: either a customs union or a multi-jurisdictional national structure.

In John Spencer's paper an attempt is made to assess the redistributive effects of the Common Agricultural Policy (CAP) from the viewpoint of static general equilibrium analysis using a Hecksher-Ohlin type model. In 1980, the total EEC budget was 16,289 million ECUs or \$US22,680 million, of which 73% was spent on agriculture. The CAP is thus of major importance to the EEC and its ramifications are such that an AGE approach seems appropriate.

The model incorporates the eight EEC member states of 1980 (Belgium and Luxembourg are treated as one country, and Greece did not join until 1981) and a residual country labelled the rest of the world (RW). Production in each country is described by a constant returns to scale Cobb-Douglas technolody for each of the two goods produced, using capital and labour as inputs. Full factor mobility is assumed within a country, but capital and labour are immobile between countries. Demand functions are generated from two level CES utility functions, and one consumer is assumed for each country. A major aspect of CAP policy is the dumping of excess agricultural produce abroad, and this is also incorporated in the model.

The most important results are those pertaining to the situation when member states leave one at a time. The most striking result is the tendency for each member state to do better outside the EEC than within it although free trade is better still in most cases.

Only Ireland is better off within the EEC than outside, and only the
Netherlands and Belgium-Luxembourg prefer a continuation of the EEC
with them outside to free trade. When a country leaves the EEC, RW
always loses but no clear pattern emerges vis-a-vis the remaining EEC
members.

      Spencer's general equilibrium calculations demonstrate the
importance of terms of trade effects, effects that are often ignored in
the analysis of customs unions and in the estimation of gains and losses
resulting from the workings of subsidy programmes such as CAP. A limita-
tion of his model is the assumption that factors of production are
immobile between EEC countries, even though, in principle at least, there
should be no obstacle to migration of factors between members of a common
market. The strong terms of trade effects that he reports may be
modified if factors of production were more mobile between countries.

      The paper by Glenn Harrison and Larry Kimbell reports on the
development and application of an AGE model of 10 Pacific Basin countries
that is designed to study the nature and extent of their economic interdependence with respect to taxes, tariffs, and non-tariff barriers. The
model is primarily neoclassical in structure, and uses the traditional
CES production function with extended and more complicated variants on
the demand side. It also uses an extended Cobb-Douglas production
structure in intermediate goods, which permits substitution between
domestic and imported corresponding commodities. Heckscher-Ohlin factor
mobility assumptions are employed, as in the Spencer model: each factor
is free to move within the sectors of each region but not between regions.
Five types of taxes are identified: factor taxes, value added taxes,
excise taxes, sales taxes and income taxes. Tariffs and non-tariff
bariers are also modelled; and a distinction is drawn between tariffs
levied on imports of intermediate inputs and those levied on imports of
final goods. Government procurement practices are approximated by a 50%
tariff applied to imports of each public household in each region.
Domestic tax systems are sometimes viewed as NTBs, and this is the
interpretation placed upon the domestic tax structures which are incorporated in the Harrison-Kimbell model.

      The policy issues considered in their paper are:
(a) The effects of multilateral "Tokyo round" tariff liberalisation;

(b) The comparative importance of multi-lateral reductions in tariffs
and NTBs;

(c) Discriminatory features of the US domestic factor tax system;

(d) The effect of multi-lateral tariff reductions with specific
factors in one region.

By and large, their results confirm those found in other
studies with similar structures (for example Whalley (1980)), and they
find that their results are qualitatively robust to parameter change.
However, their point estimate results (those conditional on all parameters
being set equal to their respective point estimates) are quite different
quantitatively from the mean welfare results (the weighted average of
welfare results from sensitivity analysis around the point estimates of
parameters).

By selecting policy simulations that correspond to several
found in the existing empirical literature, sensitivity analysis to model
structure is undertaken. Once again, qualitative results are found to be
robust to model changes insofar as these exist between the studies being
considered.

The paper by Jones et al. differs from the other trade papers
included here in a number of respects. It is a small-dimensional AGE model
of US Canadian trade; it incorporates regional effects within Canada; and
its focus is the exploration of changes in federal trade policies in Canada
on inter-regional trade. Three regions are identified; Eastern Canada
(Ontario and all provinces to its East), Western Canada (Manitoba and all
provinces to its West), and the rest of the world. Both inter-regional
and international trade occur in three commodities: manufacturing, non-
manufacturing and services.

The authors find that when revenues are redistributed according to provincial income, the West loses from unilateral abolition of
Canadian Tariffs, even though inter-regional terms of trade effects move
relatively in their favour. Small positive gains result for the East
only when the domestic import elasticity of substitution in the US is
high. The issue of how a federal government redistributes tariff revenues
by region emerges as a central issue which crucially affects regional
incidence.

The final paper in this section, by Chisholm and Tyers,
embodies the judgement that a strict general equilibrium formulation

should be sacrificed to make tractable the specification of dynamics,
price stabilisation, and storage-stockpiling issues. They report on a
multi-commodity stochastic simulation model designed to analyse the
economic effects of agricultural trade policies in world grain and meat
markets. The model incorporates dynamic production uncertainty, stockpiling behaviour, and the cross effects on both demand and supply sides,
between the five staple food commodities. To properly address the
relevant policy issues, they claim that a dynamic stochastic model must
be used, and that conventional AGE models cannot at present satisfactorily
handle short- and long-run stochastic supply and endogenous stockpiling
behaviour that interacts with insulating trade policies.

      World and domestic staple food markets are influenced by
policies that have two major dimensions - the protection of domestic food
production, and the insulation of domestic markets from world price
fluctuations. The primary focus of the paper is on the welfare impacts
of these trade policies on three major country groupings: the OECD, the
Asian region's newly industrialised countries (NICs) and the developing
countries (LDCs). The model incorporates twenty-four countries and
country groups, six of which are modelled as net trading entities only.
Storage behaviour in the model in represented by a combination of risk
neutral competitive stockpilers and public agents that respond only to
quantity triggers. Trade policies that are designed to protect and
insulate domestic markets are incorporated in the model through the
specification of the price transmission equation for each country and
commodity. Countries are assumed to insulate their domestic markets
against changing world prices by permitting short-run changes in nominal
rates of protection, while aiming to retain constant average levels of
protection in the long-run.

      The welfare effects of policy change in this model have four
components. The welfare impact on consumers is measured by the change in
the expected equivalent variation; the welfare impact on producers is the
expected change in producer surplus; the impact on government revenue is
the change in the expected net budgetary effect of consumer, producer and
trade taxes and subsidies; and the benefit to stockpilers is measured by
the expected change in profits from storage. All welfare effects are
evaluated assuming risk neutrality. The model suggests that world net
annual income would be about $70 billion (1980 US) lower with existing

agricultural trade policies in the OECD/NIC bloc as compared with free
trade. (This estimate is significantly larger than previous research has
suggested.) The predicted short-run net annual welfare gain is about
one-third of this long-run gain. The OECD/NIC bloc incurs very large net
welfare losses as a result of its own agricultural trade policies. The
major food exporters lose largely because of the unfavourable terms of
trade effects, while the major food importers lose because of the
efficiency losses associated with their own distortionary protection
policies. Disaggregation of gains by industry offers an explanation of
why these policies are pursued in the face of the aggregate losses that
stem from them. The average annual income of EEC farmers, for example,
is estimated to be about 15% higher with protection, whereas per capita
incomes of EEC consumers cum tax payers are of the order of only 1% lower.

Finally, the contribution of stockpiling to stabilise world
prices is significant in the model, and suggests that dynamic modelling
that incorporates insulating trade policies cannot properly represent
national grain market behaviour, if stockholders are excluded.

3. Tax Applications

Three papers are included in this section of the volume each
with a distinct orientation. The first two (by Slemrod and Ballard/
Goulder) use essentially Walrasian models as the basis of their work.
The third paper, by Meagher et al, attempts to link microeconomic tax
changes with macroeconomic effects.

The primary goal of the research in Joel Slemrod's paper is
to develop a methodology for integrating the information from micro unit
data files in the framework of a general equilibrium model of taxation.
The value of micro data files to research in taxation has been amply
demonstrated in a number of earlier projects - for example, the work of
Pechman and Okner (1974). The insights to be gained from general
equilibrium analysis of taxation have also been well documented, as the
work of Harberger (1962) and the later AGE literature demonstrates.
However, all previous research efforts in AGE taxation policy have been
based on the representative households approximating highly aggregated
classes of individuals. Slemrod claims two benefits for his procedure.
Firstly, the richness of statements about the vertical equity impacts of
a particular policy can be greatly increased: under the conventional

procedure, a household with income of $7,500, for example, may represent
all households in the $5,000-10,000 range. Secondly, it recognises the
fact that there is a joint distribution of household parameters covering
endowments and tastes. Within what current models refer to as "income
class" there are households with very different capital labour ratios,
very different consumption patterns, and very different portfolios.

These issues are especially interesting in the context of a
general equilibrium model with financial behaviour. This involves the
characterisation of a household with respect to risk aversion, portfolio
choice, and housing tenure status. There is more variation in these
features than in tastes amongst broad aggregates of consumption goods.

Previous work by Slemrod(1983) has attempted to integrate a
financial sector and financial behaviour into general equilibrium tax
models. In the study presented here, he assigns each tax paying unit
a value of wealth as well as a division of wealth into five net asset
categories. He assumes that expected utility is maximised subject to
the household income and wealth constraints. Expected utility is written
as a function of the expected consumption of the two types of goods,
housing services and a non-housing composite, and the riskiness of the
income flow created by its variance. The expressions for consumption
and asset demands which depend on wealth, income, relative prices, and
assets' expected returns and after tax riskiness, can all be derived.
The parameterisation of preferences is simplified by assuming an expected
utility function with constant relative risk aversion of the CES type.

Slemrod considers replacing the existing US income tax system
with a flat rate income tax and reports average percentage welfare change
and the distribution of welfare change by a real income class. His results
reinforce his claims about the benefits of incorporating micro unit data.
For example, in the real income class $20,000 and less, the average
percentage change in welfare is minus 5.5%. But 23.2% of individuals in
the class recorded a welfare gain of more than 10%, and 3.5% gained more
than 20%. Even in the income class > $20,000, where the average percent-
age change in welfare was +59.2%, 2.1% of households experienced a
welfare loss.

The primary focus of the paper by Ballard and Goulder is the
examination of alternative expectations closure assumptions in the context
of an intertemporal general equilibrium tax model. The assumptions of

myopia and of perfect foresight define polar cases concerning the availability of information about the future. They develop a consistent
general equilibrium model in which the amount of information available can
be varied systematically within these extremes. They find that the social
value of additional foresight can be negative; more foresight can lead to
lower welfare. This occurs because in the presence of distortions, the
existence of illusion in the face of the tax change can offset the
existing distortions. The welfare impact of the additional foresight is
fundamentally connected to the discrepancy between the social value of
the last dollar of saving and consumption in a second best world.

In fact, the change in the estimated impact of replacing an
income tax with a consumption tax under alternative degrees of foresight
is not great. For example, when one moves from myopia to almost perfect
foresight the welfare gain from adopting a consumption tax is reduced
by between 5 and 10%. Further, the change in welfare as a function of
the degree of foresight is greatest when myopia is replaced by a small
amount of foresight. Thereafter the relationship exhibits diminishing
returns.

The paper by Meagher and his colleagues reports a further
development in the very considerable armoury of policy facilities attached
to the ORANI model of the Australian economy. ORANI is a detailed multisectoral model of the Australian economy which can in this context be
thought of as a simple macro model with a fine commodity disaggregation.
It has 113 domestic industries, 115 commodity categories and 9 occupational categories of labour. While such a structure has considerable
detail for consideration of economy-wide changes, the very rich data base
embodied in the ORANI model suggests that it might be used for more
specific applications as well, where very fine detail may be of importance.
The paper discusses the development of a facility for tax analysis, which
makes available to a policy maker the possibility of generating macro- and
micro-forecasts of the effect of introducing a tax on wine. The macro
results seem to be generated by the particular macro closure constraints
incorporated. Nevertheless, the potential for using the very rich ORANI
data base for specific applications of this kind is amply demonstrated,
and shows how a middle course may be steered between general purpose and
specific purpose models in a policy setting.

4. Price Rigidities

The three contributions on price rigidities make progress on
a new area of application for AGE models. Two of the papers consider
explicit applications; the third approaches the conceptually thorny
issue of computing equilibria under economy-wide rationing rules.

The paper by Dale Jorgenson and Daniel Slesnick is concerned
with the measurement of social welfare. It aims to implement a new
approach to the analysis of regulatory and fiscal policies, and to
illustrate this approach by analysing alternative policies for petroleum
price regulation and taxation in the US.

The authors begin by noting that individual and social welfare
comparisons based upon index numbers are subject to very important limitations. Individual welfare measures based on index numbers provide
estimates of consumer surplus. Orderings based on consumer surplus
coincide with orderings based on individual preferences only if these
preferences are homothetic.

Measures of social welfare resulting from the compensation
principle coincide with social orderings only if individual preferences
are both identical and homothetic. Since homothetic preferences are
inconsistent with well estiablished empirical regularities in the
behaviour of individual consumers, and identical preferences for
individual consumers are inconsistent with empirical findings that
expenditure patterns depend upon demographic characteristics of households
an alternative approach is sought which avoids these features. The
authors use an econometric representation of preferences to eliminate
these restrictions, and to estimate money metric individual and social
welfare measures for alternative petroleum regulation policies.

The model which generates these results is a dynamic general
equilibrium model of the US economy reported in Jorgenson (1984).
Results are reported for the years 1980-1995 inclusive. Three policy
alternatives are considered: continued petroleum price controls, elimination of the windfall profits tax, and reform of the windfall profits
tax. Under this last policy, the windfall profits tax would be reduced
on certain categories of petroleum production beginning in 1983.

Under continued controls, all types of households gained
during the period 1980-81 and rural households continued to gain in 1982;

however, all types of families lose under continued controls beginning
1983. For example, a white urban family living in the north-east loses
$281.24 in 1983, and this rises to $1,587.43 by 1995. With the elimination of the windfall profits tax, it is found that the price of energy
is lower until 1987 and higher the remaining period 1988-95. All households experience a slight decline in welfare in 1980 and substantial
gains in welfare for the remainder of the period 1981-1995, except for
urban households in 1995 who undergo a slight decline in welfare for that
year. Under the final alternative, households gain throughout the period,
but the gains in welfare are small by comparison with those for eliminating the windfall tax after 1983. Since none of these changes yield
Pareto improvements, to choose among these policies it is necessary to
combine measures of individual welfare into an overall measure of social
welfare. Jorgenson and Slesnick attempt to do this by constructing a
social expenditure function in the spirit of Pollak (1981). The social
expenditure function is precisely analogous to the individual expenditure
function : it gives the minimum level of aggregate expenditure required
to attain a stipulated level of social welfare. Just as the individual
expenditure function and the indirect utility function can be employed in
assessing the impacts of alternative economic policies in individual
welfare, the social expenditure function and the social welfare function
can be employed in assessing the impacts of alternative policies in
social welfare.

  The level of social welfare can be translated into monetary
terms by evaluating the social welfare function at that level of welfare
for a given price system. Two different levels of social welfare can be
compared with reference to a single price system by determining the
minimum level of aggregate expenditure required to attain each level of
social welfare for the reference prices. In addition, changes in social
welfare can be decomposed into changes in efficiency and changes in
equity.

  By and large the money metric social welfare under the
assumption that the degree of inequality aversion parameter is equal to
1, approximately follows the pattern for individual welfare. However,
money metric equity is substantial and positive after 1982 under continued
controls, while it is negative but quantitatively less significant for
most years under the other two policy alternatives.

Trien Nguyen's paper presents a framework to study the issue of resource allocation and price controls from a computational general equilibrium viewpoint. The central thesis is that under price controls (that is price controls covering the whole economy, such as wage and price controls) attempts by agents to obtain trades use up real resources. They give rise to a dual price system with actual buying prices higher than controlled prices and actual selling prices lower than controlled prices. The dual price system serves as an alternative equilibrating mechanism in which resource costs are endogenously determined both at individual and market levels so as to simultaneously clear several markets under these government controls. Nguyen's study is thus distinct from the partial equilibrium literature on price controls and from the literature on fixed price equilibria which has been motivated by a desire to more rigorously specify the theoretical foundations of Keynesian macroeconomics.

This equilibrium concept under price rigidities can be thought of in the following way. At the individual level all agents behave rationally in the sense of constrained utility maximisation with respect to the dual price system. At the aggregate level, all markets clear in the sense that aggregate demands net of resource losses must not exceed aggregate endowments. As prices can be fixed either above or below market clearing levels (but not both), agents can be either on the long side or the short side of the market (but not both). Resource losses are consequently borne by only one side of the market.

The second part of the paper provides a numerical illustration to demonstrate how the approach may be used to calculate the welfare effects of price rigidities. The example used is a pure exchange economy abstracted from a benchmark equilibrium data set for the 1972 Canadian economy compiled by St. Hilaire and Whalley (1983). A constructive proof of the existence of equilibrium is established by appealing to a fixed point computational procedure.

The purpose of Imam's study is to evaluate the welfare loss suffered by the less developed countries (LDCs) due to the ceiling on the rate of interest. With an interest rate ceiling, intertemporal consumption decisions may be distorted generating sub-optimal savings. A numerical exercise is carried out for India and substantial welfare costs of interest rate controls are estimated.

The model of the Indian economy considers four consumer groups (the urban poor, the urban rich, the rural poor and the rural rich) and four commodities. The consumer group classification is designed to characterise the dual nature of the Indian economy along with consumer groups classified on the basis of income. CES production and utility functions are used. The computational technique used has been reported previously (Imam and Whalley (1982)) and constructively proves the existence of competitive equilibrium even when some economic agents face a price ceiling or floor.

5. Other Papers

Two other papers were presented at the conference. The first of these addresses the challenging problem of incorporating macrodynamic features into an AGE model. Cooper et al report on research being undertaken on this problem in the Impact project at the University of Melbourne. They begin by pointing out that if an AGE model is to be used for short run analysis, the macroeconomic environment must be prespecified. In a standard short run closure of the ORANI model, for example, the following macro variables are assigned exogenously:

    i)   one of the price level or the exchange rate (as numeraire);

    ii)   one of the real wage or the aggregate level of employment;

    iii) one of real absorption (C + I + G) or the balance of trade surplus (X-M).

The approach adopted here is to use a small macrodynamic model, MACRO, to close ORANI with respect to these variables for short run simulations (MACRO is a version of the Reserve Bank of Australia's RB II model). The models are interfaced by introducing an exogenous policy change to both models. ORANI generates a single static solution; MACRO generates a continuous sequence of changes. An attempt is then made to identify an instant after the exogenous shock when the MACRO solution is consistent with ORANI's. The elapsed time then provides an estimate of the length of the ORANI short run.

The paper provides two examples at the technique used: a shock in government spending (used to calibrate the interface) and a uniform tariff change.

The final paper in the volume is the survey by John James of applications of general equilibrium models to economic history. Over the last twenty years general equilibrium analysis has been used to try to account for differences in historical experience across countries. This has been one of the major developments in the "new economic history", the discipline which emphasises the application of formal neoclassical economic theory and quantitative techniques to historical problems. One of the distinctive characteristics of the new economic history has been the use of explicit counter factual analysis.

James begins by identifying some of the reasons why AGE models have not been used to their full potential in the new economic history. He then goes on to discuss some important applications of AGE modelling and illustrates some of the problems involved. He concludes his paper by discussing some potentially fruitful areas for the application of AGE modelling rechniques in economic history. James' paper differs from most other papers in this volume in being a survey of general equilibrium applications, rather than an application itself.

CONFERENCE THEMES

Given the increasing use of AGE models in policy formulation, it is to be expected that their range of application should be expanding. This is reflected in the conference papers. It is also natural that greater attention should now be given to what might be termed "policy usefulness". This is reflected in the stress placed on data and parameterisation issues, on the implications of alternative model closure assumptions, and on the interpretation of normative results from model simulations in the papers.

Perhaps the most easily identified innovation is more sophisticated sensitivity analysis. Up until the early 80s, it was more or less standard to vary elasticities, and sometimes share parameters as well, by a factor of 2 either way from a "best guess" figure, to test the implications of variations in their values. This approach is still widely used. But most practitioners have only a limited sense of the extent to which they are addressing the problem of errors in parameterisation. The Pagan-Shannon paper addresses this problem directly. It is a theme also stressed by Harrison and Kimbell in their contribution. They emphasise the importance of gaining a sense of the sensitivity of results to both model parameters and to model structure. They undertake a systematic sensitivity analysis for each policy simulation with respect to three sets of elasticities: the elasticities of substitution between primary factors, import demand elasticities, and own-price demand elasticities. Drawing on earlier work, they distinguish between "conditional" and "unconditional" systematic sensitivity analyses. The former refer to a series of simulations in which each parameter is perturbed from its point estimate a certain number of times conditional on all other parameters being set only to their point estimate value. The latter refer to perturbations of each parameter conditional on all other parameters also being perturbed from their point estimate a certain number of times. This set of simulations is labelled "unconditional". Because of the size of the model used in the present study (20 commodities and 12 trading regions), only conditional sensitivity analysis is employed.

A related theme contrasted the econometric approach to AGE parameterisation, associated especially with Dale Jorgenson, with the more conventional calibration approach. While most of the models represented here rely on calibration techniques for parameterisation, Jorgenson and Slesnick's paper makes use of the econometrically estimated dynamic AGE model due to Jorgenson (1984). Diewert also begins his paper by noting that the calibration approach to AGE modelling used functional forms (of the Cobb-Douglas/CES/Loentief type) to maintain tractability. These "are too restrictive and are frequently rejected by econometric tests using less restrictive functional forms". The Jorgenson approach overcomes this criticism by basing AGE models "on econometrically estimated flexible functional forms for production and utility functions".

The second major methodological strand emphasised at the conference concerned model closures. To render any AGE model operational, closure assumptions must be made across a number of areas: policy parameters, the external sector, the public sector, the treatment of time, the treatment of uncertainty, and macro relationships. The closure assumptions made can have profound implications for model outcomes.

A number of the papers addressed the closure issue in one form or another. The paper by Ballard and Goulder provides an especially clear example. In intertemporal versions of AGE models, it is typically assumed that expectations are myopic. This permits the consumer to maximise utility in each period from information available in that period. The myopic expectations assumption is an intertemporal closure assumption, but the degree of robustness of results to alternative expectations assumptions was not known. Ballard and Goulder explicitly address this problem by extending the expectations framework to incorporate varying degrees of foresight, and thus provide insight into the implications of the myopic expectations assumption for model results.

Joel Slemrod's paper addresses the financial sector closure issue in AGE models. In most AGE models, it is implicitly assumed that no financial intermediation exists. In non-Walrasian models, there is frequently a link with the macro-environment, although this macro-micro interface has not been explored in any depth. The contribution of Alan Powell and his co-workers on macro closures to the ORANI model constitutes another example of the importance of this issue.

Finally, all AGE modellers close their systems with their chosen treatment of policy parameters. The Chisholm-Tyers study, perhaps because it has its origins in the more institutionally aware agricultural economics tradition, demonstrated the care which must be taken in modelling policy interventions. This is particularly true of policies

which cannot be readily characterised as a simple ad valorem tax rate.
Chisholm and Tyers treat the interactions of domestic price stablisation
and "insulation" policies, and stockpiling with a degree of detail which
is not encountered in fully fledged AGE models. As applications of AGE
models expand to consider policy interventions such as price controls,
it is clear that the model characterisation of policy instruments will
need to be carefully examined.

The Chisholm-Tyers contribution raises major issues as to
the crude way in which institutional detail is frequently represented
in AGE models. The paper serves as a caution to those who always think
it desirable to sacrifice institutional detail to rigorous theoretical
structure. The results reported in the paper indicate that detailed
modelling of stockpiling behaviour, for example, can lead to results
which would not be evident in a model which represented such a policy
by an ad valorem tax or subsidy.

The last identifiable theme evident at the conference concerned ths use of normative criteria in policy evaluation. A number of AGE
modellers, for instance, have been concerned with the valuation of the
efficiency equity trade-off which is implicit in many comparative
outcomes of model simulations. Piggott and Whalley (1981), for example,
report average incomes by decile range in some initial situations, and
compare these with average welfare loss augmented incomes in a counterfactual situation, in order to capture both efficiency and equity
components of tax policy change. Jorgenson and Slesnick, in their paper
in Section 3 of this volume, develop an econometric approach to the
problem of estimating the money metric change associated with the change
in policy and then attempt to decompose the welfare change into equity
and efficiency components. Erwin Diewert's paper, which was written
after the conference, will doubtless inspire further efforts along these
lines.

OTHER ISSUES

In organising the conference, we aimed at a comprehensive
coverage of "new developments" in the area. The complete fulfillment
of such an aim is of course impossible. Important omissions include the
incorporation of life cycle and human capital accumulation effects with
AGE models of tax policy (Ballard (1983)); the incorporation of public
goods (Piggott and Whalley (1984)); the modelling of rent-seeking

behaviour in trade models (Hamilton, Mohammad and Whalley (1984)); and
the incorporation of increasing returns to scale in trade models
(Harris (1984)). These innovations all have the potential to make AGE
models even more useful as inputs into the policy process, and to change
our perceptions about the impacts of micro-policy instruments on allocation, distribution and welfare. They lend support to the belief that
applied general equilibrium analysis will continue to develop as an
active and innovative research programme.

Endnotes

[1] See Scarf (1967, 1973)

[2] See Shoven and Whalley (1973, 1974, 1977)

[3] See Scarf and Shoven (1984)

References

Ballard, C.L. (1983), "The Consumption Tax in an Extended Life Cycle
    Model with Demographic Change". Paper presented to the
    Applied General Equilibrium Workshop, National Bureau of
    Economic Research, Stanford, CA, February 1984.
Debreu, G. (1951), "The Coefficient of Resource Utilization", Econometrica,
    19: 273-292.
Dervis, K., J. de Melo and S. Robinson (1982), General Equilibrium
    Models for Development Policy, Cambridge, Cambridge University
    Press.
Dixon, P.B., B.R. Parmenter, J. Sutton and D.P. Vincent (1982), Orani:
    A Multisectoral Model of the Australian Economy. Amsterdam,
    North-Holland Publishing Company.
Fullerton, D., J.B. Shoven and J. Whalley (1978), "General Equilibrium
    Analysis of U.S. Taxation Policy". In 1978 Compendium on
    Tax Research. Washington, D.C. Office of Tax Analysis,
    U.S. Treasury.
Hamilton, B., S. Mohammad and J. Whalley (1984), "Rent Seeking and the
    North-South Terms of Trade", Journal of Policy Modelling,
    6, No. 4,

Harberger, A.C. (1983), "The Incidence of the Corporation Tax", Journal
        of Political Economy, 70:215-240 June.
Harris, R. (1984), Applied General Equilibrium Analysis of Small Open
        Economies with Scale Economies and Imperfect Competition.
        Mimeo, Queen's University.
Imam, H. and J. Whalley (1982), "General Equilibrium with Price
        Intervention Policies - A Computational Approach", Journal
        of Public Economics. 18(1):105-119.

Jorgenson, D.W. (1984), "Econometric Methods for Applied General
        Equilibrium Analysis", in Applied General Equilibrium
        Analysis. (Ed) Herbert E. Scarf and John B. Shoven,
        Cambridge University Press (1984).
Miller, M.H. and J.E.Spencer (1977), "The Static Economic Effects of
        the U.K. Joining the EEC: A General Equilibrium Approach",
        The Review of Economic Studies, 38, April, 175-208.
Pechman, J.A. and B.A. Okner (1974), Who Bears the Tax Burden?
        Washington, D.C.: The Bookings Institution.
Piggott, J. and Whalley, J. (1977), "General Equilibrium Investigations
        of U.K. Tax-Subsidy Policy". In Studies in Modern Economic
        Analysis. M.J. Artis and A.R. Nobay (Eds), Oxford, England:
        Blackwell.
Piggott, J. and J. Whalley (1981), "A Summary of Some Findings from a
        General Equilibrium Tax Model for the United Kingdom",
        in Carnegie. Rochester Conference Series on Public Policy,
        14, 153-200.
Piggott, J. and J. Whalley (1984), "Net Fiscal Incidence Calculations:
        Average Versus Marginal Effects". Working Papers in Economics
        and Econometrics, 112, Faculty of Economics and Research
        School of Social Services, Australian National University,
        December.
Piggott, J. (1980). A General Equilibrium Evaluation of Australian
        Taxation Policy. PhD Thesis, University of London.
Pollak, R.A. (1981). "The Social Cost of Living Index", Journal of
        Public Economics, 15, 3:311-336.
Scarf, H.E. (1967). "On the Computation of Equilibrium Prices", in
        W.M. Fellner et al. (Eds),Ten Essays in Honour of Irving
        Fisher. New York:Wiley. 207-230.
Scarf, H.E. (1973), (with the collaboration of T. Hansen), The Computation
        of Economic Equilibrium. New Haven: Yale University Press.
Scarf, H.E. and John B. Shoven (eds) (1984), Applied General Equilibrium
        Analysis, Cambridge University Press, New York.
Serra-Puche, J. (1979), A Computational General Equilibrium Model for the
        Mexican Economy: An Analysis of Fiscal Policies. PhD Thesis,
        Yale University.
Shoven, J.B. and J. Whalley (1973), "General Equilibrium with Taxes:
        A Computational Procedure and an Existence Proof", Review
        of Economic Studies, 40, October, 475-489.
Shoven, J.B. and J. Whalley (1974). "On the Computation of Competitive
        Equilibrium on International Markets with Tariffs", Journal
        of International Economics, 4, November, 341-354.
Shoven, J.B. and J. Whalley (1977). "Equal Yield Tax Alternatives: General
        Equilibrium Computational Techniques", Journal of Public
        Economics, 8, October, 211-224.
St.Hilaire and J. Whalley (1983), "A Microconsistent Equilibrium Data Set
        for Canada for Use in Tax Policy Analysis". Review of
        Income and Wealth, 29, No.2. June, 175-204.

Slemrod, J. (1983). "A General Equilibrium Model of Taxation with
     Endogenous Financial Behaviour", In Behavioural Simulation
     Methods in Tax Policy Analysis. (Ed) M. Feldstien. University
     of Chicago Press.
Whalley, J. (1975), "A General Equilibrium Assessment of the 1973 U.K.
     Tax Reform". Economica, 42, May, 139-161.
Whalley, J. (1980), "Discriminatory Features of Domestic Factor Tax
     Systems in a Goods Mobile-Factors Immobile Trade Model:
     An Empirical General Equilibrium Approach", Journal of
     Political Economy, 88, 6, December, 1177-1202.

HIDDEN CHALLENGES IN RECENT APPLIED
GENERAL EQUILIBRIUM EXERCISES

J. Whalley
University of Western Ontario

1 INTRODUCTION

The papers in this volume reflect the ways in which the
emerging field of applied general equilibrium analysis has been evolving
in recent years. The range and sophistication of policy applications has
continued to expand, but at the same time the more fundamental issues in
applying equilibrium theory to policy have hardly changed. Data remains
poor; many of the key parameters in models are little more than best
guesses; basic issues of model design (such as the use of a dynamic or
static model) remain subjective judgement calls of the modeller.

This paper reviews some of these issues, and suggests that
these problems are a reflection of wider difficulties facing the current
generation of empirical economists raised in the post-war positivist
tradition. The prerogative of the policy process establishes the need
for numerical work with clear theoretical underpinnings, but the
discipline of strict scientific principles (as in the natural sciences)
always suggests that firm conclusions are premature.

Recent applied general equilibrium analyses seeking to
contribute to policy debate therefore face a dilemma. If model results
are dismissed as too inconclusive to form the basis for policy advice,
then attempts to operationalize general equilibrium theory by selecting
values for parameters of theoretical models may be of little significance
for actual policy making. While general equilibrium theory will still

I am grateful to Rob Fisher, Michael Parkin, Herbert Scarf,
and T.N. Srinivasan for comments on an earlier draft.

25

provide an organizational framework for thinking through the issues
policy makers need to consider, on empirical grounds it may not be that
useful for deciding the precise form any particular policy should take.
On the other hand, if applied general equilibrium exercises are evaluated
as useful for policy makers, then one has somehow to reconcile the large
elements of subjectivity in the modelling process with the strong belief
in hypothesis testing in modern economics. While valuable as an input
into policy making, their place in modern empirical economics remains
unclear.

2   Empiricism and Recent Applied General Equilibrium Analyses

Much of the recent literature on applied general equilibrium
analysis has its origins in the development of general equilibrium
computational techniques by Scarf in the 1960s, and in early attempts to
use small dimensional numerical equilibrium models by Johansen (1960),
Harberger (1962) and others for policy evaluation.

This field can, perhaps, best be understood as an attempt to
use quasi realistic numerical general equilibrium models for policy and
other analyses; an effort to bridge theory and practice. This mirrors
the sense among many contemporary economists that much recent economic
theory, including that in the general equilibrium area, has become too
abstract, making it excessively remote from the practicalities of policy
making. Since the level of analytical discussion within the policy
making fraternity is often extremely limited, attempts such as those
described in this volume (or those reviewed in the recent survey paper
by Shoven and Whalley (1984)), have generally been applauded by
theorists and welcomed (although somewhat more cautiously) by policy
makers.

However, as the development of applied general equilibrium
models has steadily progressed from merely demonstrating the feasibility
of model construction and solution to serious application to policy,
disquiet has grown in the economics profession over the appropriateness
of using these models in this way. Recognizing the difficulties of
parameter specification and the necessity for choosing between rival
(and frequently contentious) assumptions, modellers have tended to
emphasize the broad themes of their results rather than the precise
numbers they produce. Builders of the tax and trade models, for
instance, have stressed how their results challenge existing perceptions

as to the impacts of policies, which they often portray as driving the
policy formation process. What seems to have prevailed in the use of
these models thus far is a form of approximate numerical investigation,
useful for exploring whether particular effects are large or small and
signing the net outcome where different effects come into play.

Because of this rough empiricism, issues such as the
frailness of the parameter specification, or the lack of statistical
testing of the models are seen by some as detracting from their
usefulness. Given the stress on broad themes of results, some have
suggested that little has been learned from these models which could not
have been guessed at as a possible outcome before the models were
constructed, especially since the models do not provide a clear guide as
to the actual outcome if real policy changes really occur.

A number of factors have contributed to this current sense of
unease. One is that key parameter values, such as elasticities, play a
pivotal role in all model calculations, but the amount that is known
about which numerical values to use remains limited. As I have remarked
on other occasions, it is quite extraordinary not only how little
we know about numerical values of elasticities, given the significance
that we attach to these in introductory courses in Economics, but how
little we think we know changes as quickly as it does. In the savings
area, for instance, 10 years ago, elasticities were thought to be small,
5 years ago they were thought to be large, and now once again they are
thought to be smaller. For many years labour supply elasticities were
thought to be small, and now they are in the process of being revised
upwards. In the international trade area researchers commonly use import
price elasticities in the neighbourhood of unity, even for small
economies, even though estimates as high as nine appear in the literature.
In many areas elasticity estimates differ in both size and sign, while
for a number of the issues in which applied modellers are interested no
relevant elasticity estimates exist. The choice of elasticity values
in applied models is therefore frequently based on contradictory, or
little or no empirical evidence. This obviously undermines confidence
in model results.

Simultaneously, however, there are no more obviously
attractive options available to policy makers who want to base their
decisions on state of the art quantification of impacts of alternative
policy changes on resource allocation and distribution. This is

especially the case if they wish to take into account relative price
effects in a logically consistent way. Whether partial equilibrium,
general equilibrium, or 'back of the envelope' quantification is used, key
parameter values must be selected, and in so many of the areas involved
in current policy debates, the applied econometrics literature is not
particularly helpful.

Another problem modellers have been forced to confront is
that of model preselection; the need to adopt key assumptions underlying
the particular applied model to be used before any model calculations can
begin. Both theoretical and applied modellers have long recognized the
need for such assumptions as full employment and perfect competition in
building general equilibrium models, and the constraints of tractibility
have been recognized for many years as an inevitable part of the modelling
process. However, in more recent work other equally important assumptions
have come to the fore. These are now widely agreed to be capable of
dramatically changing policy conclusions from models, but empirical
evidence as to which of these alternative assumptions is more
reasonable remains sparse.

An example is the set of possible assumptions one can make
as to how international factor flows take place. In tax models, the
choice between alternative assumptions substantially affects the
incidence effects of capital income taxes. If capital is internationally
mobile, it will not bear the burden of these taxes; but, in a closed
economy, domestic capital owners can be affected. Another example
arises with the treatment of time. In a static model, for example, a
tax on consumption is distorting since capital goods are tax free, but
this tax is non-distorting when analyzed in an intertemporal model.

Another issue in the applied models is the way the policies
to be analyzed are represented. In the general equilibrium tax models,
taxes have to be represented in model equivalent form, and yet for each
tax there is substantial literature disagreement as to what is the most
appropriate model treatment. In the case of the corporate tax, for
instance, the original treatment adopted by Harberger (1962) of
assuming average and marginal tax rates on capital income by industry to
be the same can bias results. Recent literature has emphasized that this
tax should be viewed as applying only to the equity return to capital
rather than to the total return, i.e., as a tax on one financing
instrument available to firms. This type of argument has even been used

by Stiglitz (1973) to argue that the tax is a lump sum tax, and, more recently, Gordon (1981) has argued that, in effect, the tax is a benefit-related tax. Whichever model treatment is adopted will change the results produced by the model. Numerical exercises obviously cannot settle disputes such as these, but some model treatment has to be adopted to analyze the policy issues; usually in full knowledge that the treatment followed may largely predetermine the conclusions.

Finally, most of the applied general equilibrium models are not tested in any meaningful statistical sense. Parameter specification usually proceeds using deterministic calibration (often to one year's data), and there is no statistical test of the model specification (see Mansur & Whalley (1984)). The issue is whether one can believe model results if there is no test of the reasonableness either of the model or of the parameter values.

This issue of testing is part of the wider issue of what we mean by empiricism in economics, to which I return to below. It is important to remember that, unlike econometric estimation, in determining parameter values by calibrating models to a single data observation, equilibrium features in the data to which calibration is applied are emphasized. Also, a characteristic of these procedures is that with enough flexibility in choice of the form of the deterministic model, it is usually possible to choose a model specification so as to exactly fit the data one is given. A purely deterministic equilibrium model in which consumers maximize utility and firms maximize profits can thus usually be constructed consistent with the observed data, provided that equilibrium conditions hold (such as demand and supply equalities).

The fact that models are not tested in a way which is acceptable to econometricians used to thinking in terms of models whose economic structure is simple but whose statistical structure is complex (rather than vice versa) should perhaps come as no surprise. In my opinion this concern with applied equilibrium exercises is not a criticism of applied general equilibrium models per se, but represents a challenge to our meaning of empiricism in modern economics, which has a wider relevance beyond these modelling exercises.

3 Precursors to Challenges

Prior to outlining the wider relevance of the experiences of
recent modelling efforts to current debates on empiricism in economics,
it is worth developing the links between the current applied general
equilibrium exercises and some earlier debates on general equilibrium
quantification.

My own opinion is that current concerns over applied general
equilibrium exercises are largely a continuation of the debate on the
feasibility of centralized calculation of a Pareto optimal allocation of
resources. This debate was begun by Barone (1908), when he implicitly
queried the operational significance of the Walrasian general equilibrium
system. As is well known, the criticism by Marx of 19th century
capitalism (in Das Kapital and the Communist Manifesto) did not provide
a concrete blueprint as to how a socialist state was to be organized, and
it was left to Barone and those who followed to deal with these questions.
Barone posed the problem of socialist organization in terms of a
Socialist Minister of Finance who must decide how to allocate state
owned but scarce means of production. Barone's solution was to note
that the only institutional change of any significance under socialism
is the transfer of ownership of the means of production from private
households to the state, and this should in no way affect the criterion
one would adopt for defining allocative efficiency. Barone therefore
suggested that a Socialist Minister of Finance should seek an allocation
of resources which is Pareto efficient.

However, since resources are state owned, deciding on an
appropriate allocation of resources involves solving the system of
equations characterizing Pareto efficiency. We know this today to be
the set of equations which also characterize a Walrasian competitive
equilibrium. Barone was pessimistic about the feasibility of such an
exercise, later termed by Wiles (1962) as "the perfect computation
of perfect competition". He emphasized how it would be necessary to
evaluate the potential profitability of all feasible activities,
including those not currently in use. The number of such activities
would be large, and Barone concluded that it would be a vast undertaking
with a large informational requirement.

The debate initiated by Barone continued on into the 1920s
and 1930s. von Mises (1924) questioned the feasibility of any meaningful
economic calculation under socialism, stressing the organic nature of

capitalist activity as producers ruthlessly search for increased profit
opportunities, and in the 1930s both Robbins (1934) and Hayek (1940)
claimed that perfect computation under socialism was completely
infeasible. Robbins raised the spectre of the millions of equations
which would need to be solved, which, in turn, would be continually
changing over time. An appropriate allocation of resources under
socialism would not be able to be determined, and therefore socialism
was regarded as infeasible as an institutional form which would achieve
economic efficiency.

The response from Lange (1936), aimed largely at von Mises,
was to suggest that it would not be necessary to make all the computations
supposedly required under socialism. The Minister of Finance could
decide upon the allocation of state owned resources in a decentralized
market environment. Even though resources are state owned under
socialism, Lange's point was that the state could rent them to private
producers, and in this way find a market clearing rental price through a
tatonnment procedure. This also proved to be the beginnings of the
literature on market socialism.

What is interesting about these debates, is that in many
ways they provided the impetus for the general equilibrium
computational work in the 1960s, which in turn lead to the applied
general equilibrium work of the 1970s and the 1980s. Schumpeter, in a
famous quotation once described Walras' work on general equilibrium as
the 'Magna Carta' of economics, and suggested that his main contribution
lay in providing a broad tapestry outlining the interconnectedness of the
economic system, rather than in generating a concrete operational framework for policy analysis. The debate on the feasibility of centralized
computation of a Pareto optimal allocation under socialism and the debate
today on the worth of applied general equilibrium models are continuations
of this same discussion.

Recent work on applied general equilibrium has, however,
also raised wider questions concerning the feasibility of centralized
calculation not fully addressed in the original debate. In the 1960s
Scarf took much of the inspiration from his work on general equilibrium
computation from the debates of the 1930s, and largely equated the
problems debated by Robbins and Lange and others with those of
computational solution, i.e. the feasibility of solving the system of
equations characterizing an equilibrium. Scarf himself thought that the

techniques he was developing would resolve the debate, and that once computation was shown to be possible it would open the way to wider developments with ultimate application both to the problem of centralized resource allocation discussed by Barone, von Mises, Robbins and others, and to that of policy evaluation in market economies.

While not directed at problems of central planning, recent applied general equilibrium work has nonetheless been concerned with problems closely related to those discussed in the socialist debate, i.e., policy evaluation in complex market-oriented economies where the alternative policy regimes to be considered each have many subtleties and important details whose impacts are not immediately apparent. What the applied models of today have been seeking is the same thing as the earlier socialist calculators; namely, to numerically determine the characteristics of an unobservable general equilibrium. This time around, its form is different. The equilibrium behaviour of a market economy under changes in economic policies is the issue rather than resource allocation in a centrally planned economy; and its implications are broader because economics has developed so much more since the 1930s.

In my opinion, recent applied equilibrium work has demonstrated that there is much more to the issue of feasibility of centralized calculation than has appeared either in the debates of the 1930s, or was assumed in the computational work of the 1960s. Issues of computational solution no longer dominate the literature. Instead, numerical specification is widely agreed to be the critical issue, since this preceeds computation. Before one solves the system of Paretian equations, one needs to write down the equations with specified parameter values.

In turn, the particular form for the Paretian equations has to be carefully specified, since model choice can substantially affect the conclusions from the analysis. The abstract general equilibrium formulation in Arrow and Debreu (1954), cleverly extended to include time through the subscripting of commodities provides an elegant general framework. Unfortunately, this is not sufficiently concrete for policy makers in complex economic systems making choices between various options. The need to adopt particular specifications in applied models for government expenditures, investment, foreign trade, tax policies, factor supplies, intertemporal behaviour, and a range of further complications is immediately apparent to anyone beginning to work with these models, and yet the treatments adopted may crucially affect the policy conclusion.

The applied general equilibrium work of the 1970s and 1980s has thus expanded the whole debate on the feasibility of centralized calculation of Pareto Optimality to one which also includes the specification of the underlying equation system. From a mechanical point of view, solution is possible. However, the sensitivity of results to assumptions and parameter values (especially elasticities), and the fact that the applied general equilibrium models are not tested are sources of concern and in some circles outright skepticism. The same arguments can, of course, also be made with respect to centralized calculations of a Pareto optimal allocation under socialism.

These issues therefore bring us back to Schumpeter and hence to Walras. The basic issue is whether there is anything more than an organizational framework implicit in the Walrasian economic system, or is there something which can be made more concrete and ultimately useful to policy makers at a practical rather than conceptual level. Recent applied general equilibrium modelling activity has forced us to face this question more forcefully than perhaps any time in the development of economics over the last 100 years, and what may be at stake is the nature of empiricism in economics itself rather than just the applied models.

My own view is that economists have perhaps tended to too easily link positivism and empirical economics, influenced in part by Friedman's essay in 1947, even though recent work by Frazer & Boland (1983) has suggested that Friedman's essay may be closer to instrumentalism than positivism. The positivists of the 1950s and 60s, of course, stressed the idea that economics is a subject much akin to the natural sciences where theory followed by hypothesis testing is the only way to proceed. Other developments in the 1940s have gone less well recognized, particularly the rival characterization of economics as a policy science (see Laswell (1951)).

Under this competing view of the world, it is impossible to definitively test propositions in the policy sciences because of the absence of controlled repeatable laboratory experiments. Policy sciences have to deal with the imperative of the policy process and are in an inevitable state of permanent flux, with schools who disagree (sometimes violently) over various propositions. The imperative of the policy process generates the need for decisions, and decision making will inevitably involve incomplete data, choosing between competing hypotheses, and subjective judgement. The contribution of policy sciences is not seen as establishing empirical laws as in the natural sciences but in raising the level of policy debate, increasing the level of understanding of how institutions may affect outcomes, challenging received wisdom, generating such data as may be relevant, and ultimately offering judgements on issues where there may be conflicting claims. Through such an adversarial process, the hope is that the policy-decision-making process will be improved. Even though definitive empirical evidence may not be at hand, such enterprises are not ruled out as unworthy scholarly activity. Indeed, they become an integral part of the policy process.

This approach both to policy making and the use of modelling in economics is something which I believe most of the applied general equilibrium modellers, many of whom were educated in the positivist tradition of the 1960s and 1970s, have inadvertently discovered for themselves. What we are witnessing in this field is a rediscovery of relevance by positivists previously seeking objective truth, and the implications of this for a generation of mathematically trained economists who have not been used to thinking in such subjective terms.

4 Challenges become Criticisms

It should by now be clear that my own view of recent applied general equilibrium analyses is that they are part of a wider challenge to empiricism in economics. This has both smaller and larger dimensions.

As far as the smaller challenges go, the problems of elasticities and other parameter values obviously suggest a reorientation of much of our empirical work in economics away from hypothesis testing and towards parameter generation. Parameter generation in recent years has been downplayed by econometricians in favour of hypothesis testing, and in the elasticity area this has become increasingly apparent to the applied modellers.

For instance, much of the work on systems of demand functions in the 1960s and 1970s has concentrated on system-wide estimation problems without concentrating in any sustained way on providing better estimates of elasticity parameters. The last survey piece on price elasticities that I have been able to find is by Hirsch in 1951. The

need is for empirical parameters more than tests of the theory. The
tradition from Schultz and others from the 1930s of an empirical concern
with parameter values _per se_, rather than with testing hypotheses seems
to have been lost in recent econometric work, and yet the need for more
reliable parameter values has been clearly revealed by the applied models.

A further challenge is whether it makes sense to continue to
develop theoretical general equilibrium theory at such a high level of
mathematical abstraction as has been true of recent work. In having to
confront both current policy problems and the difficulties of building
models to represent actual economies, the applied general equilibrium
models have not encountered mathematical difficulties, but rather the
need for special kinds of closing rules and more institutional features
in their models. This requirement for closing rules has forced some of
the models to run dangerously ahead of economic theory. Ad hoc
procedures have at times been used whose properties are not well known.
The challenge to theorists is to think in terms of more specificity as
well as more generality in their models, and to trace through the
implications of these closing rules and the specifications of
institutional arrangements for model behaviour.

There are, however, a wider set of challenges implicit in
these modelling exercises. The first is the challenge to positivism in
economics to which I have already alluded. One could perhaps
characterize current applied models as part of a move towards a new
positivism in economics. This positivism is not of the traditional
Popperian type where one attempts to positively test hypotheses, but
positivism in the sense of allowing for positive judgements on policy
options to be made by modellers. Models are to be used by analytically
trained economists attempting to improve the state of the world. Judgement is offered rather than withheld because statistical test offers no
absolute guide. The inability to definitively settle a debate does not
preclude the analyst drawing out what he sees as the implications of his
model for possible policy changes. Popperian positivism, which to my
taste has resulted in so many superbly analytically trained economists
to a large degree abdicating from the policy process, and even arguing
that economists have nothing or little to say about policy because they
cannot definitively settle their disputes, is therefore downplayed in
the use of these models. The group of economists using these models do
not show the same hesitations as the generation ahead of them in stating

their own judgements as to the desirability of possible policy changes
based on their economic modelling. This, of course, is not without its
dangers, since anything may become permissable once subjective judgement
is widely accepted as part of the economist's role. The trend, however,
seems to be clearly there in recent applied equilibrium work, and the
challenge to the next generation of modellers will be how to monitor and
evaluate the use of judgement which I believe will inevitably increase
in this and other areas of economics as the perogative of policy process
is more fully acknowledged.

Related to all this is the set of issues relating to the
meaning of empiricism in economics. Applied general equilibrium models
are complex in their economic structure and have demanding data requirements, but are statistically simple. Most of the models cannot be tested
in a conventional sense because of their dimensionality. The contrast
with modern econometric work is therefore obvious. Instead of models of
increasing statistical richness in which the economic structure is
downplayed, we now are witnessing an upsurge of interest in empirically
based models of greater economic complexity than previously, in which
concerns over economic structure dominate concerns over statistical
structure. Taken to the extreme these applied general equilibrium models
are such that a deterministic fit of models to single or even multiple
data points becomes feasible, in which case statistical testing makes
little sense.

Schumpeter's test of Walras was whether or not his general
equilibrium approach had any operational significance. If the conclusion
from recent applied general equilibrium models is that they have such
weak empirical foundations that there is little value to policy makers,
one perhaps has to go further and question whether there is much
operational significance to general equilibrium theory itself. During
the last 30 or 40 years, economics often has been presented as a
discipline much akin to natural sciences with both strong logical and
ultimately operational foundations. This I see at stake in the verdict
on the worth of applied general equilibrium exercises. Since the
essence of theory is simplification which in an exact sense must be
wrong, the constraints of tractibility perhaps dictate that economic
theory can ultimately be only an organizational framework for thinking
about economic problems. This is clearly valuable activity, but whether
we think that economic theory is merely philosophising or building the

foundation for an empirically based science makes a large difference to the way in which economic theorists proceed.

These issues also raise questions concerning the way we use models. Do we rely only on statistical tests or do we allow judgement to enter? Are we willing to examine our own perceptions of ourselves and our social institutions, in the belief that this is what shapes our policy making, rather than limit ourselves merely to attempting to track an often illusive objective reality.

My own belief is that the current applied general equilibrium models do generate insights and findings of interest to policy makers and clearly demonstrate both their relevance and the wider usefulness of economic theory. I also believe that much of the academic community and even more of the policy community remains skeptical, and that modellers must respond to this challenge of their own relevance more forcefully, and explain exactly what they see themselves as doing.

5 Future Directions for Applied General Equilibrium Analysis

Given the tone of the discussion thus far, a useful conclusion to this introductory chapter may be to lay out some of the implications of this line of argument for the future development of applied general equilibrium analysis. If I am right, and if the relevance and policy applicability of these models mark a new departure in equilibrium modelling, what types of future developments make sense?

Firstly, a change already seems to be underway in the evolution of models from the current state where there are a small number of larger scale multipurpose models (involving perhaps 20 to 30 sectors and multiple household groups) to one where there are many more models, each more issue specific and smaller. My belief is that in the future there will be less concern with developing general purpose modelling capabilities than in the last decade. The models developed in the 1970s focused on general purpose modelling capabilities partly as a continuation of the computational work of the 1960s. These models partially sought to demonstrate the feasibility of constructing applied general equilibrium models by showing they could handle much larger dimensions than theoretical models.

Model construction and solution have now both been shown to be possible. However, in applying these general purpose models to particular policy questions, a substantial amount of model detail must be carried along which is not directly applicable to the policy question at hand. In turn general purpose models applied to specific questions often need to be redesigned to target the model to the issues under investigation. As a result, recent modelling is focusing more on smaller scale issue specific models, and the themes emerging from the structure rather than the precise numbers are providing the main model output.

Another development is what, for want of a better term, I label general equilibrium econometrics. Much of the work in applied econometrics in the 1970s seems to be concerned with micro-econometrics, estimating more complex models of optimizing behaviour of households and firms than previously (such as with non-linear budget constraints). To those raised on general equilibrium theory, it is surprising that little of this activity has been taken further and used to analyze general equilibrium systems from an econometric point of view. This is, after all, the most appropriate vehicle for generating better parameter values for the equilibrium systems that modellers are now trying to solve. The basic two-person pure-exchange-economy model of economic equilibrium, for instance, emphasized in basic economic texts, has (so far as I know) never been econometrically estimated.

A further direction which also seems to be emerging is an expansion in the coverage of models to include such policy features as quantity constraints (in some cases with corresponding rent seeking activity). Such models are now widely perceived as generating more significant welfare costs of distortions than the more traditional models of tax and trade policies, because in equilibrium resources may be unused or wasted. Put simply, Krueger rectangles are bigger than Harberger triangles. Thus, a much more expansive analysis of the costs of distortions through applied general equilibrium models seems to be underway.

Other developments are occuring within the modelling fraternity itself. Modellers often complain about the necessity of being a jack of all trades. When involved in modelling activity in the applied general equilibrium area, one has to be familiar with general equilibrium theory, to be able to program (or at least communicate with programmers), to be familiar with data and be able to manipulate and convert it into a model admissible form, to be conversant with literature estimates of key parameters (including elasticities), to have a clear sense of policy issues and institutional structure, and to be

able to interpret results. With repeated modelling activity, one also
has to be something of a librarian to be able to archive and file away
results. When confronted with this range of activities it is perhaps
not surprising that it becomes difficult for graduate students and
others to enter this area. As a result, research efforts are being
focussed more and more on modelling teams similar to those which have
formed the basis for research work in the natural sciences.

Finally, it does seem clear to me that we are headed
towards an increased recognition of the inevitability of subjectivity in
both design and use of empirically based economic models. Indeed, I
would go so far as to query whether we should even think in terms of
models of particular economies or particular policy issues as constructed
in isolation from the individual doing the modelling. Since the
modellers have to make all manner of judgements including the
orientation of the model, how they chose parameter values, and which
features of results they explore and report, the models should to some
extent be seen as an extension of the mind of the modellers.

Ultimately, the future for applied general equilibrium
analysis seems likely to me to be determined by the response of the
much larger group of non modellers to the challengers outlined in this
paper. Time alone will tell whether these models lead to a new relevance
and changed empiricism in economics, or merely to further frustrations
with numerical modelling and the murky world of policy making.

References

Arrow, K.J. & Debreu, G. (1954). Existence of an equilibrium for a
    competitive economy. Econometrica, 22, 265-290.
Barone, E. (1908). Il Ministerio della Produzione nello stato
    colletivista. Giornale deqli Economistie Rivista di
    Statistica. (English translation In Collectivist Economic
    Planning, ed. F.A. Hayek, London, 1935).
Frazer, W.J. Jr. & Boland, L.A. (1983). An Essay on the Foundations of
    Friedman's Methodology. The American Economic Review,
    73, no. 1, 129-144.
Friedman,   (1947). Essays in Positive Economics, University of
    Chicago Press.
Grodon, R.H. (1981). Taxation of Corporate Capital Income: Tax
    Revenues vs. Tax Distortions. Massachusetts: National
    Bureau of Economic Research Inc., Working Paper Series
    No. 687.
Harberger, A.C. (1962). The Incidence of the Corporation Income Tax.
    Journal of Political Economy. 70, no. 3, 215-240.
Hayek, F.A. (1940). Socialist calculation: the competitive solution.
    Economica 7, 125-149.
Hirsch, W.Z. (1951). A Survey of Price Elasticities. Review of
    Economic Studies, 19, 50-60.
Johansen, L. (1960). A multi-sectoral study of economic growth.
    Amsterdam: North-Holland.
King, M.A. & Fullerton, D. (1984). The Taxation of Income from
    Capital: A Comparative Study of the United States, the
    United Kingdom, Sweden, and West Germany. (eds.)
    University of Chicago Press for the National Bureau of
    Economic Research.
Krueger, A.O. (1974). The Political Economy of the Rent-Seeking
    Society. American Economic Review, 64, 291-303.
Lange, O. (1936). On the economic theory of socialism. Review of
    Economic Studies, 4, 53-71, 123-142. Reprinted in
    O. Lange and F.M. Taylor, On the Economic Theory of
    Socialism, ed. B.E. Lippincott. Minneapolis: University
    of Minnesota Press, 1938.
Laswell, H.D. (1951). The Policy Orientation. In The Policy Sciences,
    ed. D. Lerner & H.D. Lasswell, pp. 3-15. Stanford:
    Stanford University Press.
Mansur, A. & Whalley, J. (1984). Numerical specification of applied
    general equilibrium models: estimation, calibration and
    data. In Applied General Equilibrium Analysis, ed. H.E.
    Scarf & J.B. Shoven, Cambridge University Press.
Robbins, L.C. (1934). The Great Depression. London: Macmillan.
Scarf, H. (1973). The Computation of Economic Equilibria, New Haven:
    Yale University Press.
————————— (1960). Some examples of global instability of the
    competitive equilibrium. International Economic Review,
    1, 157-172.
Shoven, J.B. & Whalley, J. (1984). Applied General Equilibrium Models
    of Taxation and International Trade. Journal of Economic
    Literature, 22, no. 3, 1007-1051.
Stiglitz, J.E. (1973). Taxation, corporate financial policy, and the
    cost of capital. Journal of Public Economics, 2, no. 1,
    1-34.

von Mises, L. (1936). Socialism: An Economic and Sociological Analysis, transalted from the German by Jacque Kuhane, London: Johnathan Cape.

Whalley, J. (1984). "Trade, Industrial Policy, and Canadian manufacturing", A Review article of a monograph by Richard Harrs. Canadian Journal of Economics, LXVI, no. 2.

Wiles, P.J.D. (1962). The Political Economy of Communism. Oxford: Basil Blackwell.

THE MEASUREMENT OF WASTE AND WELFARE IN APPLIED GENERAL
EQUILIBRIUM MODELS

W.E. Diewert
Department of Economics, The University of British Columbia,
Vancouver, British Columbia, Canada   V6T 1W5

1 INTRODUCTION

In a series of papers stemming from their Yale Ph.D. theses,
Shoven & Whalley [1972] [1973] [1974] introduced a new tool into the applied
welfare economist's toolkit, applied general equilibrium modelling.[1] The
essence of this new approach may be summarized as follows. Tax distortions
and government expenditures are introduced into a classical Walrasian
general equilibrium model. Production functions and consumer utility
functions are assumed to be of the Cobb-Douglas, C.E.S. or fixed
coefficients type or nested combinations of these functional forms. If the
functional form is of the C.E.S. type, $f(x_1, \ldots, x_N) \equiv (\Sigma_{i=1}^{N} \delta_i x_i^r)^{1/r}$, the
parameter r (which is related to the elasticity of substitution) is
determined on the basis of empirical estimates of relevant elasticities of
demand or supply. The first order parameters for the production and utility
functions in the model (e.g., the δ_i parameters in the C.E.S. functional
form) are chosen so that the general equilibrium model will have a benchmark
equilibrium as its solution. This calibration procedure determines all of
the parameters in the model.[2] Now the model may be used to simulate the
effects of alternative tax and government expenditure policies.

The above approach to general equilibrium modelling suffers from an
obvious defect which was noted by Jorgenson [1983]: the assumed functional
forms are too restrictive and are frequently rejected by econometric tests
using less restrictive functional forms. Put another way, if the number of
goods exceeds two, the Cobb-Douglas, Leontief or C.E.S. functional forms
cannot provide a second order approximation to an arbitrary functional
functional form; i.e., they are not flexible functional forms.[3] In order to
overcome this criticism, Jorgenson [1983] and his coworkers have constructed
general equilibrium models based on econometrically estimated flexible
functional forms for production and utility functions. Jorgenson's approach
to applied general equilibrium modelling might be called the econometric

42

approach, while the Shoven-Whalley approach might be called the <u>calibration</u> approach.[4]

It is not the purpose of this paper to compare and contrast the econometric and calibration approaches. Our main purpose is to discuss alternative ways for measuring the <u>waste</u> that is inherent in a tax distorted general equilibrium. Thus our discussion is relevant for both the econometric and calibration approaches to applied general equilibrium modelling. Existing applied general equilibrium models have measured waste in the following ways: (i) as an output difference or ratio; i.e., an undistorted reference equilibrium is computed and the reference equilibrium value of output is compared to the distorted equilibrium value of output, using either reference or distorted equilibrium prices to value the outputs (examples using this approach include Shoven & Whalley [1972] and Mansur and Whalley [1984]), (ii) as a sum of Hicksian [1942] compensating variations (e.g., Fullerton, Shoven & Whalley [1983]), and (iii) as a sum of Hicksian equivalent variations (e.g., Harrison & Kimbell [1983]).[5]

In this paper, we shall suggest two classes of methods for measuring the waste inherent in a tax distorted equilibrium, a <u>quantity</u> oriented method that has its origins in the work of Allais [1943][1977] and Debreu [1951][1954], and a <u>price</u> oriented method that has its origins in the work of Hicks [1942] and Boiteux [1951].

In the Allais-Debreu approach, we pick a reference nonnegative quantity vector. We then compute an artificial reference equilibrium that keeps each consumer at his distorted equilibrium level of utility, eliminates all of the tax distortions and maximizes the number of multiples of the "waste" reference vector that the economy can produce. The resulting number of wasted reference vectors is a natural measure of the resource cost of the nonoptimal tax system. Note (along with Debreu [1951]) that this measure of waste does not depend on interpersonal utility comparisons - each consumer is kept on his or her base indifference surface. In order to define formally the Allais-Debreu measure of waste, it is necessary to have an explicit economic model. Thus in section 2 below, we introduce our formal model of a small open economy that will be used throughout the paper. We then define the Allais-Debreu measure in section 3 and provide a second order approximation to it in section 4. In section 5, we consider the dependence of the approximate loss measure on second order derivatives; i.e., we develop an analytical sensitivity analysis for our Allais-Debreu loss measure.

In section 6, we define formally our Hicks-Boiteux loss measure. The measure may be described (imperfectly) in words as follows. Pick any reference Pareto optimal equilibrium for the economy and compute the corresponding equilibrium consumer prices. Let the comparison equilibrium be an observed tax distorted equilibrium. Our price oriented measure of waste may now be defined as (minus) the sum (over all consumers) of the Hicksian [1942; 128] equivalent variations, where we use the Pareto optimal consumer prices as the reference prices. We show that this measure of waste is nonnegative (which seems to be a new result).[6]

In section 7, we consider the following vexing problem: which Pareto optimal equilibrium should we choose to be the reference equilibrium in the Hicks-Boiteux loss measure? The literature on fair or equitible allocations (Foley [1967], Sen [1970], Rawls [1971], Kolm [1972], Schmeidler & Vind [1972], Varian [1974] [1976], Pazner & Schmeidler [1974][1978], Crawford [1977] and Pazner [1977] suggests an answer to this question.

The Hicks-Boiteux measure of waste can be regarded as the difference between welfare at the nondistorted and the tax distorted equilibria, where the welfare function is essentially a utilitarian social welfare function. Since we have drifted into the sea of welfare economics, it seems reasonable to pause for a swim, so in section 8, we consider properties that various authors have suggested that social welfare functions ought to have. Our approach to welfare economics follows that of Varian [1976; 255]: once we have found the "best" Pareto optimal reference equilibrium, we can construct a welfare function that can be used to make comparisons among arbitrary allocations. In section 9, we provide some concrete examples for functional forms for social welfare functions and we discuss these examples in the light of the theoretical properties listed in section 8. With one exception, the examples are taken from the work of Atkinson [1970], Blackorby & Donaldson [1978], Roberts [1980a], Deaton & Muellbauer [1980] and Jorgenson & Slesnick [1984].

In section 10, we make use of Kolm's [1969; 186] monetary measure of the injustice of an income distribution in order to decompose the loss of welfare going from a Pareto optimal equilibrium to a tax distorted equilibrium into efficiency and equity components. Our efforts in this section are similar in spirit to those of Jorgenson & Slesnick [1984].

In section 11, we return to the vexing problem raised in section 7; i.e., which equilibrium should we use as our reference equilibrium in the Hicks-Boiteux loss measure. In section 11, we discuss what to do if there is more than one fair equilibrium.

Section 12 concludes.

2 A MODEL OF A SMALL OPEN ECONOMY

We shall find it convenient to formulate our general equilibrium model of an open economy in terms of dual functions; i.e., in terms of expenditure functions and unit profit functions. Our reason for doing this is that these dual functions already contain the restrictions implied by utility or profit maximizing behavior and hence the characterization of a competitive equilibrium in the economy reduces to the solution of a certain (relatively small) system of equations or inequalities. For examples of general equilibrium models using duality theory, see Dixit & Norman [1980; ch.2] and Woodland [1982; ch.2-7]. The model that we are about to describe is very similar to that used in Diewert [1984].

Let $p \equiv (p_1, p_2, \ldots p_N)^T \gg 0_N$ denote a vector of positive domestic output and input prices and let $w \equiv (w_1, w_2, \ldots w_M)^T \gg 0_M$ denote a vector of positive world prices for internationally traded goods.[7] If the economy is actually a closed economy that does not engage in international trade, then we set $M=1$, $w_1 \equiv 1$, and the "internationally" traded good is taken to be a numeraire domestic good.

We assume that the producer side of our economy consists of K ($\leq N$) constant returns to scale sectors.[8] The technology of the kth sector is represented by a set S^k of feasible net outputs (inputs and imports are indexed negatively). Thus if $(x,y) \in S^k$, then the vector $x \equiv (x_1, x_2, \ldots, x_N)^T$ of domestic net outputs and the vector $y \equiv (y_1, y_2, \ldots, y_M)^T$ of net exports are producible by sector k. Technically, we assume that each set S^k has the following representation: for $k = 1, 2, \ldots, K$,

$$S^k \equiv \left\{ (x,y): x=a^k z_k, \ y=b^k z_k, \ (a^k, b^k) \in C^k, z_k \geq 0 \right\} \qquad (1)$$

where z_k is a nonnegative sector k scalar scale variable and C^k is a nonempty, closed convex subset of R^{N+M} that represents the sector k unit scale production possibilities. Our representation of the economy's production possibilities is broad enough to encompass both the usual neoclassical smooth production functions and the activity analysis framework. In the latter case, the sets C^k are the convex hulls of a finite number of points or activities.

Define the sector k <u>unit profit function</u> π^k which is dual to the unit scale production possibilities set C^k by[9]

$$\pi^k(p,w) \equiv \max_{a,b}\{p \cdot a + w \cdot b : (a,b) \in C^k\}, \quad k=1,\ldots,K, \qquad (2)$$

where $p \gg 0_N$ and $w \gg 0_M$. It can be shown that the π^k are (positively) linearly homogeneous and convex functions of their price arguments. Moreover, if $\pi^k(p,w)$ is differentiable with respect to its components for some k, then by Hotelling's Lemma, the solution to (2) is unique for this k and is given by $a^k = \nabla_p \pi^k(p,w)$, $b^k = \nabla_w \pi^k(p,w)$.[10]

Turning now to the consumer side of the model, we assume that there are H adult individuals in the economy. The preferences of individual h can be represented by means of an increasing,[11] quasiconcave[12] utility function, f^h, defined over a (possibly translated) orthant in R^{N+M}, Ω^h. Labor supplies are indexed negatively.

Define the individual h <u>expenditure function</u> m^h which is dual to the utility function f^h for $h=1,2,\ldots,H$ by

$$m^h(u_h,p,w) \equiv \min_{c,d}\{p \cdot c + w \cdot d : f^h(c,d) \geq u_h, (c,d) \in \Omega^h\} \qquad (3)$$

where $p \gg 0_N$, $w \gg 0_M$ and $u_h \in$ Range f^h. The functions m^h will satisfy various regularity properties which are listed in Diewert [1982;554].[13] The most important properties for our purposes are: (i) $m^h(u_h,p,w)$ is increasing in u_h and (ii) $m^h(u_h,p,w)$ is positively linearly homogeneous and concave in p,w. Moreover, if $m^h(u_h,p,w)$ is differentiable with respect to its price arguments for some h, then by Shephard's Lemma, the solution to (3) is unique for this h and is given by $c^h = \nabla_p m^h(u_h,p,w)$ and $d^h = \nabla_w m^h(u_h,p,w)$.

We also assume that each individual h possesses <u>nonnegative</u> endowment vectors of domestic and internationally traded goods, $\bar{c}^h \geq 0_N$ and $\bar{d}^h \geq 0_M$, respectively for $h=1,2,\ldots,H$. Note that, if for example the nth domestic good is a type of labour service, we assume that $\bar{c}_n^h = 0$ for all h; i.e., consumer endowments are positive only for physical goods that are transferable. Further note that if consumer h chooses the domestic net consumption vector $c^h \equiv (c_1^h, c_2^h, \ldots, c_N^h)^T$ and $c_n^h < 0$, then consumer h is supplying $-c_n^h > 0$ units of that type of labour service.

Governments appear in our model in four ways: (i) they have endowment vectors of domestic and foreign goods, (ii) they supply certain public goods and demand various inputs, (iii) they tax both domestic and internationally traded goods and (iv) they transfer revenue to or tax revenue from individuals. In order to simplify the model, we do not allow the government to optimize its choice of public goods production. Thus government functions (i) and (ii) listed above may be combined: we assume that the government has a net endowment vector of domestic goods $\bar{c}^0$; and a net endowment vector of internationally traded goods $\bar{d}^0$; i.e., $\bar{c}^0$ = government endowment of domestic goods minus government demands for domestic inputs plus government supplies of domestic goods. If $\bar{c}^0_n < 0$, then the government demand for domestic good n exceeds the sum of any supplies it produces plus its endowment of the good. Let $\tau \equiv (\tau_1, \tau_2, \ldots \tau_M)^T$ be a vector of tariffs and/or export taxes or subsidies. We assume that producers face the price vector p for domestic goods and $w+\tau$ for internationally traded goods where $p \gg 0_N$ and $w+\tau \gg 0_M$. Let $t \equiv (t_1, t_2, \ldots, t_N)^T$ be a vector of taxes or subsidies on domestic goods and $s \equiv (s_1, s_2, \ldots, s_M)^T$ be a vector of taxes or subsidies on internationally traded goods. We assume that each consumer faces the price vector $p+t \gg 0_N$ for domestic goods and $w+\tau+s \gg 0_M$ for internationally traded goods. The government's net transfer to individual h is g_h; if $g_h < 0$, then $-g_h$ is the amount of lump sum tax Mr. h pays to the government.

Assuming that consumer expenditure functions m^h and producer unit profit functions π^k are differentiable, we consider the following four sets of equations, (4)-(7):

$$m^h(u_h, p+t, w+\tau+s) = g_h + (p+t) \cdot \bar{c}^h + (w+\tau+s) \cdot \bar{d}^h \; ; \; h=1, \ldots, H. \quad (4)$$

Equation h in (4) says that expenditures on domestic and traded goods by individual h minus the value of any labour supplied, $m^h(u_h, p+t, w+\tau+s)$, equals government net transfer income, g_h, plus the value of the domestic good endowment, $(p+t) \cdot \bar{c}^h$, and plus the value of Mr. h's endowment of internationally traded goods, $(w+\tau+s) \cdot \bar{d}^h$, where all goods are valued at the consumer prices, $(p+t, w+\tau+s)$.

$$\sum_{h=1}^{H} \nabla_p m^h(u_h, p+t, w+\tau+s) = \sum_{k=1}^{K} \nabla_p \pi^k(p, w+\tau) z_k + \sum_{h=0}^{H} \bar{c}^h. \quad (5)$$

The system of N equations in (5) tells us that consumer demand for domestic goods equals producer supply plus consumer endowments, $\Sigma_{h=1}^{H} \bar{c}^h$, plus the government's net endowment vector $\bar{c}^0$.

$$0 = \pi^k(p, w+\tau) \, , \quad k=1,\ldots,K. \tag{6}$$

The K equations in (6) are the usual zero profit restrictions that apply to a competitive economy. Finally, the balance of trade constraint is:

$$\Sigma_{k=1}^{H} \, w \cdot \nabla_w m^h(u_h, p+t, w+\tau+s) = \Sigma_{k=1}^{K} \, w \cdot \nabla_w \pi^k(p, w+\tau) z_k + \Sigma_{h=0}^{H} \, w \cdot \bar{d}^h. \tag{7}$$

Equation (7) equates consumer demand for net imports to producer supply of net exports plus the value of consumer plus government (net) endowments of internationally traded goods, where all of these goods are valued at the world prices w.[14]

    We regard the system of H+N+K+1 equations (4)-(7) as a system of simultaneous equations in the following variables: $u \equiv (u_1,\ldots,u_H)^T$ (utility vector), $p \equiv (p_1,\ldots,p_N)^T$ (domestic price vector), $z \equiv (z_1,\ldots,z_K)^T$ (industry scales vector), $t \equiv (t_1,\ldots,t_N)^T$ (consumer taxes on domestic goods), $\tau \equiv (\tau_1,\ldots,\tau_M)^T$ (producer taxes on traded goods), $s \equiv (s_1,\ldots,s_M)^T$ (additional consumer taxes on traded goods) and $g \equiv (g_1,\ldots,g_H)^T$ (government transfer vector). Usually, u, p, z and one component of τ, t, s or g will be regarded as endogenous variables while the remaining components of τ, t, s and g are regarded as exogenous variables.

    A solution $(u^1, p^1, z^1, \tau^1, t^1, s^1, g^1)$ to (4)-(7) where $p^1 \gg 0_N$, $w+\tau^1 \gg 0_M$ is defined to be a <u>tax distorted competitive equilibrium</u>. It can be verified that if such an equilibrium exists, producers are competitively maximizing profits and consumers are maximizing utility subject to their budget constraints (see equations (4)). We assume that our numerical general equilibrium model has a tax distorted competitive equilibrium. In what follows, we shall refer to this equilibrium as the observed distorted equilibrium, and it will be indexed by the superscript 1.

    How can we measure the waste that is inherent in such a tax distorted equilibrium?

3 AN ALLAIS-DEBREU MEASURE OF WASTE

We first need to pick a 1+N dimensional nonnegative reference vector, $(\beta_0, \beta_1, \ldots, \beta_N) \equiv (\beta_0, \beta^T) > 0_{1+N}^T$. Recalling the definitions of the consumer utility functions f^h and the unit production possibilities sets C^k, consider the following <u>primal programming problem</u>:

$$\max_{\substack{r, z \\ c^h, d^h \\ a^k, b^k}} \left\{ r : \Sigma_{h=1}^H w \cdot d^h + \beta_0 r \leq \Sigma_{k=1}^K w \cdot b^k z_k + \Sigma_{h=0}^H w \cdot \bar{d}^h ; \right. \tag{8}$$

$$\Sigma_{h=1}^H c^h + \beta r \leq \Sigma_{k=1}^K a^k z_k + \Sigma_{h=0}^H \bar{c}^h ;$$

$$f^h(c^h, d^h) \geq u_h^1, \; (c^h, d^h) \varepsilon \Omega^h, \; h=1, \ldots, H;$$

$$\left. (a^k, b^k) \varepsilon C^k, \; k=1, \ldots, K; \; z \equiv (z_1, \ldots, z_K)^T \geq 0_K \right\}$$

where $u^1 \equiv (u_1^1, u_2^1, \ldots, u_H^1)^T$ is the utility vector which corresponds to the observed distorted equilibrium defined in the previous section.

Although (8) looks rather complex, its meaning can readily be explained: given the <u>reference resource waste vector</u> (β_0, β), we attempt to produce the maximal number (r^0 say) of multiples of this vector that the economy can produce while maintaining each consumer at his distorted equilibrium utility level and while maintaining the balance of trade constraint. Thus r^0 or $(r^0 \beta_0, r^0 \beta)$ is a natural measure of the waste that is inherent in a tax distorted equilibrium. Using (5) and (7) applied to the distorted equilibrium, it can be seen that r=0 is feasible for the maximization problem (8). Hence the maximal r which is feasible for the constraints in (8), r^0, is nonnegative.[15]

r^0 is a variant of Debreu's [1951;285] <u>coefficient of resource utilization</u> and of the <u>distributable surplus</u> of Allais [1943; 610-644], [1977;174]. Allais picks (β_0, β) to be a unit vector so that the wasted resources are measured in terms of a numeraire commodity. In our context, it is most natural to pick $\beta_0 = 1$, $\beta = 0_N$ so that we measure the waste in terms of foreign exchange. Debreu picks the reference resource waste vector to be the economy's initial endowment vector, so that in the context of our open economy model, the Debreu reference vector would be $(\beta_0, \beta) \equiv \Sigma_{h=0}^H (w \cdot \bar{d}^h, \bar{c}^h)$.

Debreu [1951;286] noted that his measure of waste had the following advantage (which also applies to our more general measure defined by (8)): if there are two distorted equilibria which both have the same utility vector solution u^1, then the measure of waste does not change. Debreu noted that Hicksian measures of waste (see section 6 below) do not share this advantage. However, our Allais-Debreu measure of waste, r^0, suffers from an obvious disadvantage: it is not invariant to the choice of the reference resource waste vector, (β_0, β). Students of index number theory will not find this lack of invariance surprising. My own preference would be to use $\beta_0 \equiv 1$ and $\beta \equiv 0_N$ as the reference vector.

We should also mention Graaff's [1977] loss measure. His model can be approximately translated into our model if we assume that all domestic goods are inputs and all internationally traded goods are outputs produced by the K sectors. Now take the constraints in (8), set $r \equiv 0$, multiply the term $\Sigma_{k=1}^{K} w \cdot b^k z_k$ by a nonnegative scalar ε and then minimize ε. Call the resulting optimal quantity ε^0. The Graaf measure of waste could then be defined by $1-\varepsilon^0 \geq 0$.

A disadvantage of the Graaff approach is that the resulting Graaff primal programming problem is not a concave programming problem and hence the solution to the Graaff problem will be harder to compute.

Since (8) is a concave programming problem, we may apply the Karlin [1959;201] - Uzawa [1958;34] Saddle Point Theorem and rewrite (8), using (3) and (4), as the following max min problem:[16]

$$r^0 = \max_{r,z} \min_{p,e} \left\{ r(1-e\beta_0-p\cdot\beta) + \Sigma_{k=1}^{K} \pi^k(p,ew)z_k \right.$$

$$-\Sigma_{h=1}^{H} m^h(u_h^1,p,ew) + \Sigma_{h=0}^{H} (p\cdot\bar{c}^h+ew\cdot\bar{d}^h);$$

$$\left. z \geq 0_K, \; p \geq 0_N, \; e \geq 0 \right\} \qquad (9)$$

where r and z are interpreted as in (8), e is a nonnegative Lagrange multiplier which was applied to the first equation in the constraints of (8) and $p \geq 0_N$ is a nonnegative vector of Lagrange multipliers applied to the next N constraints of (8). If r^0, z^0, p^0, e^0 solves (9), then z^0 is the optimal scale vector, p^0 may be interpreted as a vector of domestic prices and e^0 may be interpreted as an exchange rate that converts foreign prices into domestic prices.

Note that the primal constrained maximization problem involved 1+K+H(N+M)+K(N+M) variables whereas the essentially unconstrained max min problem (9) involves only 1+K+N+1 variables. This is an enormous reduction

in dimensionality and illustrates the power of duality theory in general
equilibrium modelling.

The Karlin-Uzawa Saddle Point Theorem may be applied (in
reverse) to the max min problem (9). Thus we may obtain a third expression
for r^0 involving another concave programming problem which has only the
price variables p and e:

$$r^0 = -\max_{e \geq 0, p \geq 0_N} \{\Sigma_{h=1}^H m^h(u_h^1, p, ew) - \Sigma_{h=0}^H (p \cdot \bar{c}^{-h} + ew \cdot \bar{d}^{-h}) : \qquad (10)$$

$$- \pi^k(p, ew) \geq 0, k=1, \ldots, K ; e\beta_0 + p \cdot \beta \geq 1\}.$$

If r^0, z^0, p^0, e^0 solves (9), then it turns out that e^0 and p^0 will solve
(10), z^0 will be the vector of optimal Lagrange multipliers for the first K
constraints in (10) and r^0 will be the optimal Lagrange multiplier for the
last constraint in (10).

Our expressions for the Allais-Debreu loss, (8), (9) and (10),
do not give much insight on how the magnitude of the loss depends on the
size of the tax distortions, τ^1, t^1 and s^1, in the observed distorted
equilibrium. In order to obtain such an insight, we turn to a second order
approximation to the loss.

4 A SECOND ORDER APPROXIMATION TO THE ALLAIS-DEBREU MEASURE OF WASTE

In order to obtain a second order approximation to the loss
measure defined by (8)-(10), we shall require some stronger assumptions. We
assume that: (i) r^0, z^0, p^0 and e^0 solves (9) (so that p^0, e^0 solves (10)),
(ii) the expenditure functions m^h are twice continuously differentiable
with respect to their price arguments at $(u_h^1, p^0, e^0 w)$ for $h=1,2,\ldots,H$,
(iii) the unit profit functions π^k are twice continuously differentiable
at $(p^0, e^0 w)$ for $k=1,2,\ldots,K$, (iv) $z^0 >> 0_K$, $p^0 >> 0_N$ and $e^0 > 0$ so that the
first order necessary conditions for the max min problem (9) hold with
equality and (v) Samuelson's [1947;361] strong order sufficient conditions
hold for the contrained maximization problem (10) when the inequality
constraints are replaced by equalities.

Consider the following system of equations in the N+1+K+1
unknowns p, e, z and r regarded as functions of a scalar parameter ξ for
$0 \leq \xi \leq 1$:

$$\Sigma_{k=1}^{K} \nabla_p \pi^k (p(\xi), e(\xi) + \tau^1 \xi) z_k(\xi) - \Sigma_{h=1}^{H} \nabla_p m^h (u_h^1, p(\xi) + t^1 \xi, e(\xi) w + \tau^1 \xi + s^1 \xi) \quad (11)$$

$$+ \Sigma_{h=0}^{H} \bar{c}^h - \beta r(\xi) = 0_N$$

$$w \cdot \left[\Sigma_{k=1}^{K} \nabla_w \pi^k (p(\xi), e(\xi) w + \tau^1 \xi) z_k(\xi) - \Sigma_{k=1}^{H} \nabla_w m^h (u_h^1, p(\xi)) \right. \quad (12)$$

$$\left. + t^1 \xi, e(\xi) w + \tau^1 \xi + s^1 \xi) + \Sigma_{h=0}^{H} \bar{d}^h \right] - \beta_0 r(\xi) = 0$$

$$\pi^k (p(\xi), e(\xi) w + \tau^1 \xi) = 0 \ , \ k = 1, 2, \ldots, K \quad (13)$$

$$1 - e(\xi) \beta_0 - p(\xi) \cdot \beta = 0. \quad (14)$$

When $\xi = 0$, define $p(0) \equiv p^0$, $e(0) \equiv e^0$, $z(0) \equiv z^0$ and $r(0) \equiv r^0$. Then when $\xi = 0$, equations (11)-(14) became the first order conditions for the max min problem (9) or the first order conditions for the Lagrangian problem that corresponds to (10).

Now consider the tax distorted equilibrium $(u^1, p^1, z^1, \tau^1, t^1, s^1, g^1)$ which satisfies equations (4)-(7). We suppose that the nonnegative reference waste vector β_0, β satisfies the following harmless normalization:

$$\beta_0 + p^1 \cdot \beta = 1. \quad (15)$$

Define $p(1) \equiv p^1$, $e(1) \equiv 1$, $z(1) \equiv z^1$ and $r(1) \equiv 0$. Then when $\xi = 1$, (11), (12), (13) and (14) become (5), (7), (6) and (15), the equations which characterize the observed tax distorted equilibrium.[17] Hence we conclude that equations (11)-(14) map the Allais-Debreu reference equilibrium into the observed tax distorted equilibrium as ξ travels from 0 to 1.

Differentiate (11)-(14) with respect to ξ and evaluate the resulting derivatives at $\xi = 0$. We obtain

$$\begin{bmatrix} S_{pp}^0 - \Sigma_{pp}^0 \ , & (S_{pw}^0 - \Sigma_{pw}^0)w \ , & A^0 \ , & -\beta \\ w^T(S_{wp}^0 - \Sigma_{wp}^0), & w^T(S_{ww}^0 - \Sigma_{ww}^0)w \ , & w^T B^0 \ , & -\beta_0 \\ A^{0T} \ , & B^{0T}w \ , & 0_{K \times K} \ , & 0_K \\ -\beta^T \ , & -\beta_0 \ , & 0_K^T \ , & 0 \end{bmatrix} \begin{bmatrix} p'(0) \\ e'(0) \\ z'(0) \\ r'(0) \end{bmatrix} \quad (16)$$

$$= - \begin{bmatrix} S^0_{pw}\tau^1 - \Sigma^0_{pw}(\tau^1+s^1) - \Sigma^0_{pp}t^1 \\ \\ w^T(S^0_{ww}\tau^1 - \Sigma^0_{ww}(\tau^1+s^1) - \Sigma^0_{wp}t^1) \\ \\ B^{0T}\tau^1 \\ \\ 0 \end{bmatrix}$$

where $S^0 \equiv \begin{bmatrix} S^0_{pp} , S^0_{pw} \\ \\ S^0_{wp} , S^0_{ww} \end{bmatrix} \equiv \Sigma^K_{k=1} \begin{bmatrix} \nabla^2_{pp}\pi^k(p^0,e^0w) , \nabla^2_{pw}\pi^k(p^0,e^0w) \\ \\ \nabla^2_{wp}\pi^k(p^0,e^0w) , \nabla^2_{ww}\pi^k(p^0,e^0w) \end{bmatrix} z^0_k ,$

$$\Sigma^0 \equiv \begin{bmatrix} \Sigma^0_{pp} , \Sigma^0_{pw} \\ \\ \Sigma^0_{wp} , \Sigma^0_{ww} \end{bmatrix} \equiv \Sigma^H_{h=1} \begin{bmatrix} \nabla^2_{pp}m^h(u^1_h,p^0,e^0w) , \nabla^2_{pw}m^h(u^1_h,p^0,e^0w) \\ \\ \nabla^2_{wp}m^h(u^1_h,p^0,e^0w) , \nabla^2_{ww}m^h(u^1_h,p^0,e^0w) \end{bmatrix} ,$$

$A^0 \equiv [a^{10},\dots,a^{K0}] \equiv [\nabla_p\pi^1(p^0,e^0w),\dots,\nabla_p\pi^K(p^0,e^0w)]$ and

$B^0 \equiv [b^{10},\dots,b^{K0}] \equiv [\nabla_w\pi^1(p^0,e^0w),\dots,\nabla_w\pi^K(p^0,e^0w)].$

In view of Hotelling's Lemma, S^0 may be interpreted as an aggregate producer substitution matrix and Shephard's Lemma implies that Σ^0 may be interpreted as an aggregate consumer substitution matrix. The N by K matrix A^0 and the M by K matrix B^0 may be interpreted as matrices of optimal input-out coefficients for domestic and foreign goods respectively.[18]

We now regard (16) as an identity in ξ, valid for ξ close to 0.[19] Premultiply both sides of (16) (regarded now as a matrix indentity in ξ valid for ξ close to 0) by $[p(\xi)^T,e(\xi),0^T_K,0]$. Using (13) and (14) and the linear homogeneity properties of the π^k and m^h in their price arguments, we obtain the following identity, valid for ξ close to 0:

$$-r'(\xi) = \xi\{\left[\tau^{1T}S_{wp}^{\xi} - t^{1T}\Sigma_{pp}^{\xi} - (\tau^1+s^1)^T\Sigma_{wp}^{\xi}\right]p'(\xi) \tag{17}$$

$$+ \left[\tau^{1T}S_{ww}^{\xi} - t^{1T}\Sigma_{pw}^{\xi} - (\tau^1+s^1)^T\Sigma_{ww}^{\xi}\right]we'(\xi) + \tau^{1T}S_{ww}^{\xi}\tau^1 - t^{1T}\Sigma_{pw}^{\xi}(\tau^1+s^1)$$

$$- (\tau^1+s^1)^T\Sigma_{ww}^{\xi}(\tau^1+s^1) - t^{1T}\Sigma_{pp}^{\xi}t^1 - (\tau^1+s^1)^T\Sigma_{wp}^{\xi}t^1 + \tau^{1T}B^{\xi}z'(\xi)\}$$

where S_{wp}^{ξ} is the bottom left submatrix of the producer substitution matrix S^{ξ} which is defined like S^0 below (16), except that the unit profit functions π^k are evaluated at the arguments $p(\xi)$, $e(\xi)w+\tau^1\xi$ instead of p^0, e^0w, etc., Σ_{pp}^{ξ} is the top left submatrix of the aggregate consumer substitution matrix Σ^{ξ} which is defined like Σ^0 except that the expenditure functions m^h are evaluated at the arguments $p(\xi)+t^1\xi$, $e(\xi)w+\tau^1\xi+s^1\xi$ instead of p^0, e^0w, etc., and $B^{\xi} \equiv [\nabla_w\pi^1(p(\xi),e(\xi)w+\tau^1\xi),\ldots,$ $\nabla_w\pi^K(p(\xi),e(\xi)w+\tau^1\xi)]$ is the M by K matrix of internationally traded goods input-output coefficients. Using (17),

$$r'(0) = 0. \tag{18}$$

In order to calculate $r''(0)$, we will require a formula for the term $\tau^{1T}B^0z'(0)$. Premultiply (16) by $[0_N^T,0,z'(0)^T,0]$ which yields:

$$\tau^{1T}B^0z'(0) = p'(0)^TA^0z'(0) + e'(0)w^TB^0z'(0). \tag{19}$$

Now premultiply (16) by $[p'(0)^T,e'(0),C_K^T,0]$ and solve the resulting expression for the right hand side of (19). This gives us the desired formula for the left hand side of (19). Call this new formula (19)'. Differentiate (17) with respect to ξ and evaluate the resulting derivatives at $\xi = 0$. Using (19)' and collecting terms, we find that

$$-r''(0) = \left[p'(0)^T,e'(0)w^T+\tau^{1T}\right]S^0\left[p'(0)^T,e'(0)w^T+\tau^{1T}\right]^T \tag{20}$$

$$- \left[(p'(0)+t^1)^T,(e'(0)w+\tau^1+s^1)^T\right]\Sigma^0\left[(p'(0)+t^1)^T,(e'(0)w+\tau^1+s^1)^T\right]^T$$

$$\geq 0$$

where the inequality follows from the positive semidefiniteness of the aggregate producer substitution matrix S^0 and from the negative semi-definiteness of the aggregate consumer substitution matrix Σ^0.

We are finally in a position to obtain a quadratic approximation to $r(0) \equiv r^0$ where r^0 is the solution to (8). We approximate $r(1)$ by $r(0) + r'(0) + (1/2)r''(0) \cong r(1)=0$. Using (18), we obtain the following quadratic approximation to r^0, the Allais-Debreu loss of output due to distortions:

$$L_{AD} = -(1/2)r''(0) \geq 0 \qquad \qquad (21)$$

where $r''(0)$ is defined by (20) and the derivatives of domestic prices $p'(0)$ and of the exchange rate $e'(0)$ are defined in (16).

Some qualitative properties of the approximate loss formula (21) may be noted. From (20) and (16), we see that the approximate loss L_{AD} may be regarded as a function of the tax distortion vectors τ^1, t^1, s^1, the aggregate producer and consumer substitution matrices, S^0 and Σ^0 respectively, and the input-output matrices, A^0 and B^0. It can readily be verified that if all of the distortion vectors increase proportionately, then the approximate loss increases quadratically; i.e., for $\lambda > 0$,

$$L_{AD}(\lambda\tau^1,\lambda t^1,\lambda s^1,S^0,\Sigma^0) = \lambda^2 L_{AD}(\tau^1,t^1,s^1,S^0,\Sigma^0). \qquad (22)$$

If all of the elements of the substitution matrices increase proportionately, then the approximate loss increases by the same proportional factor; i.e., for $\lambda > 0$,

$$L_{AD}(\tau^1,t^1,s^1,\lambda S^0,\lambda\Sigma^0) = \lambda L_{AD}(\tau^1,t^1,s^1,S^0,\Sigma^0). \qquad (23)$$

Similar quadratic approximations to the Allais-Debreu measure of waste for somewhat different models may be found in Debreu [1954] and Diewert [1983][1984].

We conclude this action by repeating our interpretation of r^0 (and of the approximate loss L_{AD} which approximates r^0 to the second order): given a waste reference vector β_0,β (which has value unity in terms of international prices - recall (14)), $r^0 > 0$ is the maximal number of multiples of this vector which can be thrown away but yet the economy can still produce enough to allow each consumer to attain his or her distorted equilibrium utility level and the balance of trade constraint is also still satisfied.

5 NUMERICAL VERSUS DIFFERENTIAL SENSITIVITY ANALYSIS

A major criticism of the use of numerical general equilibrium models of the Shoven-Whalley type is that various elasticities may be misspecified. The calibration procedure used in these models usually ensures that preferences and technology sets are well approximated to the first order but not to the second order. Hence, in recent applications of numerical general equilibrium analysis, sensitivity analysis plays a large role; i.e., instead of computing just one numerical general equilibrium model, many models are computed where the models differ only in their second order parameters. For good discussions of the techniques used, see Harrison & Kimbell [1983] and Mansur & Whalley [1984].

The same kind of sensitivity analysis issues can arise in the context of our Allais-Debreu loss measure. For different assumptions about the second order parameters of the unit profit functions π^k and of the expenditure functions m^h, the loss measure defined by (9) could be repeatedly calculated.

An alternative to the repeated calculation of many general equilibria is the derivation of an analytical formula for the derivative of the approximate loss defined by (21) with respect to a second order parameter. We term this differential sensitivity analysis. In our case, the set of relevant second order parameters is the set of elements of the aggregate producer and consumer substitution matrices S^0 and Σ^0.

Suppose the the elements of S^0 and Σ^0 depend on a real parameter θ which is initially 0. Define $L(\theta) \equiv L_{AD}(S^0(\theta), \Sigma^0(\theta))$ where L_{AD} is defined by (21), (20) and (16). Then the derivative of $L(\theta)$ with respect to θ evaluated at $\theta = 0$ is:

$$\nabla_\theta L(0) = (1/2) [p'^T, e'w + \tau^{1T}][\nabla_\theta S^0][p'^T, e'w^T + \tau^{1T}]^T \qquad (24)$$

$$- (1/2) [(p'+t^1)^T, (e'w+\tau^1+s^1)^T][\nabla_\theta \Sigma^0][(p'+t^1)^T, (e'w+\tau^1+s^1)^T]^T$$

$$+ [\nabla_\theta p'^T, \nabla_\theta e'w^T]S^0[p'^T, e'w^T+\tau^{1T}]^T$$

$$- [\nabla_\theta p'^T, \nabla_\theta e'w^T]\Sigma^0[(p'+t^1)^T, (e'w+\tau^1+s^1)^T]^T$$

where $p' \equiv p'(0) \equiv \nabla_\xi p(0)$, $e' \equiv e'(0) \equiv \nabla_\xi e(0)$, and $\nabla_\theta S^0 \equiv \nabla_\theta S^0(0)$ is the N+M by N+M matrix of derivatives of the elements of the producer substitution matrix with respect to the parameter θ evaluated at θ = 0. The N+1 derivatives with respect to θ of the price derivatives $p' \equiv \nabla_\xi p(0)$ and $e' \equiv \nabla_\xi e(0)$, $\nabla_\theta p'$ and $\nabla_\theta e'$, are determined by differentiating (16) with respect to θ and evaluating the resulting derivatives at $\theta = 0$.

Differentiating (16) with respect to θ yields the identity (25) when $\theta = 0$:

$$C[\nabla_\theta p'^T, \nabla_\theta e', \nabla_\theta z'^T, \nabla_\theta r']^T + \nabla_\theta C[p'^T, e', z'^T, r']^T = \nabla_\theta c \qquad (25)$$

where C is the square matrix on the left hand side of (16) and c is the vector on the right hand side of (16). Since C^{-1} exists, we see that (25) well defines the $\nabla_\theta p'$ and $\nabla_\theta e'$ which appear in (24). If we premultiply both sides of (25) by $[0_N^T, 0, z'^T, 0]$, we obtain the following identity which will be useful later:

$$z'^T A^{0T} \nabla_\theta p' + z'^T B^{0T} w \nabla_\theta e' = 0. \qquad (26)$$

Take the last two terms on the right hand side of (24) and rearrange terms as follows:

$$[\nabla_\theta p'^T, \nabla_\theta e' w^T] \, s^0 \, [p'^T, e' w^T + \tau^{1T}]^T$$

$$- [\nabla_\theta p'^T, \nabla_\theta e' w^T] \, \Sigma^0 \, [(p' + t^1)^T, \; (e' w + \tau^1 + s^1)^T]^T$$

$$= \begin{bmatrix} p'^T s_{pp}^0 + (e' w + \tau^1)^T s_{wp}^0 - (p' + t^1)^T \Sigma_{pp}^0 - (e' w + \tau^1 + s^1)^T \Sigma_{wp}^0 \\ \{p'^T s_{pw}^0 + (e' w + \tau^1)^T s_{ww}^0 - (p' + t^1)^T \Sigma_{pw}^0 - (e' w + \tau^1 + s^1)^T \Sigma_{ww}^0 \} w \end{bmatrix} \begin{bmatrix} \nabla_\theta p' \\ \nabla_\theta e' \end{bmatrix}$$

$$= \begin{bmatrix} - z'^T A^{0T} + r' \beta^T \\ - z'^T B^{0T} + r' \beta_0^T \end{bmatrix} \begin{bmatrix} \nabla_\theta p' \\ \nabla_\theta e' \end{bmatrix} \qquad \text{using the first two sets of equations in (16)}$$

$$= - (z'^T A^{0T} \nabla_\theta p' + z'^T B^{0T} \nabla_\theta e') \qquad \text{using (18), } r' = 0$$

$$= 0 \qquad \text{using (26).} \qquad (27)$$

Hence the last two terms in (24) are zero.

Now we are almost ready to apply the second order sensitivity analysis formula (24) (as amended by using (27)). The first thing we might think of doing is increasing the ij^{th} element of the aggregate substitution matrix Σ^0. Since Σ^0 is symmetric, we will have to also increase element ji by the same amount. However, this is not the end of the story. Since the expenditure functions m^h are linearly homogeneous in their price arguments, we may deduce that Σ^0 satisfies the following restriction:

$$[p^{0T}, e^0 w^T] \, \Sigma^0 = [0_N^T, \, 0_M^T] \, . \tag{28}$$

Hence if we increase elements ij and ji of Σ^0 by θ, in order to satisfy the restrictions (28), we must decrease element ii by $p_j^0 \theta / p_i^0$ and decrease element jj by $p_i^0 \theta / p_j^0$ where we now define $e^0 w^T = [e^0 w_1, \ldots, e^0 w_M] \equiv [p_{N+1}^0, \ldots, p_{N+M}^0]$. Define the N+M by N+M matrix M_{ij} to be a matrix of zeros except: (i) element ii is equal to $-p_j^0 / p_i^0$, (ii) element jj is equal to $-p_i^0 / p_j^0$ and (iii) elements ij and ji are equal to 1. We assume $1 \leq i < j \leq N+M$. Now set $\Sigma^0 (\sigma_{ij}) = \Sigma^0 + M_{ij} \sigma_{ij}$ where σ_{ij} is a nonnegative scalar which corresponds to an increase in elements ij (and ji) of Σ^0. Apply (24) using (27):

$$\partial L(0) / \partial \sigma_{ij} = -(1/2) \left[(p'+t^1)^T, (e'w+\tau^1+s^1)^T \right] M_{ij} \left[(p'+t^1)^T, (e'w+\tau^1+s^1)^T \right]^T \geq 0 \tag{29}$$

where the inequality follows from the negative semidefiniteness of the matrix M_{ij} and the derivatives $p' \equiv p'(0)$, $e' \equiv e'(0)$ are defined by (16). Thus as the ij^{th} element of the aggregate consumer substitution matrix Σ^0 becomes larger, the Allais-Debreu approximate loss due to the tax distortions τ^1, t^1, s^1 will generally <u>increase</u> (it can never decrease). As elements ij and ji increase (and elements ii and jj decrease in the appropriate manner so that the homogeneity restrictions (28) continue to hold), we make the aggregate substitution matrix more negative semidefinite; i.e., we increase the amount of consumer substitutability in our model. Thus the qualitative result (29) tells us that <u>more</u> consumer substitutability leads to <u>bigger</u> Allais-Debreu approximate losses. This is a new qualitative result which is consistent with our earlier qualitative result (23).

Now let us decrease the ij^{th} element of the aggregate producer substitution matrix S^0 where $i \neq j$. Since S^0 is symmetric, we must also

decrease element ji. Moreover, since the unit profit functions are linearly
homogeneous in their price arguments, we deduce that S^0 satisfies

$$[p^{0T}, e^0 w^T]\, S^0 = [0_N^T\,,\,0_M^T]. \tag{30}$$

Hence as we decrease elements ij and ji by s_{ij}, we must increase element
ii by $s_{ij}p_j^0/p_i^0$ and increase element jj by $s_{ij}p_i^0/p_j^0$. Set $S^0(s_{ij}) = S^0 - M_{ij}s_{ij}$
where M_{ij} is the same negative semidefinite matrix that was defined above
(29). Thus as we <u>decrease</u> elements ij and ji of S^0, we are making the
aggregate producer substitution matrix more positive semidefinite; i.e., we
are <u>increasing</u> the amount of producer substitutability in our model.
Applying (24) and using (27), we find that

$$\partial L(0)/\partial s_{ij} = -(1/2)\left[p'^{T}, e'w^T + \tau^{1T}\right] M_{ij} \left[p'^{T}, e'w^T + \tau^{1T}\right]^T \geq 0 \tag{31}$$

where the inequality again follows from the negative semidefiniteness of the
matrix M_{ij}. The qualitative result (31) tells us that <u>more</u> producer
substitutability leads to <u>bigger</u> Allais-Debreu approximate losses.[20]

This concludes our suggestions for the development of a
differential approach to sensitivity analysis as opposed to the numerical
approach in the context of our Allais-Debreu measure of waste. For more on
the numerical approach, see Harrison & Kimbell [1983]. For a good
discussion of the merits and demerits of the differential and numerical
approaches to general equilibrium modelling in the context of the Harberger
[1962] two sector corporate taxation model, see Shoven [1976] and Harberger
& Bruce [1976].

6 A HICKS-BOITEUX MEASURE OF WASTE

Our main task in this paper is to derive alternative measures of
the waste or deadweight loss that is inherent in a tax distorted
equilibrium. We have discussed the Allais-Debreu approach in previous
sections and we introduce the Hicks-Boiteux approach in this section.

In words, what we call the Hicks-Boiteux measure of waste is
simply (minus) the sum of the equivalent variations of Hicks [1942;128],
using the prices pertaining to <u>any</u> Pareto optimal equilibrium as the
reference (or 0) equilibrium. The observed tax distorted equilibrium is the
comparison (or 1) equilibrium. Hicks did not insist that the 0 equilibrium

be a Pareto optimal one, but Boiteux [1951;121] did; hence it seems reasonable to call this measure of loss a Hicks-Boiteux measure.

We first need to define what we mean by a Pareto optimal reference equilibrium: we specify utility levels u_h^0 for individuals $h=2,3,\ldots,H$[21] and maximize the utility of the first individual subject to the constraints of technology and trade balance and subject to attaining the given level of welfare for individuals $2,3,\ldots,H$. Hence we need to solve the following primal programming problem:

$$\max_{\substack{z \\ a^k, b^k \\ c^h, d^h}} \{f^1(c^1,d^1): \Sigma_{h=1}^H c^h \leq \Sigma_{k=1}^K a^k z_k + \Sigma_{h=0}^H \bar{c}^h ; \tag{32}$$

$$w \cdot \Sigma_{h=1}^H d^h \leq w \cdot (\Sigma_{k=1}^K b^k z_k + \Sigma_{h=0}^H \bar{d}^h) ;$$

$$z \equiv (z_1,\ldots,z_K)^T \geq 0_K ; \quad (a^k,b^k) \epsilon C^k, \; k=1,\ldots,K ;$$

$$f^h(c^h,d^h) \geq u_h^0 , \; h=2,3,\ldots,H; \quad (c^h,d^h)\epsilon\Omega^h, \; h=1,\ldots,H\}$$

where the unit scale technology sets C^k, the utility functions f^h and the consumption possibilities sets Ω^h were defined in section 2 and are assumed to satisfy the regularity conditions listed there. We now make the following additional assumptions: (i) a finite maximum for (32) exists, (ii) a feasible solution for (32) exists which satisfies the first two sets of constraints strictly and (iii) the utility function f^1 is actually concave instead of being merely quasiconcave.[22] With these extra assumptions, (32) becomes a concave programming problem and we may apply the Karlin-Uzawa Saddle Point Theorem to obtain the equivalent dual max min problem (33):

$$\max_{z \geq 0, u_1} \min_{p \geq 0, e \geq 0} \{u_1 + \Sigma_{k=1}^K \pi^k(p,ew)z_k - m^1(u_1,p,ew) \tag{33}$$

$$-\Sigma_{h=2}^H m^h(u_h^0,p,ew) + \Sigma_{h=0}^H (p \cdot \bar{c}^h + ew \cdot \bar{d}^h)\}$$

where we have set $u_1 = f^1(c^1,d^1)$ and we have also used definitions (2) for the unit profit functions π^k and definitions (3) for the expenditure functions m^h. The vector p is a vector of Lagrange multipliers (or prices) which corresponds to the first set of constraints in (32) (the domestic resource constraints) while e is a Lagrange multiplier (or exchange rate) which corresponds to the second constraint in (32) (the balance of trade constraint).

We assume that $z^0 \geq 0_K$, u_1^0, $p^0 \geq 0_N$ and $e^0 > 0$[23] solves (33) and that the functions π^k are differentiable at p^0, e^0w while the function m^k is differentiable at (u_h^0, p^0, e^0w) for $h=1,\ldots,H$.[24] Our (not necessarily unique) solution z^0, u_1^0, p^0, e^0 to (33) must satisfy the following Kuhn-Tucker conditions (see Karlin [1959;204]):

$$1 - \nabla_{u_1} m^1(u_1^0, p^0, e^0w) = 0 , \tag{34}$$

$$\pi^k(p^0, e^0w) \leq 0, \; z_k^0 \geq 0, \; k=1,\ldots,K, \; \Sigma_{k=1}^K \pi^k(p^0, e^0w) z_k^0 = 0 , \tag{35}$$

$$\Sigma_{k=1}^K \nabla_p \pi^k(p^0, e^0w) z_k^0 - \Sigma_{h=1}^H \nabla_p m^h(u_h^0, p^0, e^0w) + \Sigma_{h=0}^H \bar{c}^h \equiv x^0 \geq 0_N, p^0 \geq 0_N, p^0 \cdot x^0 = 0, \tag{36}$$

$$w \cdot \left(\Sigma_{k=1}^K \nabla_w \pi^k(p^0, e^0w) z_k^0 - \Sigma_{h=1}^H \nabla_w m^h(u_h^0, p^0, e^0w) + \Sigma_{h=0}^H \bar{d}^h \right) \equiv x_0^0 \geq 0, e^0 \geq 0, e^0 x_0^0 = 0 , \tag{37}$$

where in (37), ∇_w means calculate the gradient vector of π^k or m^h with respect to its last M arguments.

Equations and inequalities (34)-(37) characterize a Pareto optimal equilibrium, $u^0 \equiv (u_1^0, u_2^0, \ldots, u_H^0)^T$, z^0, p^0, e^0. Note the resemblance of (35) to (6), of (36) to (5) and of (37) to (7). Equation (34) may be interpreted as an equation which determines the scale of domestic prices p^0, e^0 relative to the fixed vector of international prices w. In fact, (35)-(37) are simply generalizations of (5)-(7) to allow for the possibility of negative unit profits in sectors that are not used and the possibility of free goods in equilibrium. We conclude that (35)-(37) characterize a competitive undistorted equilibrium.[25] Thus we have sketched a derivation of the Second Fundamental Theorem of Welfare Economics due to Arrow [1951]: every Pareto optimal equilibrium can be generated as a competitive equilibrium if lump sum transfers of resources are allowed.

We wish to establish a certain fundamental inequality between aggregate consumer expeditures evaluated at the distorted and undistorted equilibria. in order to do this, we must first establish some preliminary results. Premultiply both sides of (36) by p^{0T}, premultiply (37) by e^0 and add the resulting equalities. Using the linear homogeneity properties of the π^k and m^h in prices as well as (35), we obtain the following identity:

$$\Sigma_{h=1}^{H} m^h(u_h^0,p^0 . e^0w) = \Sigma_{h=0}^{H} p^0 . \bar{c}^h + \Sigma_{h=0}^{H} e^0w . \bar{d}^h. \tag{38}$$

Equations (5) and (7) applied to the distorted equilibrium may be rearranged to yield:

$$\Sigma_{h=0}^{H} \bar{c}^h = \Sigma_{h=1}^{H} \nabla_p m^h(u_h^1,p^1+t^1,w+\tau^1+s^1) - \Sigma_{k=1}^{K} \nabla_p \pi^k(p^1,w+\tau^1)z_k^1 \tag{39}$$

and

$$w . \Sigma_{h=0}^{H} \bar{d}^h = \Sigma_{h=1}^{H} w . \nabla_w m^h(u_h^1,p^1+t^1,w+\tau^1+s^1) - \Sigma_{k=1}^{K} w . \nabla_w \pi^k(p^1,w+\tau^1)z_k^1 . \tag{40}$$

Using (38)-(40), we obtain

$$\Sigma_{h=1}^{H} m^h(u_h^0,p^0,e^0w) \tag{41}$$

$$= \Sigma_{h=1}^{H} \{p^0 . \nabla_p m^h(u_h^1,p^1+t^1,w+\tau^1+s^1) + e^0w . \nabla_w m^h(u_h^1,p^1+t^1,w+\tau^1+s^1)\}$$

$$- \Sigma_{k=1}^{K} \{p^0 . \nabla_p \pi^k(p^1,w+\tau^1) + e^0w . \nabla_w \pi^k(p^1,w+\tau^1)z_k^1\}$$

$$\geq \Sigma_{h=1}^{H} m^h(u_h^1,p^0,e^0,w) - \Sigma_{k=1}^{K} \{p^0 . \nabla_p \pi^k(p^1,w+\tau^1) + e^0w . \nabla_w \pi^k(p^1,w+\tau^1)z_k^1\}$$

$$\geq \Sigma_{h=1}^{H} m^h(u_h^1,p^0,e^0w) - \Sigma_{k=1}^{K} \pi^k(p^0,e^0w)z_k^1$$

$$\geq \Sigma_{h=1}^{H} m^h(u_h^1,p^0,e^0w).$$

The first inequality in (41) follows from the definitions (3) and the fact that $\nabla_p m^h(u_h^1,p^1+t^1,w+\tau^1+s^1)$, $\nabla_w m^h(u_h^1,p^1+t^1,w+\tau^1+s^1)$ is a feasible (but not necessarily optimal) solution to the expenditure minimization problem defined by $m^h(u_h^1,p^0,e^0w)$ for h=1,2,...,H. The second inequality in (41) follows from the definitions (2) and the fact that $\nabla_p \pi^k(p^1,w+\tau^1)$, $\nabla_w \pi^k(p^1,w+\tau^1)$ is feasible for the unit profit maximization problem, $\max_{a^k,b^k}\{p^0 . a^k+e^0w . b^k : (a^k,b^k) \epsilon C^k\} \equiv \pi^k(p^0,e^0w)$, but it is not necessarily the optimal solution, for k=1,2,...,K. The final inequality in (41) follows from the nonpositivity of unit profit conditions (35) and the nonnegativity of sectoral scale conditions, $z_k^1 \geq 0$. Our method for establishing the inequality is similar to the methods used by Dixit and Norman

[1980;74] and Woodland [1982;260] to establish the existence of gains from trade.

The difference between the left hand side and right hand side of (41) defines our <u>Hicks-Boiteux Loss measure</u>:

$$L_{HB}(u^0,u^1,p^0,e^0) \equiv \Sigma_{h=1}^{H} \; m^h(u_h^0,p^0,e^0w) \; - \; \Sigma_{h=1}^{H} \; m^h(u_h^1,p^0,e^0w) \qquad (42)$$

$$= \Sigma_{h=1}^{H} \{ m^h(u_h^0,p^0,e^0w) \; - \; m^h(u_h^1,p^0,e^0w) \}. \qquad (43)$$

Thus using definition (42) and the inequality (41), we have proven

<u>Theorem 1</u>: $L_{HB}(u^0,u^1,p^0,e^0) \geq 0.$ [26]

From (42), L_{HB} is minus the sum of the Hicksian [1942;128] <u>equivalent variations</u>, $m^h(u_h^1,p^0,e^0w) - m^h(u_h^0,p^0,e^0w)$, [27] between two equilibria for our economy, where the 0 equilibrium corresponds to a specified Pareto optimal equilibrium, the 1 equilibrium corresponds to an observed distorted equilibrium and the reference prices p^0,e^0w are equilibrium prices for the Pareto optimal equilibrium.

King [1983;191] has suggested the measure (42) as an aggregate measure of deadweight loss in a many person economy, except that he did not specify that the reference prices p^0,e^0w should correspond to equilibrium commodity prices in an undistorted Pareto optimal equilibrium. It is this latter specification that ensures that the loss is nonnegative. The measure (42) seems also to be broadly consistent with Harberger's [1971] deadweight loss measures, since (42) adds together individual gains and losses in an unweighted manner.

For some purposes, it is convenient to express the loss in terms of foreign exchange (or if M=1, in terms of the resulting numeraire commodity). The resulting monetary measure may be obtained by dividing (42) through by e^0. Using the homogeneity properties of the expenditure functions m^h in their price arguments, the resulting monetary loss is

$$L_{HB}(u^0,u^1,(e^0)^{-1}p^0,1) = \Sigma_{h=1}^{H} \{ m^h(u_h^0,(e^0)^{-1}p^0,w) \; - \; m^h(u_h^1,(e^0)^{-1}p^0,w) \}. \quad (44)$$

We now attempt to provide an economic interpretation for the loss measure (44). First, we pick a reference Pareto optimal equilibrium that is "best" in some sense. (In sections 7 and 11 below, we will suggest some candidates for the "best" equilibrium). Secondly, we compute the equilibrium utility vector u^0 and the equilibrium vector of domestic commodity prices p^0/e^0 that corresponds to this equilibrium. Thirdly, evaluate the net value of commodities consumed minus the value of labour services supplied, where commodities and labour supplies are priced out at the domestic commodity prices p^0/e^0 and the international prices w. Call the resulting net value of consumption evaluated at a utility vector u and at reference prices $(e^0)^{-1}p^0$, w, <u>real income</u>, $Y(u,(e^0)^{-1}p^0,w) \equiv \Sigma_{h=1}^m (u_h,(e^0)^{-1}p^0,w)$. The inequality (41) tells us that this aggregate real income is maximized over all possible feasible utility vectors u when u $= u^0$; i.e., if u^1 is a feasible utility vector, then

$$Y(u^1,p^0/e^0,w) \le Y(u^0,p^0/e^0,w).$$

Thus $L_{HB} = Y(u^0,p^0/e^0,w) - Y(u^1,p^0/e^0,w)$ is the amount of aggregate consumption, valued at the reference prices p^0/e^0,w, that the economy is throwing away by remaining at a nonoptimal utility allocation indexed by u^1 instead of moving to the "best" utility allocation indexed by u^0. Hence L_{HB} may be interpreted as the foreign exchange equivalent value of the net consumption the economy gives up by remaining at the distorted or nonoptimal[28] equilibrium indexed by u^1.

We usually think of waste measures as measures of the amount of inefficiency in the economy. However our Hicks-Boiteux loss measure cannot be interpreted as a traditional pure loss of efficiency measure (except in the case of one consumer), since our observed distorted equilibrium indexed by u^1 could well correspond to a "nonbest" alternative Pareto optimal allocation. Thus the Hicks-Boiteux loss measure mixes welfare and efficiency considerations whereas the Allais-Debreu loss measure is a pure efficiency loss measure, since utilities are kept constant in the two situations being compared there. Both types of loss have a certain element of arbitrariness to them: in the AD measure, we must pick a reference "waste" vector, while in the HB measure, we must pick a reference "best" Pareto optimal equilibrium.

Second order approximations to the HB loss have been derived by Boiteux [1951] and by Diewert [1984].

We conclude this section by determining under what conditions the inequality in (41) will be strict so that the HB loss will be strictly positive.

Define the consumer h __substitution gain__ for $h=1,2,\ldots,H$ by

$$G^h \equiv p^0 \cdot \nabla_p m^h(u_h^1, p^1+t^1, w+\tau^1+s^1) + e^0 w \cdot \nabla_w m^h(u_h^1, p^1+t^1, w+\tau^1+s^1) \qquad (45)$$

$$- m^h(u_h^1, p^0, e^0 w) \geq 0.$$

Define the producer k __substitution gain__ for $k=1,2,\ldots,K$ by

$$G_k \equiv \pi^k(p^0, e^0 w) - \{p^0 \cdot \nabla_p \pi^k(p^1, w+\tau^1) + e^0 w \cdot \nabla_w \pi^k(p^1, w+\tau^1)\} \geq 0. \qquad (46)$$

Define the sector k __subsidy termination gain__ for $k=1,2,\ldots,K$ by

$$\gamma_k \equiv -\pi^k(p^0, e^0 w) z_k^1 \geq 0. \qquad (47)$$

The inequalities in (45)-(47) follow for the reasons explained below (41). Hence each gain term is nonnegative. If consumer h's u_h^1 indifference surface is L shaped and hence exhibits no substitution, then G^h defined by (45) will be zero. However, if the consumer's indifference surface exhibits some substitutability and commodity prices in the two equilibria are not proportional, then G^h will generally be positive. If the unit scale production possibilities set in section k, C^k, is block shaped and hence exhibits no possibilities for substitution at positive prices, then G_k defined by (46) will be zero. In particular, if C^k consists of a single point, G^k will be zero. However, if the set C^k exhibits some substitutability and prices are not proportional, then G_k will generally be positive. The consumer and producer substitution terms G^h and G_k occur in the trade literature; e.g., see Woodland [1982;266]. However, the subsidy termination term γ_k defined by (47) is new. We note that $\gamma_k > 0$ only if $z_k^1 > 0$ (so that sector k is operating in the distorted equilibrium) and if $\pi^k(p^0, e^0 w) < 0$ so that sector k makes negative unit scale profits in the reference Pareto optimal equilibrium and hence is not operated at a positive scale in the undistorted equilibrium; i.e., $z_k^0 = 0$. Hence $-\pi^k(p^0, e^0 w) z^1 = \gamma_k$ is the loss that sector k implicitly earns in the distorted equilibrium if it chooses the profit maximizing vector of input-output coefficients using the reference equilibrium prices. Hence γ_k may be interpreted as the amount sector k is implicitly being subsidized in the distorted equilibrium.

Rework the inequalities in (41) using definitions (45)-(47). A bit of algebra shows that the Hicks-Boiteux loss defined by (42) may be rewritten as follows:

$$L_{HB}(u^0,u^1,p^0,e^0) = \Sigma^H_{h=1}\ G^h + \Sigma^K_{k=1}\ G_k + \Sigma^K_{k=1}\ \gamma_k; \qquad (48)$$

i.e., L_{HB} equals the sum of the nonnegative consumer substitution gains plus the nonnegative producer substitution gains plus the nonnegative subsidy termination gains. If any of the gain terms are positive, then $L_{HB} > 0$.

7 UTILITARIAN MEASURES OF WELFARE

Recall the prices p^0,e^0 that corresponded to the Pareto optimal allocation of utilities u^0. Suppose we agree that u^0 represents the "best" allocation of utilities. Then consider the following <u>utilitarian social welfare function</u>:

$$Y(u,p^0,e^0) \equiv \Sigma^H_{h=1}\ m^h(u_h,p^0,e^0 w). \qquad (49)$$

We say that the utility vector u^1 is socially preferred to the utility vector u^2 if $Y(u^1,p^0,e^0) > Y(u^2,p^0,e^0)$. From Theorem 1 in the previous section, it can be seen that the social welfare function defined by (49) has the property that it ranks the "best" allocation of utilities u^0, the highest over all feasible utility vectors. This property of the money metric (or dual) utilitarian social welfare function (49) is closely related to Varian's [1976; 254-258] primal approach to measuring welfare. Varian, following Negishi [1960], assumes that utility functions are all concave and so the "best" allocation of utilities may be obtained by maximizing a convex combination of utilities subject to resource and technology constraints. However, our Theorem 1 does not require that utility functions be concave.

Let u^1 and u^2 be any two feasible utility allocations for the economy. Then the following identity links the utilitarian social welfare function (49) to the Hicks-Boiteux loss (42):[29]

$$Y(u^2,p^0,e^0) - Y(u^1,p^0,e^0) = -[L_{HB}(u^0,u^2,p^0,e^0) - L_{HB}(u^0,u^1,p^0,e^0)], \qquad (50)$$

i.e., the gain in utilitarian welfare moving from the equilibrium indexed by the utility vector u^1 to the u^2 equilibrium is equal to the negative of the difference in the HB losses. Thus there is a close connection between HB loss measures and utilitarian social welfare functions.

Utilitarian (or additive in individual utilities) social welfare functions have been axiomatically derived by a number of social choice theorists.[30] In addition, Deaton & Muellbauer [1980; 219-224], McKenzie [1983; 142] and King [1983] suggest the specific utilitarian social welfare function (49), which is additive in individual expenditure functions using common reference prices.[31] However, none of these authors specified that the reference prices should correspond to a Pareto optimal situation.

Which reference price vector p^0,e^0 should we choose? As Deaton & Muellbauer [1980; 225] have noted, the individual expenditure functions or money metric utility functions, $m^h(u_h,p^0,e^0w)$, provide complete scalar indicators of the objective, external economic circumstances facing each individual.[32] Elaborating on this point, define individual h's nonlabour "income" using the reference prices p^0,e^0 in period i for i=1,2 by $y_h^i \equiv m^h(u_h^i,p^0,e^0w)$ where u_h^i is the corresponding individual h utility in situation i. Then for i=1,2,

$$u_h^i = \max_{c,d}\{f^h(c,d): p^0 \cdot c + e^0 w \cdot d \leq y_h^i, (c,d)\varepsilon\Omega^h\}. \qquad (51)$$

If $y_h^1 < y_h^2$, then $u_h^1 < u_h^2$ but more than this is true: the "income" scalars y_h^i indicate the _size_ of the choice set facing _each_ individual in situations i=1,2 (using the common reference prices p^0,e^0w).

Due to the work of Harsanyi [1977; ch.4], Sen [1970; 135] and Rawls [1971; 136], economists (acting as moral philosophers) have become accustomed to the veil of ignorance idea, which suggests that social choices should be made on the assumption that each individual knows _all_ preferences and the technology sets in the economy, but that he does not know exactly who he will be. Under the circumstances, Harsayi suggests an expected utility maximization approach, while Rawls suggests a more conservative extreme risk aversion approach. We shall follow in the Rawlsian tradition (and follow Varian [1976; 251] specifically) and assume that each individual, acting behind the veil of ignorance, would prefer a society where each

individual is given an equal opportunity set. Thus consider the following
equations and inequalities:

$$m^h(u_h^0, p^0, w) = g_0^0 , \quad h=1,2,\ldots,H, \tag{52}$$

$$\Sigma_{k=1}^K \nabla_p \pi^k(p^0, w) z_k^0 - \Sigma_{h=1}^H \nabla_p m^h(u_h^0, p^0, w) + \Sigma_{h=0}^H \bar{c}^{-h} \equiv x^0 \geq 0_N, p^0 \geq 0_N, p^0 \cdot x^0 = 0, \tag{53}$$

$$\pi^k(p^0, w) \leq 0, \quad z_k^0 \geq 0, \quad k=1,2,\ldots,K, \quad \Sigma_{k=1}^K \pi^k(p^0, w) z_k^0 = 0, \tag{54}$$

$$w \cdot \left(\Sigma_{k=1}^K \nabla_w \pi^k(p^0, w) z_k^0 - \Sigma_{h=1}^H \nabla_w m^h(u_h^0, p^0, w) + \Sigma_{h=0}^H \bar{d}^h \right) = 0. \tag{55}$$

Comparing (52)-(55) with (4)-(7), we see that the above
equations characterize a competitive equilibrium where each individual
receives a common transfer g_0^0. The inequalities in (53) mean that we are
now allowing for the possibility of zero equilibrium prices for domestic
commodities. The inequalities in (54) mean that we are now allowing for the
possibility of negative unit scale profits in sectors that are run at zero
scale. We assume that the balance of trade restriction (55) holds with
equality and that the equilibrium exchange rate e^0 is positive and hence we
have renormalized prices so that $e^0 = 1$. Thus the equilibrium domestic
commodity prices $p^0 \equiv (p_1^0, \ldots, p_N^0)^T$ are denominated in units of foreign
exchange.

If the inequalities in (53) and (54) hold as equalities, then
(52)-(55) may be regarded as H+N+K+1 equations in the H+N+K+1 unknowns u^0
(utility vector), p^0 (domestic commondity price vector), z^0 (optimal
sectoral scale vector) and g_0^0 (common household transfer income).

If we premultiply (53) by p^{0T}, multiply the kth inequality
in (54) by z_k^0 and add the resulting inequalities to (55) and finally add
equations (52), we obtain the following expression for the government budget
constraint:

$$H g_0^0 = p^0 \cdot \Sigma_{h=0}^H \bar{c}^{-h} + w \cdot \Sigma_{h=0}^H \bar{d}^h. \tag{56}$$

Thus a solution to (52)-(55) may be generated by the solution techniques
used in numerical general equilibrium modelling if we simply give each
individual a net endowment vector of domestic and internationally traded
commodities equal to $H^{-1} \Sigma_{h=0}^H \bar{c}^{-h}$ and $H^{-1} \Sigma_{h=0}^H \bar{d}^h$ respectively. Thus after

government commodity requirements are met, each individual receives an equal
share of the excess total endowments of transferable commodities in the
economy. We assume that a solution to (52)-(55) exists.[33]

Unfortunately, the solution to (52)-(55) may not be unique. In
the nonunique case, we must simply select the "best" equilibrium. In
section 11, we shall return to this problem of selection, but it should be
said in advance, that we do not have any compelling criterion for picking a
best "equal opportunity equilibrium" of the type described by (52)-(55).[34]

Foley [1967; 74] defines an equilibrium to be equitable if no
individual in the society under consideration prefers someone else's
consumption allocation to his own. Varian [1974; 64] defines an allocation
to be fair if it is both equitable and Pareto optimal. If a solution to
(52)-(55) exists, then the resulting allocation is a competitive
equilibrium, and hence by the First Fundamental Theorem of Welfare Economics
(see Arrow [1951]), the allocation is Pareto optimal. Furthermore, since in
equilibrium, each household faces the same budget constraint, the allocation
is equitable as well. Thus a solution to (52)-(55) is a fair allocation.[35]
The specific fair allocation that results from a competitive equilibrium in
a pure exchange economy when endowments are divided equally is called an
"opportunity-fair" allocation by Varian [1976; 251], an "equal income
competitive equilibrium" by Crawford [1977] and the "Walrasian Choice
Correspondence from equal division" by Thomson [1983][1984].[36]

Some researchers would not call our equal opportunity
equilibrium a fair one. The problem is associated with the well known
counterexample of Pazner & Schneidler [1974] (which is repeated in Varian
[1974; 72]) which shows that fair allocations do not necessarily exist. The
problem hinges around the treatment of leisure and labour supply. Recall
that we indexed labour supplies negatively and our definition of the
consumption possibilities set Ω^h of individual h restricted h to supplying
types of labour service to types that he or she is actually capable of
supplying. If different individuals can supply the "same" type of labour
service at different efficiencies (i.e., they earn different wages), then
these types of labour service are regarded as distinct. Our conventions on
labour supply enable us to avoid the nonexistence problems encountered by
Pazner & Schmeidler, who converted the labour supply of every individual
into homogeneous leisure by subtracting hours worked from a maximal number
of hours available. Our treatment of labour supply leads however to another
problem: some researchers (e.g., Pazner [1977; 459-460] or Archibald &

Donaldson [1979; 211-213]) would not regard our equal opportunity equilibrium as being fair. The problem is that individuals who are endowed with
more valuable labour skills will be able to obtain bigger consumption
bundles (if they work). Thus Pazner [1977; 459] would probably criticize
our equal opportunity equilibrium on the same grounds that be criticized
Varian's [1974; 73-74] fair or wealth-fair allocations: both types of
allocation implicitly sanctify productivity. Thus in search of a more just
concept of fair, Pazner & Schmeidler [1978a] suggest that labour supplies
should be converted to leisure consumptions. Then household endowments of
time could be treated as transferable resources and included in the endowment vectors c^{-h} to be equally distributed across all consumers. The resulting allocation of resources generated by a competitive equilibrium is called
an <u>income-fair</u> allocation by Pazner [1977; 460], but the term <u>full income
fair</u> seems more descriptive to us.[37]   (A more descriptive term for our
"equal opportunity equilibrium" might be a <u>capital income fair</u> allocation,
because only "capital" goods or non leisure endowments of goods are equally
distributed across consumers).

A number of criticisms may be directed towards the use of full
income fair allocations. The following quotation from Pazner [1977; 461]
illustrates the first type of criticism:

> "In general, the more able a person, ceteris paribus,
> the more penalized he is relative to an unable one.
> Income-fair allocations therefore discriminate among
> people in a manner that is diametrically opposed to
> the discrimination taking place at wealth-fair
> allocations."

Another way of putting the above critism is to note that each individual's
time is confiscated by the state (presumably) and then redistributed. This
amounts to a form of slavery.[38] The second criticism is a more technical
one but is nonetheless vexing: if a given individual can supply many
different types of labour service, how can we determine which types of
labour service are to be equally shared? We might suppose that it is the
most expensive type of labour service that is to be equally distributed, but
this introduces an element of circularity since we cannot determine
equilibrium wages until we have decided which types of labour service a
multiskilled individual is going to supply to the endowment pot. Our
capital income fair concept does not suffer from this indeterminancy. A
third criticism of the full income fair concept is its lack of incentive
compatibility;[39] i.e., how is the state going to induce relatively skilled

individuals to reveal their talents? What we are arguing here is that a full income fair allocation may not in fact be feasible. This objection may at first glance appear to be morally worthless, but a second glance may change this opinion: it is no use to hold up a particular allocation as being "fair" if it is in fact not achievable.

In view of the above criticisms, we feel that a full income fair allocation is not an appropriate "just" allocation for individuals acting behind the veil of ignorance, whereas a capital income fair allocation might be appropriate. Our main reservation about the ethical justness of the equal opportunity equilibrium concept is that it shows a lack of concern for handicapped individuals; i.e., for people who have extremely low skill levels. This deficiency could be remedied by specifying that society (i.e., the government) should provide handicapped people with certain levels of services. These services would show up in the exogenously specified government net endowment vectors, $\bar{c}^0$ and $\bar{d}^0$. Thus the exogenously specified government production of public goods should also include various services for the disadvantaged.

Another way of tempering the productivity orientation of capital fair allocations would be to follow Archibald & Donaldson [1979; 211-213] by moving toward a full income fair allocation: a part of each person's time is confiscated by the state and added to the common net endowment vector to be equally distributed across all individuals. The resulting "hybrid fair" allocation would still run into the measurement and incentive compatibility problems mentioned above (and we would also need a concrete criterion for deciding on the actual portion of ones time that must be donated to the endowment pot), but it seems that this concept of fairness is worthy of further study.

Let us summarize this section as follows. (i). Pick the most desirable Pareto optimal allocation of utilities in the economy, u^0 say. (ii). Compute the corresponding prices for domestic goods that would support this Pareto optimal allocation (recall (33)), p^0, e^0 say. (iii). Measure each consumer's utility in terms of the money metric representation, $m^h(u_h, p^0, e^0 w)$, using the reference prices computed in (ii) above. (iv). Use the money metric utility functions to form the money metric utilitarian social welfare function $Y(u, p^0, e^0)$ defined by (49) above. By Theorem 1, $Y(u, p^0, e^0)$ is maximized over all feasible utility vectors u when $u = u^0$, the reference vector of utilities chosen in (i) above. (v). By (50), for two arbitrary feasible utility allocations, the gain in utilitarian welfare is equal to minus the difference in the Hicks-Boiteux losses using u^0, p^0 and e^0 as reference utilities and prices in the definition of the HB loss, (42). (vi). We follow Varian [1976] and suggest that a reasonable candidate for the most desirable Pareto optimal allocation of utilities is a solution u^0 to (52)-(55). We call such an allocation of utilities an equal opportunity allocation or a capital income fair allocation. Note that the resulting social welfare function defined by (49) depends very explicitly on the prices p^0,e^0 associated with the "best" Pareto optimal point, and thus it is not "price-independent" to use Roberts' [1980b; 278] term. Thus we agree with Roberts [1980b; 295] that it is natural to accept the fact that welfare prescriptions will be price dependent in general.[40]

8   SOCIAL MEASURES OF WELFARE

Let $u^0 \equiv (u_1^0,\ldots,u_H^0)^T$ be the "best" Pareto optimal utility vector and let p^0,e^0 be a corresponding competitive equilibrium price vector; i.e., a price solution to the max min problem (33). Recall that we used these reference prices in our definition of the utilitarian social welfare function (49). We now introduce some new notation and then we put the utilitarian welfare function on a per capita basis. Define the "income" equivalent to utility level u_h for individual h at the reference prices $(e^0)^{-1}p^0$,w by y_h:

$$y_h \equiv m^h(u_h, (e^0)^{-1}p^0, w), \quad h=1,\ldots,H \; ; \; y \equiv (y_1,\ldots,y_H)^T . \tag{57}$$

Note that each "income" y_h is now being measured in units of foreign exchange. (If there is no foreign trade in the model, then recall that w is a scalar and we set w=1. In this case y_h is being measured in terms of this numeraire good.)

We now use the "income" vector y in order to define our first example of a per capita money metric social welfare function (other examples will be given in the following section):

Example 1: Utilitarian   (e.g., McKenzie [1983; 142], King [1983]):

$$W^1(y) \equiv (\Sigma_{h=1}^H y_h)/H \equiv 1_H^T y/H \equiv \bar{y} \tag{58}$$

where 1_H is a vector of ones of dimension H, and $\bar{y}$ is the arithmetic mean
of the H components of the "income" vector y. Remember that the components
of the "income" vector are not incomes in the normal accounting sense, since
our "incomes" are relative to special reference prices and moreover correspond only to nonlabour income.

Suppose that our reference utility vector u^0 corresponds to a
capital fair allocation; i.e., u^0, p^0, z^0 and $e^0 \equiv 1$ satisfy (52)-(55).
Then Theorem 1 and equations (52) show that $W^1(y)$ is maximized over all
feasible "income" vectors y which correspond to feasible utility vectors u
at $y^* = g_0^0 1_H$; i.e., at a point where all "incomes" are equally
distributed and equal to the scalar g_0^0.

The above maximum property of the utilitarian social welfare
function is a good one; i.e., $W^1(y)$ takes on its highest value over all
feasible "income" vectors at the best income vector, $g_0^0 1_H$. The problem
with the utilitarian social welfare function occurs when we use it to rank
feasible "income" vectors y which are not optimal: the resulting ranking
shows no concern over distributional issues.[41] Thus it seems sensible to
consider alternative functional forms for a social welfare function, W(y)
say, which have the same property as the utilitarian functional form in that
W(y) is maximized over feasible y at the equally distributed income vector,
$g_0^0 1_H$, but which do not have the distributional indifference property of
the utilitarian function.

Our approach to welfare economics follows that of Varian [1976;
255]: once we have found the "best" Pareto optimal reference equilibrium, we
then introduce a welfare function that can be used to make comparisons among
arbitrary allocations.

The following property on a social welfare function expresses a
preference for a more equal distribution of money metric "incomes":[42]

Property 1: W is quasiconcave; i.e., if $0 \leq \lambda \leq 1$, then
$$W(\lambda y^1 + (1-\lambda)y^2) \geq \min \{W(y^1), W(y^2)\}.$$

Another very natural property for a social welfare function is
that it should treat individuals in an anonymous (May [1952]) or impartial
or nondiscriminatory (Kolm [1969; 188]) or symmetric (Dasgupta et al. [1973;
181]) manner. Let Py denote a permutation of the components of y. Then the
symmetry property is:

Property 2: W is <u>symmetric</u> in its arguments; i.e., $W(Py) = W(y)$ for every
permutation Py of y.

  It seems harmless to assume that social welfare is increasing
along the equally distributed "income" line. Hence we might as well scale
the social welfare function so that social welfare is equal to per capita
"income" along the equally distributed "income" line.

Property 3: <u>Cardinal scaling</u> of W; i.e., $W(\lambda 1_H) = \lambda$ for all real λ.

  The next property on W is technical in nature and seems to us to
be rather weak.

Property 4: W is <u>continuous from above</u> over its domain of definition D;
i.e., for every scalar s, the set $\{y: W(y) \geq s, y \varepsilon D\}$ is closed.

  We take D, the domain of definition of W, to be the (translated)
orthant $\{y: y \geq \tilde{y} 1_H\}$ where $\tilde{y} \leq 0$ is the lowest possible level of "income"
that could occur for any individual. If $\tilde{y} = 0$, then D is the nonnegative
orthant.

  The above 4 properties seem to us to be minimal properties that
any money metric social welfare function should have. However, the
following 3 properties are also of interest.

Property 5: W is (positively) <u>linearly homogeneous</u>; i.e., $W(\lambda y) = \lambda W(y)$ for
every $\lambda \geq 0$ and $y \geq 0_H$.

Property 6: W is <u>translatable</u>;[43] i.e., $W(y+\lambda 1_H) = W(y) + \lambda$ for all real λ
and all $y \varepsilon D$.

  The primary attractiveness of properties 5 and 6 is that they
dramatically reduce the complexity of the social welfare function W: if
property 5 holds, then each social welfare indifference surface is a radial
blowup of the unit indifference surface (assuming the domain of definition
is the nonnegative orthant); if property 6 holds, then each indifference
surface is a translation (parallel to the equal "incomes" ray) of the unit
indifference surface. Blackorby & Donaldson [1980] and Kolm [1976] relate
properties 5 and 6 to "rightist" and "leftist" measures of inequality, a

topic we will touch on in section 10. Blackorby & Donaldson [1980; 122] [1982; 254] say that W is <u>distributionally homothetic</u> if it satisfies 5 and 6. Note that properties 5 and 6 do not conflict with property 3.

<u>Property 7</u>: W is <u>nondecreasing</u>; i.e., $y^2 \geq y^1$ implies $W(y^2) \geq W(y^1)$.

        While property 7 is often placed on social welfare functions, it does not seem to be an ethically attractive property: if the distribution of "incomes" is very skewed, we may well feel that social welfare should decrease if the richest individual gets an increase in "income".
        The following Theorem formalizes some remarks made in Sen [1973; 42].

<u>Theorem 2</u>: Suppose W satisfies Properies 1-4 above. Let λ be a scalar such that the maximization problem (59) below has a feasible solution:

$$\max_{y} \left\{ W(y): \; 1 \cdot y/H \leq \lambda, \; y \varepsilon D \right\}. \tag{59}$$

Then $\lambda 1_H$ solves (59) and the maximum is $W(\lambda 1_H) = \lambda$.

<u>Proof</u>: The feasible region for (59) is $\left\{ y: \; y \geq \bar{y} 1_H, \; 1 \cdot y \leq H\lambda \right\}$, a nonempty, closed and bounded set. The existence of a maximizer y^* for (59) follows using Property 4 since the maximum of a continuous from above function over a compact set exists (see Berge [1963; 76]).
        Consider the following H points which are permutations of the components of the maximizer $y^* \equiv (y_1^*, y_2^*, \ldots, y_H^*)^T$:

$$y^1 \equiv y^*, \; y^2 \equiv (y_2^*, y_3^*, \ldots, y_H^*, y_1^*)^T, \ldots, y^H \equiv (y_H^*, y_1^*, y_2^*, \ldots, y_{H-1}^*)^T.$$

By Property 2,

$$W(y^1) = W(y^2) = \ldots = W(y^H) = W(y^*). \tag{60}$$

Define $\bar{y}^* \equiv \Sigma_{h=1}^{H} y^h/H = (1_H^T y^*/H) 1_H$. Using (60) and Property 1,

$$W(\bar{y}^*) \geq W(y^*). \tag{61}$$

Since $\bar{y}^*$ is feasible for the maximization problem (59), $W(\bar{y}^*) \leq W(y^*)$. Hence, using (61),

$$W(y^*) = W(\bar{y}^*)$$

$$= W(H^{-1}1_H^T y^* 1_H)$$

$$= 1_H^T y^*/H \qquad \qquad \text{using Property 3.} \qquad (62)$$

Again using Property 3, we may deduce that $1 \cdot y^*/H = \lambda$; i.e., our solution y^* to (59) satisfies the inequality constraint $1 \cdot y/H \leq \lambda$ with equality. Using (62), the Theorem follows.   Q.E.D.

Theorem 3: If W satisfies Properties 2 and 3 and in addition W is differentiable at the point $\lambda 1_H$, then the vector of first order partial derivatives of W evaluated at $\lambda 1_H$ is $\nabla W(\lambda 1_H) = H^{-1}1_H$.

Proof: By Property 3, $W(\lambda 1_H) = \lambda$. Differentiating with respect to λ, we obtain

$$\nabla W(\lambda 1_H) \cdot 1_H = \Sigma_{h=1}^{H} \partial W(\lambda 1_H)/\partial y_h = 1. \qquad (63)$$

By Property 2,

$$\partial W(\lambda 1_H)/\partial y_1 = \partial W(\lambda 1_H)/\partial y_2 = \ldots = \partial W(\lambda 1_H)/\partial y_H = 1/H$$

where the last equality follows using (63).

                                             Q.E.D.

Theorem 4: Let u^0, p^0, $e^0 \equiv 1$, z^0 and g_0^0 satisfy (52)-(55); i.e. they correspond to a capital income fair equilibrium. Define the money metric "income" vector y by (57). Let W(y) be any social welfare function which satisfies Properties 1 to 4. Then W(y) is maximized over all feasible "income" vectors y at the equal "income" vector $g_0^0 1_H$.

Proof: By Theorem 1,

$$g_0^0 = \max_y \{1_H^T y/H : y \equiv (y_1,\ldots,y_H)^T ; \ y_h \equiv m^h(u_h,p^0,w), \ h=1,\ldots,H ; \qquad (64)$$

$$u \equiv (u_1,\ldots,u_H)^T \text{ is a feasible utility vector}\}$$

and $g_0^0 1_H$ attains the maximum (and so is feasible in particular). By Theorem 2,

$$\max_y \{W(y) : 1_H^T y/H \leq g_0^0, \ y\epsilon D\} = g_0^0 \qquad (65)$$

and the maximum is attained at $g_0^0 1_H$, a feasible "income" vector. Since the feasible y region for (65) contains the feasible y region for (64), the Theorem follows.   Q.E.D.

Thus general social welfare functions W satisfying properties 1-4 attain their maximum over feasible money metric "income" vectors y at the equal "incomes" point $g_0^0 1_H$, the same point that maximized the utilitarian social welfare function W^1 defined by (58). However, presumably the general social welfare function W will rank nonoptimal "income" vectors in an ethically more desirable way than the utilitarian welfare function W^1. We turn now to some suggested functional forms for W.

9 EXAMPLES OF SOCIAL WELFARE FUNCTIONS

Our first example of a money metric social welfare function was the utilitarian function W^1 defined by (58). The following example has W^1 as a special case (r=1).

Example 2: Mean of Order r[44] (Atkinson [1970; 250-257]):

$$W(y) \equiv \begin{cases} (\Sigma_{h=1}^H H^{-1} y_h^r)^{1/r} & , \ r \leq 1 \ , \ r \neq 0 \ , \ y \geq 0_H \\ \\ \Pi_{h=1}^H y_h^{1/H} & , \ r = 0. \end{cases} \qquad (66)$$

Roberts [1980a; 432] provides an axiomatic characterization for W^r provided that y is restricted to be nonnegative.

The bigger r is, the smaller is the curvature of the indifference surfaces of W^r. As r approaches $-\infty$, $W^r(y)$ approaches $\min_h\{y_h: h=1,\ldots,H\}$, the Rawlsian [1971] social welfare function (see Sen [1970; 136]). W^r is discussed further by Blackorby & Donaldson [1978; 70], Roberts [1980b; 285], and Deaton & Muellbauer [1980; 236]. Blackorby & Donaldson [1982; 254-256] extend the domain of definition of W^r to all of R^H (not just the nonnegative orthant) [45] and provide an axiomatic social choice characterization for W^r.

It can be verified that W^r (restricted to the nonnegative orthant) satisfies all of the Properties listed in the previous section with the exception of Property 6, translatability. The only disadvantages that might be associated with the use of W^r in numerical general equilibrium models are: (i) the domain of definition for W^r is only the nonnegative orthant and (ii) Property 7 (nondecreasingness) is always satisfied and we may not regard this as being ethically satisfactory.

Example 3: Absolute Deviation (Roberts [1980a; 431]):

$$W^{*1}(y) \equiv \bar{y} - \gamma \Sigma_{h=1}^H |y_h - \bar{y}|/H \quad \text{where} \quad \bar{y} \equiv 1_H^T y/H \quad \text{and} \quad \gamma \geq 0. \tag{67}$$

Roberts chooses the distributional concern parameter γ to be $H/(2H-1)$ in which case W^{*1} satisfies Properties 1-7. If $\gamma=0$, $W^{*1}(y) = \bar{y}$ $= W^1(y)$, the utilitarian function. For $H=2$, and $\gamma>0$, the level curves for W^{*1} are two line segments joined at and symmetric around the 45 degree line. For $H=2$ and $\gamma>1$, the level curves are backward bending. In general W^{*1} satisfies Properties 1-6, and if γ is relatively small, it will also satisfy Property 7.

Example 4: Coefficient of Variation (Blackorby & Donaldson [1978; 70], Roberts [1980a; 431]):

$$W^{*2}(y) \equiv \bar{y} - \gamma(\Sigma_{h=1}^H (y_h - \bar{y})^2/H)^{1/2} \quad \text{where} \quad \bar{y} \equiv 1_H^T y/H \quad \text{and} \quad \gamma \geq 0. \tag{68}$$

Blackorby & Donaldson [1978; 73] graph a level set for W^{*2} with $H=3$ and $\gamma=1$ and they provide similar graphs for W^r for $r=1/2$, 0 and -2 (these graphs are repeated in part in Deaton & Muellbauer [1980; 237]). For $H=2$, the family of level curves for W^{*2} is exactly the same as for W^{*1}.

For a general H and γ, W^{*2} satisfies Properties 1-6 and it also satisfies Property 7 if γ is small enough.

Example 5: Mean of Order r in Absolute Deviations (Jorgenson and Slesnick [1984]):

$$W^{*r}(y) \equiv \bar{y} - \gamma \left[\Sigma_{h=1}^{H} H^{-1} |y_h - \bar{y}|^r \right]^{1/r}, \quad \bar{y} \equiv 1_H^T y/H, \quad \gamma \geq 0, \quad r \geq 1. \quad (69)$$

Note that W^{*r} contains examples 3 and 4 as special cases (r=1 and 2 respectively). It can be verified that W^{*r} satisfies Properties 1 through 6. The only difficult property to verify is Property 1, quasi-concavity. This property will follow if we can show that W^{*r} is a concave function, and concavity of W^{*r} will follow if we can show that $f(Y_1, \ldots, Y_H) \equiv \left[\Sigma_{h=1}^{H} H^{-1} Y_h^r \right]^{1/r}$ (where $Y_h \equiv |y_h - \bar{y}|$) is a convex function of y. But this follows since the functions $Y_h(y)$ are convex in y and the function f is convex and increasing in its arguments for $r \geq 1$ (see Hardy, Littlewood and Polya [1934]). Property 7 will hold if γ is small enough. For H=2 and $\gamma > 0$, the level curves of W^{*r} are the same family of kinked lines that occurred in Examples 3 and 4.

Unfortunately, W^{*r} is not differentiable at any point on the equal "income" ray so that the level surfaces of W^{r*} are not "flat" (or tangent to a hyperplane which is perpendicular to the equal income ray) at points on the equal income ray. Why should this lack of differentiability or "flatness" of $W^{r*}(y)$ at points $y = \lambda 1_H$ bother us? The problem is that our equal opportunity equilibrium concept has selected a particular point on society's utility possibility frontier u^0 as being the "best". What we are doing now in this section is choosing alternative functional forms (or metrics) for social welfare functions in order to measure (in some sense) how far a given utility vector u is from the "best" point u^0. However, we may not feel very certain that u^0 really is the "best" allocation of utilities, and hence for u close to u^0, we may want our social welfare function to approximate a utilitarian (or linear) money metric social welfare function. Theorem 3 shows that if W(y) is differentiable at points $y = \lambda 1_H$, then it has the same vector of first order derivatives as the utilitarian function at these equal "income" points. The functions W^{*r} do not possess this moderately desirable approximation property.[46]

The following Theorem shows that the lack of differentiability of the functions W^{*r} is a general one which will apply to any function satisfying Properties 1-6.

Theorem 5: Let W be a function which satisfies Properties 2-6 listed above in section 8. Suppose in addition that a point $y' \epsilon D$ exists such that

$$W(y') = W(1_H) = 1 \quad \text{with} \quad 1_H^T y'/H > 1 \quad \text{(hence } y' \neq 1_H\text{)}. \tag{70}$$

Then W is not differentiable at 1_H and hence using Property 6, W is not differentiable at any point $\lambda 1_H \epsilon D$.

Proof: Let $0 \leq \lambda \leq 1$. Then

$$
\begin{aligned}
W(\lambda y' + (1-\lambda)1_H) &= W(\lambda y') + (1-\lambda) &&\text{by Property 6} \\
&= \lambda W(y') + (1-\lambda) &&\text{by Property 5} \\
&= \lambda + (1-\lambda) &&\text{by (70)} \\
&= 1. &&\tag{71}
\end{aligned}
$$

Hence W is constant on the line segment joining y' to 1_H. Since $\lambda y' + (1-\lambda)1_H = 1_H + \lambda(y'-1_H)$, using (71) we have

$$\lim_{\lambda \to 0^+} \left[W(1_H + \lambda(y'-1_H)) - W(1_H) \right]/\lambda = 0. \tag{72}$$

Suppose W were differentiable at 1_H. Then by the directional derivative Theorem in calculus,

$$
\begin{aligned}
\lim_{\lambda \to 0} \left[W(1_H + \lambda(y'-1_H)) - W(1_H) \right]/\lambda &= \nabla^T W(1_H)(y'-1_H) \\
&= H^{-1} 1_H^T(y'-1_H) \quad \text{by Theorem 3} \\
&= 1_H^T y'/H - 1 \\
&> 0 \quad\quad \text{using (70).} \tag{73}
\end{aligned}
$$

But (73) contradicts (72), so our supposition is false and the Theorem follows.

Q.E.D.

Theorem 5 may be restated as follows: if the function W satisfies Properties 2-6, then W is differentiable along the equal "income" ray $\lambda 1_H$ if and only if W is the utilitarian function W^1 defined by (58). This negative result indicates to us that it would be useful to drop either Property 5 (homogeneity) or Property 6 (translatability). In the following example, we drop Property 5.

Example 6: Mean-Variance Social Welfare Function:

$$W^*(y) \equiv \bar{y} - \gamma\left[H^{-1}(y-\bar{y}1_H)^T(y-\bar{y}1_H)\right], \ \bar{y} \equiv 1_H^T y/H, \ \gamma > 0. \tag{74}$$

The first term in (74) is $\bar{y}$, the mean of the observed money metric "income" distribution, while the second term is minus a constant, γ, times the variance of the "income" distribution. The function W^* is differentiable everywhere and has the following gradient vector ∇W^* and Hessian matrix $\nabla^2 W^*$:

$$\nabla W^*(\bar{y}) = H^{-1}1_H - 2\gamma H^{-1}\left[y-\bar{y}1_H\right] \ ; \ \nabla^2 W^*(y) = 2\gamma H^{-1}\left[I_H - H^{-1}1_H 1_H^T\right]. \tag{75}$$

Since the matrix of second order partial derivatives, $\nabla^2 W^*(y)$, is negative semidefinite (of rank H-1), W^* is a concave function and hence is quasiconcave. It can be verified that Properties 1-4 and 6 hold, but Properties 5 and 7 do not hold.

Let us determine what the level surface $\{y: W^*(y) = 0\}$ looks like (the other level surfaces are translations of this surface parallel to the ray of equality). Rewrite y as $y = \bar{y}1_H + d$ where $d^T 1_H = 0$. Then y satisfies $0 = \bar{y} - \gamma\left[(y-\bar{y}1_H)^T(y-\bar{y}1_H)/H\right]$ if and only if $0 \leq d^T d = H\bar{y}/\gamma$. Thus for $\bar{y} \geq 0$, the point $y = \bar{y}1_H + d$ is on the level surface $\{y: W^*(y) = 0\}$ iff d is on the sphere of radius $(H\bar{y}/\gamma)^{1/2}$ intersected with the hyperplane $d^T 1_H = 0$. Thus the 0 social welfare level surface is a parabolic surface, symmetrically distributed around the nonnegative portion of the ray of equality and the surface is tangent to the hyperplane $\{y: 1_H^T y = 0\}$ at 0_H.

If we let H=3, then we can intersect the level surfaces of W^* on a plane, say $1^T y = 1$. Looked at in this plane, the resulting family of level curves are concentric circles centered about the point of equality, (1/3, 1/3, 1/3). This family of level curves is similar to the family of

level curves graphed by Blackorby & Donaldson [1978; 73] for the coefficient
of variation social welfare function. The only difference between the level
curves for the two families is in the labelling of the curves; in the
coefficient of variation case (mean-variance case), welfare drops propor-
tionally to (as the square of) the distance from the level curve to the
point of equality.

How should we determine the parameter γ in the definition of the
mean-variance social welfare function? Recall that "income" is measured in
terms of units of foreign exchange or if there is no foreign trade, in terms
of units of a numeraire good. Hence the components of the "income" vector y
are cardinally significant and we may simply interpret γ as a conversion
factor that converts an extra unit of variance in the "income" distribution
into an equivalent per capita reduction in "income".

There is another way in which we can determine which γ to use in
empirical applications. From (75), it can be seen that if y_h (the
"income" for individual h) is significantly larger than average per capita
"income" for the society y, then $\partial W^{\circ}(y)/\partial y_h$ will be negative. Suppose
that we can agree that if individual h's "income"exceeds average "income" by
δ, then h should be given a negative weight in the social welfare function;
i.e., we should have $\partial W(y)/\partial y_h < 0$ if $y_h - \bar{y} > \delta$. This negative
weighting scheme can be realized if we choose $\gamma = 1/2\delta$.

If we exclude the utilitarian cases, all of the social welfare
functions that we have studied in this section are reasonable in the sense
that they show some concern for the distribution of "income" or utility. We
find the lack of differentiability of the functions exhibited in Examples 3,
4 and 5 (the Jorgenson-Slesnick family of welfare functions) to be
troublesome, so we would recommend the use of either a member of the mean of
order r family (Example 2) or a mean-variance social welfare function
(Example 6). The functions $W^r(y)$ are not well defined outside of the
nonnegative orthant, but this deficiency could probably be remedied by
translating the origin in y space. The choice between W^r and W° may boil
down to ones attitude towards Property 7 (nondecreasingness): W^r always
satisfies it while W° never satisfies it globally.

Obviously, a great deal of work remains to be done in this area:
alternative functional forms for W should be suggested and complete
axiomatic characterizations should be provided.

10   THE DECOMPOSITION OF SOCIAL WELFARE LOSS INTO EFFICIENCY AND INJUSTICE COMPONENTS

Kolm [1969; 186] defined the equal equivalent of an income vector y as the scalar $K(y)$ such that $W[K(y)1_H] = W(y)$ where W is the relevant social welfare function. Atkinson [1970; 250] calls $K(y)$ the equally distributed equivalent level of income per head; $K(y)$ is the income which if given to each individual would give the same level of social welfare as that given by the original income distribution vector $y \equiv (y_1,\ldots,y_H)^T$. If W satisfies our cardinal scaling assumption, Property 3, we have $W(y) = W[K(y)1_H] = K(y)$.

Kolm [1969; 186] also defines a monetary measure of the injustice of the income distribution by

$$i \equiv \bar{y} - K(y) \qquad \text{where } \bar{y} \equiv 1_H^T y/H \text{ is average income}$$

$$= \bar{y} - W(y) \qquad \text{if W satisfies Property 3.} \qquad (76)$$

Theorem 6 (Kolm [1969; 193], Sen [1973; 42], Blackorby & Donaldson [1978; 65]):[47]

If W satisfies Properties 1-4, then $i \geq 0$.

Proof: Let $y\varepsilon D$ be given. Then by Theorem 2

$$\text{Max}_z \{W(z): 1_H^T z/H \leq \bar{y} \equiv 1_H^T y/H, z\varepsilon D\} = \bar{y}.$$

Since y is feasible for the above maximization problem, $W(y) \leq \bar{y}$ or since W satisfies Property 3, $i = \bar{y} - W(y) \geq 0$.   Q.E.D.

Kolm's [1969; 186] index of relative injustice or the Atkinson [1970; 257]-Sen [1973; 42] relative inequality index is defined as

$$\begin{aligned} I &\equiv 1 - K(y)/\bar{y} \\ &= 1 - W(y)/\bar{y} \qquad \text{if W satisfies Property 3} \qquad (77) \\ &\geq 0 \qquad\qquad \text{if W satisfies Properties 1-4 and } \bar{y} > 0. \end{aligned}$$

The above inequality follows using Theorem 6.

Thus if our social welfare function W satisfies the cardinal scaling Property 3 (as is the case with all of our examples in the previous section), then the corresponding indexes of injustice i and relative inequality I may readily be calculated using (76) and (77).

Recall our earlier expression for the Hicks-Boiteux loss (44). If we express this loss on a per capita basis (and in terms of foreign exchange), we may rewrite it as the following "efficiency" measure of loss:

$$E \equiv 1_H^T y^0 / H - 1_H^T y^1 / H \equiv \bar{y}^0 - \bar{y}^1 \tag{78}$$

where $y_h^0 \equiv m^h(u_h^0, (e^0)^{-1}p^0, w)$ is money metric "income" for individual h in the "best" Pareto optimal equilibrium and $y_h^1 \equiv m^h(u_h^1, (e^0)^{-1}p^0, w)$ is "income" for h in the observed distorted equilibrium, $h=1,\ldots,H$.

Using (76), the "injustice" in the distribution of "income" at the distorted equilibrium (assuming W satisfies Property 3) is:

$$i \equiv \bar{y}^1 - W(y^1). \tag{79}$$

Assuming that W satisfies Properties 1-4 and that the reference equilibrium is a capital income fair allocation, by Theorem 4, we have:

$$W(y^0) = \bar{y}^0. \tag{80}$$

The efficiency loss E does not take into account the possible unequal distribution of utilities in the distorted equilibrium. Hence in order to obtain an overall measure of loss that takes into account the distribution of "incomes", it is natural to add i to E:

$$E + i = \bar{y}^0 - \bar{y}^1 + \bar{y}^1 - W(y^1) \qquad \text{using (78) and (79)}$$
$$= W(y^0) - W(y^1) \qquad \text{using (80).} \tag{81}$$

Thus if W satisfies Properties 1-4 and the reference "best" equilibrium is a capital income fair one, then we may decompose the welfare change going from the "best" equilibrium to an observed distorted equilibrium into a per capita efficiency component E and an injustice or per capita loss of equity term i. Our decomposition of welfare change into efficiency and equity components is similar in spirit to the decomposition obtained by Jorgenson & Slesnick [1984].

11 ON CHOOSING THE "BEST" REFERENCE EQUILIBRIUM

Recall that we chose our reference "best" equilibrium to be an
equal opportunity or a capital income fair equilibrium; i.e., a competitive
equilibrium which satisfied (52)-(55). Could there be more than one such
solution to (52)-(55); i.e., will the Walrasian equilibrium mechanism
starting from a point where transferable endowments are equally divided
generate more than one solution? Unfortunately, the answer to this question
is yes. Debreu [1970] and Dierker [1972] show that for "most" (almost all
in a certain measure space of economies) exchange economics, the number of
equilibria will be finite and odd. Keyhoe [1980] extended this result to
certain economies with production. It is possible to make additional
assumptions on the model to ensure that the odd number of equilibria is
actually one; e.g., see Arrow & Hahn [1971; ch.9], Varian [1975b] and Keyhoe
[1980]. However, by drawing Edgeworth box diagrams for a two person, two
good economy where the economy's endowment of goods is divided equally
between the two consumers, the reader can readily verify that multiple
equilibria can occur for perferences that do not look unusual. Hence it
seems that we must accept the theoretical possibility of multiple solutions
to (52)-(55).

Assume that there are a finite number, I say, of solutions to
(52)-(55). For equilibrium i, denote the associated utility vector by
$u^i \equiv (u_1^i, \ldots, u_H^i)^T$ and the associated vector of domestic prices by
$p^i \equiv (p_1^i, \ldots, p_N^i)^T$, $i = 1, 2, \ldots, I$. Drawing on the Debreu-Dierker-
Keyhoe results referred to above, we assume that I is odd.

If H = 2 so that there are only 2 individuals in the economy,
then a natural candidate for the "best" equilibrium suggests itself. Taking
the Rawls [1971]-Harsanyi [1977] risk averse choice behind the veil of
ignorance framework, it seems likely that the two individuals would agree
that the equilibrium which gave them each their median level of utility
would be "best". If we reorder the I equilibria so that individual 1 gets
the highest level of utility in equilibrium 1, the second highest utility in
equilibrium 2, etc., then the "best" equilibrium would be number (I+1)/2.

If H > 2, then a clear candidate for the "best" equilibrium does
not seem to emerge. We outline below an approach that could be used in the
I > 1, H > 2 case.

If we graph a 3 equilibria case in an Edgeworth box for the case
of two consumers in a pure exchange economy, it is clear that the median
utility solution has the prices which are the least extreme; i.e., extreme

variations in the prices p^i will usually affect one consumer favorably and the other adversely. This suggests that we choose the "best" equilibrium to be the one which has domestic prices p^i closest to average domestic commodity prices $\Sigma_{j=1}^{I} p^j / I$; i.e., pick the i which solves $\min_i \{ D(p^i - \Sigma_{j=1}^{I} p^j / I) :$ i=1,...,I$\}$ where D is some metric ($D(x) > 0$ for every $x \varepsilon R^N$; $D(x) = 0$ only if $x = 0_N$). For example, we could take $D(x) = x^T x$.

The above procedures for selecting a "best" equal opportunity equilibrium may strike the reader as being too arbitrary. It turns out that we may follow Pazner & Schmeidler [1978b] and find another way to find a "best" reference equilibrium.

Up to now, we have been cardinally scaling individual utility functions by using a money metric scaling; i.e., we have been measuring utility by "income" along a given price expansion path. This corresponds to homogeneity of degree minus one of the corresponding indirect utility functions along a reference price ray. It also corresponds to the idea behind the Allen [1949] quantity index in the theory of index numbers. However, it is possible to give up this "dual" scaling of utility functions and use a "primal" scaling. This may be done by picking a reference nonnegative, nonzero consumption vector $(\bar{c}, \bar{d}) > (0_N, 0_M)$. Positive components of this reference vector correspond to consumer goods and not to types of labour service. Now scale each individual's utility so that

$$f^h(\lambda \bar{c}, \lambda \bar{d}) = \lambda \quad \text{for } \lambda \geq 0, \ (\lambda \bar{c}, \lambda \bar{d}) \varepsilon \Omega^h, \ h=1,2,\ldots,H. \tag{82}$$

The effect of these scaling assumptions is to measure the utility of any consumption vector (c,d) for each individual h in terms of multiples of the reference consumption vector $(\bar{c}, \bar{d})$; i.e., $f^h(c,d) = u_h$ now means that h values the bundle (c,d) in the same way that he or she values u_h bundles of $(\bar{c}, \bar{d})$.[48] This is the type of cardinal scaling used by Blackorby [1975] in order to form social judgements. This type of scaling was used by Pazner & Schmeidler [1978b] and it also corresponds to the idea behind the Malmquist [1953] quantity index in the theory of index numbers.[49]

We now follow the example of Chipman & Moore [1972] and we attempt to find a feasible allocation of resources which will acheive a maximal common level of utility for all individuals. Consider the following quasiconcave programming problem:

$$\max_{u_0,z,c^h,d^h,a^k,b^k} \left\{ u_0 : f^h(c^h,d^h) \geq u_0, \ h=1,\ldots,H \ ; \right. \tag{83}$$

$$\Sigma_{k=1}^K a^k z_k + \Sigma_{h=0}^H \bar{c}^h - \Sigma_{h=1}^H c^h \geq 0_N; \ w\cdot\left(\Sigma_{k=1}^K b^k z_k + \Sigma_{h=0}^H \bar{d}^h - \Sigma_{h=1}^H d^h\right) \geq 0;$$

$$z \equiv (z_1,\ldots,z_K)^T \geq 0_K; \ (c^h,d^h)\epsilon\Omega^h, \ h=1,\ldots,H; \ (a^k,b^k)\epsilon C^k, \ k=1,\ldots,K \Big\}.$$

The u_0 in (83) is the common level of utility that we are seeking to maximize. The other variables, functions and sets are the same as the ones which appeared in the Pareto programming problem (32).

Suppose a solution $u_0^*, \ z^*, c^{h*}, d^{h*}, a^{k*}, b^{k*}$ to (83) exists such that the first H inequality constraints in (83) are satisfied by equalities; i.e., $f^h(c^{h*},d^{h*}) \equiv u_0^* = u^*$ for $h=1,\ldots,H$. Then each consumer values his equilibrium consumption vector c^{h*},d^{h*} as being equivalent to the common consumption vector $u_0^*\bar{c}, \ u_0^*\bar{d}$, where we have used (82). We have found what Pazner & Schmeidler [1978b] (see also Pazner [1977; 463]) call an egalitarian equivalent allocation. In fact, our programming method (83) for finding such an allocation is equivalent to the more abstract method used by Pazner & Schmeidler. To emphasize that the allocation which results from solving (83) depends on the reference scaling vector $\bar{c}, \bar{d}$ that appears in (82), we call a solution to (83) a $\bar{c}, \bar{d}$ fair allocation.

Suppose we use a $\bar{c}, \bar{d}$ fair allocation as our "best" equilibrium. Can we derive a counterpart to Theorem 1; i.e., can we show that a utilitarian social welfare function is maximized over feasible allocations at the $\bar{c}, \bar{d}$ fair allocation? The answer is yes provided that we make the additional assumption that the utility functions are all concave instead of being merely quasiconcave.[50] With the concavity assumption, (83) becomes a concave programming problem. Defining $u_h \equiv f^h(c^h,d^h)$ for $h=1,\ldots,H$ and applying the Karlin-Uzawa Saddle Point Theorem plus definitions (2) and (3) yields the following equivalent expression for (83):

$$\max_{u_0,u,z\geq 0_K} \min_{\lambda\geq 0_H, p\geq 0_N, e\geq 0} \left\{ u_0 + \Sigma_{h=1}^H \lambda_h[u_h-u_0] + p\cdot\Sigma_{h=0}^H \bar{c}^h \right. \tag{84}$$

$$+ ew\cdot\Sigma_{h=0}^H \bar{d}^h + \Sigma_{k=1}^K \pi^k(p,ew)z_k - \Sigma_{h=1}^H m^h(u_h,p,ew): \ z \equiv (z_1,\ldots,z_K)^T \ ;$$

$$\lambda \equiv (\lambda_1,\ldots,\lambda_H)^T \ ; \ u \equiv (u_1,\ldots,u_H)^T \Big\}.$$

The λ_h in (84) are nonnegative multipliers corresponding to the contraints $f^h(c^h,d^h) \geq u_0$, p is a vector of nonnegative multipliers corresponding to the domestic commodity excess supply constraints, and e is a nonnegative multiplier corresponding to the balance of trade constraint. As usual, moving from a primal problem (83) to a dual problem (84) dramatically reduces the number of variables and constraints in the problem.

Assume u_0^*, u^*, z^*, λ^*, p^*, e^* solves (84). Then by the Saddle Point Theorem, there exist c^{*h}, d^{h*}, h=1,...,H and a^{k*}, b^{k*}, k=1,...,K such that $u_h^* = f^h(c^{h*},d^{h*})$ for h=1,...,H and u_0^*, z^*, c^{h*}, d^{h*}, a^{k*}, b^{k*} solves (83). In (84), set $\lambda=\lambda^*$ and $u_0 = u_0^*$, the optimal values. Then applying the Saddle Point Theorem in reverse, it can be verified that z^*, c^{h*}, d^{h*}, a^{k*}, b^{k*}, solves

$$\max_{z,c^h,d^h,a^k,b^k} \{u_0^* + \Sigma_{h=1}^H \lambda_h^*[f^h(c^h,d^h) - u_0^*] : \Sigma_{k=1}^K a^k z_k \qquad (85)$$

$$+ \Sigma_{h=0}^H \bar{c}^h - \Sigma_{h=1}^H c^h \geq 0_N ; w \cdot (\Sigma_{k=1}^K b^k z_k + \Sigma_{h=0}^H \bar{d}^h - \Sigma_{h=1}^H d^h) \geq 0 ;$$

$$z \equiv (z_1,...,z_K)^T \geq 0_K; (c^h,d^h) \varepsilon \Omega^h, h=1,...,H; (a^k,b^k) \varepsilon C^k, h=1,...,K\}.$$

Using (85), it can be seen that if u^* is a utility vector solution for (84) where $u^* \equiv (u_1^*,...,u_H^*)^T$, $u_h^* \equiv f^h(c^{h*},d^{h*})$, h=1,...,H, then

$$u^* \text{ solves } \max_u \{\lambda^* \cdot u : u \text{ is a feasible utility vector}\} \qquad (86)$$

where λ^* in (86) is a λ solution for (84). Hence under the concavity of utility functions assumption, a $\bar{c}$, $\bar{d}$ fair utility allocation generated by solving (83) maximizes a $\lambda^* \geq 0_H$ weighted utilitarian utility function over the economy's feasible utility vectors. This is the verbal translation of (86). Thus we have established our counterpart to Theorem 1.

If we assume or compute that $\lambda^* \gg 0_H$, then the $\bar{c}$, $\bar{d}$ fair utility allocation u^* is also Pareto optimal and moreover $u^* = u_0^* 1_H$ in this case. Hence as in the capital income fair allocations, the economy's "best" utility vector u^* is equally distributed. However, in the case of the $\bar{c}$, $\bar{d}$ fair allocation, we no longer have a counterpart to Theorem 4 unless all components of λ^* are positive and equal.

How could a $\bar{c}$, $\bar{d}$ fair allocation be decentralized by a central planning board? First solve (83) or (84), compute the resulting equilibrium utility and price vectors, u^*, p^*, e^* and then compute the implied required nonlabour income g_h^* for each consumer:

$$g_h^* \equiv m \ (u_h^*, \ p^*, \ e^* w) \ , \ h = 1, \ldots, H. \tag{87}$$

Assume that net transferable wealth at the p^*, $e^* w$ prices is positive; i.e.,

$$w^* \equiv \Sigma_{h=0}^{H} \ (p^* \cdot \bar{c}^h + e^* w \cdot \bar{d}^h) > 0. \tag{88}$$

Using the complementary slackness conditions associated with (84), we deduce that

$$\Sigma_{h=1}^{H} \ g_h^* = w^*. \tag{89}$$

Hence as long as each $g_h^* \geq 0$, we may give household h the fraction g_h^*/w^* of the economy's net endowment vector, $\Sigma_{h=0}^{H} \ (\bar{c}^h, \bar{d}^h)$, and the $\bar{c}$, $\bar{d}$ fair equilibrium could be supported by a competitive equilibrium. However, if any of the g_h^* are negative, we run into the incentive compatibility problems mentioned earlier; it may be difficult to force people to work for the state.

The $\bar{c}$, $\bar{d}$ fair allocations give us an alternative set of possible "best" reference equilibria for the economy. The advantages associated with the use of a $\bar{c}$, $\bar{d}$ fair allocation are: (i) they are easy to compute, especially in the case of concave utility functions and (ii) they are relatively easy to understand. Some disadvantages are: (i) it may be difficult to choose the appropriate $\bar{c}$, $\bar{d}$ reference vector (I would suggest using the average consumption vector corresponding to an observed equilibrium for the economy), (ii) although utilities may be equalized in the reference equilibrium, the corresponding money metric incomes g_h^* will not be equalized in general, (iii) if any individual gets a negative income in equilibrium, there will be an incentive compatibility problem and (iv) it will be necessary for the government to know preferences and technology sets so that it may solve the planning problem (83).

The advantages of the capital income fair allocations are: (i) they do not require an arbitrary primal scaling assumption, (ii) they give everybody the same opportunity set and (iii) the government does not have

to know preferences and technology sets: it "only" has to distribute
transferable resources equally. The disadvantage of this type of allocation
is that it may be difficult to pick out a best reference equilibrium when
there are multiple equilibria.

12 CONCLUSION

We find that there are two families of methods for measuring the
waste of resources associated with an "observed" equilibrium in a numerical
or econometric general equilibrium model.

In the Allais-Debreu approach studied in sections 3-5, we start
at the observed distorted equilibrium, pick a reference waste vector and
then determine how many multiples of this reference waste vector, r^0, can be
produced by the economy while maintaining each consumer's initial utility
level and respecting the economy's resource constraints. r^0 may be determined by solving the primal programming problem (8), the max min problem (9)
or the dual problem in prices (10). In section 4, we computed a second
order approximation to the Allais-Debreu loss r^0 to indicate how it depends
on the magnitudes of various tax distortions and "elasticities" (these
elasticities are actually first order derivatives of various supply and
demand functions). In section 5, we computed the derivatives of the second
order approximation to the Allais-Debreu loss with respect to the various
"elasticities". We called this a differential approach to sensitivity
analysis and we contrasted it with the numerical approach of Harrison &
Kimbell [1983].

In the Hicks-Boiteux approach studied in sections 6 and 7, we
start at an arbitrary Pareto optimal reference equilibrium for the economy
and compute reference utility and competitive equilibrium price vectors for
this Pareto optimal allocation. The Hicks-Boiteux loss L_{HB} defined by
(42) is the difference between aggregate money metric income at the
reference equilibrium and the "observed" equilibrium, using the prices
associated with the Pareto optimal reference equilibrium. L_{HB} turns out
to be (minus) the sum of Hicksian equivalent variations between the two
equilibria. Theorem 1 proved that L_{HB} is always nonnegative.

Roughly speaking, we can think of the Allais-Debreu measure as
starting inside the economy's utility possibilities set at the "observed"
vector of utilities and then we move out to the Pareto optimal frontier
using the reference waste vector as a direction. On the other hand, the
Hicks-Boiteux measure starts at a point on the Pareto frontier and then we

move inwards to the "observed" utility point. Mohring [1971; 362] gives a
good diagram that illustrates the difference between the two approaches in
the one consumer case.

It must be emphasized that there is an element of arbitrariness
in both approaches: in the AD approach, we must pick an arbitrary reference
waste vector; in the HB approach, we must pick an arbitrary Pareto optimal
reference equilibrium. (Of course, if there is only one consumer in the
economy, the HB reference equilibrium is uniquely determined, and so in this
not very interesting case, the HB approach is not arbitrary).

For any reference waste vector, the AD loss measure is a pure
efficiency measure in the sense that if the "observed" equilibrium is Pareto
optimal, then the AD loss is zero. On the other hand, in the many consumer
case if the "observed" equilibrium is Pareto optimal but is not the
reference "best" Pareto optimal equilibrium, then the HB loss can be
positive. Thus the HB measure of waste is not a pure efficiency measure in
the traditional sense.

Under what conditions will the HB loss (put on a proportional
basis) equal the AD loss? Complete necessary and sufficient conditions for
this equivalence are not known but some sufficient conditions are. In the
case of one consumer, Mohring [1971; 364] asserts that the losses will be
equal if: (i) the consumer's utility function is homothetic, (ii) labour
services are supplied inelastically and are treated as transferable
endowments, (iii) the technology is subject to constant returns to scale[51]
and (iv) we choose the reference waste vector to be proportional to the
economy's endowment of primary factors (capital, labour and natural
resources). Graaff [1977] proves (to the first order) a similar result for
his waste measure making similar assumptions (he has many consumers but they
are all identical in the end). King [1983; 194-195] states a result that
may be relevant. However, even under all of the above simplifying assumptions, we can only show the equivalence of the two loss measures for a
particular reference waste vector (and in the many consumer case, for a
particular reference Pareto optimal equilibrium). The point is that the two
loss measures are unlikely to give the same answer under normal
circumstances.

In section 6, we also decompose the HB loss into subcomponents
in a manner similar to the decompositions of the gains from trade made by
trade theorists such as Dixit & Norman [1980; 71-78] and Woodland [1982;
266]. Equation (48) decomposes the HB loss into a sum of nonnegative

consumer and producer substitution gains plus a sum of nonnegative subsidy termination gains.

We have already noted the dependence of the HB loss measure on the choice of a reference Pareto optimal allocation. Which reference allocation should we choose in empirical applications? This question leads us into the social choice literature (at least, superficially) and the fairness literature (more thoroughly). In section 7, we start out by showing that the gain in (money metric) utilitarian welfare moving from one distorted equilibrium to another is equal to minus the difference in the HB losses pertaining to the two distorted equilibria; see (50). We then follow Varian [1976] and suggest that an "equal opportunity" competitive equilibrium (or to use the terminology of the fairness literature, a "capital income fair" allocation) is a reasonable candidate for the "best" reference equilibrium that should be used when calculating HB losses.

Having noted that the HB loss measure can be associated with a utilitarian social welfare function, we find that we agree with Sen [1970] and others that the utilitarian functional form is not a very satisfactory one since it ranks all "incomes" summing up to a constant as being equivalent irrespective of the distribution of "incomes". Thus in section 8, we are led to study the properties of social welfare functions and in section 9, we provide some examples of social welfare functions that exhibit varying degrees of distributional concern. In section 10, we follow Kolm [1969] and decompose the loss of social welfare going from the "best" equilibrium to an "observed" equilibrium into efficiency and equity components.

The issue of what functional form should we use for a social welfare function is an important one and shows up in cost-benefit analysis where we require welfare weights for each consumer. These welfare weights may be interpreted as being proportional to the gradient vector of the economy's social welfare function with respect to utilities, evaluated at an observed distorted equilibrium. Should we follow Harberger [1971] and assume a utilitarian equal weights social welfare function or should we assume some of the other functional forms listed in section 9 that show distributional concern? Interestingly enough, if all of the distortions in the economy were eliminated systematically, it would not matter whether we used the utilitarian function W^1 defined by (58) or any social welfare function W satisfying Properties 1-4 to guide us through the tax reforms. In either case, we would eventually end up at our reference "best" equilibrium. However, it seems unlikely that all distortions will ever be eliminated in any real world economy.

We follow Varian [1976] and regard a social welfare function as a device for ordering non optimal distributions of real income or utility; different social welfare functions simply provide different metrics for measuring how far away we are from our "best" reference equilibrium.

In section 11, we take a closer look at some of the problems involved in choosing a "best" reference equilibrium. First we noted that our leading candidate for a "best" equilibrium, a capital income fair allocation, need not be unique. Following Mansur & Whalley [1984], we feel that nonuniqueness will not be a problem in empirical general equilibrium models. However, nonuniqueness does pose interesting theoretical problems, so in the first part of section 11, we suggest varous criteria for choosing a "best" capital income fair allocation. In the second part of section 11, we take a primal scaling of utility approach (as opposed to the dual or money metric scaling approach) to the construction of a "best" reference equilibrium. The resulting concept of a $\bar{c}$, $\bar{d}$ fair allocation is closely related to Blackorby's [1975] approach to measuring social welfare and is equivalent to the egalitarian equivalent allocation idea of Pazner & Schmeidler [1978b]. The programming problem (83) that enabled us to to construct a $\bar{c}$, $\bar{d}$ fair allocation is similar to one used by Chipman & Moore [1972]. The merits and demerits of capital income fair versus $\bar{c}$, $\bar{d}$ fair allocations are discussed at the end of section 11.

In trying to find the "best" reference equilibrium, we basically took the veil of ignorance approach of Rawls [1971] and Harsanyi [1977]. This approach loses much of its appeal when we move from a timeless static economy to a growing dynamic economy. An allocation which is initially fair may become an allocation which appears unfair at the start of next period (due to differential propensities to work and save).[52] Some of the other complications that we have neglected in our attempts to construct a "best" reference equilibrium are: (i) population growth (or more generally, variable populations), (ii) household equivalence problems (e.g., when does a child count as an adult), (iii) increasing returns to scale, (iv) non competitive behavior and (v) the choice of the public goods vector.

To conclude: the AD loss measure has the advantage that it is a pure efficiency measure. Moreover, we do not have to worry about determining the economy's "best" allocation. On the other hand, perhaps it is an advantage of the HB loss measure that it forces us to think about the question of which allocation is "best". Once we determine the "best" allocation, it is relatively easy to construct consistent welfare measures.

The author thanks Olga Betts for typing a difficult manuscript and C. Blackorby, R. Clarete, D. Donaldson, D. Jorgenson, J. Roumasset, S. Setboonsarng, H. Varian and J. Weymark for helpful discussions. This research was supported by the SSHRC of Canada.

FOOTNOTES

1. Jorgenson [1983] attributes the applied general equilibrium modelling methodology to Johansen [1960]. In any case, it is certainly true that Shoven and Whalley and their coauthors are responsible for popularizing the methodology.

2. The procedure is explained in detail in Mansur & Whalley [1984].

3. For examples of flexible functional forms, see Diewert [1974][1982].

4. While the econometric approach has some obvious advantages over the calibration approach, it also has some disadvantages: (i) a time series of data is required, (ii) flexible functional forms may not be globally well behaved and (iii) the required number of parameters increases as the square of the number of goods in the model and so for large numbers of goods, the econometric approach may not be feasible. The econometric and calibration approaches are compared in the context of a specific model by Mansur & Whalley [1984].

5. The approach of Jorgenson & Slesnick [1984] should also be listed but it is too complex to be summarized here.

6. Boiteux [1951] and Diewert [1984] showed that the second order approximation to the loss was nonnegative.

7. Notation: 0_N denotes a vector of zeros of dimension N, $p \gg 0_N$ means each component of the N dimensional vector p is positive, $p \geq 0_N$ means each component is nonnegative, $p > 0_N$ means $p \geq 0_N$ but $p \neq 0_N$ and $p \cdot x$ or $p^T x$ denotes the inner product of the vectors x and p.

8. If production is subject to diminishing returns to scale, we follow the example of McKenzie [1959; 66] and introduce a sector specific factor to which the profits of the firm will be imputed. This specific factor is to be regarded as an additional domestic good.

9. If the maximum does not exist, take the supremum. For additional material on unit profit functions, see Diewert & Woodland [1977; 377-378].

10. Notation: $\nabla_p \pi(p,w) \equiv [\partial \pi(p,w)/\partial p_1, \ldots, \partial \pi(p,w)/\partial p_N]^T$ denotes the vector of first order derivatives of π with respect to the components of p, $\nabla_w \pi(p,w)$ denotes the vector of first order partial derivatives of π with respect to the components of w, $\nabla^2_{pp} \pi(p,w)$ denotes the N by N matrix of second order partials of π with respect to the components of p, $\nabla^2_{pw} \pi(p,w)$ denotes the N by M matrix of second order cross partial derivatives of π with respect to the component of p and w, etc.

11. This means: if $(c^h, d^h) \epsilon \Omega^h$, $c^{h'} \gg c^h$, $d^{h'} \gg d^h$, then $f^h(c^{h'}, d^{h'}) > f^h(c^h, d^h)$.

12. This means: if $u_h \epsilon$ Range f^h, then the set $\{(c,d): f^h(c,d) \geq u_h, (c,d) \epsilon \Omega^h\}$ is convex.

13. The regularity properties listed in Diewert apply to the case where Ω^h is the nonnegative orthant. However, the appropriate properties can readily be determined for the case where Ω^h is a translated orthant. If a particular consumer h is not capable of supplying a certain type of labour service which corresponds to say the nth domestic good, then the consumption set Ω^h excludes such labour supplies; i.e., if $(c,d) \epsilon \Omega^h$, then $c_n \geq 0$ where c_n is the nth component of c.

14. There is also a government budget constraint but it is implied by the other equations.

15. We assume that a finite maximum for (8) exists.

16. In addition to the asumptions that we have already made, we require that the Slater constraint qualification condition hold; i.e., we require that a feasible solution for (8) exists that satisfies the first 1+N inequality constraints strictly.

17. Equations (4) are not needed to characterize the tax distributed equilibrium since if (5), (6) and (7) are satisfied, we may use equations (4) to define a g^1 which will be consistent with equations (5)-(7).

18. In the definitions of S^0, Σ^0 and B^0, ∇_w means differentiate the relevant function with respect to the vector of arguments $e^0 w$.

19. Our assumption that the strong second order sufficient conditions hold for the constrained maximization problem in (10) implies that the matrix on the left hand side of (16) has an inverse. Hence the Implicit Function Theorem gives us the existence of differentiable functions $p(\xi)$, $e(\xi)$, $z(\xi)$, $r(\xi)$ which satisfy equations (11)-(14) for ξ close to 0.

20. The techniques used to derive results (29) and (31) are very similar to
the techniques used by Diewert [1981; 72] to derive sensitivity results
for the Hicks-Marshall elasticity of derived demand with respect to
variations in second order parameters.

21. These specified utility levels must be small enough so that the
maximization problem (32) has a feasible solution.

22. Diewert [1973; 424] (using results due to Afriat) notes that from an
empirical point of view, if an individual has consistent preferences,
then these preferences can always be represented by means of a concave
utility function. The consistent preferences must have the property of
local nonsatiation in order for this representation to be valid. Hence
our assumption that f^1 be concave does not seem to be overly
restrictive.

23. This assumption (that the equilibrium exchange rate be positive) means
that we are assuming that trade is beneficial to the economy. We note
that e^0 is not a financial exchange rate that affects the real allocation of resources; see Whalley & Yeung [1984]. We could replace
equation (34) by the equation $e^0 = 1$ and then (34)-(37) would still
characterize a Pareto optimal allocation.

24. We only require the differentiability of $m^h(u_h^0, p^0, e^0)$ with respect to
its price arguments for h=2,3,...,H. Actually, our differentiability
assumptions are not required if we are willing to work with elements of
the subgradient correspondence in place of gradient vectors.

25. Given u^0, z^0, p^0 and e^0 as the solution to (33), we define $\tau^0 \equiv 0_N$,
$s^0 \equiv 0_M$ (so that there are no commodity tax distortions) and define
individual h's transfer by $g_h^0 \equiv m^h(u_h^0, p^0, e^0 w) - p^0 \cdot c^{-h} - e^0 w \cdot d^{-h}$ for
h=1,...,H.

26. Boadway [1974; 933] [1976; 359] illustrated this Theorem in a two
person, two good economy, with and without production. The analytical
techniques used by Foster [1976; 353-355] to establish a relationship
between his weak compensation test and Boadway's cost-benefit criterion
could be used to prove our Theorem.

27. After reading Hicks' [1946; 330-333] verbal definition of the equivalent variation, many authors (e.g., King [1983; 192]) define the
equivalent variation to be $m^h(u_h^1, p^1, w) - m^h(u_h^1, p^0, e^0 w)$ which causes
a certain amount of confusion in the literature. Hence King [1983;
190] calls our (early Hicks) definition of the equivalent variation for
individual h, $m^h(u_h^1, p^0, e^0 w) - m^h(u_h^0, p^0, e^0 w)$, the equivalent gain,

whereas Chipman & Moore [1980;935] call it the <u>generalized equivalent</u>
<u>variation</u>.

28. Nonoptimal is perhaps a better term than distorted since the u^1
    equilibrium may in fact correspond to a "nonoptimal" Pareto optimal
    allocation of utilities.

29. King [1983;192] derives the identity (50) and notes that it is true
    even if (p^0, e^0) are not equilibrium prices corresponding to a Pareto
    optimal reference equilibrium.

30. See d'Aspremont [1983] for an excellent review of this literature.

31. Measuring individual utilities cardinally by means of the individual
    expenditure functions $m^h(u_h, p^0, e^0 w)$ using constant reference prices
    $p^0, e^0 w$ is termed <u>money metric</u> utility measurement by Samuelson [1974].

32. This is not quite true in our model since different individuals may
    have different consumption possibility sets Ω^h due to differing
    abilities to be able to offer different kinds of labour services.

33. Due to our assumptions on the individual utility possibility sets Ω^h
    (i.e., that individuals cannot necessarily supply all types of labour
    service) and our assumption that the government net endowment vectors,
    c^0 and d^0, need not be nonnegative (due to government commodity
    requirements for the production of public goods), the existence of
    equilibrium is not a standard exercise. See Arrow & Hahn [1971;ch.5]
    for references to the literature on existence. For a proof of exis-
    tence in a model which treats international trade in a manner similar
    to our treatment, see Mansur & Whalley [1982].

34. In practice, the problem of selecting a "best" equilibrium may not be a
    problem. Mansur & Whalley [1984;100] state that to their knowledge, an
    example of multiple equilibria in an applied general equilibrium model
    has never been encountered.

35. Results of this type were obtained by Kolm [1972], Schmeidler & Vind
    [1972] and Varian [1974] [1976]. Varian [1975a; 244] called a solution
    to (52)-(55) a "wealth-fair allocation" or a "people's capitalism"
    equilibrium.

36. Thomson [1984] provides an axiomatic characterization of his Walrasian
    choice correspondence from equal division.

37. Becker [1965] called nonlabour income plus the value of household time,
    full income. Our terminology seems consistent with that of Archibald
    & Donaldson [1979; 211].

38. Varian [1974;75] suggests that each individual will be able to buy back his or her endowment of time in the full income fair equilibrium, but this need not be true for individuals whose services are extremely valuable.

39. For references to the incentive compatibility literature, see Dasgupta et al. [1979] and Hammond [1983].

40. Mohring [1971;367] was perhaps the first to appreciate this fact. He also raised the problem of criteria for choosing which set of reference prices should be used in a utilitarian social welfare function. Our suggestion is to follow Varian [1976] and use the prices associated with an equal opportunity equilibrium. It should be noted that Varian [1975a] discussed and compared the concepts of "capital fair" and "full income fair" allocations.

41. See the discussion in Varian [1976; 256-257], Blackorby & Donaldson [1978;71-76] and Deaton & Muellbauer [1980; 219-220].

42. Dasgupta et al. [1973;181] note that quasiconcavity reflects a tendency to prefer equality.

43. The term is due to Blackorby & Donaldson [1980;109]; the concept is due to Kolm [1969;190].

44. For the mathematical properties of means of order r, see Hardy et al. [1934].

45. Unfortunately, Blackorby & Donaldson [1982;258] also show that the global mean of order r is quasiconcave if and only if r=1 (the utilitarian function).

46. This same point was made in a slightly different manner by Blackorby & Donaldson [1978;76] who noted that the coefficient of variation social welfare function defined by (68) was unduly sensitive to changes in the distribution of income in the neighbourhood of equality compared with its sensitivity elsewhere.

47. The authors either stated or proved a result close to our Theorem 6.

48. We now assume that the consumption possibilities set Ω^h for h is a closed, nonempty, convex set in R^{N+N} which is bounded from below (i.e., $(c,d)\varepsilon\Omega^h$ implies $c \geq k1_N$, $d \geq 0_M$ where $-k \geq 0$) and exhibits free disposal (i.e., $(c',d')\varepsilon\Omega^h$, $c'' \geq c'$, $d'' \geq d'$ implies $(c'',d'') \varepsilon\Omega^h$). We assume that the point $(\lambda_h\bar{c}, \lambda_h\bar{d})$ belongs to the lowest indifference surface in Ω^h for some $\lambda_h \geq 0$, for $h=1,\ldots,H$. Thus we are now allowing for the fact that each individual needs minimal amounts of consumer goods in order to survive.

49. Deaton & Muellbauer [1980;214] argue that the Allen and Malmquist index number concepts could be used to provide natural units for making interpersonal comparisons of welfare. Note also that virtually all functional forms for consumer direct or indirect utility functions used in econometric or numerical general equilibrium models satisfy either the primal scaling assumption (82) (possibly after a translation of origin) or the dual money metric scaling. See Diewert [1974] and Lau [1977] for reviews of commonly used functional forms.

50. This is no longer (recall footnote 22) an empirically harmless assumption because the scaling assumptions (82) also have to be satisfied. We also need to assume the existence of a feasible solution for (83) such that every inequality constraint in (83) holds strictly.

51. Recall (from footnote 8) that by introducing artificial fixed factors and by using the McKenzie imputation device, our model was able to deal with diminishing returns to scale technologies. The Mohring result does not allow the use of this imputation device.

52. These types of criticisms of the fairness concept have been made by Nozick [1974] and Holcombe [1983].

REFERENCES

Allais, M. [1943], A la recherch d'une discipline économique, Vol. I, Paris: Imprimerie Nationale.

Allais, M. [1977], Theories of General Economic Equilibrium and Maximum Efficiency. In Equilibrium and Disequilibrium in Economic Theory, ed. E. Schwoediauer, pp. 129-201, Dordrecht: D. Reidel.

Allen, R.G.D. [1949], The Economic Theory of Index Numbers, Economica N.S. 16, 197-203.

Archibald, G.C. & Donaldson, D. [1979], Notes on Economic Equality, Journal of Public Economics 12, 205-214.

Arrow, K.J. [1951], An Extension of the Basic Theorems of Classical Welfare Economics. In Proceedings of the Second Berkeley Symposium on Mathematical Statistics and Probability, ed. J. Neyman, pp. 507-532. Berkeley: University of California Press.

d'Aspremont, Claude [1983], Axioms for Social Welfare Orderings, CORE Discussion paper 8349, Université catholique de Louvain, Belgium.

Atkinson, A.B. [1970], On the Measurement of Inequality, Journal of Economic Theory 2, 244-263.

Becker, E.S. [1965], A Theory of the Allocation of Time, Economic Journal 75, 493-517.

Berge, C. [1963], Topological Spaces, New York: Macmillan.

Blackorby, C. [1975], Degrees of Cardinality and Aggregate Partial Orderings, Econometrica 43, 845-852.

Blackorby, C. & Donaldson, D. [1978], Measures of Relative Equality and their Meaning in Terms of Social Welfare, Journal of Economic Theory 18, 59-80.

Blackorby, C. & Donaldson, D. [1980], A Theoretical Treatment of Indices of
    Absolute Inequality, International Economic Review 21, 107-136.
Blackorby, C. & Donaldson, D. [1982], Ratio-Scale and Translation-Scale Full
    Interpersonal Comparability without Domain Restrictions:
    Admissible Social-Evaluation Functions, International Economic
    Review 23, 249-268.
Boadway, R.W. [1974], The Welfare Foundations of Cost-Benefit Analysis,
    Economic Journal 84, 926-939.
Boadway, R.W. [1976], The Welfare Foundations of Cost-Benefit Analysis - A
    Reply, Economic Journal 86, 359-361.
Boiteux, M. [1951], Le 'revenu distruable' et les pertes economiques,
    Econometrica 19, 112-133.
Chipman, J.S. & Moore, J.C. [1972], Social Utility and the Gains from Trade,
    Journal of International Economics 2, 157-172.
Chipman, J.S. & Moore, J.C. [1980], Compensating Variation, Consumer's
    Surplus and Welfare, American Economic Review 70, 933-949.
Crawford, V.P. [1977], A Game of Fair Division, Review of Economic Studies
    44, 235-247.
Dasgupta, P., Sen, A. & Sarrett D. [1973], Notes on the Measurement of
    Inequality, Journal of Economic Theory 6, 180-187.
Dasgupta, P.S., Hammond, P.J. & Maskin, E.S. [1979], The Implementation of
    Social Choice Rules: Some General Results on Incentive
    Compatibility, Review of Economic Studies 46, 185-216.
Deaton, A. & Muellbauer, J. [1980], Economics and Consumer Behavior, London:
    Cambridge University Press.
Debreu, G. [1951], The Coefficient of Resource Utilization, Econometrica 19,
    273-292.
Debreu, G. [1954], A Classical Tax-Subsidy Problem, Econometrica 22, 14-22.
Debreu, G. [1970], Economies with a Finite Set of Equilibria, Econometrica
    38, 387-393.
Dierker, E. [1972], Two Remarks on the Number of Equilibria of an Economy,
    Econometrica 40, 951-953.
Diewert, W.E. [1973], Afriat and Revealed Preference Theory, The Review of
    Economic Studies 40, 419-425.
Diewert, W.E. [1974], Applications of Duality Theory. In Frontiers of
    Quantitative Economics Vol. II, eds. M.D. Intriligator &
    Kendrick, D.A., pp. 106-171, Amsterdam: North-Holland.
Diewert, W.E. [1981], The Elasticity of Derived Net Supply and a Generalized
    Le Chatelier Principle, Review of Economic Studies 48, 63-80.
Diewert, W.E. [1982], Duality Approaches to Microeconomic Theory. In
    Handbook of Mathematical Economics, Vol. II, eds. K.J. Arrow &
    Intriligator, M.D., pp. 535-599, Amsterdam: North-Holland.
Diewert, W.E. [1983], The Measurement of Waste within the Production Sector
    of an Open Economy, Scandinavian Journal of Economics 85,
    159-179.
Diewert, W.E. [1984], The Measurement of Deadweight Loss in an Open Economy,
    Economica 51, 23-42.
Diewert, W.E. & Woodland, A.D. [1977], Frank Knight's Theorem in Linear
    Programming Revisited, Econometrica 45, 375-398.
Dixit, A.K. & Norman, V. [1980], Theory of International Trade, London:
    Cambridge University Press.
Foley, D.K. [1967], Resource Allocation and the Public Sector, Yale Economic
    Essays 7, 45-98.
Foster, E. [1976], The Welfare Foundations of Cost-Benefit Analysis - A
    Comment, Economic Journal 86, 353-358.

Fullerton, D., Shoven, J.B. & Whalley, J. [1983], Replacing the U.S. Income
     Tax with a Progressive Consumption Tax: A Sequenced General
     Equilibrium Approach, Journal of Public Economics 20, 3-23.
Graaff, J. de V. [1977], Equity and Efficiency as Components of the General
     Welfare, South African Journal of Economics 45, 362-375.
Hammond, P. [1983], Welfare Economics, Report No. 2/83, The Institute for
     Advanced Studies, The Hebrew University of Jerusalem,
     forthcoming in Trends in Economic Theory, ed. G.R. Feiwel,
     London: Macmillan.
Harberger, A.C. [1962], The Incidence of the Corporation Income Tax, Journal
     of political Economy 70, 215-240.
Harberger, A.C. [1971], Three Basic Postulates for Applied Welfare
     Economics: An Interpretive Essay, Journal of Economic Literature
     9, 785-797.
Harberger, A.C. & Bruce, N. [1976], The Incidence and Efficiency Effects of
     Taxes on Income from Capital: A Reply, Journal of Political
     Economy 84, 1285-1292.
Hardy, G.H., Littlewood, J.E. & Polya, G. [1934], Inequalities, Cambridge:
     Cambridge University Press.
Harrison, G.W. & Kimbell, L.J. [1983], How Robust is Numerical General
     Equilibrium Analysis, Working Paper No. 8325C, Centre for the
     Study of International Economic Relations, Dept. of Economics,
     University of Western Ontario, London, Ont., Canada N6A 5C2.
Harsanyi, J.C. [1977], Rational Behavior and Bargaining Equilibrium in Games
     and Social Situations, London: Cambridge University Press.
Hicks, J.R. [1942], Consumers' Surplus and Index Numbers, The Review of
     Economic Studies 9, 126-137.
Hicks, J.R. [1946], Value and Capital, second edition, Oxford: Clarendon
     Press.
Holcombe, R.G. [1983], Applied Fairness Theory: Comment, American Economic
     Review 73, 1153-1156.
Johansen, L. [1960], A Multi-Sectoral Study of Economic Growth, Amsterdam:
     North-Holland.
Jorgenson, D.W. [1983], Econometric Methods for Applied General Equilibrium
     Modelling, Harvard Institute for Economics Research Discussion
     Paper No. 967, Harvard University, Cambridge Mass., Feb.
Jorgenson, D.W. & Slesnick, D.T. [1984], Aggregate Consumer Behavior and the
     Measurement of Inequality, Review of Economic Studies, 51,
     369-392.
Karlin, S. [1959], Mathematical Methods and Theory in Games, Programming and
     Economics, Vol. 1, Reading, Mass.: Addison-Wesley.
Keyhoe, T.J. [1980], An Index Theorem for General Equilibrium Models with
     Production, Econometrica 48, 1211-1232.
King, M.A. [1983], Welfare Analysis of Tax Returns using Household Data,
     Journal of Public Economics 21, 183-214.
Kolm, S.C. [1969], The Optimal Production of Social Justice, in Public
     Economics, eds. J. Margolis & Guitton, H., pp. 173-200, London:
     Macmillan.
Kolm, S.-G. [1972], Justice et Equite, Paris: Editions du Centre National de
     la Recherche Scientific.
Kolm, S.-G. [1976], Unequal Inequalities, I and II, Journal of Economic
     Theory 12, 416-442 and 13, 82-111.
Lau, L.J. [1977], Complete Systems of Consumer Demand Functions through
     Duality. In Frontiers of Quantitative Economics vol. IIIA, ed.
     M.D. Intriligator, pp. 59-86, Amsterdam: North-Holland.

Malmquist, S. [1953], Index Numbers and Indifference Surfaces, Trabajos de
    Estatistica 4, 209-242.
Mansur, A. & Whalley, J. [1982], A Decomposition Algorithm for General
    Equilibrium Computation with Application to International Trade
    Models, Econometrica 50, 1547-1557.
Mansur, A. & Whalley, J. [1984], Numerical Specification of Applied General
    Equilibrium Models: Estimation, Calibration, and Data. In
    Applied General Equilibrium Analysis, eds. H. Scarf & Shoven J.,
    pp. 69-127, New York: Cambridge University Press.
May, K.O. [1952], A Set of Independent Necessary and Sufficient Conditions
    for Simple Majority Decision, Econometrica 20, 680-684.
McKenzie, L.M. [1959], On the Existence of a General Equilibrium for a
    Competitive Market, Econometrica 27, 54-71.
McKenzie, G.W. [1983], Measuring Economic Welfare: New Methods, Cambridge:
    Cambridge University Press.
Negishi, T. [1960], Welfare Economics and Existence of an Equilibrium for a
    Competitive Economy, Metroeconomica 12, 92-97.
Nozick, R. [1974], Anarchy, State, and Utopia, New York: Basic Books.
Pazner, E.A. & Schmeidler D. [1974], A Difficulty in the Concept of
    Fairness, The Review of Economic Studies 41, 441-443.
Pazner, E.A. [1977], Pitfalls in the Theory of Fairness, Journal of Economic
    Theory 14, 458-466.
Pazner, E.A. & Schneidler, D. [1978a], Decentralization and Income
    Distribution in Socialist Economics, Economic Inquiry 16,
    257-264.
Pazner, E.A. & Schmeidler, D. [1978b], Egalitarian Equivalent Allocations: A
    New Concept of Economic Equity, Quarterly Journal of Economics
    92, 671-687.
Rawls, J. [1971], A Theory of Justice, Cambridge, Mass.: Harvard University
    Press.
Roberts, K.W.S. [1980a], Interpersonal Comparability and Social Choice
    Theory, The Review of Economic Studies 47, 421-439.
Roberts, K. [1980b], Price-Independent Welfare Prescriptions, Journal of
    Public Economics 13, 277-297.
Samuelson, P.A. [1947], Foundations of Economic Analysis, Cambridge, Mass.:
    Harvard University Press.
Samuelson, P.A. [1974], Complementarity - An Essay on the 40th Anniversary
    of the Hicks-Allen Revolution in Demand Theory, Journal of
    Economic Literature 12, 1255-1289.
Schmeidler, D. & Vind, K. [1972], Fair Net Trades, Econometrica 40,
    637-642.
Sen, A. [1970], Collective Choice and Social Welfare, San Francisco:
    Holden-Day.
Sen, A. [1973], On Economic Inequality, London: Oxford University Press.
Shoven, J.B. & Whalley, J. [1972], A General Equilibrium Calculation of the
    Effects of Differential Taxation of Income from Capital in the
    U.S., Journal of Public Economics 1, 281-321.
Shoven, J.B. & Whalley, J. [1973], General Equilibrium with Taxes: A
    Computational Procedure and an Existence Proof, The Review of
    Economic Studies 40, 475-489.
Shoven, J.B. & Whalley, J. [1974], On the Computation of Competitive
    Equilibrium on International Markets with Tariffs, Journal of
    International Economics 4, 341-354.
Thomson, W. [1983], Equity in Exchange Economies, Journal of Economic Theory
    29, 217-244.

Thomson, W. [1984], Characterization of the Walrasian Correspondence when Population is Variable, mimeo, Dept. of Economics, Univesity of Rochester, February.

Uzawa, H. [1958], The Kuhn-Tucker Theorem in Concave Programming. In Studies in Linear and Nonlinear Programming, eds. K.J. Arrow, L. Hurwicz & H. Uzawa, pp. 32-37, Stanford, California; Stanford University Press.

Varian, H.R. [1974], Equity, Envy, and Efficiency, Journal of Economic Theory 9, 63-91.

Varian, H. [1975a], Distributive Justice, Welfare Economics, and the Theory of Fairness, Philosophy and Public Affairs 4, 223-247.

Varian, H. [1975b], A Third Remark on the Number of Equilibria of an Economy, Econometrica 43, 985-986.

Varian, H.R. [1976], Two Problems in the Theory of Fairness, Journal of Public Economics 5, 249-260.

Whalley, J. & Yeung, B. [1984], External Sector 'Closing' Rules in Applied General Equilibrium Models, Journal of International Economics 16, 123-138.

Woodland, A.D. [1982], International Trade and Resource Allocation, Amsterdam: North-Holland.

SENSITIVITY ANALYSIS FOR LINEARIZED COMPUTABLE GENERAL
EQUILIBRIUM MODELS

A.R. Pagan
Australian National University

J.H. Shannon
Riverina College of Advanced Education

1 *INTRODUCTION*

Computable general equilibrium models (CGEM's) have now
reached the stage where attention has shifted from the feasibility of
computation and the problems arising in the construction of equilibrium
data sets to their actual application in the assessment of the effects of
alternative policies. At least one of these models - the ORANI model of
the Australian economy described in Dixon et al. (1982b) - has received
routine use in the analysis of the impact of different tariff policies
upon employment and output in particular industries and in aggregate.
Thus, the Industries Assistance Commission (IAC) have presented simulations with this model in their General Approaches to the Reduction in
Protection and more recently the inquiry into the steel industry - see
IAC (1982), (1983).

Once these models began to be used as a guide to policy
formulation, it was perhaps natural that criticism should emerge concerning the fact that CGEM's have embodied in them particular values for
various key elasticity parameters. Model builders have not been unaware
of the limitations of such a procedure, and they have occasionally
attempted to assess how sensitive the solutions really are to the assumed
parameter values e.g. Dixon et al. (1983). In some cases e.g. the IAC
Steel Inquiry, a range of simulations was presented for different values
of what was felt to be an especially important coefficient.

Perhaps the major disadvantage to the re-calibration strategies
employed above is that they only provide a very partial account of
sensitivity. Users can neither be sure that the parameters selected for
variation are the important ones nor that the combination of values
considered are not biassed towards a particular outcome. For example, it
may be that equal variations in each of two coefficients have equal
absolute effects upon model solutions but of opposite sign. Increasing

104

both by the same amount therefore has no overall impact, whereas increasing one and decreasing another would have a strong impact.

These considerations suggest that a much more comprehensive approach to sensitivity analysis is needed than is currently available. Such a need has been recognised in other areas as well e.g. Kuh et al. (1982) have tried to ascertain which coefficients in short-run econometric models are the influential ones in dynamic simulations while West (1982) has concentrated upon the mapping of the input-output coefficients into the employment and output multipliers associated with input-output analysis.

This paper provides a similar development for *linearized* CGEM's. Section 2 discusses a number of ways in which sensitivity could be analysed, beginning with the construction of some overall index and culminating in methods aimed at gauging which coefficients in the model are particularly important. In this latter development our analysis is very similar to that of Kuh et al., although certain simplifications and extensions are possible because of the lack of dynamics in many linear CGEM's. These are set out in section 3. Section 4 of the paper contains an application of the ideas to a small CGEM.

2   *SOME MEASURES OF SENSITIVITY*

There is no single measure of sensitivity for CGEM's, the requirements of individual researchers and the available information serving to delineate what is useful. Sometimes it may be desirable to focus upon the sensitivity of solutions to a particular parameter; in other situations the objective may be to construct some index of overall sensitivity. There is a further dimension centering upon the precision of information concerning the range of possible parameter values. It is therefore necessary to describe a range of indicators. The analysis below begins by examining aggregate sensitivity in the presence of non-diffuse information on parameter variation, leading ultimately to a consideration of individual coefficient sensitivity and "fuzzy" data.

(i)   *Mean/Variance Measures*

Define z as an endogenous variable in a CGEM and let θ be the ($p \times 1$) vector of unknown parameters. It is assumed that θ has been estimated previously from T observations and that $T^{\frac{1}{2}}(\hat{\theta}-\theta) \xrightarrow{d} N(0,\bar{V})$ where $\bar{V} = \plim_{T \to \infty} TV$ is the asymptotic covariance matrix of $T^{\frac{1}{2}}(\hat{\theta}-\theta)$, while V is the "small-sample" covariance matrix of $\hat{\theta}-\theta$. Since z is a function of θ we expand it in Taylor series around $\hat{\theta}$

$$z = z(\theta) = z(\hat{\theta}) + (\partial z/\partial\theta(\hat{\theta}))'(\theta-\hat{\theta}) +$$

$$\tfrac{1}{2}(\theta-\hat{\theta})'(\partial^2 z/\partial\theta\partial\theta'(\hat{\theta}))(\theta-\hat{\theta}) + 0_p(T^{-3/2}). \quad (1)$$

That the remaining terms in (1) are $0_p(T^{-3/2})$ is best seen by examining the next term in the expansion which has typical element

$$[\sqrt{T}(\theta_k-\hat{\theta}_k)][\sqrt{T}(\theta_\ell-\hat{\theta}_\ell)][\sqrt{T}(\theta_j-\hat{\theta}_j)](\partial^3 z/\partial\theta_k\partial\theta_\ell\partial\theta_j)T^{-3/2}.$$

Considering (1), if there was no uncertainty about θ, $z(\hat{\theta})$ represents the sole solution for z. Consequently, aggregate measures of sensitivity will concentrate upon the "size" of the other terms in the series expansion. Depending upon the order of terms it is regarded as desirable to keep, a large number of different estimates might be generated; but two situations are of major importance.

(a) All terms after $0_p(T^{-\frac{1}{2}})$ are ignored so that $E(z) \simeq z(\hat{\theta})$ while the variance is $D_1'VD_1$ where $D_1 = \partial z/\partial\theta(\hat{\theta})$. The "best bet" solution $z(\hat{\theta})$ is therefore retained but a variance attached to it indicating how uncertain it is.

(b) All terms to $0_p(T^{-3/2})$ are kept meaning that

$$E(z) \simeq z(\hat{\theta}) + \tfrac{1}{2}tr\, D_2\, V \quad (2)$$

where $D_2 = \partial^2 z/\partial\theta\partial\theta'$ evaluated at $\hat{\theta}$, while the variance remains at $D_1'VD_1$. For large sample sizes the term $tr\, D_2\, V$ should be small, but the sample sizes upon which $\hat{\theta}$ is based are rarely that. Hence (2) may be a better representation of the mean of z than $z(\hat{\theta})$ is. Such a preference is implicit in the work of Harrison & Kimbell (this volume), who essentially compare $z(\hat{\theta})$ with $E(z)$ in (2) for a model of the Pacific Basin.

Arguments for the retention of terms after $0_p(T^{-3/2})$ would not seem very strong, leaving the requirements for computing the mean and variance of the solution as the first and second derivatives of z with respect to θ. It is important to observe the role of V in (2). It is tempting, if V is not known precisely, to assume it to be diagonal. But this could easily lead to overstatement of the differential between $E(z)$ and $z(\hat{\theta})$ e.g. if D_2 contained positive elements and the off-diagonal terms in V were negative. Nevertheless, there does seem some scope for V to be block-diagonal between (say) coefficients representing production and demand patterns, and hence V may be relatively sparse. At all times though some care must be exercised in the specification of V.

(ii) *Extreme Bounds*

A separate approach would be to find the maximal variation in z given that parameters are constrained to be selected from an $\alpha\%$ confidence interval i.e. based on a normality assumption for $\hat{\theta}$, θ is constrained to $(\theta-\hat{\theta})'V^{-1}(\theta-\hat{\theta}) \leq \chi^2_p(\alpha)$. To solve this optimization problem set up the Lagrangean as in Leamer (1978, p.143).

$$L = z + \tfrac{1}{2}\lambda[(\theta-\hat{\theta})'V^{-1}(\theta-\hat{\theta}) - \chi^2_p(\alpha)]$$

$$\therefore \quad \partial L/\partial\theta = \partial z/\partial\theta + \lambda V^{-1}(\theta-\hat{\theta}) = 0 \tag{3}$$

$$\partial L/\partial\lambda = \tfrac{1}{2}[(\theta-\hat{\theta})'V^{-1}(\theta-\hat{\theta}) - \chi^2_p(\alpha)] = 0. \tag{4}$$

Solving (3) gives

$$\theta-\hat{\theta} = -\lambda^{-1}V(\partial z/\partial\theta) \tag{5}$$

which can be substituted into (4) to produce

$$\lambda^{-2}(\partial z/\partial\theta)'V(\partial z/\partial\theta) = \chi^2_p(\alpha) \tag{6}$$

or

$$\lambda^{-2}c = \chi^2_p(\alpha). \tag{7}$$

Consequently

$$\lambda^* = \pm(c/\chi^2_p(\alpha))^{\frac{1}{2}}. \tag{8}$$

Inserting λ^* into (5) provides those parameter values θ that produce maximal variation in z.

$$\theta = \hat{\theta} \pm [\chi^2_p(\alpha)/c]^{\frac{1}{2}}V(\partial z/\partial\theta) \tag{9}$$

The values of θ from (9) may then be used to compute values for z. This formula for aggregate sensitivity requires less information than the mean and variance to $O_p(T^{-3/2})$, in that only the first rather than second derivatives of z need to be computed.

(iii) *Individual Parameters*

Although aggregate indicators are useful as summary devices, they provide no evidence upon which parameter (or combination) is the source of any sensitivity. A decomposition into the contributions from individual parameters would therefore be highly desirable. As the variance formula $D_1'VD_1$ and $E(z)$ from (2) evidence, the mean/variance measures only allow such a separation if V is diagonal. In those circumstances (2) could be alternatively written as

$$E(z) = z(\hat{\theta}) + \sum_{j=1}^{p} (\partial^2 z/\partial\theta_j^2)v_{jj} \tag{10}$$

where v_{jj} is the j'th diagonal element in V. A suitable measure of the contribution of each coefficient θ_k to the gap $E(z) - z(\hat{\theta})$ would be

$$\phi_k = (\partial^2 z/\partial\theta_k^2)v_{kk} \left(\sum_{j=1}^{p} (\partial^2 z/\partial\theta_j^2)v_{jj} \right)^{-1}, \tag{11}$$

as this gives the fraction of the total attributed to each coefficient. A similar treatment could be given to the variance. Unfortunately, once V becomes non-diagonal there is no unique factorization into single parameters, although it may be possible to group the coefficients such that V is block-diagonal.

More progress can be made when working with the extreme bounds idea. Expanding z around $\hat{\theta}$ by the Mean-Value Theorem gives

$$z(\theta) = z(\hat{\theta}) + \sum_{j=1}^{p} (\partial z/\partial\theta_j(\theta^*))(\theta_j - \hat{\theta}_j) \tag{12}$$

where θ lies between θ and $\hat{\theta}$. Defining the proportionate changes $\dot{z} = (z(\theta) - z(\hat{\theta}))/z(\hat{\theta})$ and $\dot{\theta}_j = (\theta_j - \hat{\theta}_j)/\hat{\theta}_j$ allows (12), divided by $z(\hat{\theta})$, to be re-expressed as

$$\dot{z} = \sum S^*(z;\theta_j)\dot{\theta}_j \tag{13}$$

with $S^*(z;\theta_j) = (\partial z/\partial\theta_j(\theta^*))(\hat{\theta}_j/z(\hat{\theta}))$ as a sensitivity or S-elasticity. Notice that it is not exactly an elasticity unless $\partial z/\partial\theta_j(\theta^*)$ $= \partial z/\partial\theta_j(\hat{\theta})$, in that the derivatives are evaluated at θ^* and not $\hat{\theta}$. Because (13) is an exact formula, insertion of the extreme bounds for θ coming from (9) will produce the extreme bounds for z. Hence a decomposition of the change in the maximal variations in z into the contributions of each individual coefficient is available from (13).

Equation (13) points to some interesting features in the relation between the overall change in z and that due to individual parameters. Firstly, suppose that all coefficients change by the same proportionate amount i.e. $\dot{\theta}_j$ is the same for all j. Then the primary way to judge the relative contribution of each coefficient is by reference to its S-elasticity. Consequently, these are basic tools in the assessment of parameter sensitivity in any CGEM. Secondly, insofar as the maximal variation in θ_j signalled by (9) is not uniform across coefficients, it is the weighted elasticity which is of importance.

Two questions arise from these observations. One is how likely equality in $\dot{\theta}_j$ will be. The other is the magnitude of $\dot{\theta}_j$. To answer both requires a specific context, but some guidance to the answers is available by specializing to the case where θ contains a single coefficient i.e. $p = 1$. (9) then provides the proportionate bounds, for an $\alpha\%$ confidence level, as

$$\dot{\theta}_1 = \pm (v^{\frac{1}{2}}/\hat{\theta}_1)\sqrt{\chi_1^2(\alpha)}, \qquad (14)$$

because of the cancelling of the scalar $\partial z/\partial\theta$. Designate the t-statistic that $\theta_1 = 0$ by $t_1 = \hat{\theta}_1/v^{\frac{1}{2}}$ and the $\alpha\%$ critical value of a standard normal deviate as k_α. Then

$$\dot{\theta}_1 = \pm (k_\alpha/t_1). \qquad (15)$$

(15) highlights the role of the t-statistic and the targeted confidence level in setting the bounds. If $k_\alpha = 2 (\alpha \approx .95)$, we would obtain $\dot{\theta}_1 = 1$ if the t-statistic was two, while it would equal .5 if $t = 4$. Obviously, unless the t-values are very high for estimated elasticities, quite large changes in θ would need to be envisaged in any sensitivity analysis. In particular the variation considered in some previous studies of sensitivity - for example the 10% changes in Dixon et al. (1983) - must be regarded as far too low in the light of the magnitude of t-statistics found with economic data.

Although the S-elasticities in (13) are an important ingredient to any systematic sensitivity analysis, their exact measurement is normally impossible because of a dependence upon the unknown θ^*. This forces a consideration of ways of approximating $\partial z/\partial\theta(\theta^*)$. A first method, exact if z were linear in θ, is to estimate $\partial z/\partial\theta(\theta^*)$ by $\partial z/\partial\theta(\hat{\theta})$. The S-elasticity with such a choice is hereafter designated S_1.

A more accurate procedure arises by expanding $\partial z/\partial\theta(\theta^*)$ in Taylor series around $\hat{\theta}$, approximating $\theta^* - \theta$ by $\frac{1}{2}[\hat{\theta}-\theta]$ and retaining only the first order terms, giving

$$\partial z/\partial\theta(\theta^*) \simeq \partial z/\partial\theta(\hat{\theta}) + \frac{1}{2}(\partial^2 z/\partial\theta\partial\theta'(\hat{\theta}))(\theta-\hat{\theta}). \qquad (16)$$

(16) is then used to form a second estimate of S, designated S_2. Its rationale is best seen from the quadratic approximation to z

$$z \simeq z(\hat{\theta}) + (\partial z/\partial\theta(\hat{\theta}))(\theta-\hat{\theta}) + \frac{1}{2}(\theta-\hat{\theta})'(\partial^2 z/\partial\theta\partial\theta'(\hat{\theta}))(\theta-\hat{\theta}) \qquad (17)$$

$$= z(\hat{\theta}) + [\partial z/\partial\theta(\hat{\theta}) + \frac{1}{2}(\theta-\hat{\theta})'(\partial^2 z/\partial\theta\partial\theta'(\hat{\theta}))](\theta-\hat{\theta}) \qquad (18)$$

which may be expressed as

$$\dot{z} = \sum_{j=1}^{p} S_2(z;\theta_j)\dot{\theta}_j \qquad (19)$$

where

$$S_2(z;\theta_j) = [\partial z/\partial \theta_j(\hat{\theta}) + \tfrac{1}{2}(\theta-\hat{\theta})'(\partial^2 z/\partial \theta \partial \theta_j(\hat{\theta}))][\hat{\theta}_j/z(\hat{\theta})].$$

The approximations to S may be continued to as high an order as desired by incorporating higher-order derivative information e.g. $S_3(z;\theta_j)$ weights the first, second and third derivatives. It is unlikely that one would want to go beyond S_3, although in some cases described later it is possible to provide *exact* expressions for the elasticities, designated S_∞.

3 *SENSITIVITY AND LINEARIZED CGEM's*

In all the formulae developed in section 2, it was the various derivatives of z which formed the foundations. Hence, finding these derivatives is a primary task. For linearized CGEM's, of which the class of Johansen models is the best known, very simple expressions for these derivatives can be provided, making it an easy matter to compute the sensitivity measures given earlier.

Members of the class of linearized CGEM's may be represented as

$$Ay + Bx = 0 \tag{20}$$

where y is the $(q \times 1)$ vector of endogenous variables in the system and x is the $(r \times 1)$ vector of exogenous or control variables. It is assumed that θ are elements in A or B; in some cases there is a known functional relation which is not the identity mapping, but we ignore this extra complication. Hence our objective is to find the derivatives of y with respect to θ i.e. $\partial y/\partial \alpha_{ij}$ $(i=1,\ldots,q;\ j=1,\ldots,q)$ and $\partial y/\partial \beta_{ij}$ $(i=1,\ldots,q;\ j=1,\ldots,r)$ where $\{\alpha_{ij}\}$ and $\{\beta_{ij}\}$ are the elements of A and B respectively. The first derivatives are:

$$\partial y/\partial \alpha_{ij} = A^{-1}\,\partial A/\partial \alpha_{ij}\,A^{-1}Bx = -A^{-1}\,\partial A/\partial \alpha_{ij}\,y \tag{21a}$$

$$\partial y/\partial \beta_{ij} = -A^{-1}\,\partial B/\partial \beta_{ij}\,x \tag{21b}$$

$$\therefore \quad \partial y_m/\partial \alpha_{ij} = -\alpha^{mi} y_j \tag{22a}$$

$$\partial y_m/\partial \beta_{ij} = -\alpha^{mi} x_j \tag{22b}$$

where α^{mi} is the (m,i)'th element in A^{-1}. Provided y_m is non-zero (22a) and (22b) can be converted to the sensitivity elasticities

$$S_1(y_m;\alpha_{ij}) = -(\alpha^{mi} y_j \cdot \alpha_{ij}/y_m) \tag{23a}$$

$$S_1(y_m;\beta_{ij}) = -(\alpha^{mi} x_j \cdot \alpha_{ij}/y_m). \tag{23b}$$

The structure of these formulae reveal a number of important points. Firstly, the elasticities depend only upon information available for any particular simulation i.e. only the elements of A^{-1} and the solutions y, and computational costs to generate (23) are therefore very low. Secondly, the elasticities will vary with the experiment through the dependence of $\partial y_m / \partial \alpha_{ij}$ upon y, and the output solutions differ between simulations. Thus it is never possible to conclude that a particular coefficient is always a crucial one; it can only be asserted to be pivotal for a specified policy change or set of changes.

Higher order derivatives are also functions of the same type of information as the first derivatives e.g. the second derivatives are

$$\partial^2 y_m / \partial \alpha_{ij} \partial \alpha_{k\ell} = \alpha^{mk} \alpha^{\ell i} y_j + \alpha^{mi} \alpha^{jk} y_\ell \qquad (24a)$$

$$\partial^2 y_m / \partial \alpha_{ij} \partial \beta_{k\ell} = \alpha^{mi} \alpha^{jk} x_\ell \qquad (24b)$$

$$\partial^2 y_m / \partial \beta_{ij} \partial \beta_{k\ell} = 0. \qquad (24c)$$

When only a single coefficient is under investigation, some extra insight can be obtained into the utility of a Taylor series expansion as the basis for assessing sensitivity. (25) generalises (18) with $z = y_m$

$$(\Delta z / \Delta \alpha_{ij}) = \partial z / \partial \alpha_{ij}(\hat{\theta}) + \sum_{n=2}^{g} (n!)^{-1} (\Delta \alpha_{ij})^{n-1} \partial^n z / \partial \alpha_{ij}^n (\hat{\theta}). \qquad (25)$$

It is easily shown that

$$\partial^n z / \partial \alpha_{ij}^n = (-1)^n n! (\alpha^{ji})^{n-1} \alpha^{mi} y_j \qquad (26)$$

which can be substituted into (25) to yield

$$(\Delta z / \Delta \alpha_{ij}) = -\alpha^{mi} y_j [(1 - (\alpha^{ji} \Delta \alpha_{ij})^g / (1 + \alpha^{ji} \Delta \alpha_{ij})]. \qquad (27)$$

(27) provides a necessary condition for the existence of a Taylor series expansion viz. that $|\alpha^{ji} \Delta \alpha_{ij}| < 1$; otherwise the geometric progression implicit in (25) has no limit. Moreover, when $|\alpha^{ji} \Delta \alpha_{ij}| < 1$, it is clear that an *exact* expression for the change in $z = y_m$ in response to $\Delta \alpha_{ij}$ is available from the limit of (25) as $g \to \infty$ i.e.

$$(\Delta z / \Delta \alpha_{ij}) = -\alpha^{mi} y_j (1 + \alpha^{ji} \Delta \alpha_{ij})^{-1}. \qquad (28)$$

(28) enables the computation of an exact rather than approximate S-elasticity whenever $|\alpha^{ji} \Delta \alpha_{ij}| < 1$. Of course there is a limit to the magnitude of $\Delta \alpha_{ij}$ which can be considered; for any given model (i.e. α^{ji}), eventually the restriction for a convergent series

must be violated. If this occurs most of the measures designed to assess sensitivity described in section 2 break down. Accordingly, it is important that a check be made to ensure that the necessary conditions for a Taylor series expansion are not violated for the changes being contemplated. Unfortunately, it has not been possible to derive expressions analogous to (28) for the multi-parameter situation. No sufficient conditions for the validity of the expressions are therefore available, although one might compute the derivatives numerically and ascertain if the series appears convergent.

   4 *AN EXAMPLE*

         A small linear CGEM will be briefly examined in this section to illustrate the application of the ideas developed in the preceding sections. The model chosen for this purpose consists of ten equations constructed with the aim of elucidating the aggregate results provided by the large-scale ORANI model of the Australian economy. Termed the BOTE - Back of The Envelope - model it is fully documented in Dixon et al. (1982a) and is summarized in the Appendix to this paper. Essentially it can be viewed as a two-sector trade model with the real wage and absorption exogenously determined and with three unknown parameters - the elasticities of substitution between capital and labour in the non-exportable and exportable sectors, σ^n and σ^e respectively, and the substitution elasticity of demand between domestic and import competing goods (η_2). Values given to these coefficients were $\sigma^e = .5$, $\sigma^n = .28$ and $\eta_2 = .1$. With such choices the aggregate results from the BOTE model were quite representative of the order of magnitude of the effects of policy changes indicated by ORANI. For example a rise of .45% in absorption led to an expansion in aggregate employment of .13% in BOTE and .07% in ORANI.

         Dixon et al. analysed a number of policy experiments, but here we concentrate mainly upon the "macro" one which involved an increase in absorption of .45% with the real wage held constant. Sensitivity could be measured in terms of a number of variables, but the aggregate employment response seems the most relevant and is therefore our focus.

         Initially, it is of interest to obtain an overall picture of sensitivity with the measures described in (1) and (2). Two pieces of information are required for such calculations - the covariance matrix V of the estimates, and the first and second derivatives of z, the employment change, with respect to the three coefficients. For illustrative purposes V is taken to be diagonal, but as noted earlier this could be a very poor assumption in practice. Table 1 records the derivatives required.

Using Table 1 and defining the inverse of the squares of the t-values for n_2, σ^n and σ^e as ϕ_1, ϕ_2 and ϕ_3 so that $V = \text{diag}\{.01\phi_1, .08\phi_2, .25\phi_3\}$ we have, from section 2(i), that

$$E(z) = z(\hat{\theta}) + \text{tr} D_2 V = .133 + (.013\phi_1 - .354\phi_2 + .046\phi_3)0.5$$
$$+ 0_p(T^{-3/2}) \qquad (29)$$

and

$$\text{var}(z - E(z)) = D_1' V D_1 = (.89 \times 10^{-3})\phi_1 + .067\phi_2 + .051\phi_3. \quad (30)$$

To gain some impression of the order of magnitude of the expressions, suppose that the t-value for each coefficient was 3, making $\phi_1 = \phi_2 = \phi_3 = 1/9$. Then

$$E(z) = .133 - .016 = .117$$

and $$\text{var}(z - E(z)) = .013,$$

demonstrating the inadequacy of the point estimate once allowance is made for estimation uncertainty. Although developed from a different framework, and using the median rather than the mean, this is the same point as has been made forcibly by Harrison & Kimbell (this volume) in the context of a model of trade in the Pacific Basin.

An alternative aggregative approach, which has the advantage of requiring only first derivatives, was described in section 2(ii). This involved computing the maximal variation in z when coefficients are

Table 1
Derivatives of Employment Response, BOTE Model

1st Dervs.		2nd Dervs.		
		n_2	σ^n	σ^e
n_2	$-.2994$	1.3428	1.3351	-1.0773
σ^n	$.9170$	1.3351	-4.423	$.9095$
σ^e	$-.4537$	-1.0773	$.9095$	$.1822$

constrained to lie within a specified confidence interval. Again
assuming $\phi_j = (1/9)$ $j = 1,2,3$ and a 90% confidence interval, values from
Table 1 and $\chi_3^2(.9) = 6.25$ may be inserted into (9) to get the maximal
variation in the coefficients; $\mp.007$, $\pm.18$ and $\mp.27$ respectively.
Extreme values for z are then found to be .35 and -.32, bolstering the
previous conclusion concerning the variation in the employment response
under plausible alternative coefficient combinations.

What is the cause of this sensitivity? In section 2(iii) it
was suggested that an examination of the S-elasticities for individual
parameters could shed light upon such a question. As indicated by the
size of the variation in θ found from solving (9), quite large changes
in θ - certainly of the order of 50% - need to be considered. Consequently Table 2 presents various approximations to the S-elasticities,
including an exact one for 50% changes. The size of the critical change
above which the Taylor series expansion would not exist is also recorded.

It is now apparent that it is the factor substitution
elasticities which are responsible for the sensitivity displayed in the
employment response. These elasticities are quite large, so that a 50%
increase in σ^n combined with a 50% decrease in σ^e might be expected to
lead to a change between 140-180% in the solution for employment. As
pointed out earlier, t-values on estimated coefficients are rarely that
high as to rule out the possibility of 50% changes.

A further item of interest in Table 2 is that the first
estimate of the S-elasticity is only poor for σ^n, despite the large
changes being considered. For σ^n it is only at the fourth approximation
that a quite accurate estimate of the exact elasticity is available,
although S_3 provides a good guide.

Table 2

S-elasticities for Unknown Coefficients of the BOTE Model
Absorption Experiment, 50% Changes in Coefficients

	S_1	S_2	S_3	S_4	S_∞	Crit Change (%)
n_2	-.22	-.20	-.20	-.20	-.20	446
σ^n	1.92	1.27	1.49	1.42	1.44	148
σ^e	-1.70	-1.61	-1.62	-1.62	-1.62	1000

To emphasise a point made earlier concerning the dependence of the S-elasticities upon the particular policy configuration adopted, Table 3 replicates Table 2 for an experiment in which the domestic price of crude oil was raised 26% with absorption and the real wage held at constant values. Now it is only σ^e which is of import, and sensitivity is much less marked.

5 CONCLUSION

This paper has detailed a number of measures of the sensitivity of linear CGEM's to the parameters used to calibrate them. Each measure combines together two sources of information - model structure as reflected in the derivatives of output with respect to coefficients and uncertainty induced by the need to estimate parameters. Because there is no unique way of combining these two elements, a range of alternatives was proposed. Which one is selected depends upon the environment facing a user. With good knowledge of estimation uncertainty, as would be available if one followed Jorgenson's (1983) strategy for calibrating CGEM's, the more precise aggregative measures appeal. Otherwise tabulation of the S-elasticities defined in section 2(iii) may be the most satisfactory course of action.

Although nominally this paper was only concerned with linearized CGEM's, in fact nothing in section 2 requires that assumption. Linearity is useful only in that the derivatives needed to implement the indices described in section 2 are obtained very cheaply when that assumption holds. In non-linear systems, numerical differentiation might be performed to obtain the same information. The feasibility of such a procedure would need to be examined much more thoroughly however before any of the results of this paper could be extended more widely.

Table 3
S-elasticities for Unknown Coefficients of the BOTE Model
Oil Price Experiment, 50% Changes in Coefficients

	S_1	S_2	S_3	S_4	S_∞
η_2	.06	.06	.06	.06	.06
σ^n	.29	.19	.23	.22	.22
σ^e	.64	.61	.61	.61	.61

REFERENCES

Dixon, P.B., Powell, A.A. & Parmenter, B.R. (1982a). Farm incomes and
the real exchange rate: ORANI simulations with a back-of-the
envelope explanation. Impact Project General Paper No. G-38.

Dixon, P.B., Parmenter, B.R., Sutton, J.M. & Vincent, D.P. (1982b).
ORANI: A Multisectoral Model of the Australian Economy.
Amsterdam: North-Holland.

Dixon, P.B., Parmenter, B.R. & Rimmer, R.J. (1983). The sensitivity of
ORANI projections of the short-run effects of increases in
protection to variations in the values adopted for export
demand elasticities. In The Agricultural Sector and Economy-
wide Modelling, ed. R. Dixon. University of Melbourne,
Department of Economics.

Industries Assistance Commission (1982). General Approaches to the
Reduction in Protection. Canberra: Australian Government
Publishing Service.

Industries Assistance Commission (1983). Certain Iron and Steel Products
and Certain Alloy Steel Products. Canberra: Australian
Government Publishing Service.

Jorgenson, D.W. (1983). Econometric methods for applied general
equilibrium modelling. Discussion Paper No. 967, Harvard
Institute for Economic Research.

Kuh, E., Neese, J. & Hollinger, P. (1980). Applications of linear
analysis to econometric models. Technical Report No. 35,
Centre for Computational Research in Economics and
Management Science, Massachusetts Institute of Technology.

Leamer, E.E. (1978). Specification Searches: Ad Hoc Inference with
Non-experimental Data. New York: Wiley.

West, G.R. (1982). Sensitivity and key sector analysis in input-output
models. Australian Economic Papers, 21, 365-378.

APPENDIX

BOTE Model (all variables rate of change)

$$\xi = W_n P^n + W_m P_m^c + W_o P_o + W_e P_e \tag{1}$$

$$P^e = S_\ell^e (w + \xi) + S_k^e q^e + S_i^e \xi \tag{2}$$

$$\ell^e = \sigma^e (q^e - w - \xi) \tag{3}$$

$$x^e = V_\ell^e \ell^e \tag{4}$$

$$r^e = V_\ell^e (\ell^e + w) + V_k^e (q^e - \xi) \tag{5}$$

$$P^n = S_\ell^n (w + \xi) + S_n^k q^n + S_o^n P_o + S_e^n P^e + S_m^n P_m^n + S_i^n \xi \tag{6}$$

$$\ell^n = \sigma^n (q^n - w - \xi) \tag{7}$$

$$x^n = V_\ell^n \ell^n \tag{8}$$

$$r^n = V_\ell^n (\ell^n + w) + V_k^n (q^n - \xi) \tag{9}$$

$$x^n = \eta_1 a + (1 - \eta_1) x^e - \eta_2 (P^n - Q_m^n P_m^n - Q_m^c P_m^c) \tag{10}$$

$$W_n = .881 \qquad W_m = .050 \qquad W_o = .009 \qquad W_e = .060$$

$$S_\ell^e = .37 \qquad S_k^e = .24 \qquad S_i^e = .39$$

$$\sigma^e = .5 \qquad V_\ell^e = .61 \qquad V_k^e = .39$$

$$\sigma^n = .28 \qquad V_\ell^n = .74 \qquad V_k^n = .26$$

$$\eta_1 = .96 \qquad \eta_2 = .1 \qquad Q_m^n = .75 \qquad Q_m^c = .25$$

<u>All variables are rates of change</u>

ξ = consumer price index

P^n = price of non-exportable product

P_m^c = domestic price of imported consumption goods

P_o = domestic price of oil

P_e = price of exportable product

w = real wage rate

q^e = nominal rental value per unit of capital in the exporting industry

ℓ^e = employment in the exporting sector

q^n = nominal rental value per unit of capital in the non-exportable industry

ℓ^n = employment in the non-exportable industry

a = real domestic absorption

x^e = volume of output in the exporting sector

P_m^n = domestic price of imported inputs

THE EUROPEAN ECONOMIC COMMUNITY: GENERAL EQUILIBRIUM
COMPUTATIONS AND THE ECONOMIC IMPLICATIONS OF MEMBERSHIP

J.E. Spencer
New University of Ulster

INTRODUCTION

It is now widely recognized that the Common Agricultural Policy
(CAP) of the EEC entails not only a redistribution of resources towards
agricultural producers but also a redistribution between member states
within the EEC. These redistributive effects are not easy to measure but
clearly favour member states with certain characteristics of trade and
agricultural production which tend to persist in the long run. Such
member states are likely to receive positive net transfers each year from
their EEC partners, a situation which gives rise to serious dispute and
disharmony within the Community. While the size of the total EEC budget,
some three quarters of which results from CAP operations, is not large
relative to Community GDP, the disunity resulting from debate about its
allocation diverts attention from the fundamentals of EEC policy and
retards progress in wider issues.

Part of the difficulty arises from perceived self interest of
member states but a large part arises from the intrinsic difficulties of
interpreting the published trade data and from estimating the pattern of
gains and losses which arise.

In this paper an attempt is made to assess the redistributive
effects of the CAP from the viewpoint of static general equilibrium
analysis using a standard neoclassical model of international trade. The
study thus incorporates terms of trade effects and requires the CAP budget
to balance as total receipts are required to equal total payments. The
model is calibrated to the data of 1980, the latest year for which sufficient data was available, the first recent year in which monetary
compensatory amounts (see Buckwell et al. 1982) were not important, the
first year in which the full VAT system of budgetary transfers operated
and a year in which world food prices, trade data and the components of
the CAP budget all seemed fairly normal.

119

A fundamental assumption of the analysis is that agriculture
output is not homogeneous across member states, reflecting differences in
the mix of products, although consumers' elasticity of substitution
between the outputs can be made as large as desired. Production is
assumed to take place without intermediate goods but, more importantly,
there is no unemployment. The latter assumption along with the assumed
free internal mobility of factors of production may affect the welfare
consequences of different policies but the assumption is maintained con-
sistently across countries thereby preserving rough relative measures.
The approach, which builds heavily on the previous work of Miller &
Spencer (1977), can easily handle the inclusion of further countries such
as the new member Greece and the prospective members Spain and Portugal.

THE EEC AND THE CAP
In 1980 the total EEC budget was 16,289 million ecus or
22,680 million US dollars of which 5% was spent on administration, 73% on
agriculture, 9% on regional and social policy and 7½% on reimbursement to
member states to cover the costs of collecting the revenues paid by the
states to the budget. These revenues arise from customs duties on imports
subject to the common external tariff, agricultural import and sugar
levies and VAT revenue as required up to 1% of a standardised tax base.
These revenues belong to the Community and are known as 'own resources'.
The total budget covers most of the EEC's expenditure on
common policies with the major share going to the common agricultural
policy (CAP). The objectives of the CAP are intended to be met by means
of a unified market (common support prices) permitting free circulation
of goods and a variable levy on imports keeping out low price imports.
The common prices are set at meetings of agricultural ministers each year
and the resulting compromise has typically been prices high enough to
generate excess supplies on the home markets which have to be stored at
Community expense and ultimately disposed of partly through subsidies on
world markets. These costs (see Strasser 1981, 172-3) make up about 95%
of the agricultural spending and are channelled through the Guarantee
Section of the European Agricultural Guidance and Guarantee Fund (EAGGF
or FEOGA). The Guarantee costs need not, in principle, be high depending
as they do on demand and supply considerations and price setting. If
world prices rise, eg., Guarantee costs will tend to decline as the costs
of disposing of surpluses would correspondingly decline. Nor, on the

other hand, need the revenues with the limit on VAT revenue be sufficient
to cover EEC spending and indeed, on occasions, spending has been
uncomfortably close to the limit.

In attempting to assess the official allocation of EEC
financial costs and receipts across the various member states, several
points should be noted. First, the actual gross contributions to FEOGA
are not straightforward to measure or interpret on account of the
'Rotterdam-Antwerp' effect. Duties and levies may be collected and
returned to FEOGA in the member state where imports enter even though the
imports may be in fact merely en route to the ultimate importer.
Similarly exports qualifying for refund may be channelled through another
member state and the refunds allocated there. Secondly, if a member state
imports an agricultural good from outside the EEC it pays the levy to
FEOGA while if it imports the same good from another member state, no such
payment arises. Since the price differential is the levy, there is no
economic difference between the cases although the importer's payments to
FEOGA are higher in the first case. Accordingly, as stressed by various
writers, the net budgetary transfers are a misleading measure of the
internal distribution of gains and losses within the EEC unless accompanied by measures of trade gains and losses on intra-EEC agricultural
trade. Net exporters on intra-EEC agriculture make such gains, net
importers making corresponding losses, with the UK, already making budgetary losses, as a prime example of the latter. For UK calculations of
such gains and losses under various assumptions see Rollo & Warwick
(1979), Godley (1979), Morris (1980), Buckwell et al. (1982) and
references cited therein. Thirdly, while the CAP accounts for some three
quarters of EEC spending, other spending is not negligible and in
allocating funds from the Regional and Social Fund the EEC is not insen-
sitive to the losses incurred by some member states on the CAP. Further
the UK after difficult negotiations has managed to obtain rebates each
year since 1980. The data used in the present study relate only to agriculture Guarantee costs and take no account of these rebates which were
indeed substantial for the years 1980-82 despite lower than expected
Guarantee costs in 1980 and 1981. Finally, while the internal transfers
undoubtedly lead to internal gains and losses, the Commission has always
been reluctant to publish figures of the net transfers. It believes the
figures are misleading as a measure of economic costs and benefits for a
variety of reasons including some of those mentioned above and further

believes that calculations in order to achieve a 'juste retour' are never
likely to command agreement and in any case are alien to a spirit of
European cooperation and unity.

As regards the budget costs, the present study concentrates
only on transfers generated by FEOGA Guarantee operations. It is assumed
that each country produces only two products, agriculture and non-
agriculture, both traded internationally. The separation of agriculture
is obviously of crucial importance in modelling EEC behaviour but much
more refined disaggregation would clearly be desirable. Another limita-
tion, the significance of which is hard to assess, arises from shortcomings of the available data. As is further detailed in an appendix,
available on request from the author, tariff and levy revenues by country
have been generated from import figures despite their likely limitations.
Furthermore, the study assumes that all FEOGA costs comprise refund
expenditure on agricultural exports although in reality stocks have been
increasing and some of the expenditure relates to costs of storage and
even some unloading on occasions on domestic markets (Strasser 1981,
172-3). While the assumption that all FEOGA Guarantee costs are for
export refunds has given rise to export subsidy figures for use in the
calculations which are in fact undoubtedly too high, it is doubtful if
the results are significantly impaired. If a proportion of the surplus
supply is not exported but is destroyed, denatured or domestically subsidised, the costs and benefits are borne domestically and the relative
benefit of not being within the EEC should still be similar with the
benefits of membership still accruing to the relatively large suppliers.
Further comments on this assumption are contained in Buckwell et al.
(1982), 41-2.

THE MODEL

The model incorporates the eight EEC member states of 1980 -
Belgium and Luxembourg are treated as one country since trade data is not
available separately and Greece did not join until 1981 - and the rest
of the world (RW). It is thus a nine country model with RW importing and
exporting according to published trade figures but otherwise defined
rather arbitrarily as set out in the Appendix.

The technical specification of the model on production and
consumption closely resembles that employed by Miller & Spencer (1977).
Production in each country is described by a constant returns to scale

Cobb-Douglas technology for each of the two goods produced, X (non-agriculture) and Z (agriculture) using capital (K) and labour (L) as inputs. Each country has fixed endowments of K and L which are immobile between countries. Full factor mobility is assumed within a country so that the wage rate (w) is the same in each sector as is the rental on capital (r). As regards parameter choice, the gross domestic product (Y_F), the wage payments in each sector (wL_x, wL_z) and industry outputs ($P_x X, P_z Z$) are available from standard EEC sources (see Appendix). Choosing units of measurement so that all product and factor prices are unity and assuming production functions of the form

$$X = d_x K_x^\alpha L_x^{1-\alpha}$$

$$Z = d_z K_z^\beta L_z^{1-\beta}$$

we have, under competitive conditions, that $1-\alpha = wL_x/P_x X$, which yields α. K_x then follows as $\alpha P_x X/r$. Similarly, $\beta = 1-wL_z/P_z Z$, $K_z = \beta P_z Z/r$. d_x, d_z can now be obtained as

$$d_x = X/K_x^\alpha L_x^{1-\alpha} = (\alpha^\alpha (1-\alpha)^{1-\alpha})^{-1}$$

$$d_z = Z/K_z^\beta L_z^{1-\beta} = (\beta^\beta (1-\beta)^{1-\beta})^{-1}.$$

As in Miller & Spencer (op.cit.) none of the goods produced in the various countries are perfect substitutes (Armington 1969), although they can be made as close substitutes as desired, and the demand functions are generated from two level utility CES functions (Sato 1967, Brown & Heien 1972),

$$u = (c_x X^{-e} + c_z Z^{-e})^{-1/e}$$

where

$$X = (\Sigma a_i X_i^{-e_x})^{-1/e_x}$$

$$Z = (\Sigma b_j Z_j^{-e_z})^{-1/e_z}.$$

The constant elasticities of the lower level functions are $\sigma_x = (1+e_x)^{-1}$, $\sigma_z = (1+e_z)^{-1}$ and, at the higher level, $\sigma = (1+e)^{-1}$.

Defining

$$\phi_x = \Sigma a_i^{\sigma_x} P_{x_i}^{1-\sigma_x}, \quad \phi_z = \Sigma b_j^{\sigma_z} P_{z_j}^{1-\sigma_z},$$

the demand functions are

$$X_i = (a_i/P_{x_i})^{\sigma_x} c_x^{\sigma} \phi_x^{(\sigma_x-\sigma)/(1-\sigma_x)} Y_+/\psi$$

with an analogous expression for Z_j, where

$$\psi = c_x^{\sigma} \phi_x^{(1-\sigma)/(1-\sigma_x)} + c_z^{\sigma} \phi_z^{(1-\sigma)/(1-\sigma_z)}$$

and Y_+ is factor income plus net transfers received. The prices should be assumed to be distorted with tariffs, taxes or subsidies as appropriate.

As is noted and exploited in Miller & Spencer (op.cit.), the demand assumptions imply the validity of two stage budgeting and the existence of aggregate price indices for each class of good, X goods and Z goods. These indices are functions of X prices and Z prices, respectively, are homogeneous of degree one in those prices and are defined as

$$P_x = \phi_x^{1/(1-\sigma_x)}$$

$$P_z = \phi_z^{1/(1-\sigma_z)}.$$

The quantity indices X, Z are also functions homogeneous of degree one in the relevant quantities and are as defined above. Other properties include an implied cost function

$$c(u,P) = u.\psi(P)^{1/(1-\sigma)}$$

and an indirect utility function

$$h(P,Y) = Y.\psi(P)^{1/(\sigma-1)}.$$

The substitution elasticities can be chosen arbitrarily and are here set at $\sigma = 0.1$, $\sigma_x = \sigma_z = 3.0$ in order to reflect low

elasticities of demand for agricultural goods with respect to P_z and high
elasticities of substitution between different kinds of goods in the same
category. Since $-(\partial Z/\partial P_z)(P_z/Z) = \sigma + (1-\sigma)S_z$, where S_z is the share of
agriculture spending in total spending, the actual data with $\sigma = 0.1$
imply that the elasticity varies from just over 0.1 for the countries
with relatively low agriculture spending such as Germany to around 0.2
for the higher spenders on agriculture, Ireland and Italy. For each
country the sum of the aggregate demand elasticities for X and Z is
obviously 1+σ, so the analogous aggregate X elasticities vary from just
under 1.0 to about 0.9. Other properties aiding judicious choice of the
σ's are listed in Spencer (1981)

Given choice of σ, σ_x, σ_z, the a, b and c values are derived
from the 1980 benchmark data, recalling that units are such that prices
are unity, using the following readily established formulae:

$$a_i^{\sigma_x} = X_i(1+t_{x_i})^{\sigma_x}$$

$$b_j^{\sigma_z} = Z_j(1+t_{z_j})^{\sigma_z}$$

$$c_x^{\sigma} = (\Sigma X_i(1+t_{x_i}))^{(\sigma-\sigma_x)/(1-\sigma_x)}$$

$$c_z^{\sigma} = (\Sigma Z_j(1+t_{z_j}))^{(\sigma-\sigma_z)/(1-\sigma_z)}$$

where the X's and Z's are the observed flows and where the t's are
tariffs, taxes or subsidies. With unit prices, these parameter values
will ensure that the various consumption levels will be produced as
desired provided income is at the right level. Since, as discussed in
the Appendix, the data have been manipulated so that consumption exhausts
observed factor income plus net transfers and since factor income is
generated from the production side of each economy with unit prices, it
is clear that unit prices constitute a full general equilibrium solution
of the model. This benchmark equilibrium will accordingly replicate
observed consumption flows, observed outputs, observed factor payments
in each industry and observed international transfers of spending power
subject to some manipulation of RW import data and member states' consumption levels of own output carried out in order that the data be
consistent with the present pure trade model.

Dumping produce abroad, ie. exporting at prices below internal prices, is handled in the model, not by (a) an explicit export subsidy but by the equivalent scheme of (b) exporting at full price with the importer subsidising at the export subsidy rate and transferring the cost of the import subsidy to the exporter.

For consider an equilibrium P* under dumping (a). Suppose the importer receives imports from the exporter at a 40% discount and has total income of Y_+. Under (b) if P* still obtained, consumers in the importing country would be faced with the same prices so demands would be the same if income was the same. But in the importing country this is the case, since income is Y_+ less the subsidy cost (negative tariff income) plus the subsidy cost (since it is transferred to the exporter). Similarly, in the exporting country there is no difference in income. In case (a) the low value (60%) is obtained for the exports, in case (b) the full value along with receipt of the subsidy cost (40%). Also with P* in both cases, supplies are the same. Hence since P* is an equilibrium in one case (a), it must be in the other.

In 1980 FEOGA Guarantee Section costs according to standard EEC sources were 11.016 billion ecus, ignoring a small amount attributed to MCA's. These costs were financed with 1.802 b. ecus from agricultural levies and 5.315 b. ecus from tariff revenue (common external tariff), leaving a shortfall of 3.899 b. ecus to be financed from VAT payments. After considerable experimentation with different assumptions, it was decided for the purposes of this paper to assume a uniform tariff rate and a uniform levy rate for all EEC countries and to estimate each member state's contributions of the levy and tariff revenue as proportional to its imports of Z and X respectively from RW and its contribution of VAT revenue as proportional to its GDP figures. These assumptions were incorporated in the definition and reproduction of the 1980 data as a benchmark equilibrium. The disposition of these costs back to the member states as receipts was, however, assumed to be as officially estimated by Eurostat. Eurostat Review 1971-1980 contains official estimates of the allocation of these receipts summing to 11.306 b. ecus and these figures were accordingly used, scaled by the factor 11.016/11.306. Thus, the UK, eg. was assumed to pay 1.021 (90% tariff revenue), 0.362 (90% levy revenue), 0.713 (VAT) and to receive 0.863 as refunds yielding net receipts from FEOGA of - 1.233 (b. ecus).

Algebraicly, each member state receives $P_i(1-d_i)Z_i$ from RW for its Z exports to RW, where P_i is the price of these exports, Z_i, and d_i is the discount rate. In addition it receives $P_i d_i Z_i$ from FEOGA, so that producers receive the full price and in turn it pays its levy, tariff and VAT contributions, F_i, to FEOGA. As explained above, the equivalent, but computationally more useful, way to model this is to treat FEOGA transactions as implicit with RW paying the full price P_i but subsidising internally at subsidy rate d_i and passing on the negative subsidy revenue $-\Sigma P_i d_i Z_i$ to the EEC made up of $-F_i$ to member state i, all i. This is an allocation of the negative subsidy revenue since $\Sigma P_i d_i Z_i = \Sigma F_i$ and each member state will ultimately receive $P_i Z_i - F_i$, as required, with RW paying the correct amount for the imports of $\Sigma P_i(1-d_i)Z_i$. Illustrating for the UK, her Z exports to RW are 2.315 b. ecus at full price, $P_{UK}(1-d_{UK})Z_{UK} = 1.452$, $P_{UK}d_{UK}Z_{UK} = 0.863$ and $F_{UK} = 2.096$ (b. ecus).

When the equilibrium is varied perhaps from a tariff change or when a country leaves the EEC, it is important that the new equilibrium still characterize EEC FEOGA behaviour. If the UK leaves, eg., it is assumed that she receives discounted Z imports from the EEC members just as RW continues to do. Both RW and UK now pay full price less the dump cost transferred back to each member state in proportion to its payments to FEOGA. Since these amounts depend on tariffs and levies and are not known until the endogenous prices and incomes including transfers are known, the proportions are first approximated as relative shares of payments to FEOGA in the benchmark equilibrium excluding the UK. This typically generates an equilibrium which has the total dump cost allocated to EEC states in proportions quite closely but not fully reflecting their tariff, levy and VAT contributions, the latter being calculated as the total dump cost less tariff and levy contributions allocated over member states according to relative factor incomes. The proportions are then recalculated according to the new tariff, levy and VAT contributions and a new equilibrium found. After three or four such iterations, the proportions essentially remain constant and the appropriate new equilibrium has been found.

A further difficulty arises in assessing the effects of changing EEC membership on the refund and levy rates. When a country leaves the EEC, a new equilibrium configuration of prices emerges. Since the refund and levy rates are designed to insulate the EEC members from outside disturbance, these rates should, in principle, change in an endogenous

manner. If held constant, the outgoing member would switch demand towards
the subsidised EEC Z exports whose prices would rise and EEC supplies
would also rise. This would be a quite undesirable aspect of the model,
since the supplies of the remaining EEC members should remain broadly constant due to CAP insulation of domestic markets. For the model to have
realism the EEC P_z/P_x ratios should be roughly constant. Accordingly, when a
country leaves the EEC, a run was performed holding the d's fixed. This
indeed generated a surge of demand for EEC Z by the former member with
resulting rises in the EEC P_z/P_x ratios. This result provided endogenous
data for the necessary reduction in the d's, viz. multiplying each
country's old d by the ratio of its old Z supply to its new one. This
change resulted in Z supplies which were still high and further small
reductions were imposed until the new Z supplies and, hence, X supplies
of the member states were as before. Altering levy rates, in principle
appropriate, in accordance with the new equilibrium prices, had little
effect since price changes were not large and so the levies were left
unaltered. This had the advantage of avoiding the problem of non-uniform
changes in levies since such price changes as did emerge were not uniform
over the countries.

The algorithm used is Hansen's gradient method as used by
Miller & Spencer (op.cit.) and modified in the present study for nine
countries and a more complex transfer system. An initial vector or final
product prices is assumed and with these supplies are calculated. This
can be done, for elimination of w, r from the first order production
conditions yields

$$\pi_z = \frac{\alpha X}{\beta Z} \frac{K_z}{K_x} = \frac{(1-\alpha)X}{(1-\beta)Z} \frac{L_z}{L_x}$$

where $\pi_z = P_z/P_x$ and, using the production functions to eliminate X, Z,
the capital-labour ratios in each industry δ_x, δ_z can be found as a
function of π_z alone. Thus,

$$\delta_x(\pi_z) = K_x/L_x = \left\{ \pi_z \frac{d_z}{d_x} \left(\frac{\beta}{\alpha}\right)^\beta \left(\frac{1-\beta}{1-\alpha}\right)^{1-\beta} \right\}^{1/(\alpha-\beta)}$$

$$\delta_z(\pi_z) = K_z/L_z = \left\{ \pi_z \frac{d_z}{d_x} \left(\frac{\beta}{\alpha}\right)^\alpha \left(\frac{1-\beta}{1-\alpha}\right)^{1-\alpha} \right\}^{1/(\alpha-\beta)}$$

Since $K_x + K_z = K, L_x + L_z = L$

$$K_x = \delta_x (K - \delta_z L)/(\delta_x - \delta_z)$$

$$K_z = \delta_z (K - \delta_x L)/(\delta_z - \delta_x)$$

$$L_x = (K - \delta_z L)/(\delta_x - \delta_z)$$

$$L_z = (K - \delta_x L)/(\delta_z - \delta_x)$$

and

$$X = d_x \, \delta_x^\alpha (K - \delta_z L)/(\delta_x - \delta_z)$$

$$Z = d_z \, \delta_z^\beta (K - \delta_x L)/(\delta_z - \delta_x)$$

$$Y_F = P_x X + P_z Z \ (= rK + wL).$$

Calculation of demands, however, involves Y_+ not just Y_F as well as product prices. But the transfers depend on knowing tariff revenue which depends on knowing demands and hence Y_+. Since intra-EEC transfers are handled here as described above with extra-EEC states handing negative revenue to the EEC states and since demands are homogeneous in income of the form $X_i = f_i(P^+)$. Y_+, where $P_i^+ = P_i(1+t_i)$, a recursive ordering of countries with the extra-EEC states taken first allows solution of this problem without awkward iterative procedures. If the proportion θ_i of the tariff (or tax or subsidy) revenue on the i'th good is retained and G is the amount received from foreigners, disposable income (Y_+) may be written

$$Y_+ = Y_F + \Sigma P_i t_i \theta_i X_i + G$$

$$= Y_F + \Sigma P_i t_i \theta_i f_i(P^+) Y_+ + G$$

$$= (Y_F + G)/(1 - \Sigma P_i t_i \theta_i f_i(P^+))$$

and

$$X_i = f_i(P^+)(Y_F + G)/(1 - \Sigma P_i t_i \theta_i f_i(P^+)).$$

The first country has zero G from others but distributes to countries
lower in the order. The second country can have some G from country 1
and it transfers to countries 3, 4 etc. Given the initial vector of
product prices and total factor supplies and consequent product supplies,
demands can then be calculated for each country in turn. Total demands
and supplies are then compared, prices adjusted and a second iteration
performed and so on.

Perhaps the most important criterion in assessing each situation considered is the welfare measure. With explicit welfare functions,
no problem of measurement arises and the measure adopted is
$W = 100.u(q_1)/u(q_0)$, the zero subscript attaching to benchmark or 1980,
status quo quantities consumed. This can usefully be described in terms
of money metric utility (eg., McKenzie & Pearce 1982). Writing Y* as
the money metric utility, ie. the sum of money required at old prices P_0
to buy the welfare equivalent of the new price, income (P_1, Y_1) situation,
Y* is defined implicitly via the indirect utility function as

$$h(P_1, Y_1) = h(P_0, Y^*)$$

which solves in the present case as

$$Y^* = Y_1 (\psi(P_1)/\psi(P_0))^{1/(\sigma-1)}.$$

Accordingly,

$$Y^*/Y_0 = Y_1 (\psi(P_1))^{1/(\sigma-1)} / Y_0 (\psi(P_0))^{1/(\sigma-1)}$$

$$= h(P_1, Y_1)/h(P_0, Y_0)$$

$$= c(u_1, P_0)/c(u_0, P_0)$$

and

$$W = 100 Y^*/Y_0$$

$$= 100 c(u_1, P_0)/c(u_0, P_0)$$

ie., the cost, at old prices, of the welfare equivalent of the new
equilibrium as a percentage of the cost of the old equilibrium at old
prices (Y_o).

THE RESULTS

Table 1 gives the EEC agriculture export subsidies in the 1980
benchmark situation and the endogenously determined subsidy rates used to
hold remaining EEC supplies constant when a member state leaves. The
latter rates are invariably lower than the benchmark rates, of course,
since otherwise member states would produce more agriculture to meet
the extra demand from the former member. The relative magnitudes of the
d's are broadly similar to the benchmark situation, such differences as
there are being explained by the differing preferences of the withdrawing
member state. For example, when the UK leaves, the Ireland d falls
disproportionately to prevent the UK's demand for Ireland's Z pushing up
the Irish price and supply.

TABLE 1   EXPORT SUBSIDIES ON E.E.C. AGRICULTURE

	UK	Germany	Italy	France	Neths	Denmark	Belg./Lux.	Ireland
1980 Benchmark	.372786	.519548	.640187	.394929	.391723	.333889	.311233	.522814
UK Out	-	.4579	.5150	.3462	.3026	.2263	2687	.2416
Germany Out	.3029	-	.3761	.3036	.2219	.2349	.2198	4415
Italy Out	.3346	.3489	-	.2880	.3085	.2584	.2581	.4881
France Out	.2791	.3980	.4390	-	.2857	.2768	.2089	.3769
Neths. Out	.3258	.4357	.5930	.3564	-	.3120	.2644	.4614
Denmark Out	.3533	.4867	.6193	.3861	.3779	-	.3032	.5151
Belg./Lux. Out	.3546	.4835	.6050	.3714	.3582	.3249	-	.4990
Ireland Out	.3358	.5157	.6330	.3888	.3866	.3301	.3071	-

The welfare results are given in Table 2, results which
ultimately derive from the detailed consumption pattern of the countries
in the various cases. 1980 Benchmark, which reproduces the 1980 status
quo, assuming each country receives the refunds as officially published,
normalises the data. Autarchy (VAT) gives the welfare results from no
trade, with each EEC country continuing to charge VAT on consumption of X
as in 1980 Benchmark. The autarchy results were obtained by setting the
a_i, b_j parameters, other than own values, to zero. This gives welfare
levels equivalent to what would be obtained if all international trade in

the model ceased since in each utility function consumption of foreign production is multiplied by the appropriate a, b values. The resulting welfare levels show very large benefits from trade, especially for those countries for which imports form a large part of consumption, although no great significance can be placed on the detailed effects in a model of this kind for so drastic a change. Reducing VAT rates in the EEC to zero had a negligible effect on autarchy results and is not included. VAT, however, had more effect on the free trade results, which are accordingly given in the cases of continutation of VAT and of zero VAT. In free trade RW does slightly better if VAT is continued in the EEC countries. Throughout all the calculations, RW was assumed to have no internal tax or subsidy on X production or consumption other than a 10% tariff on X imports.

TABLE 2   WELFARE

	RW	UK	Germany	Italy	France	Neths.	Denmark	Belg./Lux	Ireland
Autarchy (VAT)	83.95	86.62	87.01	86.48	88.44	71.62	83.05	62.19	63.43
1980 Benchmark	100.	100.	100.	100.	100.	100.	100.	100.	100.
UK Out	99.94	101.00	99.97	99.97	99.97	99.87	99.94	99.87	99.22
Germany Out	99.93	100.08	100.77	100.03	100.07	99.80	100.01	99.81	100.01
Italy Out	99.95	100.09	100.07	100.90	100.07	100.05	100.10	100.03	100.06
France Out	99.92	100.19	100.16	100.12	100.53	100.09	100.20	99.91	100.10
Neths. Out	99.92	100.10	100.07	100.10	100.11	101.09	100.10	99.92	100.08
Denmark Out	99.97	100.03	100.04	100.04	100.05	100.02	100.56	100.03	100.04
Belg./Lux. Out	99.98	99.99	99.98	99.99	99.98	99.86	99.99	102.01	99.98
Ireland Out	99.99	100.02	100.04	100.04	100.04	100.04	100.04	100.04	99.67
Free Trade (VAT)	99.18	101.19	100.94	101.01	100.72	100.78	100.63	101.60	99.45
Free Trade (No VAT)	98.99	101.31	101.04	101.12	100.81	100.93	100.76	101.82	99.61

The more important results, however, are probably those pertaining to the situation when the member states leave one at a time. UK Out,eg., describes the situation when the UK withdraws from the EEC. When a country withdraws, it is assumed to continue to tariff X imports from RW as before (at 2.41655%) but it now tariffs the X imports from the EEC at the same rate. Furthermore, it now engages in free trade in agriculture with RW but benefits from the (lowered) subsidy on EEC agricultural exports. The remaining members of the EEC trade freely with each other as before but now tariff X imports and levy Z imports from the previous member just as they did and continue to do at the same rates of

2.41655% and 8.2143% respectively vis-à-vis RW.

The most striking result is the tendency for each member state to do better outside the EEC (or, more properly, the CAP) than within it although free trade is better still, particularly without VAT, in most cases. Only Ireland is better off within the EEC than outside and only Netherlands and Belgium/Luxembourg prefer the continuation of the EEC with them outside to free trade. The major gainers from withdrawal are UK, Netherlands and Belgium/Luxembourg, especially the latter, while the countries gaining least are Denmark and France with Ireland losing. The ordering is similar if the d's are unchanged with gains of about an extra ½%, principally from the larger subsidies, being obtained. Similar orderings, apart from Netherlands, were derived using different methods and less recent data by Rollo & Warwick (op.cit.), Godley (op.cit.), Morris (op.cit.) and Buckwell et al. (op.cit.).

When a country leaves, RW imports less Z from the EEC at lower subsidy rates and always loses but no clear pattern emerges vis-à-vis the remaining EEC members. They all lose when either UK or Belgium/Luxembourg withdraws and all gain if Italy or Denmark or Ireland leaves.

To analyse the patterns of gains and losses further, it is necessary to consider the terms of trade movements and other changes displayed in the remaining tables. Withdrawal from the EEC makes available export subsidies on Z imports from the country's former partners which increases external demand for these imports and accordingly their prices rise. With the export subsidy level being chosen such that each EEC country produces the same Z and hence X as before, the EEC countries' domestic P_x/P_z ratios remain constant. The terms of trade are accordingly expected to move in favour of the EEC countries relative to their former partner, an expectaion strengthened by the imposition of the common external tariff on the former partner's X exports and confirmed by Table 4. Since, however, the former member receives Z from her former partners at a discount, the international terms of trade at full price are an imperfect guide to the rate of exchange between own goods and EEC goods. Major gains to the former member arise from the cheaper Z imports, the extent of the gains depending on the extent of the price change, taking into account the subsidy, and the volume of Z imports from the EEC. Equivalently, as discussed above, the gains depend on the movement of nondiscounted prices and the size of the implicit negative transfer from the former member of the EEC. With regard to X goods, multilateral tariff

changes are involved with the erection of tariff barriers between the EEC
and the former member, and the net effects from tariff changes are
accordingly harder to predict. The main overall effects, however, derive
from the agriculture changes and it is clear that countries involved in
substantial importing of agriculture will tend to benefit from withdrawal
from the EEC.

TABLE 3   CONSUMER RELATIVE PRICE AND QUANTITY INDICES AND SHARES

		RW	UK	Germany	Italy	France	Neths.	Denmark	Belg./Lux.	Ireland
Autarchy (VAT)	Π_Z/Π_X	3.142	4.037	4.375	2.566	3.329	6.379	4.440	5.999	2.604
	$X/_Z$	38.86	47.41	58.68	17.90	36.49	54.48	57.01	55.17	21.24
	Z-share	.0748	.0785	.0694	.1254	.0836	.1048	.0723	.0981	.1092
1980 Benchmark	Π_Z/Π_X	3.396	3.606	3.870	2.618	3.317	3.723	3.830	3.748	2.775
	$X/_Z$	39.16	46.88	57.96	17.94	36.48	51.62	56.18	52.64	21.37
	Z-share	.0798	.0714	.0626	.1274	.0833	.0673	.0638	.0665	.1149
UK Out	Π_Z/Π_X	3.476	3.234	3.873	2.618	3.319	3.738	3.835	3.759	2.814
	$X/_Z$	39.25	46.37	57.97	17.94	36.48	51.64	56.18	52.65	21.40
	Z-share	.0813	.0652	.0626	.1274	.0834	.0675	.0639	.0666	.1162
Germany Out	Π_Z/Π_X	3.512	3.609	3.502	2.622	3.320	3.750	3.848	3.763	2.776
	$X/_Z$	39.29	46.88	57.39	17.94	36.48	51.66	56.20	52.66	21.37
	Z-share	.0820	.0715	.0575	.1275	.0834	.0677	.0641	.0667	.1149
Italy Out	Π_Z/Π_X	3.488	3.610	3.878	2.421	3.320	3.730	3.835	3.754	2.777
	$X/_Z$	39.27	46.88	57.97	17.80	36.48	51.63	56.18	52.64	21.37
	Z-share	.0816	.0715	.0627	.1197	.0834	.0674	.0639	.0666	.1150
France Out	Π_Z/Π_X	3.522	3.612	3.880	2.624	3.073	3.748	3.837	3.786	2.784
	$X/_Z$	39.31	46.89	57.98	17.94	36.20	51.65	56.19	52.69	21.38
	Z-share	.0822	.0715	.0627	.1276	.0782	.0676	.0639	.0670	.1152
Neths. Out	Π_Z/Π_X	3.465	3.614	3.888	2.621	3.322	2.892	3.838	3.795	2.779
	$X/_Z$	39.24	46.89	57.99	17.94	36.49	50.33	56.19	52.70	21.38
	Z-share	.0811	.0716	.0628	.1275	.0834	.0543	.0639	.0672	.1150
Denmark Out	Π_Z/Π_X	3.424	3.613	3.874	2.619	3.318	3.727	3.214	3.750	2.776
	$X/_Z$	39.20	46.89	57.97	17.94	36.48	51.63	55.20	52.64	21.37
	Z-share	.0803	.0715	.0626	.1274	.0834	.0673	.0550	.0665	.1149
Belg./ Lux. Out	Π_Z/Π_X	3.434	3.608	3.874	2.618	3.320	3.748	3.831	2.571	2.776
	$X/_Z$	39.21	46.88	57.97	17.94	36.48	51.66	56.18	50.69	21.37
	Z-share	.0805	.0715	.0626	.1274	.0834	.0677	.0638	.0483	.1149
Ireland Out	Π_Z/Π_X	3.412	3.610	3.873	2.618	3.317	3.725	3.831	3.749	2.182
	$X/_Z$	39.18	46.88	57.96	17.94	36.48	51.62	56.18	52.64	20.86
	Z-share	.0801	.0715	.0626	.1274	.0833	.0673	.0638	.0665	.0947
Free Trade (VAT)	Π_Z/Π_X	3.689	3.541	3.807	2.606	3.272	3.614	3.742	3.676	2.735
	$X/_Z$	39.49	46.79	57.87	17.93	36.43	51.47	56.05	52.53	21.34
	Z-share	.0854	.0704	.0617	.1269	.0824	.0656	.0626	.0654	.1136

Perhaps the simplest case to examine is that of Ireland.
Ireland receives considerable net transfers in the benchmark situation
which are lost on withdrawal (see Table 6). Losses on terms of trade
are particularly acute in her case (see Table 4). The loss of protection
in agriculture is accompanied by increased demand for her X good despite
the imposed tariff by the EEC. Both the internal relative consumer and
producer price of Z drops (Tables 3 and 4), producers switch from Z to X
(Table 4) and substantial switches in capital and labour occur (Table 5).

TABLE 4   PRODUCTION AND PRODUCER PRICES

		RW	UK	Germany	Italy	France	Neths.	Denmark	Belg./Lux.	Ireland
Autarchy (VAT)	X	1017.20	309.13	504.61	240.31	396.23	104.72	41.15	75.49	11.71
	Z	82.75	26.67	37.97	34.88	36.76	12.48	3.25	8.41	1.48
	P_X	5.9123	5.3831	5.5963	5.3920	5.6736	5.3803	5.3817	5.3878	5.9370
	P_Z	5.8758	5.3860	5.6182	5.3973	5.6491	5.3803	5.3805	5.3921	5.8765
1980 Benchmark	X	1000.00	316.90	513.70	243.30	392.30	105.10	38.70	78.60	9.90
	Z	100.00	18.90	28.90	31.90	40.70	12.10	5.70	5.30	3.30
	P_X	5.5556	5.5556	5.5556	5.5556	5.5556	5.5556	5.5556	5.5556	5.5556
	P_Z	5.5556	5.5556	5.5556	5.5556	5.5556	5.5556	5.5556	5.5556	5.5556
UK Out	X	995.90	322.62							
	Z	104.09	13.18							
	P_X	5.5735	5.5128	5.5625	5.5637	5.5630	5.5579	5.5636	5.5592	5.5408
	P_Z	5.5817	5.5107							
Germany Out	X	993.82		522.94						
	Z	106.17		19.64						
	P_X	5.5797	5.5672	5.5048	5.5636	5.5653	5.5466	5.5641	5.5506	5.5627
	P_Z	5.5922		5.4832						
Italy Out	X	994.88			250.89					
	Z	105.11			24.30					
	P_X	5.5758	5.5691	5.5644	5.4628	5.5642	5.5647	5.5707	5.5630	5.5669
	P_Z	5.5861			5.4492					
France Out	X	992.90				402.29				
	Z	107.09				30.66				
	P_X	5.5834	5.5749	5.5678	5.5656	5.4673	5.5644	5.5767	5.5530	5.5696
	P_Z	5.5977				5.4078				
Neths. Out	X	997.11					109.64			
	Z	102.89					7.56			
	P_X	5.5762	5.5706	5.5666	5.5728	5.5728	5.4387	5.5716	5.5581	5.5697
	P_Z	5.5820					5.4387			
Denmark Out	X	998.58						40.75		
	Z	101.42						3.65		
	P_X	5.5777	5.5745	5.5750	5.5767	5.5771	5.5737	5.3949	5.5747	5.5749
	P_Z	5.5806						5.3939		
Belg/Lux. Out	X	998.53							80.79	
	Z	101.47							3.11	
	P_X	5.5691	5.5643	5.5630	5.5651	5.5636	5.5575	5.5656	5.4873	5.5642
	P_Z	5.5720							5.4845	
Ireland Out	X	999.21								11.17
	Z	100.79								2.03
	P_X	5.5917	5.5848	5.5912	5.5914	5.5915	5.5905	5.5906	5.5905	5.2959
	P_Z	5.5933								5.2580
Free Trade (VAT)	X	981.66	319.72	518.99	246.69	398.38	108.22	40.01	80.04	10.77
	Z	118.28	16.08	23.60	28.51	34.60	8.98	4.39	3.86	2.43
	P_X	5.4741	5.6273	5.6046	5.6098	5.5780	5.5330	5.5233	5.6125	5.4624
	P_Z	5.5107	5.6262	5.5920	5.6035	5.5409	5.5330	5.5227	5.6105	5.4356

Prices are normalized to sum to 100 in each case. Blank entries have X and Z as for 1980 Benchmark
and $P_X = P_Z$ for E.E.C. member states.

The net result is a loss to Ireland from withdrawal despite substantial imports of Z from the EEC under EEC subsidies.

The case of German withdrawal is less clear. It might perhaps be expected that Germany would gain more on withdrawal but the costs of the CAP to Germany in terms of transfers are small relative to her GDP (Table 6). German demand for the agriculture of her former partners rises with the

TABLE 5   FACTOR ALLOCATION AND SHARES

		RW	UK	Germany	Italy	France	Neths.	Denmark	Belg./Lux.	Ireland
Total K		410.	97.09	198.03	111.58	151.04	41.05	15.79	28.09	4.53
Total L		690.	238.71	344.57	163.62	281.96	76.15	28.61	55.81	8.67
Autarchy (VAT)	K_Z	8.12	6.02	5.65	4.66	2.03	4.29	1.25	2.29	0.68
	L_Z	74.62	20.65	32.32	25.23	34.73	8.19	2.00	6.12	0.80
	K-share	.3776	.2875	.3611	.4038	.3519	.3502	.3539	.3322	.3254
1980 Benchmark	K_Z	10.0	4.24	4.24	8.79	2.28	4.16	2.18	1.43	1.45
	L_Z	90.0	14.66	24.66	23.11	38.42	7.94	3.52	3.87	1.85
	K-share	.3727	.2891	.3650	.4055	.3488	.3503	.3556	.3348	.3432
UK Out	K_Z	10.46	2.94							
	L_Z	93.64	10.23							
	K-share	.3716	.2903							
Germany Out	K_Z	10.69		2.84						
	L_Z	95.48		16.80						
	K-share	.3710		.3689						
Italy Out	K_Z	10.57			6.61					
	L_Z	94.54			17.69					
	K-share	.3713			.4095					
France Out	K_Z	10.79				1.66				
	L_Z	96.30				29.00				
	K-share	.3707				.3565				
Neths. Out	K_Z	10.32					2.60			
	L_Z	92.57					4.96			
	K-share	.3719					.3505			
Denmark Out	K_Z	10.16						1.40		
	L_Z	91.26						2.25		
	K-share	.3723						.3542		
Belg./ Lux. Out	K_Z	10.16							.83	
	L_Z	91.31							2.28	
	K-share	.3723							.3366	
Ireland Out	K_Z	10.09								.92
	L_Z	90.70								1.11
	K-share	.3725								.3307
Free Trade (VAT)	K_Z	12.07	3.60	3.43	7.81	1.90	3.09	1.57	1.04	1.09
	L_Z	106.22	12.48	20.17	20.70	32.70	5.89	2.71	2.82	1.34
	K-share	.3675	.2897	.3672	.4073	.3535	.3504	.3547	.3360	.3346

Blank entries have K_Z, L_Z and K-share at 1980 Benchmark levels for E.E.C. member states.

export subsidy but the benefits are again small relative to GDP. Her
supply of Z falls and her exports of Z to each country declines. Her X
exports to the EEC also fall but she exports more X to RW. Within the
EEC there is a clear tendency for internal trade to expand at the expense
of trade with RW and Germany although the case of Netherlands X imports
is the most varied with smaller amounts bought by Netherlands from UK,
Italy, France and Denmark. In the benchmark situation, almost a quarter
of Netherlands X imports came from Germany, a higher proportion than that
of any other EEC members. This preference for German X goods works against
Netherlands when Germany leaves as it gives rise to high transfers to FEOGA

TABLE 6   INTERNAL E.E.C. TRANSFERS

		UK	Germany	Italy	France	Neths.	Denmark	Belg./Lux.	Ireland	Total
1980 Benchmark	G.D.P.	932.78	1507.22	764.44	1202.78	325.56	123.33	233.06	36.67	
	Total Payments	5.822	8.414	4.447	6.336	2.689	.814	1.822	.256	30.600
	Refunds	2.397	6.644	4.947	7.658	4.181	1.667	1.578	1.528	30.600
	Net Receipts	-3.425	-1.769	.500	1.322	1.492	.853	-.244	1.272	0.
UK Out	G.D.P.	925.58	1509.09	765.55	1204.38	325.69	123.51	232.21	36.57	
	Total Payments		8.710	4.534	6.509	2.939	.899	2.052	.535	26.178
	Refunds		6.143	4.343	7.161	3.939	1.739	1.478	1.376	26.178
	Net Receipts		-2.567	-.191	.652	1.000	.840	-.574	.841	0.
Germany Out	G.D.P.	934.62	1493.02	765.46	1204.73	324.99	123.51	232.82	36.71	
	Total Payments	5.102		4.243	5.670	3.032	.819	2.128	.239	21.233
	Refunds	2.135		3.657	6.945	4.044	1.591	1.474	1.388	21.233
	Net Receipts	-2.968		-.586	1.275	1.012	.772	-.655	1.149	0.
Italy Out	G.D.P.	935.01	1509.53	751.44	1204.59	326.07	123.66	233.36	36.74	
	Total Payments	5.031	7.446		5.585	2.444	.708	1.681	.229	23.123
	Refunds	2.174	5.599		6.987	3.863	1.584	1.467	1.448	23.123
	Net Receipts	-2.857	-1.846		1.403	1.419	.876	-.214	1.220	0.
France Out	G.D.P.	935.64	1509.92	765.52	1182.12	325.94	123.75	232.85	36.74	
	Total Payments	4.277	6.231	3.647		2.319	.601	1.892	.215	19.182
	Refunds	2.062	5.562	3.618		3.693	1.525	1.406	1.317	19.182
	Net Receipts	-2.215	-.670	-.029		1.375	.924	-.486	1.102	0.
Neths. Out	G.D.P.	935.34	1510.28	766.85	1206.56	318.72	123.69	232.17	36.76	
	Total Payments	5.162	7.887	3.836	5.366		.744	2.196	.232	25.422
	Refunds	2.315	6.063	4.534	7.519		1.604	1.895	1.492	25.422
	Net Receipts	-2.847	-1.824	.698	2.153		.861	-.301	1.260	0.
Denmark Out	G.D.P.	936.01	1512.59	767.40	1207.51	326.64	119.77	233.87	36.80	
	Total Payments	5.598	7.899	4.190	5.840	2.580		1.733	.243	28.082
	Refunds	2.232	6.410	4.759	7.527	4.109		1.543	1.504	28.082
	Net Receipts	-3.366	-1.489	.569	1.686	1.529		-.190	1.261	0.
Belg./ Lux. Out	G.D.P.	934.19	1509.15	765.71	1204.45	325.65	123.55	230.18	36.72	
	Total Payments	5.950	8.881	4.564	6.774	3.134	.835		.263	30.400
	Refunds	2.529	6.653	4.822	8.198	4.990	1.672		1.536	30.400
	Net Receipts	-3.421	-2.227	.258	1.424	1.856	.837		1.273	0.
Ireland Out	G.D.P.	938.03	1517.45	769.65	1211.00	327.72	124.16	234.60	34.91	
	Total Payments	5.800	7.937	4.221	6.000	2.623	.780	1.764		29.126
	Refunds	2.508	6.628	4.924	7.662	4.178	1.657	1.568		29.126
	Net Receipts	-3.292	-1.309	.702	1.662	1.555	.878	-.197		0.

Multiplication of the 1980 Benchmark figures by 0.36 translates units into thousand million ecus.

and accordingly worsens Netherlands net receipts on internal transfers
(Table 6). Even worse losses for Italy are offset by terms of trade gains
so that the value of her GDP rises by more than the loss in net receipts
(Tables 4 and 6) and small net gains are made overall (Table 2).

Belgium/Luxembourg benefits most from withdrawing from the EEC
and CAP. In this case the very substantial benefits of the export subsidy
are augmented by ceasing to make transfer losses on CAP and are less
diminished by terms of trade losses since the prices of her major trading
partners in the Benchmark situation, Netherlands and Germany, rise less
than those of others.

The most surprising case is Netherlands Out as it is widely
held that Netherlands does well from the CAP. Substantial net transfers
are lost on withdrawal (Table 6) and the movement in terms of trade does
not seem particularly favourable yet Netherlands obtains the second
highest gains from leaving. The answer lies in her unusually high degree
of trade, especially, like Belgium/Luxembourg, in agricultural imports,
and the relatively high increase in agricultural consumption on leaving
the EEC (Table 3), an increase of some $3\frac{1}{2}\%$ and second only to Belgium/
Luxembourg. The gains of these two member states from leaving could well
be overstated in accordance with any over-statement of their trade due to
the Rotterdam/Antwerp effect.

Table 3 reports on consumer relative price and quantity
indices. The price indices, defined above, include tariff, tax and subsidy
information so π_z/π_x is expected to fall when a country leaves the EEC,
as is X/Z, aggregate X consumption relative to aggregate Z. This is
confirmed in all cases, especially in that of Belgium/Luxembourg. When a
country leaves, π_z/π_x tends to rise for the remaining countries, including
RW, due to the increased total demand for their Z output, although the
effects are typically small.

Table 5 reports the factor movements and shares. As is well
known, factor movements in models of this type tend to be unrealistically
large. Accordingly, the welfare levels of the withdrawing country,
especially in the cases of withdrawal of Ireland and Denmark, might be
somewhat exaggerated as they involve considerable relative shifts of
factors out of agriculture, such shifts being notoriously difficult to
achieve in practice.

Returning to the 1980 benchmark and before proceeding to
further analysis of all these cases, it is worth noting the results of

several computer runs in which the common external tariff was increased
in steps assuming other things equal - in particular, no retaliation from
RW. One might expect that such increases would benefit all EEC members
at first, but as the tariff gets high, the terms of trade gains would be
offset by the ensuing distortions earlier for the countries with the
bigger relative stake in agriculture. Although such runs were not carried
out in great detail, gains were made for all EEC member states, up to
around 1.5% (more for the Netherlands) until the tariff reached about 50%
when Denmark, Belgium/Luxembourg and Ireland ceased gaining. Italy and
then France ceased gaining shortly afterwards and when tariffs of 60% were
tried all gains ended.

A run was performed increasing each country's efficiency in
Z production by multiplying their production functions by 1.2. No other
changes were made and the results are given in Table 7. RW gains about
1.3% while within the EEC Italy gains most and Denmark least. Percentage
increases in supply of the two goods vary quite markedly with Ireland
and Denmark increasing agriculture supply most and the UK and Germany
increasing X most. Terms of trade change favour UK, Germany and Belgium/
Luxembourg, while the pattern of internal transfers within the EEC are
broadly as before with total payments overall declining due to the fall
in the price of agriculture generally.

TABLE 7

INCREASE IN EFFICIENCY OF AGRICULTURE PRODUCTION
OF 20% IN E.E.C. AND RW

	RW	UK	Germany	Italy	France	Neths.	Denmark	Belg./Lux.	Ireland	Total
Welfare	10 1.34	101.39	101.22	102.30	101.48	101.12	100.96	101.29	101.36	
G.D.P.	3191.24	977.34	1578.91	799.24	1255.98	339.58	128.07	243.82	37.93	
Payments		5.218	7.418	3.980	5.520	2.457	.720	1.684	.227	27.225
Refunds		2.112	5.873	4.387	6.865	3.714	1.494	1.394	1.385	27.225
Net Receipts		-3.106	-1.545	.407	1.345	1.257	.774	-.290	1.158	
P_X	.60724	.60895	.60888	.60773	.60721	.60622	.60350	.60802	.60145	
P_Z	.50352	.50736	.50648	.50571	.50296	.50519	.50287	.50659	.50010	
X	1013.78	319.75	517.97	247.68	397.82	106.84	39.46	79.41	10.29	
Increase	13.8 %	9.0%	8.3%	1.8%	1.4%	1.7%	2.0%	1.0%	3.9%	
Z	103.42	19.26	29.55	33.02	42.19	12.43	5.93	5.39	3.49	
Increase	3.4%	1.9%	2.2%	3.5%	3.7%	2.7%	4.0%	1.7%	5.8%	

If the increase in efficiency is confined to the EEC countries
and is accompanied by a concomitant cut in the levy and export refund rates,
the pattern of gains was similar, again with Italy doing best.

A limited number of runs were performed as a robustness check
on the model. First, the size of the capital and labour endowments of
RW, essentially an arbitrary choice in the base run, were substantially
increased. Such runs showed, as expected, little change in the patterns
of gains and losses within the EEC, although the checks were not extensive.
Terms of trade changes vis-à-vis RW were, of course, smaller as RW got
bigger. Secondly, σ_z was increased from 3 to 5 in order to see if
increased substitution elasticities and hence demand elasticities for Z
would have marked effects. This change produced welfare figures in the
various runs which were close to the figures in the main runs for which
σ_z was set at 3. There was, however, a systematic tendency for the rest
of the EEC to do slightly better than before when one of the member states
withdrew from the union, but the improvement was generally of small order
and typically around 0.05%. Thirdly, in order to overcome the 'Rotterdam-
Antwerp' effect, some runs were tried in which Germany, Netherlands and
Belgium/Luxembourg were combined into one trading block. Suppose that
the UK imported a unit from Germany but that the import came via
Netherlands so that the original data recorded the transaction as
Netherlands importing from Germany and the UK importing from Netherlands.
Treating Germany, Netherlands and Belgium/Luxembourg as one country,
Germany Plus, recorded internal trade between these three countries is
treated as domestic consumption of domestic output. Such consumption
would accordingly be overstated with the operation of the 'Rotterdam-
Antwerp' effect, but the crucial external trade data would be 'correct'
with Germany Plus exporting one unit to the UK. Manipulating all the
data in this way for the base run and then repeating the other runs
with the three countries treated as one throughout led to a very similar
pattern of gains from withdrawal from the EEC for the other EEC members
as that previously estimated. The UK gained most from withdrawal (1.02%),
Italy gained 0.90% from withdrawal, Germany Plus gained 0.58%, France 0.53%,
Denmark 0.48% and Ireland lost 0.32% from withdrawal.

Finally, it should be stressed that other ways of measuring
the costs and benefits of the CAP can easily be devised. For example,
each country could remain within the CAP but could pay its own subsidy

cost rather than subscribe to common financing and general equilibrium
methods can again be readily applied (Spencer 1984).

CONCLUSION

This paper has endeavoured to calculate the economic implications of membership of the EEC as defined with respect to the common
agricultural policy. Special attention has been paid to the balancing of
the budget within the EEC and the general equilibrium calculations have
demonstrated the importance of terms of trade effects, effects often ignored
in the analysis of customs unions and in the estimation of gains and losses
consequent on the workings of the CAP. The question as to which country does
best and which worst from the CAP is ill-defined without reference to an
alternative policy assumption, such assumptions being widely varied in the
literature. From the results in this paper, Ireland would have most to
lose from a general swing towards free trade and Belgium/Lumembourg and
UK most to gain. In a movement to autarchy, Belgium/Luxembourg and Ireland
would lose most but all would lose considerably. Given the continuation
of the EEC/CAP system, Belgium/Luxembourg, Netherlands and the UK would
gain most by leaving unilaterally and eliminating agricultural protection
while still maintaining X tariffs at EEC levels, although all countries
but Ireland would also gain by so doing. If Germany, Belgium/Luxembourg
and Netherlands are combined to form one country in order to offset upward
biases in trade figures through the 'Rotterdam-Antwerp' effect, the
UK is estimated as the country with most to gain from withdrawal. The case
where more than one, but not all, withdraw has not been examined. The
pattern of gains and losses has not taken account of other EEC policies,
especially the rebates recently granted to the UK and no account was taken
of gains to Belgium/Luxembourg from the siting of major EEC institutions,
offices and personnel in their capitals.

It is fairly clear that member states see political advantages
in membership. Such advantages are perhaps impossible to measure but
undoubtedly help to explain the coherence of the EEC and could perhaps be
assumed to spread evenly across membership. It is certain, however, that
the uneven distribution of gains and loses from the CAP puts real strain
on the unity of the EEC and it is hoped that the methods applied in this
paper may contribute towards an assessment of these gains and losses and
accordingly contribute towards an acceptable system of rebate financing.

BIBLIOGRAPHY

Armington, P.S. (1969). The geographic pattern of trade and the effects of
        price changes. International Monetary Fund Staff Papers, 16,
        179-201.
Brown, M. & Heien, D. (1972). The S-Branch utility tree. A generalisation
        of the linear expenditure system. Econometrica, 40, no.4,
        737-47.
Buckwell, A.E., Harvey, D.R., Thomson, K.J. & Parton, K.A. (1982). The
        Costs of the Common Agricultural Policy. London & Canberra :
        Croom Helm.
Godley, W. (1979). The system of financial transfers in the EEC. In
        The Net Cost and Benefit of EEC Membership, ed. M. Whitby,
        pp.20-33. C.E.A.S. Seminar Paper No.7 : Wye College, Kent.
McKenzie, G.W. & Pearce, I.F. (1982). Welfare measurement - a synthesis.
        American Economic Review, 72, no.4, 669-682.
Miller, M.H. & Spencer, J.E. (1977). The static economic effects of the
        UK joining the EEC : a general equilibrium approach.
        Review of Economic Studies, 44, 71-93.
Morris, C.N. (1980). The common agricultural policy. Fiscal Studies, 1,
        17-35.
Rollo, J.M.C. & Warwick, K.S. (1979). The CAP and resource flows among
        EEC member states. Government Economic Service Working
        Paper No.27, Ministry of Agriculture, Fisheries and Food,
        London.
Sato, K. (1967). A two-level constant-elasticity-of-substitution
        production function. Review of Economic Studies, 34, 201-18.
Spencer, J.E. (1981). Discussion of Simmons' large generalised strongly
        separable demand system. In Macroeconomic Analysis, eds.
        D. Currie, R. Nobay & D. Peel, pp.174-7. London : Croom Helm.
Spencer, J.E. (1984). Trade Liberalisation Through Tariff Cuts and the
        European Economic Community : A General Equilibrium Evaluation
        Forthcoming.
Strasser, D. (1981). The Finances of Europe. Revised Edition.
        Luxembourg : Office for Official Publications of the European.
        Communities.

The author wishes to thank Brendan O'Kane of the NUU Computer Centre
for painstaking and expert assistance with computer routines far beyond
the call of duty.

ECONOMIC INTERDEPENDENCE IN THE PACIFIC BASIN: A GENERAL
EQUILIBRIUM APPROACH

G. W. Harrison
University of Western Ontario

L. J. Kimbell*
University of California - Los Angeles

1. INTRODUCTION

This paper reports on the development and application of a
numerical general equilibrium (GE) model of ten Pacific Basin countries
that is designed to study the nature and extent of their economic interdependence with respect to taxes, tariffs and non-tariff barriers. The
model is firmly neoclassical in structure and is empirically calibrated
to represent the structure of the Pacific Basin economy as of 1975. It
represents an application of the techniques for inter-regional GE
analysis developed in Kimbell and Harrison (1984), the solution methods
introduced in Kimbell and Harrison (1983), and the techniques of
systematic sensitivity analysis of numerical GE models presented in
Harrison et al. (1985).

Our model incorporates two major "novelties" from the
perspective of general methodology. The first is a simple technique for
allowing intermediate input substitutability that does not involve
significant increases in computational expense. This feature is
particularly important for international trade models in the face of
the empirical significance of trade in intermediates and prevailing
estimates of non-zero import price elasticities. The second novelty is
the use of systematic sensitivity analyses in order to determine how

*Harrison is Assistant Professor, Department of Economics,
University of Western Ontario; Kimbell is Professor and Director, UCLA
Business Forecasting Project, Graduate School of Management, UCLA. We
are grateful to the National Science Foundation, the Reserve Bank of
Australia, the UCLA Pacific Basin Economic Study Center, the ASEAN-
Australia Economic Relations Research Project, and the Social Sciences
and Humanities Research Council of Canada for support at various stages
of this project.

143

robust or fragile are the policy results obtained from our model. Our overall model specification is presented in Section 2.

A number of policy simulations are reported in Section 3, along with sensitivity analyses of our results. In terms of aggregate welfare effects in each region, we generally conclude that (i) global multilateral tariff and NTB reductions have small but qualitatively robust effects on the major trading blocs (the U.S., EEC and Japan); (ii) those reductions do, however, have significant and qualitatively robust effects on most other Pacific Basin countries; and (iii) in terms of relative importance, the effects of NTB liberalization dominate tariff liberalization. We also discuss the relationship between these conclusions and the existing literature.

2. MODEL SPECIFICATION

By way of perspective, we employed three broad criteria in specifying our model. The first was that it be understandable, in the sense of having a (neoclassical) structure that would be readily familiar to all economists despite great sectoral detail and a large number of trading regions. The second was that it be readily operational with existing data sources. The third requirement was that it be repeatedly soluble for the purposes of systematic sensitivity analysis. A number of additional requirements, specific to our intended policy applications, are of secondary importance but have nonetheless influenced our chosen specification. Harrison (1985 a) provides a detailed exposition of many of the technical features of the model.

2.1 Trading Regions

The model identifies eleven trading regions, listed in Table 1 along with several aggregate statistics, plus a residual "Rest of World". These regions represent a diverse range in terms of degree of industrialization, size, and "openness" to international trade. In terms of geographic coverage, our model subsumes the three region (U.S., Japan, EEC) model presented in Whalley (1980 a,b) (1982) (1984 a,b) and Brown and Whalley (1980), while providing certain country-specific detail for less-developed countries abstracted from in the 7-sector (U.S., Japan, EEC, Other Developed Countries, OPEC, Newly Industralized Countries and Less Developed Countries) model presented in

Whalley (1984 a,b).

2.2 Commodities

Each region produces twenty commodities, and these are listed in Table 2. In addition to the commodities listed, each household in each trading region allocates income to "savings", which are in turn allocated to the purchase of a bundle of investment goods (primarily, but not exclusively, in the household's own region).

2.3 Production Structure

Each of the commodities in Table 2 are assumed to be produced in each region and are, in principle, tradeable. Each commodity is distinguished by producing region, implying that our model has 240 commodities. This is the familiar "Armington assumption" distinguishing products by point of production. Each sector uses intermediate inputs from its own region and from all other regions, as well as primary

TABLE 1

Trading Regions

	Region	GDP	Exports	Imports	Population	GDP per capita
1.	Australia	87.3	11.7	9.5	13.8	6326
2.	Canada	165.2	33.9	34.3	22.7	7277
3.	Indonesia	30.5	6.9	5.5	135.2	226
4.	Malaysia	9.3	3.8	3.5	11.9	781
5.	Philippines	15.8	2.3	3.5	42.1	375
6.	Singapore	5.6	5.1	7.5	2.3	2435
7.	Thailand	14.6	2.2	2.8	41.9	348
8.	Korea	20.6	5.0	6.7	35.3	583
9.	Japan	501.9	54.7	49.7	111.6	4497
10.	U.S.A.	1518.3	107.1	98.1	213.6	7108
11.	E.E.C.	1373.2	146.3	148.0	258.0	5323

Notes: GDP, Exports (fob) and Imports (fob) are measured in billions of U.S. dollars in 1975, and were obtained from lines 99b, 77aad and 77abd, respectively, of the International Financial Statistics of the IMF (period average exchange rates used). Population is measured in millions, and is obtained from line 99z of the IFS. GDP per capita is measured in U.S. dollars. Note that the Exports and Imports listed here are not the model-equivalent values. The model also includes a twelfth region, a residual "Rest of World".

factors (labour and capital). Although it is useful to visualize the use
of intermediate inputs in the form of a complete multi-regional
(international) input-output table, an important feature of the present
model is that the implied technical coefficients are not fixed with
respect to relative input prices. That is, we do not employ a Leontief
technology in the use of intermediate inputs, but assume instead a
Cobb-Douglas technology. Thus intermediate inputs are substitutable and,
as a composite, substitutable with a composite of primary inputs.
Primary inputs, in turn, are characterized with a standard CES
technology.

TABLE 2

Elasticities of Substitution Between Primary Factors
"Australian Estimates"

	Cross-Section		Time Series	
Sector	Point Estimate	Standard Error	Point Estimate	Standard Error
1. Agriculture, Forestry and Fishing	0.640	0.640	0.780	0.200
2. Minerals and Extractive Ores	0.500	0.500	0.110	0.540
3. Energy Products	1.132	0.790	0.858	0.683
4. Food, Beverage and Tobacco	1.044	0.173	0.801	0.140
5. Textiles, Clothing, Footwear and Leather	1.293	0.170	1.317	0.100
6. Lumber and Wooden Products	0.925	0.172	0.995	0.235
7. Pulp, Paper and Printing	1.105	0.107	0.328	0.173
8. Chemicals	1.462	0.337	0.599	0.152
9. Rubber and Plastic Products	1.041	0.135	0.450	0.212
10. Non-Metallic Mineral Products	0.828	0.422	1.453	0.160
11. Basic and Fabricated Metal Products	1.141	0.128	0.567	0.224
12. Industrial Machinery	0.701	0.179	0.460	0.563
13. Electrical and Other Machinery and Equipment	0.662	0.260	0.736	0.222
14. Motor Vehicles	1.706	0.362	1.030	0.250
15. Other Transport Equipment	0.871	0.220	0.327	0.339
16. Electricity, Gas and Water Supply	0.167	0.167	0.360	0.050
17. Construction	0.324	0.324	0.324	0.324
18. Trade, Transport and Communications	0.970	0.970	0.970	0.970
19. Services	0.970	0.970	0.240	0.400
20. Public Administration and Community Services	0.970	0.970	0.970	0.970

Note: A Standard Error exactly equal to the Point Estimate indicates
that no data-based error estimate is available (see text for
discussion).

We adopt a Cobb-Douglas technology for intermediate inputs here for three reasons. The first is the comparative unease that economists have in accepting unchanging "trade coefficients" (viz., the off-diagonal blocks of the multi-regional IO table) in an international, as opposed to inter-regional (sub-national), context. The second reason is the need to calibrate our model to (own-price) import elasticities that are significantly different from zero. These elasticities typically reflect imports intended for intermediate use and also directly for final demand; the available estimates do not differentiate between these two, and must therefore be somehow allocated to each. Employing a Leontief technology in intermediates implies an inordinately high import elasticity for final demand; employing a Cobb-Douglas technology in intermediates implies much more reasonable final demand import elasticities.

The third reason for adopting a Cobb-Douglas technology, rather than a more general CES specification, is computational tractability. Whalley (1980 b; p. 1185) notes the significant computational expense involved in solving his 33-sector model when CES intermediate input substitutability is allowed. Indeed the additional expense is such as to force him to aggregate his model to five sectors in most applications (see, for example, Whalley 1980 a). In the nature of things, we have reinvented the wheel of Cobb-Douglas intermediate input substitutability apparently first developed by Boadway and Treddenick (1978; p. 430 ff.).

The two primary factors employed in each sector are characterized by a CES technology. In general, Heckscher-Ohlin (HO) factor mobility assumptions are adopted: each factor is free to move within the sectors of each region but not between regions. Alternative Ricardo-Viner (RV) factor mobility assumptions could also be examined, with capital in one region being specific to either Manufacturing or Non-Manufacturing sectors (and mobile within the sectors of each block). Kimbell and Harrison (1984) discuss the procedure for calibrating the model to these alternative factor mobility assumptions. Whalley (1980 a,b) (1982) (1984 a) and Brown and Whalley (1980) adopt the HO approach; Whalley and Wigle (1984) adopt, inter alia, the RV approach.

We now provide a formal derivation of the production relationships of the model. Let there be n industries competitively producing output X_i (i=1,...,n) using n intermediate inputs

X_{ji} (j=1,...,n) and a value-added composite V_i. Assume that the production function is Cobb-Douglas:

$$X_i = A_i \prod_{j=1}^{n} X_{ji}^{\alpha_{ji}} V^{\delta_i} \tag{1}$$

for i=1,...,n, and where A_i is the scale parameter, α_{ji} is the expenditure share of intermediate input j, and δ_i is the share of value-added. Assume for the moment that there are no primary factor taxes or taxes on intermediate transactions. With constant returns to scale we have

$$\sum_{j=1}^{n} \alpha_{ji} + \delta_i = 1 \tag{2a}$$

or

$$\delta_i = 1 - \sum_{j=1}^{n} \alpha_{ji} \tag{2b}$$

It is easy to show from the first-order profit maximizing conditions that per-unit factor demands for value-added (v_i) are a function of all intermediate input prices (p_j, j=1,...,n):

$$v_i = A_i^{-1} \left(\frac{\delta_i}{p_{v,i}}\right)^{1-\delta_i} \prod_{j=1}^{n} \left(\frac{p_i}{\alpha_{ji}}\right)^{\alpha_{ji}} \tag{3}$$

for i=1,...,n, where $p_{v,i}$ is the per-unit price of the composite value-added input in sector i. The first-order conditions are:

$$p_{v,i} = \frac{p_i \delta_i X_i}{V_i} \tag{4a}$$

and

$$p_j = \frac{p_i \alpha_{ji} X_i}{X_{ji}} \quad (j=1,...,n) \tag{4b}$$

for i=1,...,n. The zero-profit condition tells us that per-unit product prices are the weighted sum of payments to all inputs, with the optimal unit factor demands used as weights. Thus we have

$$p_i = \sum_{j=1}^{n} a_{ji} p_j + v_i p_{v,i} \tag{5a}$$

or

$$p_i X_i = \sum_{j=1}^{n} p_j X_{ji} + v_i p_{v,i} \tag{5b}$$

for i=1,...,n, where

$$a_{ji} \equiv \frac{X_{ji}}{X_i} \qquad (i,j=1,\ldots,n) \qquad (6)$$

is the usual intermediate input-output coefficient.

Substituting (4a) and (4b) into (5b) provides

$$P_i = \frac{P_{v,i}\, v_i}{1 - \sum\limits_{j=1}^{n} \alpha_{ji}} \qquad (7)$$

for $i=1,\ldots,n$. Substituting (3) into (7) for v_i and using (2b) leads to

$$P_i = \left[A_i^{-1}\, \delta_i \left(\frac{P_{v,i}}{\delta_i}\right)^{\delta_i} \prod_{j=1}^{n} \left(\frac{P_i}{\alpha_{ji}}\right)^{\alpha_{ji}} \right] \Big/ 1 - \sum_{j=1}^{n} \alpha_{ji}$$

$$= \left[A_i^{-1}\, \delta_i \left(\frac{P_{v,i}}{\delta_i}\right)^{\delta_i} \prod_{j=1}^{n} \left(\frac{P_i}{\alpha_{ji}}\right)^{\alpha_{ji}} \right] \Big/ \delta_i$$

$$= A_i^{-1} \left(\frac{P_{v,i}}{\delta_i}\right)^{\delta_i} \prod_{j=1}^{n} \left(\frac{P_i}{\alpha_{ji}}\right)^{\alpha_{ji}} \qquad (8)$$

for $i=1,\ldots,n$. By converting (8) to a log-linear form we may solve
directly for the vector of product prices (also the vector of intermediate
input prices) for given values of each $p_{v,i}$ ($i=1,\ldots,n$). In full matrix
notation we have

$$\ell n\ p = [I - A']^{-1} (\ell n\ D - \bar{\alpha}\ \ell n\ \alpha) \qquad (9)$$

where
$$\underset{(n \times 1)}{\ell n\ p} \equiv \begin{bmatrix} \ell n\ p_1 \\ \ell n\ p_2 \\ \vdots \\ \ell n\ p_n \end{bmatrix},$$

$$\underset{(n \times n)}{A} \equiv \begin{bmatrix} \alpha_{11} & \alpha_{12} & \cdots & \alpha_{1n} \\ \alpha_{21} & \alpha_{22} & \cdots & \alpha_{2n} \\ \vdots & \vdots & & \\ \alpha_{n1} & \alpha_{n2} & \cdots & \alpha_{nn} \end{bmatrix},$$

$$
\ln_{(n \times 1)} D \equiv
\begin{bmatrix}
\ln(A_1^{-1} \, P_{v,1}^{\delta_1} \, \delta_1^{-\delta_1}) \\[2mm]
\ln(A_2^{-1} \, P_{v,2}^{\delta_2} \, \delta_2^{-\delta_2}) \\[1mm]
\vdots \\[1mm]
\ln(A_n^{-1} \, P_{v,n}^{\delta_n} \, \delta_n^{-\delta_n})
\end{bmatrix} , \text{ and}
$$

$$
\bar{\alpha} \, \ln \bar{\alpha} \equiv
\begin{bmatrix}
\sum\limits_{j=1}^{n} \alpha_{j1} \, \ln \alpha_{j2} \\[3mm]
\sum\limits_{j=1}^{n} \alpha_{j2} \, \ln \alpha_{j2} \\[2mm]
\vdots \\[2mm]
\sum\limits_{j=1}^{n} \alpha_{jn} \, \ln \alpha_{jn}
\end{bmatrix}
$$

Note that the Leontief Inverse of the _transpose_ of A is used in (9), not the "regular" Leontief Inverse.

Messy as (9) may look, it is relatively trivial to evaluate as alternative iterations over the relative primary factor inputs generate different values for $p_{v,i}$. Once the vector of intermediate input prices are obtained from (9), we may solve back for the usual intermediate input-output coefficients using

$$
a_{ij} \equiv \left(\frac{p_i}{p_i} \right) \alpha_{ij} \qquad (i,j=1,\ldots,n) \tag{10}
$$

These coefficients may then be used _as if_ they were constants in any solution algorithm that assumes no intermediate input substitutability.

In the above derivation we assume that $p_{v,i}$ is given. If the composite value-added production is CES then we may write

$$
V_i = \left(\sum_{f=1}^{N_f} \gamma_{f,i} \, F_{f,i}^{\rho_i} \right)^{1/\rho_i} \tag{11}
$$

for $i=1,\ldots,n$, where N_f denotes the number of primary factor inputs ($N_f = 24$ in our model), $F_{f,i}$ denotes the usage of primary factor f in producing value-added in sector i, and $\rho_i \equiv 1 - (1/\sigma_i)$, σ_i being the elasticity of primary factor substitution in sector i. Per-unit value-added factor intensities may be derived from (11) in the usual way:

$$F_{f,i} = \frac{\gamma_{f,i}^{\sigma_i} \; P_f^{-\sigma_i}}{\left(\sum_{f=1}^{N_f} \gamma_{f,i}^{\sigma_i} \; P_f^{1-\sigma_i}\right)^{1/\rho_i}} \tag{12}$$

for $f=1,\ldots,N_f$ and $i=1,\ldots,n$. Solving for the Langrangian multiplier in this derivation yields a composite price index for value-added:

$$P_{v,i} = \left(\sum_{f=1}^{N_f} \gamma_{f,i}^{\sigma_i} \; P_f^{1-\sigma_i}\right)^{1/(1-\sigma_i)} \tag{13}$$

for $i=1,\ldots,n$. Composite output is obtained by substituting the optimal values for $F_{f,i}$ back into (11).

The foregoing derivations may be readily modified to allow for input taxes. Primary factor taxes lead to new equations to replace (12) and (13):

$$F_{f,i} = \frac{\gamma_{f,i}^{\sigma_i} \; t_{f,i}^{-\sigma_i} \; P_f^{-\sigma_i}}{\left(\sum_{f=1}^{N_f} \gamma_{f,i}^{\sigma_i} \; t_{f,}^{1-\sigma_i} \; P_f^{1-\sigma_i}\right)^{1/\rho_i}} \tag{12'}$$

for $f=1,\ldots,N_f$ and $i=1,\ldots,n$, where $t_{f,i}$ is the tax rate (in "ad valorem" form) on the use of factor f in sector i, and

$$P_{v,i} = \left(\sum_{f=1}^{N_f} \gamma_{f,i}^{\sigma_i} \; t_{f,i}^{1-\sigma_i} \; P_f^{1-\sigma_i}\right)^{1/(1-\sigma_i)} \tag{13'}$$

for $i=1,\ldots,n$. Allowing for intermediate input taxes requires modification to equations (8):

$$P_i = A_i^{-1} \left(\frac{P_{v,i}}{\delta_i}\right)^{\delta_i} \prod_{j=1}^{n} \left(\frac{t_{ji}P_j}{\alpha_{ji}}\right)^{\alpha_{ji}} \tag{8'}$$

for $i=1,\ldots,n$. Equation (9) is correspondingly modified in an obvious way, and (10) becomes

$$a_{ij} \equiv \left(\frac{P_i}{P_i t_{ij}}\right) \alpha_{ij} \qquad (i,j=1,\ldots,n) \tag{10'}$$

since the α_{ij} are defined gross of intermediate tax payments.

The benchmark calibration of the production function of each sector with intermediate input substitutability is trivial given the Cobb-Douglas functional form. Note that no scale (or "efficiency") parameter is used in the CES value-added specification in equation (11);

the scale parameter A_i in the Cobb-Douglas specification in equation (1)
is available for the purposes of benchmark calibration (see Mansur and
Whalley 1983; Section III.D).

There are two major data sources required to calibrate this
production structure: a complete multi-regional IO table for the regions
listed in Table 1 (including sectoral value-added data), and extraneous
estimates of the elasticities of substitution between labour and capital.
The Institute of Developing Economies (1982) and Harrison (1985 b)
describe the construction of the IO table. The relative availability of
national IO data for 1975 determined the dating of our model.

Table 2 lists the point estimates of the elasticity of
substitution for each of the Australian sectors based on 1947/67 U.S.
time-series estimates from Mayor (1971), U.S. cross-section estimates for
Manufacturing sectors from Zarembka and Chernicoff (1971), and estimates
for all other sectors from Piggott and Whalley (1985; Table 6.1) or
Whalley (1980 b; p. 1191, fn. 5).[1] Standard errors for each point
estimate are also shown, and are used in our sensitivity analysis
(discussed in Section 2.7). A standard error exactly equal to the point
estimate indicates that no data-based error estimate is available. This
is common in non-manufacturing sectors, and is consistent with a
reasonably diffuse prior on the point estimate. The sensitivity analysis
reported below employs the time series estimates in Table 2.

The estimates for Manufacturing sectors shown in Table 2
represent value-added weighted averages of estimates obtained at the IO
level of aggregation (109 sectors in the Australian case). They are
"Australian" estimates simply because Australian value-added weights
were employed to compute the averages. Thus each trading region has
different elasticities corresponding to those in Table 2 to the extent
that the share of each sector in that region's total value added differs
from the corresponding Australian share.

2.4 Demand Structure

The demand pattern in each trading region is represented by a
single private household and a single public household. Thus the model
identifies 24 households in all.

Private households maximize a nested utility function with
three levels. The "top" level is a Klein-Rubin utility function, leading

to an Extended Linear Expenditure System (ELES) defined in principle over eight commodity groupings (Food, Clothing, Housing, Durables, Personal Care, Transportation, Recreation, and Other Services) and savings. The "middle" level is a CES function defined over the commodities within each of these eight commodity groupings. Thus "Agriculture, Forestry and Fishing" and "Food, Beverage and Tobacco" from Table 2 are combined in a CES function to form the composite grouping "Food".[2] Finally, the "bottom" level is a CES function defined over each of the commodities listed in Table 2 differentiated by origin.

The consumption problem of the private household may therefore be viewed in three stages. Given the income to be allocated to consumption (i.e., non-savings), the allocation of expenditure to the eight commodity groupings is decided. Then, conditional on the expenditure for each group, the allocation to each of the (varying number of) commodities within each group is decided. Finally, the household decides between alternative sources of each commodity given the expenditure allocated to that commodity. Specific functional forms aside, this type of utility nesting structure is common to recent international trade GE models.

We now provide a formal statement of the calibration procedure adopted for the ELES specification. Howe (1975) has shown that ELES may be derived from an instantaneous Klein-Rubin utility function which directly includes Savings as an argument and which assumes that "subsistence savings" (or "precommitted savings") are zero. An alternative interpretation of the consumer's maximization problem leading to ELES was advanced by Lluch (1973) and is discussed in Lluch, et al. (1977; p. 14). We shall adopt the Howe (1975) interpretation for the purposes of calibration.

Assume that the utility function is specified as

$$U = \sum_{i=1}^{n} \beta_i \, \ln(q_i - \gamma_i) \tag{14}$$

where n is the number of commodities ("commodity groupings" in the context of our GE model), q_i is the quantity of good i consumed, β_i is the marginal budget share of good i, γ_i denotes "subsistence" consumption of good i, and we further require

$$q_i > \gamma_i \tag{15a}$$

and $\qquad \beta_i > 0$ $\qquad\qquad\qquad\qquad\qquad\qquad$ (15b)

for each i, and

$$\sum_{i=1}^{n} \beta_i = 1 \qquad\qquad\qquad\qquad (15c)$$

We shall assume that the nth good represents savings, adding the further restriction

$$\gamma_n = 0 \qquad\qquad\qquad\qquad (15d)$$

It can be shown that the demand functions obtained by maximizing (14) subject to the constraint

$$\sum_{i=1}^{n} p_i q_i = y \qquad\qquad\qquad\qquad (15e)$$

where y denotes disposable income, are

$$q_i = \gamma_i + \beta_i \left(y - \sum_{k=1}^{n} p_k \gamma_k \right) \Big/ p_i \qquad\qquad (16)$$

for $i=1,\ldots,n$. Expenditure is therefore given by

$$p_i q_i = \gamma_i p_i + \beta_i \left(y - \sum_{k=1}^{n} p_k \gamma_k \right) \qquad\qquad (17)$$

for $i=1,\ldots,n$. We may define the expenditure share on good i as

$$s_i \equiv \frac{p_i q_i}{y} \qquad\qquad\qquad\qquad (18)$$

We know that because (14) is additive the "Frisch formula" relating elasticities to expenditure elasticities may be used; thus

$$\eta_{ik} = -\epsilon_i s_k \left(1 + \frac{\epsilon_k}{\omega} \right) + \delta_{ik} \frac{\epsilon_i}{\omega} \qquad\qquad (19)$$

for $i,k=1,\ldots,n$, where $\delta_{ik} = 1$ if $i=k$ and $\delta_{ik} = 0$ for $i \neq k$, ϵ_i is the expenditure elasticity of good i, η_{ik} is the elasticity of demand for good i with respect to the price of good k, and ω denotes the "Frisch parameter".

$\qquad$ Given values for the average savings share, S_n, from the benchmark equilibrium and the Frisch parameter, ω, equation (2.11) of Lluch, et al. (1977) implies a marginal propensity to consume, μ, given by

$$\mu = \frac{1 - S_n}{1 - S_n - S_n \omega} \qquad\qquad\qquad\qquad (20)$$

Since $\gamma_n = 0$ from (15d) we have

$$\beta_n = 1 - \mu \tag{21}$$

Given values for each ϵ_i and S_i, $i=1,\ldots,n-1$, we solve backwards for

$$\beta_i = \epsilon_i S_i \tag{22}$$

for $i=1,\ldots,n-2$,

$$\beta_{n-1} = 1 - \sum_{k=1}^{n-2} \beta_k - \beta_n \tag{23}$$

and

$$\gamma_i = \left[- \left(\eta_{i\ell} S_i \right) \Big/ \beta_i \right] y/p_i \tag{24}$$

where $\ell \neq i$ in the last equation (for i=1 use $\ell=2,\ldots,n-1$, and for i > 1 use $\ell = 1$).

Equation (22) is implied by the formula for total expenditures elasticities given in Lluch, et al. (1977; Table 2.2, p. 18) or equation (14.28) in Dixon, et al. (1982; p. 101). Equation (23) is implied by the normalization restriction (15c). Equation (24) is implied by equations (14.29)-(14.32) of Dixon, et al. (1982; p. 101).

The basic data to parameterize the top level of our utility function for each private household are obtained from Lluch, et al. (1977) (LPW) and input-output data on final demand expenditure shares. LPW (pp. 74/80) estimate an approximate relationship between the ELES "Frisch parameter"[3] and real GNP per capita. This relationship is used to estimate the value of this "parameter" for those countries in our model that are not directly included in the LPW study.[4] Expenditure elasticities, and their implied asymptotic standard errors, are obtained from Table 3.12 of LPW (p. 54); for those countries not directly covered by their estimates the average estimates for "real GNP per capita" class intervals are used.[5]

The middle and bottom levels of our utility function are calibrated to uncompensated own-price elasticities using the procedures outlined in Mansur and Whalley (1984) and widely used in other models. The relevant elasticities, and implied standard errors, for the middle level calibration are obtained from LPW (Table 3.13, p. 55) in the same manner as the expenditure elasticity estimates discussed above. Where available, import price elasticities obtained from Alouze (1977), Stern, et al. (1976; pp. 15/24) and Stone (1979) were similarly used to calibrate the bottom level. Such data were available for Australia,

Canada, Japan, U.S.A. and the EEC. For every other country in our model the own-price elasticity estimates used at the middle level were also used at the bottom level.[6]

Household savings are allocated entirely to the purchase of a Cobb-Douglas composite of commodities from all regions for the purpose of capital formation. These expenditures refer to purchases of real goods and services.

Public households in each region spend their revenues on various own-region and foreign commodities. A Cobb-Douglas utility function is used for these households, and is calibrated using expenditure shares by each government (for current consumption purposes and capital formation).

Private household income is generated from the sale of their factor endowment to own-region industries and from transfers received from their government. Each government receives revenue from the taxes, tariffs and non-tariff barriers that it levies on own-region and foreign economic activity; these policy instruments are discussed in more detail in the next section. In principle the model allows for inter-government transfers, in the form of (untied) aid; in practice we have been unable to obtain adequate data to include these transfers in the present model.

Although each and every household has a "balanced budget" in equilibrium, there is no explicit or implicit presumption in the model that bilateral trade flows between any two regions balance.

2.5 Tariffs and Non-Tariff Barriers

In principle the model incorporates a wide range of taxes, tariffs and non-tariff barriers (NTB's) differentiated by commodity, region and stage-of-production of (legal) incidence, and taxing government. In practice, however, data limitations severely circumscribe the detail, coverage and accuracy of our "model equivalent" estimates of these policy instruments. Harrison (1985 a,b) provides details on the data sources for the estimates used.

The basic source of data on tariffs was the international input-output table presented in Institute of Developing Economies (1982) and Harrison (1985 b). We draw a distinction between tariffs levied on imports of intermediate inputs and those levied on imports of final goods. Recall that we allow a given sector to import intermediates from

all other sectors in all regions. Thus the total import duties paid by
this sector reflects the various tariff rates applicable to the range of
intermediates it imports, weighted by the expenditure on each imported
intermediate. The "ad valorem" tariff implied by this procedure need
bear no similarity to the posted tariff on imports of the commodity of the
sector in question.[7] Moreover, the same tariff rate applies to all
intermediate input imports of the given sector. The implied tariff rates
on final demand imports bear a direct similarity to posted rates (due
allowance being made for "water in the tariff", such as might be expected
on tariffs on ASEAN imports of snow-making machines). Although our model-
equivalent tariff rates on intermediate input imports do not correspond
directly to posted rates, they can be reconciled satisfactorily with the
1976 rates used by Whalley (1980 b; Table 2) for the U.S., EEC and Japan.

The available data on "ad valorem equivalents" of NTB's are
notoriously poor. We rely heavily on the aggregative estimates listed in
Whalley (1984 a; Table A1) and the detailed estimates employed in Whalley
(1980 a), Yeats (1978) and Hamilton (1984). We adopt the measures of the
"ad valorem" equivalent of agricultural NTB's in Japan and Korea reported
in Saxon and Anderson (1982) and Anderson (1981), respectively. The
measures adopted for Australia, Canada, Indonesia, Malaysia, the
Philippines, Singapore and Thailand were derived from Tyers and
Chisholm (1982; Table A1). Government procurement practices are
approximated by a 50% tariff applied to imports of each public household
in each region, following Whalley (1982; p. 356).

Domestic tax systems are often viewed as NTB's (see Lloyd
1973; Ch. 7), and their discriminatory features are included in the model.
Asher and Booth (1983) provide an excellent description of the comparative role of indirect taxes in ASEAN countries. Our model reflects many
of their estimates of sales, excise and foreign trade taxes.

Five types of taxes are identified: factor taxes, value-
added taxes, excise taxes, sales taxes and direct (income) taxes.
Factor taxes are levied by each region's government on the use of
Capital and Labour in own-region production. Value-added taxes are
levied in the EEC only on own-region production. The legal incidence
of these factor and value-added taxes is on own-region economic activity
because the present model assumes no international factor mobility and/or
no international ownership of the factors of a given region.

Sales taxes are defined here as being levied at any "intermediate" stage of production, and excise taxes as falling initially on goods (from any region) when they are cleared for own-region consumption. With input-output data recorded at "basic values", information on "net indirect taxes" indicates (net) taxes paid by the users of the commodities on which the taxes were levied. In the absence of a reconciliation of transactions at "basic values" and "producers' prices" it is not possible to identify from the available data the appropriate intermediate stage to incorporate the tax (as a sales tax), or even to decide how much of the tax should be treated as a sales tax and how much as an excise tax. For example, the Australian input-output tables supplied by the Australian Bureau of Statistics (1981) do allow clarification of both of these issues, the Canadian tables due to Statistics Canada (1981) only resolve the second issue, and the U.S. tables provided by the Bureau of Economic Analysis (1981) resolve neither issue. If the available data could not resolve these issues we treated all such taxes as excise taxes.

Direct (income) taxes are computed on a residual basis in the benchmark equilibrium such that each region's government (after collecting revenue from all other taxes, tariffs and NTB's) had total revenue equal to its total expenditure.

The model theoretically allows for a wide range of "border tax adjustments" (BTA), such as discussed by Johnson and Krauss (1970), Harberger (1974; Ch. 14), Floyd (1973) (1977) and others. The present empirical version assumes no BTA's at all. Given the importance of the internationally discriminatory features of domestic tax systems emphasized by Whalley (1980 b), the role of BTA's demands empirical attention in future research.

2.6 Solution Procedures

A benchmark equilibrium solution for 1975 was obtained by solving "backwards" for certain parameter values in the usual fashion. Apart from the treatment of intermediate input substitutability these procedures were standard to the literature. Mansur and Whalley (1984; Section 3) and Piggott and Whalley (1985; Ch. 4) provide general discussions of these procedures, and Kimbell and Harrison (1984; Section 3.2) discuss the calibration of models with immobile factors (i.e., our

Heckscher/Ohlin assumption). Given some counterfactual policy change, we solve the model for a new equilibrium using the Factor Price Revision Rule introduced by Kimbell and Harrison (1983). The substitutability of intermediate inputs is algorithmically transparent in the sense that any procedure that can solve models with fixed intermediate requirements will also be able to solve models assuming (Cobb-Douglas) substitutability. Moreover, this new feature only adds one matrix operation during each iteration of the algorithm.

2.7 Sensitivity Analysis

The policy-relevance of numerical GE models, and their avowedly "empirical" nature, render them open to casual criticism. Most economists are deeply familiar with their underlying neoclassical structure. We are _not_ therefore concerned to defend them here from criticisms based on rejection of that structure. On the

other hand, criticism based on suspicion of the particular _empirical calibration_ adopted currently leads to non-systematic and/or uninformed debate. The general techniques used to calibrate numerical GE models are discussed in the references given above. Given, then, that users of numerical GE models are increasingly "informed" as to the various sources of data embodied in their simulations, how is one to identify the robustness of the results for some particular policy decision? Our response to this important question is to undertake a systematic sensitivity analysis of our policy simulations in Section 3.

A number of critical dimensions to such analysis may be readily identified from any discussion of the procedures used to calibrate GE models (see Harrison (1985 d) for numerous illustrations in the trade policy context). For one obvious example, consider the elasticities of substitution listed in Table 3 that are used to calibrate the CES production functions of each sector. Popular calibration procedure is to employ the vector of point estimates based on a search of the available econometric literature. Such estimates are usually accompanied by standard errors, such as those also listed in Table 2. The vectors of estimates formed by considering all combinations of estimates within (say) one standard error either side of the point estimate for each sector provides a continuum of distinctly calibrated

GE models whose comparative static (policy) properties need not be identical.

There are many ways to weight the results of a large sensitivity analysis such as the ones undertaken in Section 3. For illustrative purposes we now provide a simple hypothetical numerical example of the weighting procedure adopted in the present study.

Assume that we are concerned with the sensitivity of a model to different estimates for two parameters, β_1 and β_2. The model may have many more parameters than just these two, in which case the sensitivity results are of course conditional on the estimates used for the other parameters. To simplify matters, assume in Case A that the prior probability density function (pdf) of the second parameter estimate (β_2)

TABLE 3

Hypothetical Numerical Examples of Weighting Procedure

CASE A

Simulation	Marginal Probability of β_1	Marginal Probability of β_2	Joint Probability	Normalized Joint Probability
1	0.5	0.5	0.25	0.25
2	0.5	0.4	0.20	0.20
3	0.5	0.1	0.05	0.05
4	0.5	0.5	0.25	0.25
5	0.5	0.4	0.20	0.20
6	0.5	0.1	0.05	0.05
Sum			1.00	1.00

CASE B

Simulation	Marginal Probability of β_1	Marginal Probability of β_2	Joint Probability	Normalized Joint Probability
1	0.5	0.5	0.25	0.3968
2	0.5	0.1	0.05	0.0794
3	0.5	0.1	0.05	0.0794
4	0.4	0.5	0.20	0.3175
5	0.4	0.1	0.04	0.0635
6	0.4	0.1	0.04	0.0635
Sum			0.63	1.00

is discrete and consists of three values: the point estimate with probability 0.5, one other estimate with probability 0.4, and a final estimate with probability 0.1. We also assume that the prior pdf of the first parameter estimate (β_1) is discrete, but in this case it is uniform and takes on two values only with equal probability.

A complete enumeration of all possible simulations in Case A is presented in Table 3. In simulation 1 the two point estimates are adopted, each with a marginal probability of 0.5. Assuming independence of the random variables β_1 and β_2, we may calculate their joint probability as the product of their marginal probabilities. This is shown in column 4 for Case A. Simulation 2 holds constant the value of β_1 and adopts the second value of β_2, with resulting joint probability 0.2; similarly, simulation 3 adopts the final value of β_2, which has the lowest marginal probability of the three values considered. Simulations 4, 5 and 6 repeat the sequence of β_2 values with the second value of β_1 (which also have marginal probability 0.5). By the laws of probability, and the knowledge that we have completely enumerated the joint distribution of the two parameters, we note that the sum of the joint probabilities is one. Thus we do not need to "normalize" the joint probability values, and simply repeat the values in column 4 in column 5.

In Case B we consider a more likely situation in which complete enumeration of the pdf of one or more of the parameters is not possible (presumably because it would be too expensive, even if possible). Two interpretations of this case are valid. The first is to think of the prior pdf for β_1 as having three or more discrete values, only two of which are considered (having marginal probabilities that sum to only 0.9), and the prior pdf for β_2 as having four or more discrete values, only three of which are considered (having marginal probabilities that sum to only 0.6). The second interpretation is that we are only evaluating discrete approximations to the continuous prior pdf of each parameter. This latter interpretation is in practice the most likely: in most cases we are able to assume that the prior pdf for each parameter is Gaussian (e.g., the asymptotic distribution of the elasticities of factor substitution).

Irrespective of the interpretation, we note from Table 3 that the joint probabilities of the six simulations for Case B do not sum to one. Thus we normalize (by the constant of proportionality

1.5873015 = 1/0.63) so that the joint distribution is _proper_. Alternatively, we could have normalized each of the marginal distributions.

In Case A and Case B, the normalized joint probabilities for
each simulation provide the weights used when reporting the results of the
simulations. Assume that the endogenous variable we are concerned with is
the percentage change in employment in a certain sector from the benchmark equilibrium as the result of some tariff change. Hypothetical values
are listed in Table 4 for each simulation. For pedagogic purposes assume
that the same employment impacts obtained in Case A as in Case B. The
weighted average percent change in employment is zero in Case A and
0.1111 in Case B. Note that other descriptive statistics could be
computed once we know the pdf of the employment changes. The comparison
of Cases A and B also illustrate the obvious point that the pdf of
employment changes is sensitive to the weights attached to given parameter
values by the prior pdf.

In the present case we undertake a systematic sensitivity
analysis for each policy simulation with respect to three sets of
elasticities: the elasticities of substitution between primary factors
(Section 2.3), the import demand elasticities (Section 2.4), and the own-
price demand elasticities (Section 2.4). In the first and third cases we
have available well-defined standard errors and a presumption that the
distribution of each parameter estimate is well-behaved (i.e., follows a
t-distribution); we may therefore completely define a Bayesian prior
distribution for these elasticities.[8] In the case of the import
elasticities we adopt the aggregative standard errors compiled in
Harrison, _et al._ (1985; Appendix A) _or_ the same prior as used for the

TABLE 4

Weighting Procedure Applied to Simulation Results

| | | CASE A | | CASE B | |
Simulation	Percent Change in Employment	Normalized Joint Probability	Weighted Employment Change	Normalized Joint Probability	Weighted Employment Change
1	1.00	0.25	0.25	0.3968	0.3968
2	1.00	0.20	0.20	0.0794	0.0794
3	1.00	0.05	0.05	0.0794	0.0794
4	-1.00	0.25	-0.25	0.3175	-0.3175
5	-1.00	0.20	-0.20	0.0635	-0.0635
6	-1.00	0.05	-0.05	0.0635	-0.0635
Sum		1.00	0.0	1.00	0.1111

demand elasticities when we had no separate import elasticity estimates
available.

Harrison, et al. (1985) distinguish between "conditional" and
"unconditional" systematic sensitivity analyses. The former refers to a
series of simulations in which each parameter is perturbed from its point
estimate a certain number of times (four in the present case) conditional
on all other parameters being set only to their point estimate value.
The latter refers to perturbations of each parameter conditional on all
other parameters also being perturbed from their point estimate a certain
number of times; thus the set of simulations is "unconditional". Clearly
the latter type of analysis is more complete than the former, but at a
severe cost in terms of the number of required simulations. Given the
size of the present model and the large number of parameters subject
to perturbations (720), we have opted for the conditional systematic
sensitivity analysis.[9]

We shall consider five values for each parameter, including
the point estimate. Thus we have four perturbations for each parameter.
Two of these perturbations will be one-half of a standard error above and
below the point estimate, and the other two will be one standard error
above and below the point estimate. The exact marginal probabilities for
these values depend on the relevant degrees-of-freedom for the parameter
estimate; where we are unable to infer that value from published data it
is assumed large enough for asymptotic results to hold. We therefore
require 2881 simulations for each policy change (720 relevant parameters
times 4 perturbations per parameter, plus one simulation with all
parameters equal to their point estimate). In all cases reported in
Section 3 we initially solved the model for the given policy change with
all parameters set equal to their point estimates. Given the solution
values for this simulation as starting values for the sensitivity
analysis simulations involving a perturbed elasticity, we were able to
find the new solution values extremely quickly.

3. POLICY RESULTS

In this section the welfare incidence of a series of hypothetical global trade liberalization strategies is reported. The welfare
change for the private household in each region is measured by the

Hicksian equivalent variation between the benchmark equilibrium (the GE solution that replicates the observed data in the base year, 1975) and the various counterfactual equilibria (the GE solution with some policy change that does not, in general, correspond to any observed historical episode). This measure is then expressed as a percentage of GDP in the base year in order to allow comparisons between regions of such diverse size.

Table 5 presents the welfare impacts of two separate global policies, one that eliminates tariffs in all regions and another that

TABLE 5

Welfare Impact of Global Trade Liberalization

Policies	Impacted Region	Point Estimate	Mean	Standard Deviation	Probability of Welfare Gain
Tariffs	Australia	0.03	0.49	0.08	0.91
	Canada	0.26	0.41	0.04	0.87
	Indonesia	-0.56	-0.70	0.03	0.28
	Malaysia	1.93	2.65	0.04	0.94
	Philippines	-0.80	-0.98	0.04	0.16
	Singapore	1.65	2.01	0.02	0.95
	Thailand	-1.94	-1.75	0.08	0.18
	Korea	1.34	2.34	0.07	0.98
	Japan	1.11	1.79	0.03	0.95
	U.S.A.	0.21	0.24	0.02	0.87
	EEC	0.41	0.61	0.06	0.94
NTB	Australia	1.26	1.43	0.19	0.93
	Canada	1.82	1.96	0.13	0.96
	Indonesia	1.67	1.78	0.23	0.90
	Malaysia	2.41	2.36	0.39	0.79
	Philippines	2.75	2.82	0.31	0.84
	Singapore	2.87	3.01	0.41	0.96
	Thailand	4.31	4.81	0.50	0.98
	Korea	3.59	3.73	0.46	0.76
	Japan	0.92	1.05	0.09	0.85
	U.S.A.	-0.44	-0.38	0.07	0.31
	EEC	0.37	0.41	0.08	0.77

eliminates NTB's in all regions. The Point Estimate column reflects the
impacts of the policy in the counterfactual equilibrium conditional on
all parameters being set equal to their respective point estimates. The
remaining three columns report summary statistics for the set of counterfactual equilibria implied by our sensitivity analysis. The Mean
Welfare impact is the average change in the welfare impacts, with the
prior probability density functions mentioned earlier being used to
weight the results. The Standard Deviation of the welfare impact is
similarly computed from the pdf of welfare impacts.[10] The final column
reports the Probability of Welfare Gain, obtained by numerically
evaluating the (proper) pdf of welfare gains. This column provides a
useful measure of the confidence one can attach to qualitative
inferences about welfare impacts in the model.

Several features of the results in Table 5 are noteworthy.
First, it is apparent that NTB liberalization confers greater benefits
than tariff liberalization to each nation except the U.S.A. Note that
the benchmark year tariffs are those applying prior to the Tokyo Round
multilateral tariff reductions, suggesting that our conclusion about the
relative importance of liberalizing NTB's is of even greater relevance
for current circumstances. This conclusion is echoed in results obtained
in the Whalley (1984 b) GE trade policy models. Whalley (1980 a; p. 224)
concludes that:

> Abolitions of tariff barriers alone would increase
> world trade by [1973] US$10 bill. While abolishing
> non-tariff barriers would increase trade by US$20
> bill. The two sets of policies thus have a compound-
> ing effect on the level of world trade. The effects
> of these two areas of policy appear unequally
> balanced and suggests that more stress should be
> placed on non-tariff barriers in the current Tokyo
> Round negotiations.

The simulations reported in Brown and Whalley (1980; Table 14,
Experiments 6 and 10) indicate that the global welfare gains from
(multilateral) NTB liberalization are roughly double those from tariff
liberalization. Whalley (1982) concludes that "...under some assumptions
the changes in the NTB codes in the [Tokyo Round] Agreement may be more
significant than the tariff cuts" (p. 360), although quantification of
the negotiated NTB reduction is particularly speculative in this case.

Second, the results in Table 5 are qualitatively identical
to, but proportionately larger than, those reported in Harrison (1985 c)

for <u>fifty percent</u> tariff and NTB reductions. It is not too surprising
that a one hundred percent reduction in a set of distortions (such as
shown in Table 5) generates greater welfare impacts, but what is notable
is that the welfare losses incurred by some countries are less severe and
the welfare gains incurred by <u>some</u> countries are more than double those
reported in the other studies. These findings are easily explained--
<u>removing</u> all distortions of a certain type not only reduces the size of
the distortion, but it "equalizes" it (by definition, at "zero") across
all sectors and all regions. The latter effect is present in the results
shown in Table 5 but not in the simulations reported elsewhere.

Third, to the extent that the results for tariffs and NTB's
in Table 5 are additive and symmetric, they support a widespread and
cynical view of the last few decades of multilateral trade "liberalization". Hamilton and Whalley (1983; p. 3), for example, note that:

> Those who are pessimistic about the GATT process
> argue that successive GATT rounds have not produced
> substantive progress in limiting and reducing non-
> tariff barriers. They also argue that non-tariff
> barriers are increasingly being used as a way of
> offsetting reductions in protection produced by
> negotiated tariff cuts. A cynical view of trade
> liberalization sometimes expressed is that
> countries participate in GATT tariff cuts hoping
> that partners will take the tariff cut seriously,
> with the reduction in own protection subsequently
> offset by an erection of non-tariff barriers.

This view is supported in the present model. The results in Table 5 are
approximately additive in the sense that removing tariffs <u>and</u> NTB's
together results in welfare impacts close to those implied by adding
the impacts shown for each policy separately. The results for NTB's are
also approximately symmetric in the sense that an across-the-board
increase leads to welfare impacts that are roughly equal in size and
opposite in sign to those impacts resulting from a decrease in NTB's.[11]
These approximations are much more exact if one is looking at <u>partial</u>
reductions (e.g., fifty percent) or increases in the particular policies
rather than their complete elimination.

Fourth, the welfare impacts may seem "small" when one
considers the radical policy changes involved (viz., complete elimination
of certain trade barriers for all countries). However, it should be
noted that these impacts represent <u>annual</u> gains or losses that could
accrue over many years to represent "large" impacts. Moreover, the

welfare gains for Malaysia (2.65%), Singapore (2.01%), Korea (2.34%) and
Japan (1.79%) due to _tariff_ liberalization are hardly small. Similarly,
the gains to ASEAN nations (especially Thailand) from NTB liberalization
are quite large in relation to previous estimates. Also note that many
of the stated welfare impacts are extremely robust to uncertainty about
the parameters of the model (i.e., high values for Probability of Welfare
Gain), even if the Mean impact is deemed "small" by some standard.

     The results in Table 6, reported in Harrison and Rutström
(1985), demonstrate how the overall welfare gains shown in Table 5 are
reduced when one only considers the multilateral liberalization of
protection (tariffs _and_ NTB's) directed at Manufacturing sectors. We
define "Manufacturing" as sectors 4 through 15 (recall Table 2). This
implies that we _are_ reducing protection, _inter alia_, on the "Textiles,
Clothing, Footwear and Leather" sector. This sector has, of course, been
one of the holiest of Sacred Cows in recent GATT-ordained multilateral
trade negotiations, even though it has been desecrated with the distortions of the Multi-Fibre Agreement.

     The importance of the results in Table 6, when compared with
those in Table 5, is the focus they place on Agricultural protection by

TABLE 6

Welfare Impact of Global Manufacturing Trade Liberalization

	Impacted Region	Point Estimate	Mean	Standard Deviation	Probability of Welfare Gain
Tariffs and NTB	Australia	0.85	0.84	0.12	0.94
	Canada	0.91	0.91	0.10	0.97
	Indonesia	1.30	1.26	0.19	0.91
	Malaysia	1.89	1.72	0.28	0.82
	Philippines	1.72	1.65	0.30	0.86
	Singapore	2.41	2.44	0.34	0.93
	Thailand	1.01	1.04	0.21	0.71
	Korea	2.80	2.85	0.31	0.75
	Japan	0.94	0.93	0.12	0.87
	U.S.A.	-0.31	-0.33	0.10	0.28
	EEC	0.14	0.16	0.06	0.73

Source: Harrison and Rutström (1985; Table 5).

NTB's. Consider, for example, the large gains for Japan and Korea in Table 5 and their relatively meager gains in Table 6. These results for Japan and Korea reflect two powerful, but contrasting, effects: the efficiency gains in production from removal of distortions favouring Agricultural and Food Products, and the significant decline in incomes of their farming sector due to changes in the terms-of-trade (TOT). In each case the former effect dominates. This result is consistent with the findings of Anderson (1981; p. 41) with respect to NTB agricultural protection in Korea that

> ...partial equilibrium analysis...suggests that the policies of the late 1970's were responsible for transferring about $4 billion per year to producers, but at a cost to consumers-cum-taxpayers of about $4.8 billion, the difference (about 1.6 percent of GNP) being a net loss to the economy because of foregoing the opportunity to take advantage of the gains from international trade. (The loss that would be calculated using general equilibrium analysis would be even larger, since it would also measure the increase in the value of production that is possible with the more efficient employment in manufacturing, etc. of the labour and other resources that would be freed from the removal of agricultural protection.)

Similar remarks also apply to Thailand, although here there is also a significant worsening of the TOT.

The TOT effects just noted are also a feature of the Tokyo Round simulations reported by Whalley (1982), given that the tariff reductions negotiated during that Round are heavily concentrated on Manufacturing goods (notwithstanding the treatment of Textiles). The expansion of trade in those goods which follows such tariff or NTB reductions outweighs the direct effect on Manufacturing prices, leading to a net move in the trade-weighted TOT against countries that largely export non-Manufacturing goods. These countries are generally LDC's whose export trade is currently oriented towards Agricultural products and/or Mining.

4. CONCLUDING REMARKS

The numerical general equilibrium model presented has been applied to study numerous policy issues. Harrison (1985 c) considers alternative unilateral and multilateral tariff liberalization policies, Harrison and Rutström (1985 a) consider various global and regional manufacturing trade liberalization strategies in the Pacific Basin, Harrison and Rutström (1985 b) examine the possibility of ASEAN forming a customs union, and Harrison, et al. (1985) evaluate partial equilibrium numerical results on the impact of allowing free international labour mobility.

Although these policy applications are important, we caution against the present version of our model being considered definitive in any sense. It is our firm belief that numerical general equilibrium models are only beginning to reach the point at which they can be used to indicate policy-relevant effects of trade or tax policies. Harrison and Rutström (1985 a; Section 4) argue in detail that significant re-formulations of the qualitative structure of existing general equilibrium models, including the present model, is necessary to address many trade policy issues of importance in the Pacific Basin. These include an allowance for resource-wasting rent-seeking activities in the context of non-tariff trade barriers, allowance for economies of scale in manufacturing sector production in small economies, and the implications of recognizing the presence of alternative formulations of labour markets in developing economies. Given the "ad hockery" or inadequacy of alternative quantitative techniques currently in use, we urge careful consideration of the above issues in future developments in applied general equilibrium analysis.

FOOTNOTES

[1] Whalley (1980 b; p. 1191, fn. 15) attributes his estimates primarily to the compendium in Caddy (1976), although Caddy only presents estimates for Manufacturing sectors. Mayor (1971) does present estimates for several non-manufacturing sectors, and we use these for our sectors 1, 2, 16 and 19 (time series estimates). Harrison, et al. (1985) present new estimates for use in the Whalley model.

[2] In several cases, given the level of commodity aggregation adopted, this level of the utility tree is redundant (e.g., the grouping "Clothing" includes only one commodity from Table 2, "Textiles, Clothing, Footwear and Leather") or ambiguous (e.g., the commodity "Services" in Table 2 is allocated to two groupings, "Recreation" and "Other Services"). The full ELES disaggregation is retained, in the face of such redundancy and ambiguity, for three reasons: (i) data exist for two trading regions (Australia and the U.S.) to split up commodities between commodity groupings, removing any ambiguity; (ii) it is possible to simply aggregate commodity groupings to remove any remaining ambiguity; and (iii) we hope to employ greater commodity disaggregation in future research (and do not wish to recode the model or data).

[3] The "Frisch parameter" under LES is the expenditure elasticity of the marginal utility of expenditure. This "parameter" is well-defined under ELES, and is the concept we are directly concerned with.

[4] Korea, Thailand, Australia and the U.S. are directly covered by LPW.

[5] An alternative approach might be to use the regressions across countries of expenditure elasticity against GNP per capita reported in Table 3.18 (p. 62) of LPW. However, the explanatory power of four of the eight regressions is extremely low.

[6] The bottom level of the utility function for these countries is obviously redundant with this formulation. It is retained for coding convenience and to allow for the possible future use of import elasticities for these countries.

[7] Unless, of course, all of those imports were directed solely to the corresponding domestic sector (i.e., the off-diagonal elements of the off-diagonal trade blocks in our international IO table are all zero). This is not the case in the present IO table.

[8] There is an implicit presumption here that the off-diagonal elements of the covariance matrix of our elasticity estimates are all zero. Although non-zero elements are theoretically available for certain blocks of elasticity estimates (e.g., the demand elasticities) this presumption is adopted in the present model.

[9]Pagan and Shannon (1985) propose a technique which may be used to provide a computationally feasible approximation to an unconditional systematic sensitivity analysis. Harrison, et al. (1985) examine the accuracy of the approximation involved, and illustrate that their technique is often quite accurate.

[10]Note that there is absolutely no presumption that the policy impacts (welfare impacts in this case) have a Gaussian distribution. One should not therefore assume that the Mean and Standard Deviation are in any way "sufficient statistics" of that distribution. In fact, many of the policy impact pdf's encountered elsewhere are slightly skewed.

[11]The simulations underlying these claims of additivity and symmetry are not reported here. Whalley (1985) and Harrison (1985 c) provide examples of sets of trade policies that are neither additive nor symmetric (e.g., compare unilateral cuts in trade barriers with multilateral cuts).

REFERENCES

Alouze, C. M. (1977). Estimates of the elasticity of substitution between imported and domestically produced goods classified at the input-output level of aggregation. Working Paper No. 0-13, IMPACT Project, Melbourne, October.

Anderson, Kym (1981). Northeast Asian agricultural protection in historical and comparative perspective: the case of South Korea. Research Paper No. 82, Australia-Japan Research Centre, Australian National University, May.

Asher, Mukul G. & Booth, Anne (1983). Indirect Taxation in ASEAN. Singapore: Singapore University Press.

Australian Bureau of Statistics (1981). Australian National Accounts. Input-Output Tables 1974-75 (ABS Cat. No. 5209.0). Canberra: Commonwealth Government Printer.

Boadway, R. & Treddenick, J. (1978). A general equilibrium computation of the effects of the Canadian tariff structure. Canadian Journal of Economics, V. 11, 424-46.

Brown, F. & Whalley, J. (1980). General equilibrium evaluations of tariff-cutting proposals in the Tokyo Round and comparisons with more extensive liberalization of world trade. Economic Journal, V. 90, 838-66.

Bureau of Economic Analysis (1981). Summary Input-Output Tables of the U.S. Economy: 1973, 1974, and 1975 (BEA-SP 81-037). Washington, D.C.: Department of Commerce.

Caddy, V. (1976). Empirical estimation of the elasticity of substitution: a review. Preliminary Working Paper No. OP-09, IMPACT Project, Melbourne, November.

Dixon, P. B., Parmenter, B. R., Sutton, J. & Vincent, D. P. (1982). ORANI: A Multisectoral Model of the Australian Economy. Amsterdam: North-Holland.

Floyd, R. H. (1973). GATT provisions on border tax adjustments. Journal of World Trade Law, V. 7, 489-99.

Floyd, R. H. (1977). Some long-run implications of border tax adjustments for factor taxes. Quarterly Journal of Economics, V. 91, 555-78.

Hamilton, Bob & Whalley, John (1983). Geographically discriminatory trade arrangements. Working Paper No. 8321C, Centre for the Study of International Economic Relations, University of Western Ontario, November.

Hamilton, Carl (1984). Voluntary export restraints on Asia: tariff equivalents, rents and trade barrier formation. Seminar Paper No. 276, Institute for International Economic Studies, University of Stockholm, April.

Harberger, A. C. (1974). Taxation and Welfare. Boston: Little, Brown and Company.

Harrison, Glenn W. (1985 a). Economic interdependence between ASEAN and Australia: a general equilibrium approach. Working Paper, ASEAN-Australia Economic Relations Research Project, Australian National University.

Harrison, Glenn W. (1985 b). Structural interdependence between ASEAN and Australia: an input-output approach. Working Paper, ASEAN-Australia Economic Relations Research Project, Australian National University.

Harrison, Glenn W. (1985 c). A general equilibrium analysis of tariff reductions. In General Equilibrium Trade Policy Modelling, eds. T. N. Srinivasan and J. Whalley. Cambridge: MIT Press.

Harrison, Glenn W. (1985 d). Sensitivity analysis and trade policy modelling. In General Equilibrium Trade Policy Modelling, eds. T. N. Srinivasan and J. Whalley. Cambridge: MIT Press.

Harrison, Glenn W., Jones, Richard, Kimbell, Larry J. & Wigle, Randall (1985). How robust is applied general equilibrium analysis? Working Paper No. 8501, Centre for the Study of International Economic Relations, University of Western Ontario, January.

Harrison, Glenn W. & Rutström, E. E. (1985 a). The effect of manufacturing sector ptoection on ASEAN and Australia: a general equilibrium analysis. In The Political Economy of Manufacturing Sector Protection in Australia and ASEAN, eds. C. Findlay and R. Garnaut. Sydney: George Allen and Unwin.

Harrison, Glenn W. & Rutström, E. E. (1985 b). ASEAN as a customs union. ASEAN Economic Bulletin, V. 2, forthcoming.

Howe, H. J. (1975). Development of the extended linear expenditure system. European Economic Review, V. 6, 305-10.

Institute of Developing Economics (1982). International Input-Output Table for ASEAN Countries: 1975. IDE Statistical Data Series 39. Tokyo: Asian Economic Press.

Johnson, H. G. & Krauss, M. (1970). Border taxes, border tax adjustments, comparative advantage, and the balance of payments. Canadian Journal of Economics, V. 34, 595-602.

Kimbell, Larry J. & Harrison, Glenn W. (1983). On the solution of general equilibrium models. Working Paper No. 8301C, Centre for the Study of International Economic Relations, Department of Economics, University of Western Ontario, January.

Kimbell, Larry J. & Harrison, Glenn W. (1984). General equilibrium analysis of regional fiscal incidence. In Applied General Equilibrium Analysis, eds. H. E. Scarf and J. B. Shoven. New York: Cambridge University Press.

Lloyd, P. J. (1973). Non-Tariff Distortions of Australian Trade. Canberra: Australian National University.

Lluch, C. (1973). The extended linear expenditure system. European Economic Review, V. 4, 21-32.

Lluch, C., Powell, A. A. & Williams, R. A. (1977). Patterns in Household Demand and Saving. New York: Oxford University Press.

Mansur, A. & Whalley, J. (1984). Numerical specification of applied general equilibrium models: estimation, calibration, and data. In Applied General Equilibrium Analysis, eds. H. E. Scarf and J. B. Shoven. New York: Cambridge University Press.

Mayor, T. H. (1971). Equipment expenditures by input-output industries. Review of Economics and Statistics, V. 53, 26-36.

Pagan, Adrian R. & Shannon, J. (1985). Sensitivity analysis for linearized computable general equilibrium models. In New Developments in Applied General Equilibrium Analysis, eds. J. Piggott and J. Whalley. New York: Cambridge University Press.

Piggott, J. & Whalley, J. (1985). Economic Effects of U.K. Tax-Subsidy
       Policies: A General Equilibrium Appraisal. New York:
       Cambridge University Press.
Saxon, E. & Anderson, K. (1982). Japanese agricultural protection in
       historical perspective. Research Paper No. 92, Australia-
       Japan Research Centre, Research School of Pacific Studies,
       ANU, Australia.
Statistical Office of the European Communities (Eurostat) (1983).
       National Accounts ESA. Input-Output Tables 1975.
       Brussels: Eur o stat.
Statistics Canada (1981). The Input-Output Structure of the Canadian
       Economy 1971-77. Catalogue 15-201E. Ottawa: Statistics
       Canada.
Stern, R. M., Francis, J. & Schumacher, B. (1977). Price Elasticities
       in International Trade: An Annotated Bibliography.
       London: Macmillan.
Stone, J. (1979). Price elasticities of demand for imports and exports:
       industry estimates for the U.S., the EEC, and Japan.
       Review of Economics and Statistics, V. 61, 306-12.
Tyers, Rod & Chisholm, Anthony (1982). Agricultural policies in
       industrialized and developing countries and international
       food security. Unpublished Manuscript, Research School of
       Pacific Studies, Australian National University, February.
Whalley, J. (1980 a). General equilibrium analysis of U.S.-EEC-
       Japanese trade and trade distorting policies. Economie
       Applique, V. 33, 191-230.
Whalley, J. (1980 b). Discriminatory features of domestic factor tax
       systems in a goods mobile-factors immobile trade model: an
       empirical general equilibrium approach. Journal of Political
       Economy, V. 88, 1177-1202.
Whalley, J. (1982). An evaluation of the Tokyo Round trade agreement
       using general equilibrium computational methods. Journal
       of Policy Modelling, V. 3, 341-61.
Whalley, J. (1984 a). The north-south debate and the terms of trade: an
       applied general equilibrium approach. Review of Economics
       and Statistics, V.
Whalley, J. (1984 b). Trade Liberalization Among Major World Trading
       Areas: A General Equilibrium Approach. Cambridge: MIT
       Press.
Whalley, J. (1985). Impacts of a 50% tariff reduction in an eight-
       region global trade model. In General Equilibrium Trade
       Policy Modelling, eds. T. N. Srinivasan and J. Whalley.
       Cambridge: MIT Press.
Whalley, J. & Wigle, Randall (1983). Are developed country multilateral
       tariff reductions necessarily beneficial for the U.S.?
       Economics Letters, V. 12, 61-7.
Whalley, J. & Wigle, Randall (1984). Adjustment to trade policy
       changes: alternative formulations and initial calculations.
       In Structural Adjustment in Trade Dependent Advanced
       Economies, ed. C. Jungenfelt. New York: St. Martin's Press
       and IEA.
Yeats, A. J. (1980). Trade Barriers Facing Developing Countries.
       London: Macmillan.
Zarembka, P. & Chernicoff, H. B. (1971). Further results on the
       empirical relevance of the CES production function. Review
       of Economics and Statistics, V. 53, 106-10.

REGIONAL IMPACTS OF TARIFFS IN CANADA: PRELIMINARY RESULTS
FROM A SMALL DIMENSIONAL NUMERICAL GENERAL EQUILIBRIUM MODEL

Rich Jones and John Whalley of the University of Western
Ontario and Randall Wigle of the University of Saskatchewan

The first two authors wish to acknowledge research support
from the Social Sciences and Humanities Research Council.
Helpful comments were received from the Economics Workshop at
the University of Saskatchewan.

Introduction

This paper presents some preliminary results from a small
dimensional applied general equilibrium model of U.S.-Canadian trade
which incorporates regional effects within Canada, and explores impacts
of changes in federal trade policies in Canada on interregional trade.
Unlike the recent general equilibrium work by Harris (1984) on Canadian
trade policy no scale economy features are included.

Regional Dimensions of Canadian Trade Policy

Since Confederation most Canadian policy debates have involved
discussion of their regional effects. Regional economic structures among
Canadian provinces are sharply differentiated, and as a result the impacts
of federal policies can be quite pronounced across regions.

Interprovincial trade is dominated by exports of manufactures
by Central Canada (Ontario and Quebec) to Western and Atlantic Canada in
return for resources and agricultural products. In international trade
Canada is a net importer of manufactures, and a net exporter of
resources.[1] Tariff protection is primarily on manufactures and has
traditionally been viewed as hurting the West and Atlantic Canada and
helping Central Canada since manufactures from Central Canada can be sold
to the West behind the protection of a tariff barrier.

Several policy elements besides the tariff have regional
effects. Price controls on energy products under the National Energy
Program hurt the West and help Central Canada. Grain transportation
subsidies help the West. Equalization payments transfer money to low
income provinces. Unemployment insurance benefits Atlantic Canada. The
federal income tax redistributes against higher income provinces. The
federal manufactures sales tax is thought to be harmful to Central Canada,
although this effect is partially offset by the manufacturing and
processing incentive in the corporate tax which lowers corporate tax

175

rates for manufacturing.

In short, Canada is a patchwork quilt of conflicting regional interests which come into play in debate on almost every national policy issue. Provinces not only have substantial autonomy but frequently form coalitions on an issue by issue basis to promote or block various policy initiatives. The role of the provinces in policy making in Canada is therefore pivotal and the perception as to what are the regional impacts of policies such as the federal tariff is key to the Canadian policy process.

Regional Impacts of the Canadian Tariff

The conventional wisdom on the regional impact of the Canadian tariff is that it increases the Canadian market price for manufactures, forcing Western buyers to pay higher gross of tariff prices for manufactures. In more popular discussion, the increased employment and income generated in Central Canada's manufacturing industry are seen as the major benefit of the tariff.

In the sparse academic literature on this subject, a small number of attempts have been made to both identify and quantify these effects. Most of this literature examines regional consequences of a unilateral abolition of tariffs by Canada, although it is well recognized in Canada there are sharp differences between a unilateral and multi-lateral tariff abolition.

One of the best known studies of regional impact is that by Hazledine (1978) who models Canada as a small open economy (SOE) in trade in resources and agricultural goods. His model seeks to have Canada as a price taker for resources and agriculture, but a price maker for manufactures. Estimates of changes in manufacturing shipments by province under a tariff change are generated using shipments elasticities, and form the basis for estimates of employment changes both nationally and by province. Changes in GNP, GDP, and GRP,[2] and changes in absorption[3] resulting from unilateral tariff abolition and other policy experiments are all calculated.

The regional consequences of unilateral tariff abolition by Canada in Hazledine's model are decreased employment and GRP in all regions (with the highest reduction in Atlantic Canada and Ontario). Somewhat paradoxically, absorption (in all regions) is financed by increased trade deficits (or reduced surpluses) since there is no trade balance condition to restrict imports. The policy implication seems to

be that tariffs help maintain employment everywhere in Canada, but reduce
welfare in all regions since trade deficits fall and consumption is
reduced. No clear interregional effects emerge from Hazledine's calculations since effects among regions are dominated by national effects.

      A further study of interregional effects of the tariff is that
by Pinchin (1979) who estimates that unilateral abolition of tariffs by
Canada would lead to a 19 percent reduction in manufacturing employment
(or a 4 percent reduction in total employment), along with a 10 percent
devaluation of the Canadian dollar. The pattern of interregional
transfers implied by the tariff is strongly in favour of Ontario and
Quebec, at the expense of the Prairies, British Columbia and the Atlantic
region. Aside from the interregional transfers which this reallocation
would imply, the total losses estimated by Pinchin are so large that no
federal government would reasonably be expected to argue for removing the
tariff.

      Despite the widely held popular perception that the tariff
helps Central Canada and hurts Western and Atlantic Canada, no clear
consensus emerges from this literature as to the regional impacts in
Canada of a movement to a free trade, either unilaterally or bilaterally,
or multilaterally. With the exception of Hazledine (1978) calculations do
not come from exercises in which the equilibrium structure used and
parameter values are clearly displayed. Much of the analysis involves
mutually inconsistent assumptions making results difficult to interpret.

The Modelling Approach

      The starting point for the present study is the 1974 Statis-
tics Canada interprovincial trade data which give bilateral trade flows
by product between provinces as well as trade outside Canada, and 1974
provincial input-output tables (also obtained from Statistics Canada)
which give demand, production, and value added data by province. These
are combined with information from a previously constructed 1972 micro
consistent data set for Canada for general equilibrium tax policy due to
St-Hilaire and Whalley (1983) to provide a micro consistent data set for
regional applied general equilibrium analysis. Previous studies of the
interregional effects of the federal tariff have had the disadvantage of
working with provincial manufacturing shipments data which do not allow
researchers to identify interprovincial trade in agriculture and
resources, or the destination of interprovincial shipments. The destination by province of imports from outside Canada is also unknown from this

data.

We use our data in a small dimensional interregional applied general equilibrium model similar to the trade models described in Shoven and Whalley (1984). Three regions appear, representing Eastern Canada (Canada from the Manitoba-Ontario border East), Western Canada (Canada from the same border West) and a residual rest of the world (ROW). Both interregional and international trade occur in three commodities; manufactures, and non-manufactures, and services.

As with other bench mark data exercises, constructing this regional data set requires a number of modifications to meet the conditions required for micro consistency. Trade balance by region and demand supply equalities for commodities are all imposed. For example, it is necessary to assure that in the benchmark data the total production of Eastern Canada Manufacturing goods is exactly equal to direct and indirect use at home and abroad. A similar condition holds for all other products.

The computer code used is based on the seven-region international trade model used by Whalley (1982) to investigate trade liberalization issues in the global economy. This model is best thought of as an empirical analogue of a Hecksher-Ohlin trade model, although similar products produced by different regions are treated as qualitatively different (cars in the U.S. and Japan), and technology, which is country specific, is represented by different parameter values in each country. The model uses nested CES production and demand functions with the hierarchies chosen to allow the key substitution possibilities which enter the model. The assumption of product heterogeneity by country (the 'Armington' assumption) is used to accomodate cross hauling in bilateral trade flow data. This allows literature estimates of trade elasticities to be more adequately incorporated into the approach than is possible in a homogeneous products trade model. Two factors of production are considered and are mobile among industries within each region, but are immobile between regions.

In adapting the code to the regional issues analyzed here the Armington structure in demand is retained, as are the factor mobility assumptions. This formulation thus allows East and West manufactured and non-manufactured output to be close but not perfect substitutes, and the elasticity of substitution between types of commodities to be varied within the model.

One necessary modification arises from the treatment of each

region as an independent state in the international trade model. Revenues
generated by a given region's government equal expenditures of that same
authority. In the current model application the relevant constraint is
that total revenue accruing to the federal government from both the East
and the West of Canada equal total expenditures by the federal government.

Three sources of revenue exist for the federal government in
this model. First, a manufacture's sales tax of 12 percent is levied on
final demand in both Canadian regions for all manufactured goods,
including imports from ROW. Second, there are factor taxes on capital
and labour in the three sectors in each of the Canadian regions. Similar
rates are assumed for both East and West, determined from the 1972 micro
consistent data set. Third, are the tariffs on non-manufactured and
manufactured goods imported from ROW.

At the time our modelling work was done, interprovincial
trade data was unavailable for years other than 1974 (it has since become
available for 1979). It was therefore impossible to estimate the
elasticities of demand in interprovincial trade for use in the model.
As a result, the same elasticities are assumed to apply to international
and interprovincial trade, with their values set equal to a best guess
estimate of these values from econometric literature. Values for the
rest of the world are assumed to be U.S. estimates. It is well known
that results of numerical trade models are sensitive to these elasticities. Sensitivity analyses on results are therefore also performed.

In setting tariff rates in the model further problems arise.
For aggregate manufacturing our procedure for estimating the tariff rate
is to calculate the total duty payable on manufactured imports and
determine this as a proportion of the pre-tariff value of imports. This
procedure cannot be applied separately for each region, even though the
average tariff on manufactures in Eastern Canada tends to be lower than
that on manufactures in the West due to the higher proportion of autos
and auto parts in the former (duty free under the U.S.-Canada auto pact).
Subsequent sensitivity analysis also investigate this issue.

The procedure used to analyse policy changes in the model
follow the calibration/counterfactual equilibrium analysis approach
outlined in Mansur and Whalley (1984). This is outlined in Figure 1.
Once the functional forms for production and utility functions are
specified, and elasticities are set, the model is calibrated to the 1974
benchmark data set. Calibration determines the values of the share

Figure 1

Flow Chart of Model Use

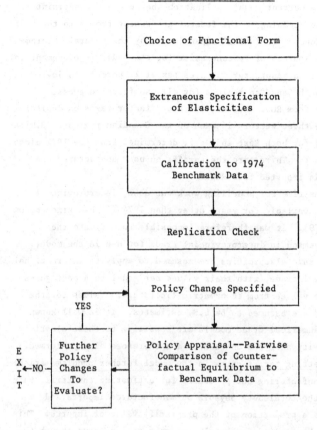

parameters consistent with the elasticities and the observed data set, using the assumption that firms are minimizing cost and consumers are maximizing utility subject to their budget constraints. The accuracy of the computer code is checked by confirming that the equilibrium outcomes of cost minimization and utility maximization given the inferred share parameters correspond to the original data. The desired policy change is then introduced and a counterfactual equilibrium solution computed. Policy appraisal proceeds using a pairwise comparison of the benchmark equilibrium data and each counterfactual equilibrium solution.

Interregional Impacts of the Federal Tariff

        Results are presented in Table I for a unilateral elimination of tariffs in Canada . This change worsens both welfare and the terms of trade for both the East and West, with an improvement in the Rest of the World.

        To a large extent these results reflect the values of the trade elasticities used. Canada is not modelled as a small open economy, and the ROW obtains a welfare gain at the expense of both Canadian regions as a result of the unilateral tariff abolition by Canada. This result can be seen simply as an illustration of the well known optimal tariff argument that countries which can influence their terms of trade will typically suffer a terms of trade deterioration by setting their own tariff to zero. In this case, results suggest that existing tariffs in Canada are closer to optimal tariffs than are zero tariffs.

        The more interesting feature of Table I is that, while as expected the East experiences a larger terms of trade deterioration, the West appears to lose almost as much from tariff abolition as the East. This is opposite to the belief that in relative terms the East gains interregionally from the tariff at the expense of the West.

        This latter result, however, is a direct consequence of the treatment of government revenues in the model. Regions are given a share of federal revenues equal to the amount paid by the region in the 1974 benchmark data. Since the East imports more than the West, their relative contribution of tariff revenues to the federal government is large. When Canadian tariffs are eliminated this reduces the West's share of tariff revenues returned to them in lump sum form. This is larger than the West's actual tariff payments, and thus the West loses from tariff elimination. This result therefore suggests that the way in which the revenues raised by the tariff are redistributed, interregion-

Table I

Unilateral Abolition of the Federal Tariff

A. Specification

 - government revenue redistributed to regions proportional to regional benchmark contribution to total federal
 benchmark revenues

 - elasticity of substitution between own and external
 goods (other province production) in both intermediate
 production and consumption set equal to literature
 estimates of national import price elasticities

B. Results

REGION	WELFARE EFFECTS[1]	TERMS OF TRADE CHANGE[2]
East	-.98	-4.20
West	-.88	-1.18
ROW	.11	4.75

---

[1] Change in welfare measured as the Hicksian equivalent
variation as a percentage of GRP.

[2] Percentage change in index of export to import producer
prices (+ve indicates improvement).

ally may be a more important determinant of the regional impacts of the tariff than the conventionally discussed price effect from protection on the interregional terms of trade.

In Table II we report results for the unilateral elimination of tariffs by Canada where we make an adjustment to the model so that the reduction in revenues received is proportional to each region's import share. In this case, regional results are closer to the terms of trade effects.

The implications of these results are that the federal tariff typically will produce a relative interregional terms of trade improvement in favour of the East, but the interregional income redistribution effect from tariff revenues is also important.

Varying Elasticities of Substitution

In the results presented in Tables I and II, both Canadian regions lose from unilateral tariff removal. These results largely reflect our modelling of Canada with respect to ROW. Our A priori expectation is that the elasticity of substitution between domestic and imported commodities in demand and production in ROW should be important for the welfare and terms of trade impacts produced by the model. In the extreme case, if the elasticity of substitution between domestic products and imports in the ROW is infinite, then Canada becomes a small open price taking economy in which case the cost of the tariff is borne exclusively by importing regions. At the opposite extreme, if Canada can influence its terms of trade, a substantial improvement could result from a tariff .

Results in Table III suggest that as the import domestic substitution elasticity in ROW gets higher, the terms of trade effects get smaller. The changes in the terms of trade effects for both the East and the West are as might be expected for the various elasticity specifications. The welfare results, however, suggest that the East gains from the removal of tariff when ROW's elasticity is high. The West continues to lose but by less.

Varying Tariff Rates by Region

In Table IV results using different relative tariffs by region are reported. These analyses are included because, due to the Auto Pact, the effective average tariff on Eastern imports of manufactures is lower than that on Western imports. In these cases the relative size of tariffs in the East is changed by reducing the tariff in the East

Table II

Unilateral Abolition of Tariffs by Canada with
Distribution of Federal Revenues Changes from Table I

	Revenue Returned to Region Proportional to Benchmark Contribution	Revenue/Change Distributed Proportional to Imports
Welfare Effects		
(Hicksian Evs as % of GRP)		
East	- .98	-1.19
West	- .88	- .37
ROW	.11	0.11
Terms of Trade Effects		
(% change, +ve indicates improvement)		
East	-4.20	-4.42
West	-1.18	-0.67
ROW	4.75	4.69

Table III

Sensitivity of Results to the

Import/Domestic Substitution Elasticity in ROW

(Unilateral Tariff Abolition with

Government Revenue Returned to Regions as in Table I)

	Elasticity Value		
	1.66[1]	10	20
Welfare Impacts (Hicksian Equivalent Variations as % of Income)			
East	− .98	.05	.19
West	− .88	−.30	−.27
ROW	.11	.03	.02
Terms of Trade (% change, +ve indicates improvement)			
East	−4.20	−.87	−.35
West	−1.18	−.09	−.25
ROW	4.75	.86	.45

---

[1]This is the value used in Tables I and II. Values of 1.3 were used for both East and West, and are also used in this table and those following.

Table IV

Sensitivity of Table I Results to Variations
in the Relative Size of East to West Tariffs
(Unilateral Tariff Abolition with
Government Revenue Redistributed to Regions)

	East Tariff equals West Tariff	East Tariff equals 1/2 West Tariff	East Tariff equals 1/4 West Tariff
	A. Welfare Impacts		
	(Hicksian EV as % of GRP)		
East	- .98	- .78	- .68
West	- .88	- .17	.20
ROW	.11	.07	.05
	B. Terms of Trade Effects		
	(% change, +ve indicates improvement)		
East	-4.20	-2.58	-1.75
West	-1.18	-0.79	-0.64
ROW	4.75	2.94	2.02

holding the Western tariff unchanged.

These results reflect the feature that the redistribution effect with tariffs is reversed between cases 1 and 3. In case 3, with considerably higher tariffs in the West, the majority of federal tariff revenues come from the West. When the tariff is eliminated, the West's contribution to national revenues drops by more than the transfer the West receives. In this case, unlike case 1, the West gains from the elimination of the tariff. These results therefore once again emphasize the importance of revenue redistribution effects in evaluating the regional impact of tariffs.

Conclusion

In this paper we report preliminary results from a small dimensional numerical general equilibrium model of U.S.-Canadian trade which incorporates regional effects within Canada. Under all assumptions of elasticities when revenues are redistributed by GRP, the West loses from unilateral abolition of Canadian tariffs, even though interregional terms of trade effects move relatively in their favour. Small positive gains result for the East only when the domestic import elasticity of substitution in the U.S. is high due to international terms of trade effects. The issue of how the federal government redistributes tariff revenues by region emerges as a central issue which crucially affects regional incidence.

ENDNOTES

1. Although bilateral U.S.-Canadian trade in autos and auto parts under the free trade Auto Pact accounts for 25 percent of U.S.-Canadian trade.

2. Gross Regional Product.

3. Absorption equals consumption plus capital formation and is suggested by Hazledine as a measure of the welfare impacts of the tariff change.

References

Harris, R. with Cox, D. (1984). Trade, Industrial Policy and Canadian
    Manufacturing. Toronto, Canada: Ontario Economic Council
Hazledine, T. (1978). The Economic Costs and Benefits of the Canadian
    Federal Customs Union. In The Political Economy of
    Confederation, Ottawa: Economic Council of Canada
Mansur, A. & Whalley, J. (1984). Numerical specification of applied
    general equilibrium models: estimation, calibration and
    data. In Applied General Equilibrium Analysis, ed.
    H.E. Scarf & J.B. Shoven, Cambridge University Press.
Pinchin, H. (1979). The Regional Impact of the Canadian Tariff.
    Ottawa: Economic Council of Canada.
Shoven, J. & Whalley, J. (1984). Applied General Equilibrium Analysis
    of Tax and Trade Policy Issues, Journal of Economic
    Literature, 22, no. 3, 1007-1051.
St-Hilaire, F. & Whalley, J. (1983). A Micro Consistent Data Set for
    Canadian Tax Analysis. Review of Income and Wealth.
Whalley, J. (1980). Discriminating Features of Domestic Factor Tax
    Systems in a Goods Mobile-Factors Immobile Trade Model:
    An Empirical General Equilibrium Approach. Journal of
    Political Economy, 88, no. 6, 1177-1202.
————— (1982). An Evaluation of the Tokyo Round Table Agreement
    Using General Equilibrium Computational Methods. Journal
    of Policy Modelling, 4, 341-361.

AGRICULTURAL PROTECTION AND MARKET INSULATION POLICIES:
APPLICATIONS OF A DYNAMIC MULTISECTORAL MODEL

Anthony H. Chisholm
The Australian National University

Rodney Tyers
The Australian National University

INTRODUCTION

Policies affecting international trade in agricultural
commodities have been a subject of considerable interest to economists
and policy-makers during the past decade. In this paper a multi-commodity
stochastic simulation model is used to analyze the economic effects of
agricultural trade policies in world grain and meat markets. Previous
studies on the welfare effects of agricultural trade policies in a global
context have modelled a single commodity, usually in a comparative-static
framework.[1]

The model presented in this study goes beyond this research.
Five international commodity markets are simulated - rice, wheat, coarse
grains, ruminant meats and non-ruminant meats.[2] The model incorporates
dynamic production uncertainty, stockpiling behaviour, and the cross-
effects, on both the demand and supply side, between the five staple-food
commodities. International markets are fully distinguished from domestic
markets and linked through the use of price transmission equations, and
all prices are endogenous.

While the model is more advanced than previous agricultural
trade models, it is not a complete general equilibrium model. To
properly address the policy issues that are the focus of this paper we
believe it is essential that a dynamic stochastic model be used. General
equilibrium models cannot, at present, satisfactorily handle short- and
long-run stochastic supply and endogenous stockpiling behaviour that
interacts with insulating trade policies. The modelling of these
components has necessarily led to the sacrifice of a complete general
equilibrium formulation.[3]

World and domestic staple-food markets are influenced by
policies that have two major dimensions. First, policies may serve

either to protect or tax domestic food production. Second, policies may
aim to insulate domestic markets from world price fluctuations.[4] A primary
focus of the paper is on the welfare impacts of these trade policies on
three major country groupings - the OECD, the Asia-Pacific regions' newly
industrialized countries (NICs), and the developing countries (LDCs). The
protectionist and insulating components of the policies will be discussed
in turn.

The most important forms of intervention in agricultural
commodity markets are trade and pricing policies that directly affect
product prices. Tariff and non-tariff barriers (NTBs) introduce a wedge
between domestic and border prices. In the OECD and NICs (South Korea,
Malaysia, Singapore, and Taiwan) domestic food prices are commonly set at
levels above world prices. Protection levels are particularly high in the
major food-importing regions - Japan, EEC, South Korea and Malaysia. By
maintaining domestic food prices at levels above world prices, domestic
production is stimulated in these countries and domestic consumption is
constrained. The effect of these protectionist policies is to lower world
trading prices.

The developing countries, in contrast to the protectionist
policies prevalent in the OECD and NICs, commonly adopt policies which
serve to tax food production (subsidize consumption) by maintaining
domestic food prices at levels below world prices, particularly for rice
and wheat (Peterson 1979). Since these policies act to increase domestic
demand and suppress domestic supply they place an upward pressure on world
trading prices.

Whether the combined effects of positive protection in the
OECD-NIC bloc and negative protection in the developing-country bloc
result in a higher, or lower, world price for a particular commodity is
an empirical issue. The results will be largely determined by the
relative sizes of the trading blocs, levels of protection, and
elasticities of excess supply and demand. The developing country bloc is
by far the largest producer and consumer of rice with a level of
production of around five times that of the OECD-NIC bloc and its trade
policies thus have a major impact on the world rice market. In the other
commodity markets, the production/consumption levels and trade policies
of the OECD-NIC block are the dominant force. However, liberalization
of trade policies in the developing country bloc would have very

significant effects, particularly in the case of wheat for which the
developing country bloc is the major importer.

The inherent instability of agricultural production is lore,
though ˜the sole prominence often given to stochastic production in
explaining the instability of world prices in agricultural commodity
markets is folklore. As Johnson (1975, 1981) has persuasively argued in
the context of world grain markets, man and not nature, is responsible for
a large part of the variability in world prices. In both developed and
developing countries, most domestic markets are heavily insulated from
world price fluctuations. Changes in world prices are not transmitted
into these domestic markets, at least in the short-run, and excess demands
adjust only very sluggishly to world price movements. The impact of
natural fluctuations in world production on world price volatility is
thus exacerbated. The burden of adjustment is carried by consumers and
producers in the few countries which do not insulate their domestic
markets and by those public and private stockpilers that face world prices.

The most notable cases of trade policies that are designed to
insulate their domestic consumers and producers from world price movements
are the system of variable import levies (and variable export subsidies)
employed by the EEC, (Sampson and Snape 1980), and the monopoly power over
controlling commodity trade volumes directly that is exercised by
governments in Japan, China, the Soviet Union and most developing
countries (Amat 1982; and Siamwalla 1981). The major non-insulated
domestic markets are the North American cereal markets in which fluctuations in world prices have been relatively freely transmitted into
domestic markets.

Finally, private and public stockpiling play an important role
in stabilizing domestic and international commodity prices. The method of
incorporating private and public stockpiling behaviour and the other major
features of the model are described in the following section. The usefulness and potential of the model is then illustrated by analysing the
effects of several agricultural trade liberalization scenarios.

OVERVIEW OF THE MODEL

In the simulation model, the world is disaggregated into
twenty four countries and country groups, six of which are modelled as net
trading entities only (Table 1). A mathematical description of the model

is given in Appendix 1. The model is a revised version of the one first
presented by Tyers and Chisholm (1981, 1982). The equations represented
in the model are based primarily on econometric analysis of time series
data for the period 1960 to 1980. A full description of the revised
model, the results of the econometric analysis and the parameters adopted
is given in Tyers (1984).

The main innovative characteristics of the model are:

(1) It is a multi-commodity model that, for each country, incorporates
both the own- and cross-price elasticities of demand and supply in the
interdependent markets for five commodities.

(2) It distinguishes and links domestic and international commodity
markets through price transmission equations that aim to quantify the
net effects of domestic protectionist and insulating policies.

TABLE 1
COUNTRIES AND COUNTRY AGGREGATES IN THE MODEL

Countries in which Domestic Markets are Simulated	Countries Studies as Net Trading Entities
OECD	Africa
Australia	China
Canada	Central & South America
European Community (EEC)	USSR
Japan	Middle East & Other Asia
New Zealand	Other Europe
United States	
NICs	
South Korea	
Malaysia	
Singapore	
Taiwan	
LDCs	
Bangladesh	
Burma	
India	
Indonesia	
Pakistan	
Philippines	
Sri Lanka	
Thailand	

(3) It incorporates stockpiling equations for each country for each of the grain commodities; it distinguishes between purely private speculative stockpiling and stockpiling behaviour in countries in which government-held stocks are dominant.

(4) The model is dynamic and stochastic and calculates the annual forecast means and variances of domestic and world prices, consumption, production, trade, storage, and a variety of welfare measures for each country.

Consumption behaviour in each country is assumed to be characterized by constant income, own-price, and cross-price elasticities of demand as shown by equation (1) in Appendix 1. Production behaviour is represented by a Nerlovian "partial adjustment" model which is linear in the logs of production and producer prices, as shown in equations (2) to (6). The model thus estimates short- and long-run supply responses and the underlying price elasticities are permitted to vary considerably in accordance with the empirical data. Production in each country and country group is subject to multiplicative random disturbances from the distribution of residuals to the fitted model.

The bulk of the theoretical research on commodity price stabilisation has focussed on the role of storage, usually in the context of a closed economy. This research has been of a normative nature focussing on "optimal" stockpiling policies and the factors influencing the distribution, between consumers and producers, of the welfare effects of storage.[5] Muth (1961) made a seminal contribution to the positive economic analysis of storage behaviour and this research has been expanded by Turnovsky (1979), Aiyagari et al. (1980), and Wright and Williams (1982). However, these models have not been applied in an international trade setting.

Storage behaviour in the model presented here (equation 7) is represented by a combination of risk-neutral competitive stockpilers and public agents that respond only to quantity triggers. The formulation of competitive stockpiling behaviour is an empirical adaptation of the model originally developed by Muth. Our model permits stock levels to respond to either domestic or international prices, depending upon which price series gave the best results, for each country and commodity, in the econometric time series analysis of stockpiling. To explain changes in stock levels in countries where government-held stocks dominate (e.g. Indonesia), stockpiling is modelled to respond to quantity triggers,rather than to domestic or international prices. This formulation captures public storage behaviour in the presence of insulating trade policies.

Trade policies that are designed to protect and insulate domestic markets are incorporated in the model through the specification of a price transmission equation for each country and commodity.[6] Countries are assumed to insulate their domestic markets against changing world prices by permitting short-run changes in nominal rates of protection while aiming to retain constant average levels of protection in the long-run. Thus, in the present version of the model, the econometrically-based price transmission elasticities are less than unity in the short-run but are assumed equal to unity in the long-run and to approach unity through a partial-adjustment type of lag distribution (equation 8). With this formulation, the smaller the short-run transmission elasticity, the greater the degree of market insulation and the more sluggish is the eventual transmission of any sustained change in a commodity's world price.

The excess demand behaviour of large country aggregates and the centrally planned countries are incorporated through the use of a linear version of the "partial adjustment" model (equations 9 to 12). Aggregate net imports adjust only partially to international price movements in a single year and they are disturbed annually by additive random errors.[7]

Finally, the welfare effects of a counterfactual policy change have four components. The welfare impact on consumers is measured by the change in the expected equivalent variation in income; the welfare impact on producers is the expected change in producer surplus; the impact on government revenue is the change in the expected net budgetary effect of consumer, producer and trade taxes and subsidies; and the benefit to stockpilers is measured by the expected change in profits from storage. All welfare effects are evaluated assuming risk-neutrality. A detailed mathematical description of the welfare measures is given in Appendix 2.

APPLICATIONS TO TRADE LIBERALIZATION

This section compares a reference projection with a number of counterfactual simulations which have been selected to illustrate the usefulness and potential of the model. In the reference projection, the equations reflect the trade policies which were in place over the period

1960 to 1980. Most of the model's parameters are based on econometric
analysis for this time interval, although corrections have been made in
cases in which significant changes occurred in the mid-to-late 1970s.
The reference levels of protection and market insulation for each country
and commodity are given in Table 2. In the reference case, these trade
policies and the underlying behavioural parameters are projected to be
applicable over the period 1980 to 1990.

The reference case, and all counterfactual simulations in
which both protection and market insulation are liberalized, are based on
100 ten-year simulations that generate forecast means and standard
deviations. As a consequence of the model's size and complexity, multiple
simulations are expensive. Since the variances of domestic and world
food prices are most sensitive to each country's degree of market
insulation, market stability is relatively unaffected by changes in pure
protection. Single simulations are therefore sufficient for the counterfactual analysis involving changes in protection only.

The model is first applied to estimate the effects of three
multilateral trade liberalization scenarios: complete trade liberalization
in the OECD-NIC bloc, in the LDCs, and in all eighteen countries
identified in the first column of Table 1, respectively. Trade scenarios
are then analyzed in which reference levels of protection are partially
liberalized while maintaining market insulation. Finally, some
simulation results are presented that show the important role of market
insulation and stockpiling behaviour.

Complete trade liberalization in the OECD-NIC bloc
To estimate the effects of OECD and NIC trade policies, the
model compares the reference projection with the estimated situation in
the absence of protection and market insulation in the OECD-NIC bloc.
The impact of trade liberalization on world prices and trade are shown in
Table 3.

First, world prices of rice, wheat, coarse grains and ruminant
meats would be considerably higher if the OECD-NIC bloc completely
liberalized its trade in these products. Second, the instability of
world prices is considerably reduced following OECD-NIC liberalization.
For example, the coefficient of variation of world wheat prices is
reduced by about one half while for coarse grains and ruminant meats it

TABLE 2

REFERENCE LEVELS OF PROTECTION AND MARKET INSULATION[a]
(per cent)

	Rice	Wheat	Coarse Grain	Ruminant Meat	Non-ruminant Meat
OECD					
Australia					
Consumer subsidy	-87	-20	0	0	0
Producer subsidy	14	4	0	0	0
Degree of insulation	11	11	13	5	40
Canada					
Consumer subsidy	0	-12	0	0	-5
Producer subsidy	0	15	0	0	5
Degree of insulation	51	37	11	79	50
EEC					
Consumer subsidy	-47	-110	-83	-94	-40
Producer subsidy	47	110	83	94	40
Degree of insulation	100	100	100	91	76
Japan					
Consumer subsidy	-250	-62	-15	-274	-40
Producer subsidy	317	362	325	293	46
Degree of insulation	91	100	50	88	17
New Zealand					
Consumer subsidy	0	0	0	0	0
Producer subsidy	0	0	0	0	0
Degree of insulation	20	100	74	10	100
United States					
Consumer subsidy	-30	0	0	0	0
Producer subsidy	30	15	0	0	0
Degree of insulation	41	0	0	40	5
NICs					
South Korea					
Consumer subsidy	-175	-54	-15	-282	-148
Producer subsidy	183	108	141	301	148
Degree of insulation	100	69	74	99	62
Malaysia					
Consumer subsidy	-50	-30	-27	-41	-11
Producer subsidy	65	30	27	48	11
Degree of insulation	30	50	13	79	0
Singapore					
Consumer subsidy	0	0	0	0	0
Producer subsidy	0	0	0	0	0
Degree of insulation	29	86	80	70	50
Taiwan					
Consumer subsidy	-113	0	-2	-127	0
Producer subsidy	105	85	64	127	0
Degree of insulation	88	73	10	99	87

Table 2 continued

	Rice	Wheat	Coarse Grain	Ruminant Meat	Non-ruminant Meat
LDCs					
Bangladesh					
Consumer subsidy	10	10	0	0	0
Producer subsidy	-10	-10	0	0	0
Degree of insulation	46	27	60	10	23
Burma					
Consumer subsidy	25	0	0	0	0
Producer subsidy	-25	0	0	0	0
Degree of insulation	50	50	50	80	80
India					
Consumer subsidy	6	0	0	0	0
Producer subsidy	-6	0	0	0	0
Degree of insulation	83	85	36	60	86
Indonesia					
Consumer subsidy	18	-71	4	0	0
Producer subsidy	-10	0	-4	0	0
Degree of insulation	92	91	85	80	80
Pakistan					
Consumer subsidy	40	10	0	0	0
Producer subsidy	-40	-10	0	0	0
Degree of insulation	79	92	60	80	80
Philippines					
Consumer subsidy	16	0	-38	-9	-7
Producer subsidy	-20	0	17	9	7
Degree of insulation	100	47	48	92	76
Sri Lanka					
Consumer subsidy	10	10	10	0	0
Producer subsidy	-10	-10	-10	0	0
Degree of insulation	78	90	90	90	90
Thailand					
Consumer subsidy	25	0	7	0	0
Producer subsidy	-25	0	-7	0	0
Degree of insulation	67	51	43	80	82

[a] Distortions are here expressed as percentages of the border price of each commodity. The degree of insulation is the complement of the short-run elasticity of price transmission $(1-\emptyset$, where $\emptyset$ is the elasticity of price transmission) also expressed in percentage terms. Consumer and producer subsidy equivalents are derived by comparing the average domestic wholesale and producer prices with the corresponding border prices, for the interval 1978-80.

TABLE 3
WORLD PRICE AND TRADE VOLUME CHANGES WITH COMPLETE TRADE LIBERALIZATION

	Rice	Wheat	Coarse Grains	Ruminant Meat	Non-ruminant Meat
WORLD PRICE[a] (Per Cent Change)					
Free Trade LDCs 1981	-8 (-71)	10 (-40)	1 (-7)	1 (-9)	1 (-8)
Free Trade LDCs 1990	-10 (-71)	-5 (-55)	2 (-12)	2 (-12)	-0.1 (-14)
Free Trade OECD/NICs 1981	45 (-10)	36 (-37)	28 (-27)	38 (-36)	23 (-18)
Free Trade OECD/NICs 1990	17 (-12)	21 (-46)	16 (-26)	26 (-22)	3 (3)
Free Trade 18 Countries 1981	8 (-71)	32 (-54)	26 (-30)	37 (-39)	22 (-23)
Free Trade 18 Countries 1990	6 (-70)	20 (-63)	16 (-32)	27 (-27)	2 (-11)
WORLD TRADE[b] (Difference & Per Cent Change)					
Free Trade LDCs 1990	1.4 (10)	1.5 (2)	4.1 (4)	0 (0)	0 (0)
Free Trade OECD/NICs 1990	2.4 (18)	-4.7 (-6)	27.6 (27)	2.5 (73)	3.3 (61)
Free Trade 18 countries 1990	3.3 (25)	-3.8 (-5)	28.3 (27)	2.4 (72)	3.2 (60)

Note:
[a] The numbers presented for world prices are per cent changes in forecast means with changes in standard deviations in parentheses (based on one hundred simulations), for the first year (1981) and the tenth year (1990) after trade liberalization, respectively.

[b] The numbers presented for world trade volumes are quantity changes as of 1990, measured in million metric tons with per cent changes in parentheses.

drops by over one quarter. Third, there is an overall increase in the
volume of world trade in grains and meats following OECD-NIC liberalization.[8]

In the wheat and coarse grains markets, trade liberalization
in the EEC is a dominant force leading to higher and more stable world
prices. Trade liberalization in the EEC, together with liberalization in
Japan, is a major factor accounting for higher and more stable ruminant
meat prices. In the rice market, trade liberalization in Japan, South
Korea and the United States provides the major force generating a higher
world price.

The impacts on annual economic welfare (1990) of trade
liberalization in the OECD-NIC bloc are shown in Table 4. The measure of
aggregate economic welfare is the sum of consumers' surplus, producers'
surplus, net government revenues, and stockpiling profits (Appendix 2). A
diagrammatic illustration of the effects of trade liberalization on the
above welfare measures is presented in Appendix 3.

The impact of OECD-NIC trade liberalization on the welfare of
the LDCs derives solely from the terms of trade effects. Most developing
countries are net importers of staple foods and the higher world prices
impose welfare loss on these countries. The country aggregates, including
Africa, China, Central and South America, and the USSR, are also net
importers of food and suffer a welfare loss as a result of the
unfavourable terms of trade effects.

The impact of trade liberalization on the economic welfare of
countries within the OECD-NIC bloc is a function of both the terms of
trade effects and the gains arising from the elimination of efficiency
losses. Trade liberalization results in a substantial rise in economic
welfare for all countries in the OECD-NIC bloc. For the major food
exporters - Australia, New Zealand, Canada, and the United States - the
welfare gains arise predominantly from the favourable terms of trade
effects.

Among the major food importers in the OECD-NIC bloc, Japan
and South Korea stand out in terms of the very high levels of protection
given to their agricultural producers (Table 2).[9] The substantial welfare
gains accruing to these two countries result from the elimination of
efficiency losses.[10] The terms of trade effects are unfavourable for these
food importing regions.

TABLE 4
WELFARE IMPACTS (1990) OF COMPLETE TRADE LIBERALIZATION (Change in Forecast Mean Annual Welfare(1980)US$)

	Free Trade (LDCs)		Free Trade (OECD-NICs)		Free Trade (18 countries)	
	Total($mill.)	Per Capita($)	Total($mill.)	Per Capita($)	Total($mill.)	Per Capita($)
OECD						
Australia	-27	-2	1,098	67	1,126	69
Canada	-87	-3	650	25	697	27
EEC	-426	-2	34,157	129	34,156	129
Japan	240	2	30,923	247	30,896	246
New Zealand	40	13	607	193	637	202
United States	356	1	3,805	16	4,158	17
TOTAL	96		71,240		71,670	
NICs						
South Korea	-11	0	6,959	156	7,036	158
Malaysia	-46	-3	-269	-16	-289	-17
Singapore	6	2	-44	-16	-36	-13
Taiwan	30	1	1,291	61	1,229	58
TOTAL	-21		7,937		7,940	
LDCs						
Bangladesh	-33	0	-106	-1	-150	-1
Burma	-19	0	5	0	3	0
India	-346	0	-1,647	-2	-1,830	-2
Indonesia	375	2	-337	0	-66	0
Pakistan	-77	-1	41	0	-54	0
Philippines	-93	-2	-93	-2	-166	-3
Sri Lanka	7	0	-13	-1	-12	-1
Thailand	72	1	28	0	234	4
TOTAL	-114		-2,122		-2,041	
COUNTRY AGGREGATES						
Africa	231	0	-1,264	-2	-1,025	-2
China	-60	0	-66	0	-181	0
Central & South America	64	0	-1,053	-2	-1,016	-2
USSR	79	0	-492	-2	-424	-1
Middle East & Other Asian Countries	142	0	-1,157	-4	-1,027	-3
Other European Countries	-46	0	-170	0	-62	0
TOTAL	410		-4,202		-3,735	

The substantial welfare gain made by the EEC is also attributable to the elimination of efficiency losses. Following trade liberalization, the EEC switches from being a large exporter of wheat and a small exporter of ruminant meats to being a major importer of both commodities. The overall terms of trade effects are thus also unfavourable for the EEC, given that with free trade the region is a net importer of all commodities except non-ruminant meats.

In sum, agricultural trade liberalization in the OECD-NIC bloc has unfavourable terms of trade effects for food importers and favourable terms of trade effects for food exporters. As net food importing regions, the developing-country bloc and the country aggregates thus incur a welfare loss as a result of trade liberalization in the OECD and the NICs. The trade liberalizing countries, on the other hand register a substantial gain in economic welfare. For food exporting countries, the welfare gains stem primarily from favourable terms of trade effects, whereas for food importers the welfare benefits are attributable to the efficiency gains arising from the elimination of domestic market distortions.[11]

Complete trade liberalization in the LDCs

In the second simulation, trade barriers in all the developing countries are eliminated whilst maintaining existing trade policies in the OECD-NIC bloc. Removal of the mainly negative levels of producer protection and the insulating policies in the developing countries results in a significant decline in the world rice price, a small decline in the world wheat price and a marginal increase in the world prices of coarse grains and ruminant meats (Table 3). In the world rice market, the lower price is mainly attributable to the increase in supply in Burma, Thailand, Pakistan and the Philippines following removal of the negative levels of protection to rice growers in these countries.

With the exception of the world rice market, the impact of trade liberalization in the LDCs on mean world prices is small compared with that resulting from trade liberalization in the OECD-NIC bloc. In contrast, trade liberalization in the LDCs has as large an impact overall on the stability of world prices as does OECD-NIC trade liberalization (Table 3). In particular, the trade insulating policies of the LDCs are the predominant cause of instability in world rice prices and are about

an equal force, with the OECD-NIC countries, in contributing to the
instability of world wheat prices.

The terms of trade effects resulting from trade liberalization
in the LDCs provide small overall gains in economic welfare to the OECD-
NIC bloc and the country aggregates (Table 4). Trade liberalization by
the LDCs results in a modest welfare loss to the bloc as a whole. With the
major exception of Indonesia, the terms of trade effects are unfavourable
for the developing countries, and they dominate the efficiency gains
arising from removal of domestic price distortions.

Complete trade liberalization in all countries

In the third simulation, agricultural trade is liberalized in
all eighteen countries. It is most insightful to compare the results from
this simulation with those for trade liberalization in the OECD-NIC bloc
alone. The major difference between the world prices generated by these
two simulations is a lower world rice price, and more stable world
commodity prices, when all eighteen countries liberalize their trade. In
the world rice market following trade liberalization, the pressures toward
higher world prices generated by increased excess demand in the OECD-NIC
bloc are largely counter-balanced by the forces toward lower world prices
generated by trade liberalization in the LDCs. There are only small
differences between the impacts of trade liberalization in the OECD-NIC
bloc, and liberalization in all eighteen countries, on the total welfare
of each country (Table 4).

Partial liberalization of protection and sensitivity testing[12]

The reference consumer and producer subsidy/tax components of
the trade policies detailed in Table 2 are now reduced by fifty per cent
and the market insulation component of trade policies is assumed to
remain unchanged. Following the initial adjustment of domestic price
levels, subsequent movements in world food prices continue to be only
partially transmitted into most domestic markets. This type of trade
scenario is probably a more realistic representation of one possible outcome of actual multilateral agricultural trade negotiations.

The estimated changes in world prices and trade volumes
resulting from partial liberalization of protection in the OECD-NIC bloc,
and in the LDCs, are shown in Table 5. The impact of partial trade

TABLE 5
WORLD PRICE AND TRADE VOLUME CHANGES WITH 50 PER CENT REDUCTION IN PROTECTION[a]

	Rice	Wheat	Coarse Grains	Ruminant Meat	Non-ruminant Meat
WORLD PRICE (Per cent change)					
Reduced Protection in LDCs	-7 (-10)	0 (-5)	0 (2)	0 (2)	0 (0)
Reduced Protection in OECD/NICs	5 (17)	13 (21)	8 (16)	9 (26)	0 (3)
Reduced Protection in 18 Countries	-3 (6)	12 (20)	7 (16)	9 (27)	1 (2)
WORLD TRADE (Difference)					
Reduced Protection in LDCs	-0.3 (1.4)	-0.5 (1.5)	-2.5 (4.1)	0 (0)	-0.1 (0)
Reduced Protection in OECD/NICs	-1.8 (2.4)	-5.2 (-4.7)	14.8 (27.6)	0 (2.5)	1.6 (3.3)
Reduced Protection in 18 Countries	-0.2 (3.3)	-4.2 (-3.8)	9.9 (28.3)	0 (2.4)	1.1 (3.2)

Note:

[a] World price and trade volume (million metric tons) changes are measured for the year 1990 with consumer and producer protection levels (Table 2) reduced by 50 per cent. The market insulation component of trade policies has been left unchanged. The numbers in parentheses are the corresponding changes for complete trade liberalization from Table 3.

TABLE 6

WELFARE IMPACTS (1990) OF 50 PER CENT REDUCTION IN PROTECTION(Change in Forecast Mean Annual Welfare (1980) US$)

	Trade Liberalization(LDCs)		Trade Liberalization(OECD-NICs)		Trade Liberalization(18 countries)	
	Total($mill.)	Per Capita($)	Total ($mill.)	Per Capita($)	Total ($mill.)	Per Capita ($)
OECD						
Australia	-19	-1	321	20	338	21
Canada	-10	0	250	10	244	9
EEC	-7	0	21,731	82	22,223	84
Japan	356	3	13,834	110	13,266	106
New Zealand	1	0	194	62	213	68
United States	-125	-1	586	2	475	2
TOTAL	196		36,916		36,759	
NICs						
South Korea	-12	0	3,239	73	2,313	51
Malaysia	-24	-1	-131	-8	-124	-7
Singapore	6	2	-17	-6	-12	-5
Taiwan	23	1	708	33	425	20
TOTAL	-7		3,799		2,602	
LDCs						
Bangladesh	14	0	-66	-1	-51	0
Burma	5	0	0	0	7	0
India	133	0	-738	-1	-576	-1
Indonesia	134	1	-138	-1	43	0
Pakistan	-43	0	-5	0	-49	0
Philippines	-50	-1	-38	-1	-77	-1
Sri Lanka	0	0	-12	-1	-11	-1
Thailand	-74	-1	-14	0	-45	0
TOTAL	119		-1,011		-759	
COUNTRY AGGREGATES						
Africa	108	0	-712	-1	-575	-1
China	-73	0	-117	0	-184	0
Central & South America	17	0	-531	-1	-509	-1
USSR	24	0	-348	-1	-302	-1
Middle East & Other Asian Countries	58	0	-503	-2	-481	-2
Other European Countries	24	0	133	-1	-9	0
TOTAL	158		-2,078		-2,060	

liberalization on world prices and trade volumes is substantial, but as
would be expected, generally smaller than the impact of complete trade
liberalization (Table 3). A similar trend in the welfare effects is
shown in Table 6. One interesting result is that the LDCs have an
aggregate welfare gain with partial trade liberalization compared with
the aggregate welfare loss incurred with complete trade liberalization.
This result indirectly indicates the significance of market insulating
policies which are fully operative in the partial trade liberalization
simulation but are eliminated in the complete trade liberalization
simulation.

       The role of market insulation is tested directly in a
simulation in which the degree of market insulation in all countries is
reduced by 20 per cent. The reference projection and the OECD-NICs 50
per cent reduced protection simulation are then repeated. The results
shown in Table 7 indicate that the size of world price changes is
sensitive to the reference levels of market insulation. In particular,
the higher the reference levels of market insulation the greater will be

TABLE 7
SENSITIVITY OF WORLD PRICE CHANGE TO THE DEGREE OF MARKET INSULATION[a]

	Rice	Wheat	Coarse Grains	Ruminant Meat	Non-ruminant Meat
The effect of 50% less protection in the OECD/NICs					
1981					
Reference Market Insulation	24.7	11.5	18.5	27.5	11.4
20% less Market Insulation	15.3	10.0	16.2	21.1	10.2
1990					
Reference Market Insulation	4.8	12.9	7.8	8.9	0.3
20% less Market Insulation	5.5	8.9	6.2	8.8	1.8
Elasticity of price changes to Market Insulation					
1981	1.9	0.7	0.6	1.2	0.5
1990	−0.7	1.6	1.0	0.1	−25.0

Note:
   [a]The results given in the table are derived by reducing the degree
of market insulation in all countries by 20 per cent and repeating
the reference projection and the OECD/NICs 50 per cent reduced
protection analysis. The reference levels of market insulation
are given in Table 2.

the changes in world prices attributable to trade liberalization.

The results given in Table 8 similarly show that the welfare impacts of trade liberalization are reasonably sensitive to the estimated reference levels of market insulation. The impact of a changed reference level of market insulation on the estimated welfare gain/loss for a particular country is dependent on the differences in both the terms of trade effects and in the rates of transmission of world price movements into the domestic market. In most cases these effects combine so that the

TABLE 8
SENSITIVITY OF WELFARE IMPACTS TO THE DEGREE OF MARKET INSULATION[a]
Annual Welfare Impact of 50% Less Protection in the OECD/NICs(1990)

| | Per Capita ($) | | |
	Reference Market Insulation	20% Lower Market Insulation	Elasticity to degree of Market Insulation[b]
OECD			
Australia	19.7	18.3	0.3
Canada	9.6	7.9	0.9
E.E.C.	81.8	68.3	0.8
Japan	110.3	113.6	-0.2
New Zealand	61.7	58.6	0.3
U.S.A	2.5	2.5	0
NICs			
South Korea	72.8	66.0	0.5
Malaysia	-7.7	-6.9	0.6
Singapore	-6.4	-6.1	0.3
Taiwan	33.2	33.9	0
LDCs			
Bangladesh	-0.56	-0.40	1.4
Burma	0	0.05	-
India	-0.89	-0.71	1.0
Indonesia	-0.79	-0.75	0.3
Pakistan	-0.05	0.08	13.0
Philippines	-0.63	-0.38	2.0
Sri Lanka	-0.68	-0.47	1.6
Thailand	-0.23	-0.15	1.7

Note:

a
  See note a, Table 7.

b
  These elasticities measure the per cent change in the welfare estimate which results from a one per cent change in the levels of market insulation made simultaneously in all 18 countries listed in Table 1.

lower the reference level of market insulation the smaller the impact of trade liberalization on the welfare gain or loss. But in a few countries, for example Japan and Pakistan, a lower reference level of market insulation increases the size of the welfare change. Market insulation clearly assumes an important role in the model and misspecification of reference levels of market insulation will introduce errors into the estimates of the impact of trade liberalization on world prices and the economic welfare of individual countries.

Finally, the important role of endogenous private and public stockpiling in the model may be investigated via a counterfactual simulation in which stock levels are not permitted to respond to price or production fluctuations. In the absence of responsive stockpiling, countries with a high degree of market insulation cease to make any contribution to the absorption of shocks arising from short-run fluctuations in world production. Adjustments to fluctuations in world production now fall entirely on consumers in countries with relatively uninsulated markets. A substantial increase in the volatility of world prices for all grains occurs. Most notably, in the absence of storage, the forecast standard deviation of world wheat prices increases sixfold and this vast increase in price instability results in a significant increase in the forecast mean world wheat price.[13]

Because trade policies which insulate domestic markets increase the instability of world prices an interdependency exists between stockpiling and trade insulating policies. This is best illustrated by considering first a counterfactual reference projection for a world in which market insulating trade policies are eliminated in all countries, while endogenous stockpiling is retained. The forecast standard deviation of world wheat prices in this reference projection (no-insulation) is one-third the size of the forecast obtained in the presence of existing market-insulating policies. If now, stockpiling is eliminated in the no-insulation reference simulation, the forecast standard deviation of world wheat prices increases by around 50 per cent. While this represents a substantial increase in world wheat price volatility, it is considerably smaller than the sixfold increase obtaining when stockpiling was eliminated and existing market-insulating policies retained. Stockpiling thus assumes an even more important role in the presence of trade policies that insulate domestic markets and exacerbate world price instability, than in the absence of such policies.

CONCLUDING COMMENTS

The major innovative features of the agricultural trade model presented in this paper are its multi-commodity structure and its treatment of protectionist and insulating policies in combination with endogenous stockpiling behaviour.

World net annual income is estimated to be about 70 billion dollars (1980 U.S.$) lower with existing agricultural trade policies in the OECD-NIC bloc as compared with free trade, allowing a ten-year period for long-run supply adjustment to free trade. The predicted short-run net annual welfare gain is about one third of the long-run gain. The OECD-NIC bloc trade policies have terms of trade effects which have a favourable impact on the economic welfare of the LDCs and country aggregates. These countries are net importers of grains and meats from the OECD and gain from the lower world prices attributable to the trade policies of the OECD-NIC bloc.

The OECD-NIC bloc incurs very high net welfare losses as a result of its own agricultural trade policies. The major food exporters - Australia, Canada, New Zealand, and the United States - lose largely because of the unfavourable terms of trade effects. The large welfare losses incurred by regions which are major food importers - Japan, the EEC, and South Korea - stem from the efficiency losses associated with their own distortionary protectionist policies.

Examination of the welfare impacts in a more disaggregated form enables some insight to be gained into the question of why the above countries impose trade policies that result in substantially lower economic welfare than that attainable with free trade. Firstly, consumer surplus is greater, and producer surplus smaller, in all countries - except Japan, the EEC, South Korea, Malaysia and Taiwan - as a consequence of the agricultural trade policies of the OECD-NIC bloc. In the three major highly protectionist regions - the EEC, Japan and South Korea - the annual gains to farmers from existing protectionist policies are highly concentrated. The average annual income of EEC farmers, for example, is estimated to be about fifteen per cent, or 750 dollars (1980 U.S.$) higher with protection, whereas per capita incomes of EEC consumers-cum-taxpayers are of the order of only one per cent lower. In the political process - as analysed by Stigler (1975), Peltzman (1976) and others - this concentration of benefits facilitates the formation of powerful interest groups (producers) who successfully lobby governments for protectionist policies that effectively tax a larger dispersed group (consumers) at a relatively low per capita rate.

Trade policies in the LDCs have small welfare impacts compared with those in the OECD-NIC bloc. The major impact of the LDCs policies is to significantly increase the mean world rice price. The terms of trade effects of trade distortions, in both the North and the South, are favourable overall to the LDCs and unfavourable to the rest of the world. For the LDCs, the favourable terms of trade effects are dominant and their aggregate economic welfare is higher than it would be with free trade.

The domestic-market insulating policies of the OECD-NICs and the LDCs have about an equal overall impact on the instability of world prices. The contribution of stockpiling to stabilising world prices is evidenced by the very large sixfold increase in the forecast volatility of world grain prices when it is eliminated from the model. Dynamic models that incorporate insulating trade policies cannot properly represent international grain market behaviour if stock-holders are excluded. The inclusion of these behavioural characteristics in our model, however, has necessarily involved the sacrifice of a full general equilibrium framework.

Notes

The revision of our 1983 conference paper has benefited from comments of David Vincent (discussant), the editors, and a referee. We are grateful to John Freebairn for valuable comments on our research. Thanks are due to George Fane and Ted Sieper for helpful discussions and to Chris Jankovic for research assistance provided in the preparation of tables. Any remaining shortcomings are the responsibility of the authors alone.

1. Single-commodity international markets with endogenous world prices have been modelled in static equilibrium by Shei and Thompson (1977) and Valdes and Zeitz (1980) and with excess supply uncertainty by Zwart and Meilke (1979).

2. The meat of ruminants comprises cattle and sheep and that of non-ruminants, pigs and poultry. Coarse grains and wheat are both consumed directly and also used as inputs for meat production.

3. In particular, the model assumes fixed foreign exchange rates and predetermined income, population and productivity growth rates. The research does not incorporate analysis of protection to markets for agricultural inputs for which reliable data is generally unavailable; nor does it take account of the structure of protection existing elsewhere in an economy.

4. The term "protection" refers to the long-run average divergence between domestic and border prices, while the term "insulation" refers to the degree to which short-run world price movements are transmitted into the domestic market.

5. For surveys of this theoretical research see Turnovsky (1978), Newbery and Stiglitz (1981), and Chisholm (1982). Much of the earlier theoretical research on stabilization confounded the analysis of the economic consequences of the disturbances themselves with the more difficult problem of the economic benefits of storage (Wright 1979, Chisholm 1982).

6. Price transmission equations were first used as a means of making endogenous the intertemporal adjustments that governments make to trade policies which affect domestic commodity prices by Bredahl et al. (1979) and Cronin (1979). In the earlier research of Tyers and Chisholm (1981 and 1982), both the protection and insulation components of trade policy were represented through linear relationships between the logs of domestic and border prices. Following a proposal by Abbott (1979a,b) that inter- temporal changes in food trade policies may be better described by a lagged adjustment model, this formulation was fitted for selected countries and found to be generally superior and is adopted in the present model. Price transmission equations have been applied in single commodity trade models by Abbott (1979a,b), Lattimore and Sehuh (1979) and Sarris and Freebairn (1983). In the multi-commodity trade model presented here, the combination of price transmission equations and endogenous stockpiling behaviour is an important one.

7. Since net trade is the difference (residual) between domestic production and consumption, small disturbances in production can cause large proportional changes in the net trade of country-aggregates. For this reason, additive disturbances and linear excess demands are used in these cases.

8. Trade liberalization will usually increase the volume of world
trade, though when protection takes the form of substantial export
subsidies (e.g. EEC wheat exports) it is possible for the volume of world
trade to be smaller with free trade. For example, the volume of world
wheat trade declines by 6 per cent with OECD-NIC trade liberalization.
The fall in world wheat trade is largely a consequence of the EEC switch-
ing from exporting 15 million tons of wheat to importing 4 million tons
following elimination of protection.

9. The domestic and border prices for a number of the countries
identified in Table 2 are based on a research program on Western Pacific
agricultural trade coordinated by the Research School of Pacific Studies
at the Australian National University. Particular attention has been
given to problems of varietal and quality differences in the selection of
domestic and border commodity prices; see, for example, Saxon and
Anderson (1982) and Anderson (1983).

10. To simplify the exposition, the term "elimination of efficiency
losses", is used here as if the "small country" assumption always applied.
The simulation results, of course, incorporate the impact on world prices
of "large country" trade liberalization, but no attempt is made in this
paper to estimate the "optimum tariff" for large food importers or
exporters.

11. Following the presentation of the conference draft of our paper, a
number of revisions to the model and data were completed and all results
reported in the present paper are based on the revised version of the
model. Further detailed studies have been undertaken, using the revised
model, of the economic effects of the Common Agricultural Policy of the
EEC (Anderson and Tyers, 1983 and Tyers, 1984) and of East Asian
agricultural policies (Tyers and Anderson, 1984).

12. A more comprehensive sensitivity testing of the model structure is
presented in Tyers (1984).   This research includes an examination of the
sensitivity of the results to EEC production elasticities which are
especially difficult to estimate. Pagan and Shanon (1984) propose that
the elasticities of particular results to the values adopted for
particular parameters could be evaluated by repetitions of the analysis
or by deriving these elasticities endogenously. Harrison and Kimbel(1984)
use simple a priori probability distributions of their parameter estimates
and many repetitions of their analysis to derive probability distributions
of their important results. Tyers selectively evaluates elasticities of

sensitivity using repeated simulations. For the large stochastic model
presented here, evaluation of a more comprehensive set of these
elasticities would be costly and impractical, while the stochastic nature
of the model rules out their endogenous estimation.

13. The change in the forecast mean world wheat price resulting from
the increase in price instability derives from the non-linear structure
of the model so that stochastic production disturbances do not lead to
mean-preserving spreads. Changes in forecast mean world price tend to
exert a dominant effect on the measure of welfare change attributable to
a more unstable world price regime.

References

Abbott, P.C. (1979a). Modeling international grain trade with government-
    controlled markets. American J. Agricultural Economics 61:
    22-31.

————————— (1979b). The role of government interference in inter-
    national commodity trade models. American J. Agricultural
    Economics 61:135-40.

Aiyagari, S.R. et al.(1980). Rational expectations, inventories and price
    fluctuations. Economic Growth Center Discussion Paper no.363,
    Yale University.

Amat, S. (1982). Promoting national food security: the Indonesian
    experience. In Food Security: Theory, Policy and Perspectives
    from Asia and the Pacific Rim, eds. A.H.Chisholm and R.Tyers,
    pp. 145-70. D.C. Heath & Co., Lexington Books, Mass.

Anderson, K. (1983). Growth of agricultural protection in East Asia.
    Food Policy 8 (4):327-36.

Anderson, K. and R. Tyers (1983). European Community grain and meat
    policies and U.S. retaliation: effects on international
    prices, trade and welfare. Discussion Paper no.83, Centre
    for Economic Policy Research, Australian National University,
    December.

Brendahl, M.E. et al. (1979). The elasticity of foreign demand for U.S.
    agricultural products: the importance of the price trans-
    mission elasticity. American J. Agricultural Economics 61:
    58-63.

Chisholm, A.H. (1982). Commodity price stabilization: microeconomic
    theory and policy issues. In Food Security: Theory, and
    Perspectives from Asia and the Pacific Rim, eds. A.H.Chisholm
    and R. Tyers, pp.67-103.

Cronin, M.R. (1979). Export demand elasticities with less than perfect
    markets. Australian J. Agricultural Economics 23:69-72.

Harrison, G. and L. Kimbell (1984). General equilibrium analysis of
    regional economic policy in the Pacific Basin. This vol.Ch.

Johnson, D.G. (1975). World agriculture, commodity policy and price
    variability. American J. Agricultural Economics 57:823-28.

————————— (1981). Grain insurance, reserves and trade: contribution to
    food security for LDC's. In Food Security for Developing
    Countries, ed. A. Valdes. Boulder, Colo. Westview Press.

Lattimore, R.G. and G.E. Schuh (1979). Endogenous policy determination:
    the case of the Brazilian beef sector. Canadian J.
    Agricultural Economics 27:1-18.
Muth, S.F. (1961). Rational expectations and the theory of price move-
    ments. Econometrica 29:315-336.
Newbery, D.M.G. and J.E. Stiglitz (1981). The Theory of Commodity Market
    Stabilization. Oxford University Press.
Pagan, A. and J.H. Shannon (1984). Sensitivity analysis for linearized
    computable general equilibrium models. This vol. Ch.
Peltzman, S. (1976). Toward a more general theory of regulation. J. Law
    and Economics 19:211-48.
Peterson, W.L. (1979). International farm prices and the social costs
    of cheap food policies. American J. Agricultural Economics
    61:12-21.
Sampson, G.P. and R.H. Snape (1980). Effects of the EEC's variable import
    levies. J. Political Economy 88:1026-39.
Sarris, A.H. and J.Freebairn (1983). Endogenous price policies and
    international wheat prices. American J. Agricultural
    Economics 65:214-24.
Saxon, E. and K. Anderson (1982). Japanese agricultural protection in
    historical perspective. Pacific Economic Papers no.92,
    Australia-Japan Research Centre, Australian National University.
Shei, S. and R.L. Thompson (1977). The impact of trade restrictions on
    price stability in the world wheat market. American J.
    Agricultural Economics 59:628-38.
Siamwalla, A. (1981). Security of rice supplies in the ASEAN region. In
    Food Security for Developing Countries, ed. A. Valdes.
    Boulder, Colo. Westview Press.
Stigler, G.J. (1975). The theory of economic regulation. In The Citizen
    and the State: Essays on Regulation, Ch.8, University of
    Chicago Press, Chicago.
Turnovsky, S.J. (1978). The distribution of welfare gains from
    stabilization: a survey of some theoretical issues. In
    Stabilizing World Commodity Markets, eds. F.G. Adams and
    S.A. Klein, D.C. Heath and Co., Lexington Books, Mass.
Turnovsky, S.J. et al. (1980). Consumer surplus, price instability and
    consumer welfare. Econometrica 48:135-52.
Tyers, R. and A.H. Chisholm (1981). Food security and agricultural policy
    in Asia and the Pacific: applications of a multi-commodity
    stochastic simulation model. East West Resource Systems
    Institute Working Paper WP.31-19, Honolulu, Hawaii.
———————————————— (1982). Agricultural policies in industriali-
    zed and developing countries and international food security.
    In Food Security: Theory, Policy and Perspectives from Asia
    and the Pacific Rim, eds. A.H. Chisholm and R. Tyers, pp.307-
    53, D.C. Heath and Co., Lexington Books, Mass.
Tyers, R. (1984). Agricultural protection and market insulation: analysis
    of international impacts by stochastic simulation. Pacific
    Economic Papers no.111, Australia-Japan Research Centre,
    Australian National University.
Tyers, R. and K. Anderson (1984). Price, trade and welfare effects of
    agricultural protection: the case of East Asia. Pacific
    Economic Papers no.109, Australia-Japan Research Centre,
    Australian National University.
Valdes, A. and J. Zeitz (1980). Agricultural protection in OECD countries:
    its cost to less developed countries. Research Report no.21
    International Food Policy Research Institute,Washington, D.C.

Wright, B.D. (1979). The effects of ideal production stabilization: A
     welfare analysis under rational behavior. J. Political
     Economy 87:1011-33.
Wright, B.D. and J.C. Williams (1982). The Economic Role of Commodity
     Storage. The Economic J. 92:596-614.
Zwart, A.C. and K.D. Meike (1979). The influence of domestic pricing
     policies and buffer stocks on price stability in the world
     wheat industry. American J. Agricultural Economics 61:434-47.

Appendix A1   The Model

Consumption:

$$c_{ilt} = c_{ilo}^T \left(\frac{N_{lt}}{N_{lo}}\right) \left(\frac{y_{lt}}{y_{lo}}\right)^{n_{il}} \prod_j^m \left(\frac{p_{jlt}}{\bar{p}_{jlo}}\right)^{a_{ijl}} \tag{1}$$

Production:

$$q_{ilt}^* = q_{ilt}^T \prod_j^m \left\{ \left(\frac{p_{jlt}}{\bar{p}_{jlo}} \lambda_{ilt}\right)^{b_{1ijl}} \left(\frac{p_{jlt-1}}{\bar{p}_{jlo}} \lambda_{ilt-1}\right)^{b_{2ijl}} \left(\frac{p_{jlt-2}}{\bar{p}_{jlo}} \lambda_{ilt-2}\right)^{b_{3ijl}} \right\} \tag{2}$$

Partial adjustment to target, q^*: $q_{ilt} = q_{ilt}^T \left(\frac{q_{ilt-1}}{q_{ilt-1}^T}\right)\left(\frac{q_{ilt}^*}{q_{ilt}^T} / \frac{q_{ilt-1}}{q_{ilt-1}^T}\right)^{\delta_{il}} e^{\varepsilon_{ilt}} \tag{3}$

Production shifter: $q_{ilt}^T = q_{ilo}^T e^{g_{il}t} \tag{4}$

Change in producer/consumer price ratio: $\lambda_{ilt} = (\rho_{ilt}^P / \rho_{ilt}^C)/(\rho_{ilo}^P / \rho_{ilo}^C) \tag{5}$

Random disturbances: $\varepsilon_{lt} \sim N(\underline{0}, U_l) \tag{6}$

Closing stocks:

$$s_{ilt}/z_{ilt} = \alpha_{il}[p_{ilt+1}^S - (1 + r_l) p_{ilt}^S - \theta_l (s_{ilt}/ \bar{s}_{ilt-1})]$$
$$+ \beta_{il}[q_{ilt} + s_{ilt-1} - \bar{q}_{ilt} - \bar{s}_{ilt}] / z_{ilt} + \gamma_{il} \tag{7}$$

Price transmission:

$$p_{ilt} = \rho_{ilt}^C x_l h_{il}^{\beta}{}_{io} \left(\frac{p_{ilt-1}}{\rho_{ilt-1}^C x_l h_{il}^{\beta}{}_{io}}\right)^{1-\phi_{ilt}} \left(\frac{p_{it}}{\bar{p}_{io}}\right)^{\phi_{ilt}} \tag{8}$$

Net imports:

$$m_{ilt} = c_{ilt} + s_{ilt} - q_{ilt} - s_{ilt-1} \tag{9}$$

Net-trading aggregates:

Target imports: $m_{ilt}^* = m_{ilt}^T + b_{il}(p_{it} - \bar{p}_{io}) \tag{10}$

Partial adjustment: $m_{ilt} = m_{ilt}^T + m_{ilt-1} - m_{ilt-1}^T$
$$+ \delta_{il}[m_{ilt}^* - m_{ilt}^T - (m_{ilt-1} - m_{ilt-1}^T)] + \varepsilon_{ilt} \tag{11}$$

Net import shifter: $m_{ilt}^T = c_{ilo}^T \left(\frac{N_{lt}}{N_{lo}}\right) \left(\frac{y_{lt}}{y_{lo}}\right)^{n_{il}} - q_{ilo}^T e^{g_{il}t} \tag{12}$

International market clearing: $\sum_l^n m_{ilt} = 0 \tag{13}$

Appendix A1 (continued)   Nomenclature

Quantities: c_{ilt} = consumption (domestic disappearance) of commodity i in country l in year t.

c_{il0}^T = trend consumption of i in country l in the base year, 1980.

q_{ilt} = production of commodity i in country l in year t.

q_{ilt}^T = trend production of commodity i in country l. For t=0 this is trend production in 1980. For t>0 this would be trend production if producer prices were to remain constant.

$\bar{q}_{ilt}$ = an equally-weighted moving average of production in the three years prior to and including t.

m_{ilt} = net imports of commodity i to country l in year t.

m_{ilt}^T = trend net imports of i to country or country-aggregate l in year t. For t=0 this is the trend of net imports in 1980. For t>0 this would be trend net imports were the border price to remain constant.

z_{ilt} = denominator in storage equation; equal to $\bar{q}_{ilt}$ where commodity i is not imported, and to an equally weighted moving average of consumption where the commodity is imported.

ε_{ilt} = random disturbance to the production of i in country l, or to the net imports of i to country aggregate l, in year t.

U_l = variance-covariance matrix of random disturbances to the production or (in the case of country aggregates) net imports of all commodities i (from 1 to m) in country l.

s_{ilt} = closing stock of commodity i in country l in year t.

$\bar{s}_{ilt-1}$ = equally-weighted moving average of closing stocks of commodity i in the three years prior to t.

Prices: p_{ilt} = domestic wholesale price of i in country l in year t.

$\bar{p}_{il0}$ = average domestic wholesale price in the years 1978 through 1980.

p_{ilt}^s = price at which stocks are traded. Depending on the commodity and the country this may be either the border price or the domestic wholesale price - which ever gave the best econometric results.

p_{ilt+1}^s = expected stock trading price in year t+1. In the version of the model presented here, this is set to a four-year equally-weighted moving average of stock trading prices, including the price in year t.

P_{it} = standard international trading price of commodity i in year t, based on f.o.b. export prices at the major ports in Thailand (rice), Canada (wheat), USA (maize), Australia (beef) and USA (pork and poultry).

$\bar{P}_{i0}$ = average standard international price in the years 1978 through 1980.

Fixed
parameters: n_{il} = income elasticity of demand for commodity i in country l.

a_{ijl} = the elasticity of the demand for i with respect to the price of j in country l.

b_{ijl} = elasticities of the target-level of production of i with respect to the producer price of j.

b_{1ijl} = very short-run supply elasticity - non-zero only for ruminant meats.

b_{2ijl} = one-year response elasticity.

b_{3ijl} = two-year response elasticity - non-zero only for ruminant meats.

δ_{il} = partial adjustment elasticity in the production (net import) of i in country (aggregate) l.

g_{il} = growth rate in the trend of production of commodity i in country l which would be sustained with constant real producer prices.

θ_l = average cost of cereal storage in country l at stock level $\bar{s}_{ilt-1}$.

Appendix 1A (continued)

Fixed
parameters
(continued): $\alpha_{il}, \beta_{il}, \gamma_{il}$ = estimated parameters determining the response of closing stocks to expected
profits, a quantity trigger and working storage requirements, respectively.

x_l = the exchange rate of country l in domestic currency per US\$(1980).

h_{il} = the ratio of the import or export unit value of commodity i in country l to the standard
international price, P_{i0}, reflecting shipment costs, quality differences and access to
concessional sales, in the base period, 1978-80. These divergences from the standard
prices are assumed to remain constant throughout all simulations.

r_l = the real rate of interest in country l.

Exogenously
projected
variables: N_{lt} = the population of country or aggregate l in year t.

y_{lt} = the per capita income in country or aggregate l in year t.

Exogenous
policy
variables: ρ^C_{ilt} = the ratio of domestic wholesale to border price of commodity i in country l. This is uni
minus the rate of consumer subsidy on the purchase price of the commodity.

ρ^P_{ilt} = the ratio of domestic producer to border price of commodity i in country l. This is the
familiar nominal protection coefficient. The time subscript refers to the intertemporal
changes due to the phased introduction of a new policy.

ϕ_{ilt} = the short run elasticity of price transmission permitted by the government of country l
between the domestic and international prices of commodity i. In the formulation given
in equation (8) the corresponding long run transmission elasticity is unity.

Appendix A2   Welfare Measure

Consumer benefit from a policy change:

Expected Equivalent Variation (linear approximation)[a]: $B_{lt}^C = E \{ V_{lt}^{New} - V_{lt}^{Ref} \}$ (14)

Where: $V_{lt} = -\frac{1}{2} c_{lt}' A_l^{-1} c_{lt} - (-\frac{1}{2} c_{lt}^{u'} A_l^{-1} c_{lt}^u)$ (15)

Slutsky Matrix approximation[b]: $A_l = \{ a_{ijl}^c \, c_{ilt} / p_{jlt} \}$ (16)

Compensated price elasticities: $a_{ijl}^c = a_{ijl} + \eta_{il} \dfrac{p_{jlt} \, c_{jlt}}{N_{lt} \, y_{lt}}$ (17)

Utility-constant consumption, at prices $\bar{p}_{l0}$: $c_{lt}^u = c_{lt} + A_l (\bar{p}_{l0} - p_{lt})$ (18)

Trend consumption: $c_{ilt}^T = c_{il0}^T \left(\dfrac{N_{lt}}{N_{l0}} \right) \left(\dfrac{y_{lt}}{y_{l0}} \right)^{\eta_{il}}$ (19)

Producer benefit from a policy change:

The expected change in producers' surplus[d]: $B_{lt}^P = E \{ S_{lt}^{New} - S_{lt}^{Ref} \}$ (20)

Where: $S_{lt} = \sum_i (q_{ilt} p_{ilt}^P - C_{ilt})$ (21)

Ex post producer price: $p_{ilt}^P = p_{ilt} (p_{ilt}^P / p_{ilt}^C)$ (22)

Production cost: $C_{ilt} = \displaystyle\int_{k_{ilt}}^{q_{ilt}} p_{ilt}^* \, dq_{ilt}$ (23)

Planned (expected) production[e]: $\hat{q}_{ilt} = q_{ilt} \, e^{-\varepsilon_{ilt}}$ (24)

Planning prices to achieve expected output q_{lt} (linear approximation): $p_{lt}^* = B_l^{-1} (g_{lt} - f_l)$ (25)

Linear supply response matrix: $B_l = \{ b_{ij} \}_l = \{ (b_{1ijl} + b_{2ijl} + b_{3ijl}) \, q_{ilt}^T / \bar{p}_{jl0}^P \}$ (26)

Linear production intercept: $f_{il} = q_{ilt}^T [1 - \sum_j^m (b_{1ijl} + b_{2ijl} + b_{3ijl})]$ (27)

Lower integration bound: $k_{ilt} = \text{Max} \{ 0 , f_{il} + \sum_{j \neq i} b_{ijl} p_{jlt}^* \}$ (28)

Government revenue benefit from a policy change:

Expected change in net revenue from taxes and subsidies: $B_{lt}^G = E \{ G_{lt}^{New} - G_{lt}^{Ref} \}$ (29)

Where: $G_{lt} = \sum_{i \in M} G_{ilt} + \sum_{i \in X} G_{ilt}$ (30)

Appendix A2   (continued)

Net revenue on imported
commodities:
$$G_{i\ell t} = m_{i\ell t} (P_{i\ell t} - x_\ell h_{i\ell} P_{it}) + q_{i\ell t} (P_{i\ell t} - P_{i\ell t}^P) \qquad (31)$$

Net revenue on exported
commodities:
$$G_{i\ell t} = - m_{i\ell t} (x_\ell h_{i\ell} P_{it} - P_{i\ell t}^P) + c_{i\ell t} (P_{i\ell t} - P_{i\ell t}^P) \qquad (32)$$

Benefit to holders of grain stocks of a policy change:

Expected change in profits:
$$B_{\ell t}^S = E \{ \sum_i^m (R_{i\ell t}^{New} - R_{i\ell t}^{Ref}) \} \qquad (33)$$

Intra-year
profit on i:
$$R_{i\ell t} = x_\ell h_{i\ell} P_{it} (s_{it-1} - s_{it}) - \theta_\ell (s_{i\ell t} / \bar{s}_{i\ell t-1}) s_{i\ell t} \qquad (34)$$

Total welfare impact of a policy change:

The sum of the component benefits:
$$W_{\ell t} = B_{\ell t}^C + B_{\ell t}^P + B_{\ell t}^G + B_{\ell t}^S \qquad (35)$$

Net trading aggregates:
$$W_{\ell t} = E \{ S_{\ell t}^{New} - S_{\ell t}^{Ref} \} \qquad (36)$$

Where $S_{\ell t}$ is the area under the single-
commodity excess demand curve:
$$S_{\ell t} = \frac{1}{2} \sum_i^m (m_{i\ell t}^2 / b_{i\ell}) \qquad (37)$$

Variables not defined in Table A1:

$c_{\ell t}$ = an m-component vector of total consumption levels (direct consumption plus consumption
by livestock) in country ℓ in year t.

$q_{\ell t}$ = an m-component vector of production levels in country ℓ in year t.

$P_{\ell t}$ = an m-component vector of consumer prices in country ℓ and year t.

$\varepsilon_{\ell t}$ = an m-component vector of random disturbances to production in country ℓ and year t.
These are derived as the exact additive equivalents of the multiplicative disturbances
applied to equation (3) of Table A1.

$b_{i\ell}$ = the slope of the linear target excess demand function for commodity i of net-trading
aggregate ℓ.

[a] In this non-linear, multivariate and stochastic model, the Equivalent Variation (EV) is estimated
using a linear approximation. Compensated demand elasticities are evaluated at the endogenous prices,
$P_{\ell t}$, and used to assemble the local Slutsky Matrix of compensated demand coefficients. A linear,
utility-constant demand function is then drawn through ($P_{\ell t}, c_{\ell t}$) and the EV is measured relative to the
base period prices, $P_{\ell 0}$ (which are the same for every simulation). The consumer benefit, associated
with some New set of simulations which incorporate a policy change, is then the expected value of the
New EV (relative to the base period prices, $P_{\ell 0}$) minus the expected value of the Reference EV (also
evaluated relative to the base period prices). This indirect method of calculating the consumer
benefit helps to minimize the errors associated with the linear approximation. Note also the embedded
assumption that consumers are risk neutral.

[b] A_ℓ excludes the terms linking grain consumption to meat prices since these represent the consumption
behaviour of the livestock sector and only direct consumption parameters are relevant here.

[c] $c_{\ell t}^u$ excludes the consumption of grain by livestock. This is assumed to make up a fixed proportion of
coarse grain consumption, set separately for each country.

[d] Producer surplus is evaluated as the difference between a posteriori revenue at the endogenous producer
prices and production levels ($P_{\ell t}, q_{\ell t}$) and the cost associated with planned production.

[e] Note that planned production differs from the Nerlovian target production of equation (2). It is the
level of production which would be expected to occur in the absence of the random disturbance introduced
in equation (3).

Appendix A3   Illustration of Impact of Trade Liberalization on Welfare

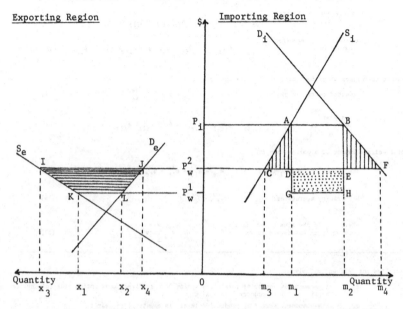

Exporting Region   Importing Region

In the above figure, the world is represented by a highly protectionist importing region and a free trade exporting region. The world price is P_w^1 and the domestic price in the importing region is P_i. The wedge between the high domestic price and the low world price is maintained by a variable levy on imports which raises revenue equal to the area ABGH. With free trade, the world price rises to P_w^2 and imports increase from $m_1 m_2$ to $m_3 m_4$. The resultant welfare changes in the exporting region derives solely from the terms of trade effect, whereas the welfare impacts in the importing region are attributable to both terms of trade effects and the removal of protection. The welfare impacts of trade liberalization are summarised below.

Welfare Change	Importing region	Exporting region
Consumer surplus	P_w^2 FBP$_i$	$-P_w^1$ LJP$_w^2$
Producer surplus	$-P_w^2$ CAP$_i$	P_w^1 KIP$_w^2$
Government revenue	$-$GABH	$-$
Net Welfare	ADC + BEF $-$ GDEH	LKIJ

A GENERAL EQUILIBRIUM MODEL OF TAXATION THAT USES MICRO-UNIT
DATA: WITH AN APPLICATION TO THE IMPACT OF INSTITUTING A
FLAT-RATE INCOME TAX

Joel Slemrod
University of Minnesota and the National Bureau of Economic
Research

I INTRODUCTION

In recent years, micro-unit data files with detailed information on income sources and taxes have become increasingly available. Also
in the last decade computable general equilibrium models of the effects
of taxation have grown in both detail and sophistication. The primary
goal of the research described here is to begin to develop a methodology
for integrating the information from micro-unit data files into the framework of a general equilibrium model of taxation. It is hoped that this
integration will be valuable for providing a detailed understanding of the
impact of taxation, especially the taxation of capital income. In order
to illustrate this value, the methodology is applied to a study of the
economic impact of instituting a flat-rate income tax system.

The potential contribution of micro-unit data sets to research
in taxation has been amply demonstrated in a number of applications.
Several different files have been the basis of econometric investigations
of the responsiveness of particular aspects of behavior to changes in the
tax system. Among the aspects studied so far have been charitable contributions, capital gains realizations, demand for housing, and labor supply.
Micro-unit data have also been used to provide detailed accounts of the
impact of a particular aspect of the tax law, or the probable impact of a
potential change in it. For example, the files have been applied to
capital gains taxation and the integration of the corporate and personal
income tax systems. Often the results of an econometric analysis are
used to simulate behavioral responses to a particular policy.

The insights to be gained from a general equilibrium analysis
of taxation have also been well documented.[1] Harberger's (1962, 1966)
original one-consumer, two-sector model has been extended to include many
consumer groups and many sectors by the work of Shoven and Whalley and
their collaborators. The interaction between taxation and financial

221

behavior has recently been introduced into general equilibrium modeling
by Slemrod (1980, 1982, 1983). All previous research efforts have been
based on representative households standing in for highly aggregated
classes of individuals, and usually feature no more than 20 different
classes, and often less than that.[2] These classes are distinguished by
their endowment of capital and labor in efficiency units, family size,
preferences concerning consumption goods, and possibly also their preferences concerning risk and their tax rates.

In this paper we propose to replace that state-of-the-art
procedure of considering a small number of representative households,
each of which can represent up to several million actual households, with
a procedure where the number of households is expanded to a much higher
order of magnitude. In particular, the number of representative households is expanded toward the sample size of a micro-unit data set, which
may go as high as over 90,000 households, in the case of the U.S. Treasury
Tax File. In what follows I first consider the incremental benefits of
such a procedure and then the incremental costs.

The most obvious benefit from extensive further disaggregation
is that the richness of statements about the distributional impact of a
particular policy can be greatly increased. In the current models, a
household with income of $7500 may represent all households in the $5000-
$10,000 range. The welfare impact of a policy on the household with
$7500 of income may be an inaccurate indicator of the impact on a $5000
income or a $10,000 income household. In a micro-unit data set there are
likely to be households with income within a few dollars of $5000 and
$10,000, so the welfare impact on them need not be extrapolated from the
impact on a $7500 income household.

A more important advantage of using a micro-unit data base is
that it recognizes the fact that there is a joint distribution of the
household parameters of endowment and tastes. Thus, within what the
current models refer to as "income class," there are households with very
different capital-labor ratios, very different consumption patterns, and
very different portfolios. In the event of such variation, the state-of-
the-art methodology might conclude that policy change X would cause a
dollar-equivalent welfare increase of $Y to group Z, but in fact there is
a distribution of welfare effects whose mean is approximately $Y. The
dispersion of the distribution of welfare losses is a relevant and perhaps
critical piece of information to policymakers contemplating a tax reform.[3]

This information is certainly the most important input to any discussion
of the horizontal equity implications of a policy. That is, it will
allow us to investigate to what extent a policy has greatly varying welfare effects on households of essentially the same means.

This issue of the distribution of impact within an income
class is especially interesting in the context of a general equilibrium
model with financial behavior (GEFB). The key additional household characteristics that enter a GEFB model are the degree of risk aversion, which
affects portfolio choice, and the housing tenure status. Intuition suggests that there is as much, if not more, variation in these areas than
in, for example, tastes among broad aggregates of consumption goods.

There are two principal incremental costs from using a micro-
unit data base for general equilibrium tax analysis. The first and most
obvious is the additional computational expense involved. Even with the
most efficient machine currently available, the computational expense of
calculating equilibrium is not trivial. However, further technological
advances in computational efficiency are likely to make this a less
critical consideration.

Another issue arises due to the tremendous informational
requirements of a general equilibrium analysis with micro-unit data.
Current models already require a large amount of information and parameterization. In particular, for each representative household we require
the endowment of capital and labor in efficiency units, and the household's equilibrium bundle of goods, including labor supply. Because in
the baseline equilibrium the observed data must be the outcome of a consumer optimization problem, the usual procedure is to assume a particular
functional form for the utility function and then solve "backwards" for
the function's parameters which would generate the observed data as the
optimal consumer choice. The basic approach is the same when the data
base is actual household data rather than stylized households which represent an average of many households. The GEFB model, though, also
requires information on the portfolios of households. However, the data
set which has detailed information on income sources and the tax situation of households, the Treasury Tax File, has only indirect information
about asset holdings. In particular, it has the flow of annual capital
income for some kinds of income, such as shares of stock, and no information at all about other assets such as tax-exempt bonds and pension
wealth. Thus, one critical set of data must be imputed to the households.

Once these imputations are made, the parameters of the utility function
can be solved backwards so as to be consistent with the imputations.
However, the preference parameters are only as accurate as the data imputations.

The earlier work of Pechman & Okner (1974) employed an approach
which is similar to that of this project, although the goal (to study the
personal incidence of the total U.S. tax system) was somewhat different.
Their results were based on a micro-unit data file of a sample of 72,000
families. This study was distinguished by the fact that in developing its
assumptions about the incidence of particular taxes, it attempted to take
seriously modern theoretical developments in incidence analysis, which are
based on general equilibrium considerations. Specifically, one variant of
incidence assumptions allocated all taxes on capital income, regardless of
the statutory bearer, to property income earners in general. This is an
incidence story that would emerge from a general equilibrium analysis
assuming perfect mobility of capital among sectors, price flexibility,
and perfect competition. A second variant of assumptions allocated the
burden of the corporate income tax to stockholders in proportion to the
dividends they received, and allocated the burden of the property tax on
dwellings in proportion to the cash on imputed rents of households. These
incidence assumptions are consistent with the view that capital is immobile among various uses.

The incidence assumptions used by Pechman & Okner are not,
however, derived from an explicit theoretical framework, and thus can be
internally inconsistent. For example, in discussing the incidence of the
corporation income tax, they state ". . .assuming that the total supply of
saving is fixed, the earnings of labor remain unchanged, and capital bears
the entire tax" (p. 31). This statement is not, in general, correct
within the context of the Harberger model, where the effect of a partial
capital income tax on the wage rate need not be zero, and depends on the
relative factor intensities of production in the two sectors, the two
elasticities of substitution, and the demand substitutability.

There is no possibility of internal inconsistency when an
analysis of the impact of taxes is carried out within the context of an
explicit general equilibrium model, where the vector of prices assures
supply and demand are equal for each market. The aim of this paper is to
utilize the richness of the micro-unit data, as did Pechman & Okner,
within the context of such a general equilibrium model of the effects of

taxation. Before we proceed to lay out this model, we describe our
approach to the imputation of some important data that is absent from our
data file; this is done in Section II. Section III sets out the procedure
for recovering the parameters of the expected utility function that are
consistent with the household data, actual and imputed. In Section IV,
we describe the general equilibrium model in which the micro-unit household data is imbedded, and describe the baseline equilibrium solution.
The model is illustrated in Section V by simulating the impact of replacing the current U.S. income tax with a flat-rate system which yields the
same revenue. Some concluding thoughts are offered in Section VI.

II   IMPUTATION OF HOUSEHOLD INFORMATION

Each year the Internal Revenue Service (IRS) draws a large
stratified random sample of income tax returns and makes the information
publicly available. Thus, for each sample taxpaying unit, we have
detailed information on the sources of income, the amounts and kinds of
deductions and exemptions taken, marital status, state of residence,
whether any household member is over 65 years of age, and other demographic information. Using a tax calculator developed at the National
Bureau of Economic Research, we can calculate from this information the
marginal tax rate for each household. The data base for this study is a
random subsample of 459 taxpaying units taken from the IRS sample for
1977.

Unfortunately, no direct information about household portfolios is available on this data set. One approach to remedying this
absence is to merge the tax return information with another data set that
does have this information; an exact match would be ideal, but a synthetic
match would be acceptable. This was not pursued, though, because there
is no single micro-unit file which contains up-to-date information on
households' complete pattern of wealth holdings. The Federal Reserve
Board's Survey of Financial Characteristics of Consumers does have such
information, but it refers to year-end 1962 and thus is too out-of-date
to be a candidate for a merge with the tax return sample.

The approach taken in this paper is to impute the household
portfolios. The imputation procedures utilize the information on the tax
file containing capital income flows and other household data that con-
veys information about wealth holdings. These imputations also utilize
econometric evidence about the determinants of wealth holdings, where

relevant.   In addition, the procedures are constrained to be consistent
with known aggregate information about wealth holdings, which is in some
cases disaggregated by income class.   The goal is to construct a distribution of wealth holdings that represents the actual U.S. economy of 1977.

As is presented in detail in Section III, in the general equilibrium model household portfolio choice is based on an expected utility-
maximizing framework that includes a portfolio of five assets.   The assets
are corporate equity, owner-occupied housing, other residential capital,
tax-free bonds, and net taxable interest-bearing instruments.   For the
purposes of imputation the last category will be split into several assets
and liabilities components.   Specifically, holdings of taxable bonds,
demand deposits, savings deposits, and home mortgage liabilities will be
imputed separately.   Specific procedures for imputing each category of
asset will now be outlined.

II.A   Corporate equity

The tax file contains the dollar value of dividends received
for each taxpaying unit.   If the dividend-price ratio was identical for
all shares, it would be a trivial matter to capitalize the dividend flow
into asset value.   Of course, the dividend-price ratio does vary among
different stocks.   In fact, it is likely that that ratio varies systematically with the tax situation of the household.   Shares of corporations
that retain a relatively large portion of their earnings would be preferred by relatively high tax bracket individuals.   Ignoring this systematic relationship by applying a constant capitalization rate to all
households' dividends would, therefore, underestimate the concentration
of stockholdings among the highest income earners, because income is
positively correlated with tax rate.

In order to avoid this bias, we utilize the evidence collected
by Blume et al. (1974) on the observed dividend-price ratios by income
class in 1970.   Two adjustments to their published figures are made.
First, the income brackets used by Blume et al. are indexed to represent
the same real income brackets in 1977.   Second, each household's imputed
stockholdings are adjusted proportionately so that the imputed aggregate
equals the Flow of Funds entry for total corporate equity held by individuals in 1977.[4]

II.B Owner-occupied housing

II.B.1. Tenure choice. The first step in imputing the value of owner-occupied housing to households is to decide which taxpayers own a home. Non-owners will, of course, be assigned zero assets in this category.

In 1977, approximately one-half of all homeowners itemized their deductions. Identifying these homeowners is fairly straightforward. If the home mortgage interest and/or property tax deduction is present, then the household is considered to be a homeowner. This procedure relies on two assumptions. The first is that practically every homeowner pays some mortgage interest or property tax. The second is that practically all property taxes reported on Schedule A of Form 1040 (itemized deductions) correspond to homes. Property taxes on other assets, such as business or rental capital, are generally reported in other places, such as in the expenses section of Schedules C and E (which pertain to business and rental incomes, respectively).

A different procedure is necessary to identify those homeowning households that did not itemize their deductions, presumably due to insufficient mortgage interest, property tax, and other itemizable deductions. The total number of owner-occupied houses is listed by income class in the Census of Housing. Subtracting the number found to be owned by itemizers will yield the number of nonitemizing families that must have owned a house. Ownership will be assigned to this number of nonitemizing returns on the basis of estimated probabilities of ownership. Recently, much valuable work has been done on estimating the demand for housing, including the tenure choice decision, of which Rosen (1979 b) is one example. Rosen used cross-section data to estimate the probability that a family will be an owner-occupier. The tax file contains information on most of the explanatory variables used by Rosen, including income, tax price, number of dependents, and whether the head of household is elderly. Other variables such as race, sex, and other age categories are not available. Using Rosen's regression results, we estimate the probability of a household owning housing using the former set of variables, with the latter set subsumed into the constant term. As mentioned above, we can calculate how many nonitemizers owned a house in 1977; by extension, we know what percentage of nonitemizers owned. The estimated probabilities will be adjusted proportionately so that their average equals this percentage. Finally, whether any particular nonitemizing household owns housing is determined using a random process that has the (corrected) estimated probability of ownership.

II.B.2. <u>Value of owner-occupied housing</u>. The next step is to impute the value of housing held by the owners. Again, Rosen's econometric analysis forms the basis of our procedure. He estimated quantity of housing, using the same variables as in the tenure choice equation. Thus, we can predict the value of housing using the variables on which we have information, and include a constant term to reflect the others.

For nonitemizers, this procedure is the only one we can use. For itemizers, however, there is an alternative imputation procedure suggested by Hendershott & Slemrod (1983). The idea is that property tax payments can provide an estimate of house value. If the effective property tax rate were known for each household's municipality, tax payments could be capitalized into an accurate estimate of house value. Such information is not available. However, the state of residence of each household is known, and by utilizing information on statewide average effective property tax rates,[5] we can (with some unavoidable error) capitalize property tax payments into house value. Lacking any obvious way to combine both sources of information about the house value of itemizing households, the imputed value is the simple average of the two. For nonitemizers, the first-mentioned measure is the imputed value. All imputations are then adjusted proportionately so that the imputed aggregate value of housing stock matches the aggregate net value of owner-occupied housing for 1977, reported in Musgrave (1981).

II.C <u>Net taxable "bonds"</u>

Although, in reality, there are innumerable different kinds of taxable financial instruments with fixed nominal return, in the general equilibrium model used here all such assets are aggregated into a category called "bonds." Nevertheless, in the imputation stage it seems valuable to separately estimate the holdings of a few important categories of assets and liabilities, and then sum their values to arrive at a value of net taxable "bond" holdings.

II.C.1. <u>Bonds, time deposits, and demand deposits</u>. For each household, the tax file provides a value for interest received. This figure includes interest on securities that earn the current market rate of interest and

also interest on time deposits, which in 1977 earned a lower-than-market
rate of return. There is no information on zero-yielding demand deposits,
whose return presumably comes in the form of economizing of transaction
costs that holding wealth in this form allows. Survey evidence suggests
that the ratio of time and demand deposits to short- and long-term bond
holdings is larger for lower income households, and that the former is a
major portion of their asset holdings. Thus, ignoring these low-yielding
assets will cause an overestimation of the inequality in the distribution
of wealth. The procedure outlined below is designed to avoid this error.

       Using survey data, we estimate the mean and standard deviation
of the holding of time and demand deposits by income class. Then, assuming that these holdings are distributed according to a truncated (at zero)
normal distribution, we generate imputed values for each household by
drawing from a random normal distribution of the appropriate mean and
variance, and setting negative values to zero. Multiplying the estimated
deposits by the average 1977 rate of interest on these accounts yields an
estimate for the interest received on time deposits. Then the difference
(if positive) between the reported interest and the interest received on
time deposits provides an estimate of interest received on securities
that yield the market return. Using an average maturity for bonds held
by households, we can calculate the real value of the assets that would
correspond to this flow of interest receipts. Thus, this procedure yields
separate values for demand deposits, time deposits, and bond holdings.[6]
These values are then summed to give the imputed value for taxable "bond"
assets.

II.C.2. <u>Home mortgage debt</u>. For households that itemize their deductions,
the tax file contains information on the amount of mortgage interest paid.
The approach[7] to imputing the real value of itemizers' mortgage debt from
current mortgage payments relies on the institutional fact that, in 1977,
most outstanding mortgages were of a standard form: fixed payment and a
30-year maturity. We assume that all mortgages were of this type and that
the ratio of the original loan to the house value was uniformly 0.80.
Looking backward in time from 1977, an outstanding mortgage could have
been issued any time between 1947 and 1977. Using the average rate of
interest on mortgages issued in any of these years, the ratio of the
remaining principal to the original value of the house can be calculated.
If we assume that all house values have increased by the rate of price

increase in the average house, we can calculate the ratio of the outstanding principal to the current house value for a mortgage issued in any year
from 1947 to 1977. Multiplying this by the interest rate at issue yields
the ratio of current interest payments to current house value. It turns
out, though this need not be true, that the relationship between time of
issue and the ratio of current interest payments to current house value is
virtually monotonic. Because of this monotonicity, for any observed ratio
of interest payments to house value, we can determine the time to maturity
of the outstanding mortgage. Knowing the time to maturity, interest rate
at issue, and the long-term interest rate in 1977 is sufficient information to calculate the real value of the remaining mortgage debt. In sum,
this procedure uses the imputed house value and known mortgage interest
payments to generate a value for mortgage debt.

No information on mortgage payments by nonitemizing households
is available. For these households, the sum of mortgage payments and all
other itemizable deductions is probably less than the applicable standard
deduction.[8] This ensures that any outstanding mortgage is not large. We
assume that the real value of the mortgage liability of nonitemizers is
zero.

II.C.3. Total "bond" holdings. The imputed figure for total net taxable
bonds is simply the sum of the imputed values of demand deposits, time
deposits, and bonds, minus the imputed real value of mortgage debt.

II.D   Non-owner-occupied residential capital

All tax returns in the sample include a value for net rent
received. A straightforward procedure for obtaining the value of non-
owner-occupied residential capital (real estate) is to use a common capitalization rate to convert these flows into stocks. A natural capitalization rate to choose is one that generates an aggregate imputed stock
equal to the estimated aggregate from Musgrave (1981). A serious obstacle
becomes immediately apparent, though. In 1977, almost as many returns
(2.43 million) reported a net loss on rental property as reported a net
gain (2.60 million). These negative flows cannot be sensibly converted
into negative asset holdings. The approach taken here is to capitalize
the absolute value of reported rental income, on the grounds that the
generation of losses requires capital in proportion to the reported loss.
This procedure is unsatisfactory, but no superior procedure is apparent.

II.E Tax-exempt bonds

No information on the income from tax-exempt bonds is available on the tax file. Survey evidence from the 1962 Survey of Financial
Characteristics of Consumers indicates that, as expected, the predominance
of these assets increases with income. This survey also indicates that
not all high income households hold tax-exempt bonds and the extent of
holdings varies greatly. In the light of this evidence, one possible
imputation procedure is to estimate a mean and variance of tax-exempt
bonds by income class and then randomly draw holdings for households.
This is essentially the procedure used for imputing demand and time
deposits.

This procedure, though, seems to be inadequate in this context for the following reason. It is likely that if a household in a
high tax bracket does not hold tax-exempt bonds, then it is holding some
alternative tax-preferred asset. Thus, to assume that households in this
position are not taking advantage of the tax "shelter" would be incorrect.
A more satisfactory approach is to assume that all households take advantage of tax-preferred assets to the extent it is worthwhile. This suggests an approach to the imputation of these assets which is different
from those already described. We assume that the household holds that
amount of tax-exempt bonds that would be predicted by the maximization of
a particular expected utility function for given market rates of return,
the household's tax rate, and the appropriate wealth and income constraints. This procedure is described in detail in Section III.

II.F Labor supply

Each household is assumed to supply labor completely inelastically. One natural measure of a household's labor supply in efficiency
units is its wage and salary income, which is known for each household.[9]
This procedure is not, however, adopted here. Because the portfolio
imputation procedures do not ensure that imputed taxable property income
equals actual reported property income subject to tax, using actual wage
and salary income as a measure of labor supply implies that imputed taxable income will be different from actual taxable income. Furthermore,
tax liability in the baseline equilibrium will be different from actual
tax liability. Because the change in the distribution of tax liability
is one of the critical objects of investigation in this study, we have
imputed labor supply as the residual between actual taxable income and

imputed taxable property income plus exemptions and deductions. The virtue of this procedure is that it guarantees that the baseline equilibrium
distribution of tax liability is identical to that observed in 1977 while
at the same time retaining in the baseline equilibrium the actual distribution of deductions and exemptions. If actual wage and salary income
were used as the measure of labor supply, either the tax liability (and
tax rate) or the amount of deductions and exemptions would have to be
imputed as a residual. Because both of these last two are critical to the
impact of instituting the flat-rate tax and the distribution of labor
income (in this model with inelastic labor supply) is not, it was decided
to calculate the latter as a residual. It is reassuring that the total
and distribution of imputed labor supply are not drastically different
from the observed distribution of labor income in 1977.

II.G Rental housing services

For households that do not own their own housing, a value for
rental housing services consumed is needed. Our procedure for imputing
this value is to utilize the regression equation for rental housing estimated by Rosen (1979 b)[10] in a manner analogous to that described above for
owner-occupied housing. As with owner-occupied housing, the predicted
value is adjusted proportionately to yield an aggregate value consistent
with the observed U.S. total in 1977.

III PORTFOLIOS AND EXPECTED UTILITY MAXIMIZATION

III.A An expected utility maximization framework

At this stage, each taxpaying unit has assigned to it a value
of wealth as well as a division of wealth into five net asset categories.
We will assume that this portfolio maximizes expected utility subject to
the household's income constraint and constraint on total wealth. We can
write these constraints as:

$$C_i = P_L L_i + r_B B_i + r_E E_i + r_M M_i + r_N N_i - \delta_H H_i - \pi W_i$$

$$- TAX(P_L L_i + r_B B_i + \gamma r_E E_i + r_N N_i - DEDEX_i) + TRAN_i \quad (3.1)$$

$$W_i = B_i + E_i + M_i + N_i + H_i \quad (3.2)$$

where the notation is defined as follows:

C	:	expected consumption of non-housing good
P_L	:	wage rate
L	:	labor supply
r_B	:	nominal rate of return to taxable bonds
B	:	taxable bond holdings
r_E	:	expected nominal rate of return to equity
E	:	equity holdings
r_M	:	expected nominal rate of return to tax-exempt bonds
M	:	tax-exempt bond holdings
r_N	:	expected nominal rate of return to real estate
N	:	real estate holdings
δ_H	:	rate of depreciation of housing capital
H	:	owner-occupied housing
W	:	total wealth
π	:	fully anticipated rate of inflation
TAX	:	individual income tax function
γ	:	fraction of equity income subject to individual income tax
DEDEX	:	adjustments, exemptions, and deductions from gross income to taxable income
TRAN	:	transfer received from the government

In expression (3.1), consumption of the composite corporate good is equal to labor income plus nominal property income minus depreciation on owner-occupied housing, the decline in the real value of assets due to inflation, and tax liability, plus transfers received from the government. Tax liability is written as a function of taxable income, which is equal to labor income, plus taxable property income minus allowable deductions and exemptions. Income from tax-exempt bonds is not included in taxable income, and only a fraction of the income from equity is included, due to the preferential tax treatment of capital gains.

In order to simplify the consumer's problem, we assume that expected utility can be written as a function of the expected consumption of the two types of goods, housing services and a non-housing composite good, and the riskiness of the income flow, measured by its variance.[11] This assumption allows us to write down relatively simple expressions for consumption and asset demands that depend on wealth, income, relative prices, and assets' expected returns and after-tax riskiness.

We further simplify by imposing a particular form on the
expected utility function, one in which the risk term is separable from
the two expected consumption terms and which implies constant relative
risk aversion. Specifically, we assume that

$$EU_i = U_i(C_i, H_i) - \frac{\beta_i R_i}{2W_i} \qquad (3.3)$$

where β_i is a measure of relative risk aversion and R_i is the after-tax
variance of the income stream. In (3.3) and hereafter it is assumed that
one unit of housing capital produces one unit of housing services. For
the U_i function, we use the constant elasticity of substitution form. It
can be written as:

$$U_i = (\alpha_i C_i^{-\mu_i} + (1-\alpha_i)H_i^{-\mu_i})^{-1/\mu_i} \qquad (3.4)$$

where the elasticity of substitution between C_i and H_i is equal to $1/1+\mu_i$.

The variance of the income stream depends on the portfolio
chosen and also on the risk associated with the government transfer payment. On the assumption that the returns of the risky assets (E, M, and N)
are uncorrelated, the variance of the household's income stream can be
approximated by[12]

$$R_i = \sigma_E^2 (E_i(1-t_{Ei}) + s_i t_{EA} E)^2 + \sigma_M^2 M_i^2$$
$$+ \sigma_N^2 (N_i(1-t_{Ni}) + s_i t_{NA} N)^2 . \qquad (3.5)$$

In equation (3.5) the σ^2 terms refer to the before-personal-
tax variance of the return, s_i refers to the share of total transfers that
is paid to household i, and t_{EA} and t_{NA} are the average economy-wide tax
rates on equity and real estate income, respectively, weighted by holdings
of the assets.[13]

Collecting equations (3.1) through (3.5), we can write the
household's problem as:

$$\text{Maximize}_{C_i, H_i, E_i, B_i, M_i, N_i} (\alpha_i C_i^{-\mu_i} + (1-\alpha_i)H_i^{-\mu_i})^{-1/\mu_i} - \frac{\beta_i R_i}{2W_i} \qquad (3.6)$$

subject to

$$C_i = P_L L_i + r_B B_i + r_M M_i + r_N N_i - \delta_H H_i - \pi W_i$$
$$- TAX(p_L L_i + r_B B_i + \gamma r_E E_i + r_N N_i - DEDEX_i) + TRAN_i \qquad (3.7)$$
$$W_i = B_i + E_i + M_i + N_i + H_i \qquad (3.8)$$

$$R_i = \sigma_E^2 \, (E_i(1-t_{Ei}) + s_i t_{EA} E)^2 + \sigma_M^2 M_i^2$$
$$+ \sigma_N^2 \, (N_i(1-t_{Ni}) + s_i t_{NA} N)^2 \qquad (3.9)$$

$$M_i \geq 0 \qquad\qquad\qquad\qquad\qquad\qquad\qquad (3.10)$$

The first-order conditions of this maximization problem yield closed-form expressions for all the choice variables. As they stand, though, these expressions have certain properties that make them inadequate for our current purpose, which is to have the predicted optimal consumer choices be consistent with the imputed portfolios.

The first undesirable property of this modeling as it stands is that, in order to consume housing services, the household must own its own housing. In fact, only about 65% of households are owner-occupiers. In order to generate rental as well as owner-occupying, we assume that housing services obtained by rental (HR) are not necessarily perfectly substitutable for services obtained from owned housing (HO). The rate of substitution may be thought to depend on such things as family size and expected mobility. Thus, we can rewrite the first part of the expected utility function of expression (3.4) as:

$$[\alpha_i C_i^{-\mu_i} + (1-\alpha_i)(\theta_i HO_i + (1-\theta_i) HR_i)^{-\mu_i}]^{-1/\mu_i} \qquad (3.4')$$

where θ_i is one if the household is an owner-occupier and zero otherwise. It is assumed that the two tenure possibilities are mutually exclusive.

The price of housing services will generally differ depending on which tenure choice is made. The rental price is the same for everyone, but the price of owner-occupied housing includes the foregone after-tax interest receipts, the magnitude of which depends on the applicable tax rate. A household will prefer renting to owning housing if the relative cost advantage of renting versus owning is not outweighed by its relative preference for owner-occupation.[14] We do not inquire into the determinants of tenure choice, and take the imputed classification to be exogenously fixed.[15]

The consumer problem now has a sequential nature. First the household decides whether to own or rent housing. Then the household decides how to apportion its wealth among the available assets, which includes owner-occupied housing, if in the first stage the choice was made to be an owner. The amount of owner-occupied housing chosen in this second stage depends on its price and on the household taste parameters, α_i and μ_i. The only additional changes to be made in the foregoing description of the consumer problem is that the left-hand side of (3.7) becomes $C_i + R \cdot HR_i$ where R is the rental price of housing, and the correct interpretation of H_i in expressions (3.7) and (3.8) is HO_i, the amount of owned housing.

The remaining asset demands depend on the pattern of after-tax expected returns, the riskiness of the asset, and the measure of risk aversion, which may vary from household to houshold. However, this single varying parameter is not sufficient to generate the observed variations in the mix of risky assets held by households in the same tax situation. Moreover, it cannot explain why so many households do not hold any of a particular asset.[16]

One explanation of household differences in the mix of risky assets held is that portfolio decisions are made on the basis of subjective expectations of the return to various assets, which differ from the objective return distribution and which vary among households. Those with high subjective estimates of the return to an asset are the ones who hold it. If the distribution of these subjective evaluations is not perfectly correlated among different assets, then there will be variation in the mix of assets held.

Another possible explanation of this phenomenon is that households differ in the objective rate of return that can be earned from a particular capital investment. This argument applies mostly to real estate and less to equity and tax-exempt bonds.[17] Some people's talents are more applicable to real estate management than others', and they earn a higher return than others. A part of that return is, strictly speaking, a return to the particular talents, but for some reason it cannot be marketed separately from ownership of real estate.

In sum, households facing the same opportunity set may choose different portfolios for a number of reasons: (i) they have different tastes for owner-occupied versus rental housing; (ii) if they are owner-occupiers, they have different tastes for housing services versus non-housing goods; (iii) they have different degrees of risk aversion; and (iv) they have different subjective or objective expectations of the returns to the available assets.

Our preferred procedure draws on both of the possible explanations discussed above. First, we assume that the subjective rate of return on equity does not vary from household to household. This leaves only one free parameter in the equity demand equation, the risk aversion

coefficient. Using the actual equity holdings, the equity demand equation
can be solved "backwards" to yield the household's implied risk-aversion
coefficient.[18] Second, we assume that households do differ in the rate of
return they can (or believe they can) earn on real estate holdings. Using
the risk-aversion coefficient derived from the equity equation, the real
estate demand equation is solved backwards to determine the adjustment to
the expected return to real estate that is consistent with the imputed
holding of each household. Finally, the asset demand equation for tax-
exempt securities, using the derived risk-aversion coefficient, is used to
generate an imputed holding for each household.

One aspect of this procedure makes it more difficult than
described above. In order to solve the equity demand equation backwards
for the risk-aversion coefficient, a value for W_i (household wealth) is
needed. This value is calculated as the sum of the imputed values of E_i,
H_i, B_i, M_i, and N_i. A problem arises since our procedure that generates
a value of M_i requires the value of β_i. Thus, the risk-aversion coefficient (β_i), M_i, and wealth (W_i) must be obtained through the backward
solution of a system of three simultaneous equations.

III.B Details of recovering preference parameters from household choices

We begin with the demand for housing and the composite corporate consumption good. From the first-order conditions of the constrained
expected utility maximization problem, the following housing demand function can be derived:

$$H_i = \frac{a_i y_i}{p_{Hi}^{\varepsilon_i} + a_i p_{Hi}} \tag{3.11}$$

where $a_i = (1-\alpha_i/\alpha_i)^{\varepsilon_i}$. In (3.11) ε_i is the elasticity of substitution
between housing and the composite good and p_{Hi} is the price of housing
services to household i, which is R for renters and $r_B(1-t_i) - \pi + \delta_H$ for
owner-occupiers. H_i is properly interpreted as HO_i for homeowners and
HR_i for renters. y_i is real income, equal to the right-hand side of
equation (3.7) plus the imputed rental value of owner-occupied housing.
We assume that the elasticity of substitution is the same for all households and equal to 0.5; this assumption enables us to solve (3.11) for a_i
for each household.

The demand function for C_i is:

$$C_i = \frac{y_i}{1 + a_i p_{Hi}^{1-\epsilon}} \quad . \tag{3.12}$$

Knowing a_i, y_i, and p_{Hi} allows us to compute C_i. C_i, H_i, and α_i are sufficient to calculate U_{Ci}, the marginal utility of an expected unit of consumption, which is needed in the backward solution of the risky asset demand equations.

The asset demand equations for equity and tax-exempt bonds, respectively, are:

$$E_i = \frac{W_i U_{Ci} [r_E(1-\gamma t_i) - r_B(1-t_i)]}{\beta_i \sigma_E^2 (1-\gamma t_i)^2} - \frac{s_i t_{EA} E}{(1-\gamma t_i)} \quad . \tag{3.13}$$

and

$$M_i = \max\left[\frac{W_i U_{Ci} [r_M - r_B(1-t_i)]}{\beta_i \sigma_M^2}, \; 0\right] \quad . \tag{3.14}$$

Note that the second term of (3.13) reflects the covariance between the transfer received from the government and the risk from equity returns. The form of (3.14) reflects the assumption made in (3.10) that households cannot borrow at the tax-exempt interest rate.

Since our goal is to calibrate the baseline equilibrium to represent a stylized U.S. economy of 1977, we set r_B, r_M, and r_E to be consistent with rates of return prevalent at that time; specifically, we use 0.09, 0.058, and 0.12, respectively. We assume that s_i, the share of government transfers that goes to household i, is equal to the ratio of the household's adjusted gross income to aggregate adjusted gross income. Thus Σs_i is equal to one. The value of $t_{EA} E$ is the weighted average marginal tax rate on equity income, which can be calculated from imputed equity holdings and households' marginal tax rates.

Finally, E_i, M_i, and W_i are linked through the wealth identity:

$$W_i = B_i + E_i + M_i + N_i + H_i \quad . \tag{3.15}$$

Given values of E_i, r_E, r_B, r_M, t_i, γ, s_i, $t_{EA}E$, σ_ϵ^2, and σ_M^2, the three equations (3.13), (3.14), and (3.15) can be solved for U_{Ci}/β_i, M_i, and W_i. Using the value of U_{Ci} obtained as described above and U_{Ci}/β_i, we can simply obtain β_i for each household.

The final step is to determine the subjective/talent factor
that generates the asset demand for real estate. The asset demand function is:

$$N_i = \frac{W_i U_{Ci} [r_N(1-t_i) - \zeta_i - r_B(1-t_i)]}{\beta_i \sigma_N^2 (1-t_i)^2} - \frac{s_i t_{NA} N}{(1-t_i)} \qquad (3.16)$$

where ζ_i is the subjective/talent factor. In (3.16), all values other
than r_N and ζ_i have already been determined. Calibrating the baseline
equilibrium to satisfy a particular value of r_N (in this case, $r_N = 0.10$)
then allows us to calculate ζ_i for each household.

IV INCORPORATION OF A GENERAL EQUILIBRIUM MODEL

Upon completion of the procedures outlined in Sections II and
III, the following information is available: all of the 1040 information,
total wealth, net holdings of each of five assets, and taste parameters
that generate the observed portfolios from an expected utility maximization problem. The aggregate portfolio holdings are consistent with known
information about economy-wide asset holdings.

The next step is to integrate this information with a general
equilibrium model of taxation. Essentially, several economy-wide parameters, such as the wage rate, and the yields on the menu of assets, are
determined endogenously by a system of equations that represent the equilibrium conditions. A general equilibrium model with endogenous financial
behavior (GEFB) has already been developed by Slemrod (1980, 1982, 1983).
This model is a generalization of the Harberger and Shoven-Whalley models,
which feature a simple capital market equilibrium condition that the
after-tax rates of return on all assets be equal. In the GEFB models,
this is replaced by explicit market-clearing relationships for each of
the several assets. Asset demands are derived from expected utility maximization by risk-averse individuals. Asset supplies may also be made
endogenous.

The goal in designing the general equilibrium model to be
used here was to construct a very simple model that would allow us to
analyze the major aspects of tax policy proposals, and highlight the usefulness of a micro-unit data base. The model has two real factor inputs,
capital (K) and labor (L), and two outputs, a composite corporate good
(C), and the services from housing, which may be either owner-occupied
(HO) or rented (HR). Corporate output is produced with a Cobb-Douglas

production function, and housing services require only capital input.
Labor is supplied inelastically. Without loss of generality, it is
assumed that one unit of housing capital produces one unit of housing
services.

In equilibrium all markets must clear. The market-clearing
conditions of this model are:

$$\Sigma_i E_i^* = (1-b)K_c \tag{4.1}$$

$$\Sigma_i N_i^* = \Sigma_i HR_i^* \tag{4.2}$$

$$\Sigma_i M_i^* = \bar{M} \tag{4.3}$$

where an asterisk superscript indicates that the value is the optimal
choice of the ith household given its income and wealth constraints.
Expression (4.1) says that the aggregate demand for equity must equal its
supply, which is equal to the corporate capital stock multiplied by the
exogenously specified corporate equity-capital ratio (1-b). Expression
(4.2) represents market-clearing for rental housing: the left-hand side
is the aggregate demand for rental housing capital, and the right-hand
side is the aggregate demand for rental housing services. The aggregate
demand for tax-exempt bonds is set equal to the exogenous supply, $\bar{M}$, in
(4.3). There is no explicit market for owner-occupied housing. Market-
clearing in the markets for bonds and the composite corporate consumption
good are assured by Walras' Law applied to the wealth constraint and
income constraint, respectively.

The federal government purchases no goods; it merely returns
its revenues, minus real payments on its debt, to households. Each household receives a fixed share, s_i, of whatever revenues are returned. We
write this relationship as:

$$TRAN_i = s_i(\Sigma_i TAX_i + TAXCORP - (r_M - \pi)\bar{M} - (r_\beta - \pi)\bar{B}_G) \tag{4.4}$$

where $\bar{B}_G$ is outstanding federal government debt, taken to be exogenous.

Corporation income is subject to a flat-rate corporate income
tax at rate t_c. Payments to debt-holders are deductible from taxable
income, as is a depreciation allowance, δ_c^*, per unit of capital. The
depreciation allowance differs from actual depreciation, δ_c, both because
of historic cost depreciation and because the schedule of allowances differs from true economic depreciation even in the absence of inflation.
Corporate capital income after corporation income tax is paid to either

bond holders or equity owners. Thus, we can write a corporate earnings
exhaustion equation in the form:

$$br_B + (1-b)r_E = f_k - \delta_c - t_c(f_k - br_B - \delta_c^*) + \pi \qquad (4.5)$$

where f_k is the gross earnings of a unit of capital. Total corporation
income tax revenues are described by:

$$TAXCORP = t_c K_c (f_k - br_B - \delta_c^*) . \qquad (4.6)$$

Competition in factor markets and in the market for rental
housing enforces the following relationships:

$$f_k = g \left[\frac{K_c}{\bar{L}} \right]^{g-1} \qquad (4.7)$$

$$P_L = (1-g) \left[\frac{K_c}{\bar{L}} \right]^{g} \qquad (4.8)$$

$$R = r_N + \delta_H - \pi . \qquad (4.9)$$

Equation (4.7) requires the gross earnings of capital to equal the gross
marginal product of capital; (4.8) requires the wage rate to be equal to
the marginal product of labor; (4.9) represents the relationship between
the rental price of housing and the return to real estate.

An equilibrium for this system is a vector of expected returns
for each asset, a price for rental housing services, and a portfolio allocation and consumption decision for each household, which implies aggregate totals for each asset (including the allocation of real capital).
Because all consumer decisions are based on expected utility maximization,
a value for expected utility can be calculated for each household.

V A SIMULATION EXPERIMENT: THE EFFECTS OF INSTITUTING A FLAT-
RATE INCOME TAX

V.A A description of the policy experiment

In this section the methodology is illustrated by simulating
the general equilibrium impact of replacing the 1977 income tax system
with a flat-rate income tax.[19] The flat-rate system that we consider has
a particularly simple form. It completely eliminates any personal exemptions, all currently itemizable deductions other than interest paid, and
the standard deduction. It retains the exempt status of interest on
state and local securities and the preferential treatment of capital
gains. Thus, the tax base becomes adjusted gross income minus interest
paid instead of (what in 1977 was called) taxable income. All of the tax

base, starting from the first dollar, is subject to a constant proportional tax rate. The tax rate is chosen so that the same amount of revenue is raised under the flat-rate system as is raised under the 1977
individual income tax system.[20]

Under this flat-rate income tax system, all households with
positive adjusted gross income face the same marginal and average tax
rate. The impact effect (before any general equilibrium considerations)
of such a tax change is to shift the burden of taxation from the wealthy
to the lower- and middle-income groups. However, because the extent to
which households under the current system take deductions varies widely,
the impact within income groups is not uniform. Households that took
extraordinary advantage of deductions under the old system may pay more
tax even though their average tax rate declines, because the base on which
tax is assessed goes up so much. This detailed look at the distributional
impact of taxation is the virtue of a micro-unit data base.

V.B The general equilibrium response

The general equilibrium effects of the switch to a flat-rate
tax are substantial, and tracing their impact provides some important
insights. The policy change induces large portfolio shifts. For those
high-income households that formerly had high marginal tax rates, the
lower tax rate makes tax-favored assets such as tax-exempt bonds and equi-
ties relatively less attractive. The relative attractiveness of taxable
debt and real estate increases. The marginal opportunity cost of owner-
occupied housing increases dramatically, causing a flight from this asset.
For those low-income households that face a higher marginal tax rate under
the flat-rate system, the financial response may also be large. These
households are not usually real estate owners or holders of tax-exempt
securities, so their portfolio reallocation is away from nominal debt
holdings toward owner-occupied housing and equity holdings. These shifts
in asset demand cause changes in the assets' pre-tax rates of return and
the cost of housing which, in turn, induce behavioral response. In this
paper we consider only the situation when the system comes to rest at a
new equilibrium position. Table 5.1 presents some summary statistics of
the two equilibria.

The flat-tax rate which generates the same revenue as the
baseline tax system is 0.152. With this tax rate, the tax disadvantage
of holding taxable bonds (and the tax advantage of borrowing) declines;

Table 5.1 Characteristics of the Baseline and Flat-Rate Tax Equilibria

	Baseline	Flat-Rate
Expected rate of return to taxable bonds	0.0900	0.0800
Expected rate of return to tax-exempt bonds	0.0580	0.0731
Expected rate of return to equity	0.1200	0.1221
Expected rate of return to real estate	0.1000	0.0898
Rental price of housing	0.0850	0.0748
Corporate capital stock ($ billion)	1388.3	1409.2
Owner-occupied housing stock ($ billion)	1320.0	1303.1
Rental housing stock ($ billion)	395.0	391.0
Individual income tax revenue ($ billion)	184.4	184.4

- -

(Fraction Held by Low-Income* Households)		
Total wealth	0.40	0.40
Taxable bonds	1.10	0.72
Tax-exempt bonds	0.02	0.40
Equity	0.09	0.33
Real estate	0.65	0.67
Owner-occupied housing	0.21	0.25

---

*Low-income is defined as having a real income in the baseline case of $20,000 or less.

the increased demand for this asset forces down its equilibrium nominal rate of return from 0.0900 to 0.0800. Conversely, the tax advantage derived from holding tax-exempt bonds drastically declines, inducing an increase in its expected nominal return from 0.0580 to 0.0731. Note that the premium earned by taxable bonds compared to tax-exempt bonds falls from 35.6% of the taxable bond yield to just 8.6%. The equilibrium expected return to equity, the income from which is partially tax-favored but not tax-exempt, does not change substantially.

The impact on the allocation of capital is not particularly large. As Table 5.1 indicates, the corporate capital stock increases by 1.4%, the owner-occupied housing stock decreases by 1.3%, and the rental housing stock decreases by 1.0%. That the change in capital allocation is not larger may seem surprising at first glance, because the opportunity cost of housing presumably increases greatly as a result of the decreased marginal tax rate. Two factors work against this intuition. First, the change to this flat-rate system does not reduce the marginal tax rate of all homeowners. In fact, it increases the marginal tax rate from zero to 0.152 for a large number of low-income homeowners, thus reducing their user cost. Second, the before-tax user cost of housing for all households declines as a result of the drop in the riskless rate of return from 0.0900 to 0.0800. This implies that the critical tax rate is 0.246: households that, in the baseline equilibrium, had a marginal tax rate lower than this experience a lower user cost; those households that had a tax rate above this face a higher cost under the flat-rate equilibrium. Though the aggregate owner-occupied housing stock is only slightly smaller under the flat-rate equilibrium, it is certainly more efficiently allocated because all households face the same user cost, while in the baseline equilibrium the price varied widely across households due to differences in marginal tax rates.[21] The fact that the rental housing stock declines even though its relative price falls is due to the decline in real income of the low-income households who tend to be renters of housing services.

Although the allocation of capital among sectors is not greatly altered, the distribution of asset ownership is very different. Table 5.1 documents the fact that, under the flat-rate system, asset ownership is much less segmented. Households with incomes less than $20,000 expand their share of equity ownership from 9% to 33%, and of tax-exempt bonds from 2% to 40%. High-income households that in the baseline equilibrium

held negative amounts of taxable bonds, own 28% of taxable bonds in the
flat-rate equilibrium. The low-income households expand their share of
owner-occupied housing from 21% to 25%.

V.C   The differential incidence of the flat-rate tax system

In this section we investigate the distributional impact of
instituting the flat-rate income tax system. For two important reasons,
this is not identical to simply investigating how the pattern of tax
liabilities changes. First, there are distributional implications to the
change in the pattern of rates of return and relative prices. For example, high-income households, which were previously induced to hold the
low-yielding but tax-exempt bonds, may now hold a portfolio with a higher
before-tax expected return but with a higher tax liability.[22] The second
reason arises because households in this economy are risk averse. A
change in the tax system may induce them to hold more or less risky portfolios. Thus, any change in tax paid may be offset by the change in the
amount of risk borne. For example, a portfolio shift away from tax-
preferred equity toward fully taxable bonds may be accompanied by larger
expected tax payments, but may be a preferred position due to the diminished riskiness of the income stream.

As is well known, there is no unambiguously superior measure
of change in welfare. In what follows, the measure used is the amount of
certain real income that would have to be given to the household in the
baseline equilibrium to provide a change in welfare equivalent to the
change caused by the switch to the flat-rate tax system. This amount is
expressed as a percentage of the household's certainty equivalent real
income in the baseline equilibrium.

The second column of Table 5.2 shows the average percentage
change in welfare by real income class.[23] As expected, the higher-income
households experience a welfare increase, while the lower-income households are, on average, worse off. The average percentage welfare gain
increases monotonically with real income. It should be kept in mind that
this is a comparative equilibrium analysis. Thus it does not account for
the capital gains and losses on existing assets that would undoubtedly
arise in the event of a move to a flat-rate income tax. For example, tax-
exempt bonds would decline in value, and their predominantly high-income
owners would suffer a capital loss.

Table 5.2 Average Percentage Welfare Change and Distribution of Welfare Change, by Real Income Class

Real Income	Average Percentage Change in Welfare	Percentage of Households Whose Change in Welfare is:							
		Less Than -10%	-5% to -10%	-5% to 0	0 to +5%	+5% to +10%	+10% to +15%	+15% to +20%	More Than +20%
$0 - $20,000	-5.5*	23.2	24.2	35.0	14.1	0	0	0	3.5
$20,000 - $50,000	+1.6	4.1	0	15.9	66.3	11.5	1.8	neg.	0.4
$50,000 - $100,000	+18.3	0	neg.	5.5	11.6	15.4	6.4	23.2	37.8
$100,000 - $200,000	+35.1	0	0	0	0	0.7	8.5	15.4	75.3
More Than $200,000	+59.2	0	0	2.1	1.1	0	0.5	0.5	95.7

*This figure does not include a small number of households whose baseline income was close to zero, yielding very large percentage changes in welfare.

neg. = negligible.

The last several columns of Table 5.2 provide information
about the dispersion of the distributional impact within real income
groups. For the $0-$20,000 income group, more than 80% of the households
are made worse off, though the extent of the welfare decline varies quite
a bit. Almost two-thirds of the households in the $20,000-$50,000 group
experience a slight (less than 5%) gain in welfare, although the other
one-third experience a wide range of impact. The dispersion among the
$50,000-$100,000 group is also very large, with nontrivial numbers of
households experiencing a welfare decline and also welfare increases in
excess of 20%. Above $100,000, the fraction of households with a welfare
increase less than 20% decreases, although even in the highest income
group some households would be worse off under this flat-rate system.

Because these simulation results rest on a very simple model
of the economy, which has neither labor supply nor savings responsiveness,
and also rest on a particular data imputation procedure and parameterization, the results should certainly not be taken literally as a guide to
policy decisions. Nevertheless, they do indicate the additional insights
that can be provided by using micro-unit data in the context of an explicit general equilibrium framework. The micro-unit data base certainly
allows a more disaggregated view of the impact of a policy change, and
the general equilibrium framework picks up the effect of changing prices
on the distributional impact of the switch to a flat-rate tax.

VI CONCLUSIONS

The purpose of this section is to assess the potential value
of a general equilibrium policy analysis that uses micro-unit data.
Because this paper is only a first step in the direction of a full-
fledged modeling effort, some of what is said will be speculation. As
it turns out, some of the speculation could have been made before this
research was begun. Hopefully, though, grappling with building such a
model has produced some additional insights of value.

As of this writing, the computational cost associated with
calculating an equilibrium with several thousand agents is not trivial.
However, within a few years, the computational cost will likely not be an
important constraint on the investigator. The enduring question, then,
is whether it is worth bothering with at all, whatever the cost. The
answer to this question, I think, depends on two factors: (i) the quality

of the micro-unit data base and (ii) the amount of confidence we can have
in the specification of the households' utility functions.

The issue of the quality of the data base is central to any
use of micro-unit data, be it general equilibrium or not. The investigator is using differences in household data to make predictions about the
differential impact of a policy change. The predicted dispersion in impact will be overestimated to the extent that the variations in data are
due to errors in measurement. This problem is especially relevant to this
study where several household variables of interest had to be imputed.
Clearly, the results stated here about the differential impact of policy
rest to some degree on the accuracy of these procedures. This concern,
though, also applies to the numerical general equilibrium models without
financial behavior, where among the key data needed are expenditures by
type of good. In highly disaggregated models which feature many different
goods, individual household expenditure data is the likely data base and
is undoubtedly subject to substantial measurement error problems.

The other critical factor in my assessment of the potential
of the technique explored in this paper has to do with the specification
of households' utility functions. The standard procedure for recovering
preference is to assume a particular functional form for the utility
function and also a critical parameter, which is assumed not to vary
across households. Then, the observed decisions of a household force the
remaining parameters to take certain values. In this paper, the constant
elasticity of substitution utility function is assumed to prevail with a
given elasticity of substitution. Observed decisions of households then
determine the remaining free parameter of the utility function. Similarly, a constant relative risk-aversion expected utility function is
assumed and the risk aversion parameter is determined by observed equity
holdings. The choice of different functional forms or the choice of a
different set of free parameters would clearly imply a different picture
about how tastes differ between individuals. For example, an alternative
assumption about how preferences vary is that all households have the
same share parameter (α_i) but differ in their elasticity of substitution
(ϵ_i) between housing services and the composite corporate good. The
values of ϵ_i could, as before, be recovered from observed consumption
decisions. The implications of the distribution of taste parameters for
the efficiency costs and the incidence of a tax change could, conceivably,

be quite different from the implications obtained using the other procedure for determining household utility functions. Because the detailed
incidence conclusions rest so heavily on the way in which household utility functions differ, the reliability of any predictions depends on reducing the arbitrariness of the specification of utility.

In spite of these caveats, the usefulness of the marriage of
micro-unit data sets with computable general equilibrium clearly is
unquestionable. The combination allows the analyst to trace the effects
of policy on the complete range of households in the economy and at the
same time can incorporate in a rigorous way the response of the economy
to policy changes.

NOTES

1. See the survey by Fullerton et al. (1983).

2. Although, see Piggott & Whalley (forthcoming), where 100
different consumer types are represented in the model.

3. King (1981, 1983) has stressed the importance to policy
decisions of disaggregated welfare analysis.

4. Note that no adjustment is made for the fact that divi-
dend/price ratios actually differ among households within an income class,
nor have we tried to account for any systematic underreporting of dividends. Details of this procedure are available from the author.

5. These data were obtained from the Advisory Commission of
Intergovernmental Relations (1974).

6. Details of this procedure are available from the author.

7. This procedure is a more general version of the approach
adopted in Hendershott & Slemrod (1983). Details are available from the
author.

8. Potential itemizable deductions may exceed the standard
deduction for a nonitemizing household if the household is unwilling to
spend the effort required to document the deductions.

9. A more accurate measure of labor supply would include
some portion of the net return to business, profession, farm, and partner-
ship activities as an approximation to the labor input share in self-
employment, plus employer contributions for social insurance programs and
other fringe benefits.

10. This regression equation is not included in the published
version of Rosen's paper, and was graciously provided by the author.

11. See, among others, Tobin (1958), Mossin (1969), and
Feldstein (1969), for discussion concerning the mean-variance framework
for portfolio choice.

12. Equation (3.5) is an approximation because it ignores
the fact that in a progressive tax system with less than perfect loss
offset provisions, the after-tax variance depends not just on the marginal tax rate, but on, in general, the entire schedule of tax rates.

13. See Slemrod (1982) for the derivation of this expression.

14. See Hendershott & Slemrod (1983) for a detailed discussion of the tax components of the relative price of owning, versus renting, housing.

15. Although, see Gordon & Slemrod (1983), for a numerical
general equilibrium model where the fraction of households that own housing is determined endogenously.

16. The theory predicts that as long as each risky asset
earns an expected premium over the riskless asset, all households should
hold some of each risky asset (in the case of zero covariances among
returns).

17. It would also seem applicable to capital in unincorpo-
rated enterprises, which is not treated in this study.

18. The method of "backwards" solution to obtain parameters
is discussed in Mansur & Whalley (1983).

19. The parameter values for this simulation experiment are
as follows: $\gamma = 0.625$, $\sigma_E^2 = 0.0304$, $\sigma_M^2 = 0.015$, $\sigma_N^2 = 0.009$, $b = 0.4$,
$\pi = 0.05$, $g = 0.15624$, $t_c = 0.46$, $\delta_H = 0.035$, $\delta_c = 0.036$, $\delta_c^* = 0.004$,
$\bar{M} = 3.566 \times 10^{11}$, $\bar{K} = 3.65 \times 10^{12}$, $\bar{B}_G = 1.904 \times 10^{11}$, $\bar{L} = 1.2181 \times 10^{12}$.
Space constraints do not allow a discussion here of the choice of these
values. See, though, Slemrod (1980) and also Gordon & Slemrod (1983) for
a treatment of related parameter choice issues.

20. In the new equilibrium, the revenue raised by the corporation income tax may, though, be different from that in the baseline
equilibrium.

21. See Slemrod (1982) for a discussion of the efficiency
cost of differing user costs for owner-occupied housing.

22. The low return earned on tax-preferred assets may be
thought of as an implicit tax. This point has been stressed by Galper &
Toder (1982).

23. The classification variable is real income in the baseline equilibrium situation.

REFERENCES

Advisory Commission on Intergovernmental Relations (1974). The Property
     Tax in a Changing Environment. Washington, D.C.

Blume, M., Crockett, J., & Friend, I. (1974). Stockownership in the
     United States: Characteristics and trends. Survey of Current
     Business.

Feldstein, M. (1969). The effects of taxation on risk-taking. J. of
     Political Economy, 77.

Fullerton, D., Shoven, J., & Whalley, J. (1983). General equilibrium
     analysis of U.S. taxation policy. In 1978 Compendium of Tax
     Research. Washington, D.C.: Office of Tax Analysis, U.S.
     Treasury.

Fullerton, D., Henderson, Y., & Shoven, J. (1983). A comparison of meth-
     odologies in empirical general equilibrium models of taxation.
     In Applied General Equilibrium Analysis, eds., H. Scarf &
     J. Shoven. New York: Cambridge University Press.

Galper, H. & Toder, E. (1982). Transfer elements in the taxation of
     income from capital. Presented at a National Bureau of
     Economic Research Conference on Income and Wealth, Madison,
     Wisconsin, May 14-15.

Gordon, R. & Slemrod, J. (1983). A general equilibrium simulation study
     of subsidies to municipal expenditures. J. of Finance, 38.

Harberger, A. (1962). The incidence of the corporation income tax. J.
     of Political Economy, 70.

Harberger, A. (1966). Efficiency effects of taxes on income from capital.
     In Effects of Corporation Income Tax, ed., M. Krzyzaniak.
     Detroit, Mich.: Wayne State University Press.

Hendershott, P. & Shilling, J. (1982). Capital allocation and the eco-
     nomic recovery tax act of 1981. Public Finance Quarterly, 10.

Hendershott, P. & Slemrod, J. (1983). Taxes and the user cost of capital
     for owner-occupied housing. AREUEA J., 10.

King, M. (1981). Welfare analysis of tax reforms using household data.
     National Bureau of Economic Research Technical Working Paper
     #16.

King, M. (1983). The distribution of gains and losses from changes in
     the tax treatment of housing. In Behavioral Simulation Meth-
     ods in Tax Policy Analysis, ed., M. Feldstein. Chicago, Ill.:
     University of Chicago Press.

Mansur, A. & Whalley, J. (1983). Numerical specification of applied general equilibrium models: Estimation, calibration, and data. In Applied General Equilibrium Analysis, eds., H. Scarf & J. Shoven. New York: Cambridge University Press.

McLure, C. (1975). General equilibrium analysis: The Harberger model after ten years. J. of Public Economics, 4.

Mossin, J. (1968). Taxation and risk-taking: An expected utility approach. Economica, 35.

Musgrave, J. (1981). Fixed capital stock in the United States: Revised estimates. Survey of Current Business.

Pechman, J. & Okner, B. (1974). Who Bears the Tax Burden? Washington, D.C.: Brookings Institution.

Piggott, J. & Whalley, J. (forthcoming). Economic Effects of U.K. Tax-Subsidy Policies: A General Equilibrium Appraisal. New York: Macmillan Press.

Projector, D. & Weiss, G. (1966). Survey of Financial Characteristics of Consumers. Washington, D.C.: Board of Governors of the Federal Reserve System.

Rosen, H. (1979). Owner-occupied housing and the federal income tax: Estimates and simulations. J. of Urban Economics, 6.

Rosen, H. (1979). Housing decisions and the U.S. income tax: An econometric analysis. J. of Public Economics, 8.

Shoven, J. (1976). The incidence and efficiency effects of taxes on income from capital. J. of Political Economy, 84.

Shoven, J. & Whalley, J. (1972). A general equilibrium calculation of the effects of differential taxation of income from capital in the U.S. J. of Public Economics, 1.

Slemrod, J. (1980). A general equilibrium model of capital income taxation. Unpublished Ph.D. dissertation, Harvard University.

Slemrod, J. (1982). The allocation of capital among sectors and among individuals: A portfolio approach. NBER Working Paper #951.

Slemrod, J. (1983). A general equilibrium model of taxation with endogenous financial behavior. In Behavioral simulation methods in tax policy analysis, ed., M. Feldstein. Chicago, Ill.: University of Chicago Press.

Tobin, J. (1958). Liquidity preference as behavior toward risk. Review of Economic Studies, 25.

CONSUMPTION TAXES, FORESIGHT, AND WELFARE:
A COMPUTABLE GENERAL EQUILIBRIUM ANALYSIS

C.L. Ballard
Michigan State University, East Lansing, Michigan 48824

L.H. Goulder
Harvard University, Cambridge, Massachusetts 02138

Paper prepared for Conference on Numerical Micro Models,
Australian National University, Canberra, Australia,
August 1983. We are grateful to Peter Dixon, Frank Milne, and
David Starrett for helpful comments and suggestions. We are
responsible for any remaining errors. We also wish to thank
Karl Scholz for fine research assistance and Nancy Evans for
expert typing of the manuscript.

1 INTRODUCTION

In recent years the policy significance of consumers'
expectations has gained increasing recognition. Lucas (1976) and others
have argued convincingly that individuals' beliefs about what a policy
might do could significantly affect what the policy would do. Although
researchers generally acknowledge the potential policy impacts of
expectations, most of the attention to this issue has been in the context
of short-run stabilization policy. For example, the ways that an
announced monetary policy can lead to higher inflation by generating
inflationary expectations—even when the policy itself is not "intrinsi-
cally" inflationary—have been widely examined. There has been less
attention to the ways that expectations might affect policies oriented
toward long-run growth—a consumption tax, for example. Even fewer
studies attempt to quantify these effects.

Our purpose here will be to explore how consumers'
expectations (and, in particular, their ability to anticipate future
prices) can influence the attractiveness of adopting a consumption tax
in the U.S. To do this we employ a multisector general equilibrium model
which allows for alternative specifications about consumers' foresight.

Large applied general equilibrium models often use one of two
basic approaches to expectations. One approach is to assume that the
current behavior of economic agents depends only on previous or current
prices and not on any prices to be realized in the future. Both static

253

expectations (where only current prices determine expectations and influence behavior) and adaptive expectations (where previous prices also enter in) are consistent with this approach. This approach achieves plausibility to the extent that it is believed that futures markets are limited and economic agents have little information about the prices which will have to be paid later on. There are also some practical advantages to this approach: since all current behavior is independent of actual future prices, the path of an economy over time can be determined relatively simply, by solving successively for the general equilibrium of each period on the basis of the prices up to that period. There is no need to employ a more complex, fully intertemporal model in which the equilibrium prices of all periods are solved for simultaneously. Computational general equilibrium models adopting this approach include Borges and Goulder (1982), Fullerton, Shoven, and Whalley (1983), Hudson and Jorgenson (1978), and Dervis, de Melo, and Robinson (1982).

The other popular approach is to assume perfect foresight on the part of key economic agents. Under this approach, expectations about future prices are right on the mark; and thus to calculate the behavior of economic agents in a given period one must determine the future prices which are (correctly) anticipated. This implies that the prices of all periods must be solved for simultaneously. Although it may pose computational complexities, this approach is attractive to the extent that one believes that, because of futures markets or for other reasons, economic agents have considerable information about the prices which they will face at some later time. Computational general equilibrium models incorporating this approach include Auerbach, Kotlikoff, and Skinner (1983), Chao (1982), Manne and Preckel (1983).

The assumptions of static expectations and of perfect foresight stand as polar cases. They represent extremes concerning the availability of information about the future. Our objective is to develop a single, consistent model in which the amount of information available can be varied systematically within these extremes. We believe this can provide considerable insight regarding the value of such information, and a fuller appreciation of the significance of the treatment of expectations in other models.

We have developed a model with "variable" foresight by modifying a large-scale general equilibrium model originally developed by Fullerton, Shoven and Whalley (FSW, 1983). The FSW model assumes

myopic expectations, and thus takes the first of the two basic approaches
described above. In the FSW model, consumers make their consumption-saving
decisions by assuming that the relative prices of the current period will
continue to prevail in all future periods.

In order to examine most effectively the implications of
consumer foresight, a number of modifications of the FSW model were
required. To begin with, we enabled the model to incorporate different
"degrees of foresight" on the part of consumers, ranging from static
expectations to perfect foresight. Here, foresight is measured according
to the number of years into the future that consumers can forecast prices
correctly. A second modification was to replace the consumption component
of the FSW model with a more general submodel which captures intertemporal
effects more fully.

Using the new model, we have investigated how foresight can
influence the consequences of adopting a pure consumption tax in the U.S.
We are especially concerned with the implications of foresight for consumer
welfare, and in making welfare assessments we take account of consumers'
well-being during the transition period after the policy change as well
as during the eventual new steady state.

In the next section, we describe our model's treatment of
consumer behavior and the way we have incorporated variable degrees of
foresight. In Section 3, we present other features of the model (many
of which are common to the FSW model) with emphasis on welfare calculations. Section 4 reports and interprets the results of our simulations.
The paper concludes with Section 5.

2 THE MODEL OF CONSUMER BEHAVIOR

In a previous study (see Ballard and Goulder, 1982), we
examined the importance of foresight using a consumption submodel similar
to that contained in the FSW model. While a number of insights into the
effects of expectations were gained using that submodel, for this study
we have developed a different and more general submodel with greater
potential to bring out the implications of different foresight specifications. The most important advantage of the new submodel is that it allows
a consumer's planned consumption path to depend on the consumer's expected
future incomes (as well as current income).

2.1 The Consumer's Maximization Problem

For a representative consumer, the new model employs the additively separable lifetime utility function:

$$\tilde{U} = \sum_{t=1}^{\infty} \frac{1}{(1+\rho)^{t-1}} \; U_t(C_t, \; H_t) \tag{1}$$

where ρ is the subjective rate of time preference, C_t is consumption in period t, and H_t is hours worked in period t. As in the FSW model, we treat households as extending infinitely through time. The labor-leisure choice is captured through the substitutability between C_t and H_t in the instantaneous utility function, U_t.

Let C_t^* represent minimum required consumption in period t. Then define

$$\hat{C}_t \equiv C_t - C_t^* \tag{2}$$

as discretionary consumption in period t. Also, let H_t^* denote maximum potential hours of work. Then define

$$\hat{H}_t \equiv H_t^* - H_t \tag{3}$$

as (discretionary) leisure time.

For the instantaneous utility or "felicity" function, U_t, we choose a single isoelastic form for all periods:

$$U_t = \begin{cases} \dfrac{Z_t^{\,1-\delta}}{1-\delta} & , \; \delta \neq 1 \\[2ex] \ln Z_t & , \; \delta = 1 \end{cases} \qquad \text{all } t \tag{4}$$

where Z_t is a Cobb-Douglas composite of discretionary consumption and leisure:

$$Z_t = \hat{C}_t^{\,\alpha} \; \hat{H}_t^{\,1-\alpha} \tag{5}$$

The parameter δ is the inverse of the intertemporal elasticity of substitution for Z_t.

Combining the above expressions, we can write a given consumer group's lifetime utility (from year 1) as

$$\tilde{U} = \sum_{t=1}^{\infty} \frac{1}{(1+\rho)^{t-1}} \frac{\left[(C_t - C_t^*)^{\alpha} (H_t^* - H_t)^{1-\alpha}\right]^{1-\delta}}{1-\delta} \tag{6}$$

Consumers maximize U subject to the constraint that the present value of lifetime consumption must not exceed the present value of lifetime resources. This constraint can be written as

$$\sum_{t=1}^{\infty} \frac{p_t C_t}{\prod_{s=1}^{t} (1+r_s)} \leq W_1 + \sum_{t=1}^{\infty} \frac{w_t H_t + Y_t}{\prod_{s=1}^{t} (1+r_s)} \tag{7}$$

where $r_1 \equiv 0$ and where W_1 is the value of inherited capital, Y_t is the value of transfers received in period t, r_s is the rate of return in period s, and p and w denote the price of consumption and labor, respectively. Expression (7) thus states that the present value of lifetime consumption must not exceed the value of inherited capital plus the present value of lifetime earnings and transfers. (Expression (7) is easily modified to account for taxes on consumption, capital, or labor. For expositional convenience we disregard such taxes here.)

The variable H_t^*, which denotes maximum possible labor time in period t, is specified exogenously for each period. We specify H_t^* as growing at a constant rate, Θ. This rate is meant to reflect both population growth and labor productivity growth, since labor time is measured in efficiency units.

The system represented by (6) and (7) will be well-behaved only if Θ is less than the rate of return, r, which prevails in the long run. (If this were not the case, discounted potential lifetime earnings would be infinite, and there would be no effective constraint on consumption.) A characteristic of this infinite-horizon model is that there is one rate of return which the economy will always approach in the long run (see Starrett, 1982). We calibrate the model to yield a long-run rate of

return of four percent, and we specify a value of 2.8 percent for θ.
(See subsection 2.3 below.)

There are several features of this submodel which can be useful
in a study of consumer foresight. First, consumers have the flexibility
to plan for varying amounts of consumption in different future periods.
This is in contrast to the FSW model, where consumers must plan for a
constant level of consumption in all future periods. Second, this new
model allows each consumer's planned allocations of consumption over time
to be based on expected lifetime income, rather than on current income
alone. In the FSW model and in our previous work, tax policy affected
consumption-savings choices by influencing the expected relative prices of
present and future consumption and by influencing current income. With
the new model, policy changes can influence the consumption-savings decision not only through these channels but also through effects on expected
future incomes.

2.2 Solving the Model

From expressions (6) and (7), we can write the Lagrangean
function for the consumer's maximization problem as

$$
L = \sum_{t=1}^{\infty} \frac{1}{(1+\rho)^{t-1}} \frac{\left[(C_t - C_t^*)^{\alpha} (H_t^* - H_t)^{1-\alpha} \right]^{1-\delta}}{1-\delta}
$$

$$
+ \mu \left\{ W_1 + \sum_{t=1}^{\infty} \left[(w_t H_t + Y_t - p_t C_t) \prod_{s=1}^{t} (1+r_s)^{-1} \right] \right\}
$$

(8)

Differentiating equation (8) with respect to C_t and H_t we get
the first-order conditions for a maximum. These have the usual interpretations: namely, that the marginal utility of discretionary consumption
in each period equals the marginal utility of wealth times the effective
price of consumption in the period, and that the marginal utility of work
equals the marginal utility of wealth times the effective wage rate.

After dividing the equations for the first-order conditions by
each other, we get an expression which states that the marginal rate of
substitution between consumption and work equals the relative price of
work and consumption:

$$\frac{(C_t-C_t^*)\,(1-\alpha)}{(H_t^*-H_t)\,\alpha} = \frac{w_t}{P_t} \tag{9}$$

This can be rewritten in a form which shows the relationship between leisure and discretionary consumption in each period:

$$(H_t^*-H_t) = (C_t-C_t^*)\,(\frac{1-\alpha}{\alpha})\,\frac{P_t}{w_t} \tag{10}$$

If we substitute equation (10) into the first-order condition for consumption, we get an expression for $C_t-C_t^*$ in terms of prices and parameters:

$$(C_t-C_t^*)^{-\delta} = [\frac{(1+\rho)^{t-1}}{\alpha}]\,(\frac{1-\alpha}{\alpha})\,(\frac{P_t}{w_t})^{(1-\alpha)(\delta-1)}\,\frac{\mu P_t}{\prod\limits_{s=1}^{t}(1+r_s)} \tag{11}$$

Using equation (11) we can calculate the ratio of discretionary consumption in any two adjacent periods, that is $(C_t-C_t^*)/(C_{t-1}-C_{t-1}^*)$. Recursive calculation of this ratio generates the equation of motion for discretionary consumption:

$$(C_t-C_t^*) = (C_1-C_1^*)\,\Omega_t^{1/\delta}\,\Psi_t^{\frac{(\delta-1)(1-\alpha)}{\delta}} \tag{12}$$

where

$$\Omega_t = (\frac{P_1}{P_t})\,\frac{\prod\limits_{s=1}^{t}(1+r_s)}{(1+\rho)^{t-1}}$$

and

$$\Psi_t = (\frac{w_t}{P_t})\,(\frac{w_1}{P_1})^{-1}$$

Combining equations (10) and (12), we get an equation of motion for leisure:

$$(H^*_t - H_t) = (C_1 - C^*_1) \, \Omega_t^{1/\delta} \, \psi_t^{\frac{(\delta-1)(1-\alpha)}{\delta}} \, (\frac{1-\alpha}{\alpha})(\frac{P_t}{w_t}) \tag{13}$$

We thus have equations of motion for $H^*_t - H_t$ and $C_t - C^*_t$ in terms of $C_1 - C^*_1$, prices, and known parameters. From the point of view of the consumer, the prices are also parametric. Thus, all that remains to solve the consumption submodel is to determine $C_1 - C^*_1$ (or, more precisely, C_1, since C^*_1 is not a choice variable). This can be done by substituting the expressions for $C_t - C^*_t$ given by equation (12) into the lifetime resource constraint, (7). This yields the expression

$$C_1 - C^*_1 = \frac{\sum\limits_{t=1}^{\infty} [(w_t H^*_t + Y_t - p_t C^*_t) \prod\limits_{s=1}^{t} (1+r_s)^{-1}] + W_1}{\alpha^{-1} \sum\limits_{t=1}^{\infty} [p_t \Omega_t^{1/\delta} \psi_t^{\frac{(\delta-1)(1-\alpha)}{\delta}} \prod\limits_{s=1}^{t} (1+r_s)^{-1}]} \tag{14}$$

Equation (14) can be used to solve for consumption in period 1 as a function of given parameters and the prices of consumption, the wage rates, and the rates of return of every period. The relevant variables for consumption calculations are the consumer's _expected_ prices of consumption, wage rates, and rates of return.

Equation (14) is an expression for consumption in period 1, but perfectly analogous expressions allow the calculation of consumption in other periods. In every period each consumer projects a path of lifetime consumption; but if foresight is not perfect, actual consumption will generally differ from planned consumption in every period except the current one. When consumers do not have perfect foresight, they continually modify their expectations and hence their planned path of future consumption. However, the planned path and the actual path of consumption do conform to one another in the current period, since expectations are treated as unchanging within any given period. Thus, for each period τ, we use the relationships in equation (14) to calculate C_τ based on the set of expectations held by consumers during period τ. Once C_τ is known, H_τ can be calculated using equation (10).

The above discussion shows how the consumer may calculate a path of consumption based on initial wealth (W_1), expected transfers (Y), and expected prices (p) and wages (w). We still need to show how expectations are formed. One possibility would be to incorporate explicitly a model of the costs of information acquisition or information processing, and to determine endogenously the amount of information available to consumers, that is, to model consumers as purchasing information in some optimal way. Consumers' expectations would be based on the information purchased. We have not taken this approach, for two reasons. First, the theoretical literature in this area has progressed very slowly. In addition, data on information acquisition costs are not available, implying that any attempt to specify information costs explicitly would be ad hoc.

Instead, we have chosen to specify the expectational structure exogenously. We assume that consumers are able to predict the movements of relative prices perfectly for a certain number of years. Beyond that, however, they anticipate constant prices. For example, if the "expectational horizon" is 10 years, then consumers can predict prices $P_1, \ldots, P_{10}$, and $P_{K1}, \ldots, P_{K10}$ correctly, but for subsequent years, they assume (incorrectly) that P_{10} and P_{K10} will continue to hold. In the limit, as the expectational horizon becomes large, this amounts to perfect foresight.[1] Note that "correct prediction" has a special meaning here. The predictions are correct until the expectational horizon, given the structure of expectations. A longer expectational horizon leads, in general, to different behavior, which in turn leads to different prices about which consumers form expectations.

We employ an iterative technique to ensure that consumers correctly anticipate prices over the specified number of years of foresight. We start off by assigning consumers certain initial expectations[2] about future prices. Given these expectations, consumer behavior can be determined in the model. We therefore run the model using these expectations and see what prices actually emerge over time. If the expected prices and the actual prices do not match, we modify the expected prices and solve the model again. The new expected prices are a weighted average of the old expected prices and the old actual prices. This modified Gauss-Seidel technique is employed repeatedly until the expectations conform (for the specified number of years ahead) to the actual prices within some desired level of accuracy.

Our procedure offers no guarantee of convergence. However, in practice, convergence has always been achieved. It usually takes between 15 and 30 iterations for expected prices and actual prices to become within .01 percent of each other for every year for which we have required expectations to be correct.

Given any set of expectations, we can solve in each period for the set of current equilibrium prices of goods and services consistent with those expectations. One important feature of production in our model is that, in a given period, the current prices of all intermediate goods and all consumer goods can be calculated once the current prices of the primary factors, labor and capital, are known. Labor is the numeraire, with price equal to 1. The future price of capital is therefore the key to predicting goods prices in some future period, since all goods prices can be determined once the capital price, technology, and budget shares are known. We use a tatônnement algorithm developed by Kimbell and Harrison (1983) to determine equilibrium factor prices in each period.

Table 1 gives an example of a typical pattern of consumer expectations. In this example, equilibrium periods are spaced two years apart, and consumers are regarded as being able to see ahead three periods, or six years. As indicated by the table, expectations must be defined with respect to both the period about which they are held and the period in which they are held. In Table 1, the elements along the diagonal are "correct" prices. Note that consumers expectations are correct only for the specified number of periods into the future.

Table 1. Expected Prices of Capital*

Periods in which Expectations are Held	1	2	3	4	5	6	7	8
1	1.006	.9720	.9445	.9220	.9220	.9220	.9220	.9220
2		.9720	.9445	.9220	.9037	.9037	.9037	.9037
3			.9445	.9220	.9037	.8888	.8888	.8888
4				.9220	.9037	.8888	.8767	.8767
5					.9037	.8888	.8767	.8670

*Equilibria are spaced two years apart. The number of years of foresight is six: consumers can correctly predict prices three, two-year periods ahead.

A much larger table would be necessary to describe expectations over the usual simulation interval of 80 years. In fact, if equilibria are two years apart and consumers are able to see three periods ahead, then in order to compute behavior over an 80-year simulation period we must calculate 44 equilibria. The first 41 equilibria span an interval of

80 years and represent the actual equilibria on the basis of which we make
welfare evaluations. The remaining three equilibria are computed to calculate the (correctly) expected prices for periods 42-44, which enter into
consumers' expectations from periods 39-41.

In general, if T is the number of periods in which expectations
are held, the model requires simultaneous over T + S periods, where S is the
number of periods of correct foresight. It should be noted that the number
of independent capital prices which must be solved is also T + S: the T
"real" prices plus the S prices expected from period T for periods beyond T.
The number of equilibrium prices of capital is therefore no less than the
number of equilibrium periods, and consequently we are able to avoid problems of non-uniqueness of relative capital prices which might otherwise
occur.

2.3 Parameter Selection and Steady-State Properties

We have constructed this new model so that in the base case (or
status quo) simulation, it exactly replicates the steady state of the FSW
model and of our previous foresight study (Ballard and Goulder, 1982). This
is appealing for two reasons. Because the base case exhibits steady-state
growth from the initial (or benchmark) year, the economic impacts of any
policy alternative can be observed most easily, since all departures from
the steady state can be attributed to the alternative policy. And since
the model replicates the results of the other models in the base case, we
obtain a common standard for comparing model results under different policy
scenarios.

The steady-state and replication features of the model imply
certain restrictions on model parameters. In this model, an exogenous
parameter γ describes the relationship between stocks of capital goods and
flows of capital services: each unit of capital goods produces exactly γ
units of capital services in all future periods. Following FSW, we use a
value of .04 for γ. There is no depreciation in the model. Under these
circumstances, if P_S represents the price of new capital goods and P_K the
price of capital services, then r_t, the rate of return in any given period
t, can be expressed by:

$$r_t = \frac{P_{Kt}\gamma}{P_{S,t-1}} + \frac{P_{St} - P_{S,t-1}}{P_{S,t-1}} \tag{15}$$

Thus, the rate of return consists of a capital service flow term and a
capital gains term.

We will calibrate the model to generate steady-state growth in the base case, with all prices unchanging and equal to 1. In the steady state of the base case, equation (15) reduces to $r_t = \bar{r}$, where $\bar{r}$ is the steady-state rate of return, equal to γ.

The equation of motion (12) implies that for any two adjacent periods in the steady state,

$$\frac{C_t - C^*_t}{C_{t-1} - C^*_{t-1}} = \left(\frac{1 + \bar{r}}{1 + \rho}\right)^{1/\delta} \tag{16}$$

Let Θ represent the steady-state growth rate of the system. (The choice of Θ will be discussed below.) In the steady state $C-C^*$ must grow at the rate Θ. Thus from (16), we have

$$\left(\frac{1 + \bar{r}}{1 + \rho}\right)^{1/\delta} = 1 + \Theta \tag{17}$$

Equation (17) implicitly defines combinations of δ and ρ which are consistent with a given steady-state growth rate Θ and a given steady-state rate of return $\bar{r}$.

Given equation (13), the growth of $C-C^*$ at the rate Θ, and the condition that relative prices remain unchanged in the steady state, it follows that leisure (or H^*-H) must grow at the same rate as does $C-C^*$ in the steady state. We specify C^* (non-discretionary consumption) and H^* (total potential labor time in efficiency units) as growing at the rate Θ, so that the model generates balanced growth in the steady state, with C and H (as well as $C-C^*$ and H^*-H) growing at the rate Θ.

Given the observed benchmark values of C and H, specified benchmark values for C^* and H^*, and the benchmark values for p and W (equal to 1), the value of α can be inferred based on equation (10) above.

The remaining parameter to be specified is Θ, the steady-state growth rate of the system. The value of Θ is determined from the requirement that the steady-state growth path include the observed benchmark equilibrium as a point on this path. If transfers (Y) grow at the rate Θ, then in the steady state, with prices unchanging and equal to 1, equation (14) above can be rewritten as

$$C_1 - C_1^* = \frac{a + W_1}{b} \tag{18}$$

where

$$a = \sum_{t=1}^{\infty} \frac{(H_1^* + Y_1 - C_1^*)(1 + \Theta)^{t-1}}{(1 + \overline{r})^{t-1}}$$

and

$$b = \alpha^{-1} \sum_{t=1}^{\infty} \frac{(1 + \Theta)^{t-1}}{(1 + \overline{r})^{t-1}}$$

When Θ is less than $\overline{r}$, the expressions for a and b can be rewritten as

$$a = (H_1^* + Y_1 - C_1^*)\left(\frac{1 + \overline{r}}{\overline{r} - \Theta}\right)$$

$$b = \alpha^{-1}\left(\frac{1 + \overline{r}}{\overline{r} - \Theta}\right)$$

Thus, in the steady state, equation (14) becomes

$$C_1 - C_1^* = \frac{(H_1^* + Y_1 - C_1^*)\left(\frac{1 + \overline{r}}{\overline{r} - \Theta}\right) + W_1}{\alpha^{-1}\left(\frac{1 + \overline{r}}{\overline{r} - \Theta}\right)} \tag{19}$$

or

$$C_1 - C_1^* = \alpha(H_1^* + Y_1 - C_1^*) + \alpha W_1\left(\frac{\overline{r} - \Theta}{1 + \overline{r}}\right) \tag{20}$$

Equation (10) implies that in the steady state

$$\alpha = \frac{C - C^*}{C - C^* + H^* - H} \tag{21}$$

If we substitute for α in equation (20) we get an expression for C_1 with two roots. These are:

$$C_1 = C_1^* \tag{22}$$

and

$$C_1 = H_1 + Y_1 + \bar{r} W_1 - \Theta W_1 \tag{23}$$

The interesting case is given by equation (23). By definition, capital income in period 1, K_1, is equal to $\bar{r} W_1$, and by definition $C_1 = H_1 + Y_1 + K_1 - S_1$. Thus, for the steady-state path to include the benchmark equilibrium, we must have

$$S_1 = \Theta W_1 \tag{24}$$

or

$$\Theta = \frac{S_1}{W_1} \tag{25}$$

That is, the benchmark equilibrium lies on a steady-state path only if savings enable wealth to grow at the steady-state growth rate Θ. Therefore, to allow the model to replicate the benchmark data as an equilibrium on a steady-state path, we choose Θ based on the observed values of S and W (or K, since $W = K/\bar{r}$) in the benchmark data set. The parameter Θ then defines the rate at which we augment the values of H^*, C^*, and Y from year to year.

The value of Θ given by equation (25) is the same value as that used in our previous foresight study and in the FSW model. Consequently, in the base case our new model generates a steady-state growth path identical to that of these other models.

Table 2 summarizes the bases for specifying parameter values and indicates the values of these parameters in the model.

Table 2. Summary of Parameterization Methods and Parameter Values

Parameter	Basis for Determining Value	Value in Model
θ	S_{1/W_1}	.0288
γ	exogenous	.04 (as in FSW model)
$\bar{r}$	$\bar{r} = \gamma$ in steady state [equation (15)]	.04
δ	exogenous	1.1
ρ	equation (17), given $\bar{r}$, δ	.0112
C_{1*}	exogenous	630,301 [or $0.8(C_1)$]
H_{1*}	exogenous	933,123 [or $1.2(H_1)$]
α	equation (21), given $C*,H*$	.5933

*Subscript "1" denotes benchmark year.

The restriction on the values of ρ and δ implied by equation (17) is a stringent one. We cannot take arbitrary values for one of these parameters without running the risk of getting very unrealistic values for the other parameter. We looked at a number of ρ-δ combinations, and chose a combination for which each seemed to be at least roughly compatible with the econometric literature. The value of 1.2 for δ is the range of values suggested in the literature [see, for example, the survey in Davies (1981)], and recent work by Hansen and Singleton (1982) is consistent with our choice. The value for δ implies a value for ρ of about 1.1 percent, which is in the plausible range for this parameter. Note that, in each simulation, both ρ and δ are taken to be constants. Having a constant value of ρ is a sufficient condition for consistent dynamic optimization in the sense of Strotz (1955-1956).

3 OTHER ASPECTS OF THE MODEL

3.1 General Features

We have already described our submodel of consumer behavior in some detail. Other aspects of our model correspond to those of the FSW model (except for the features used to make welfare comparisons; these will be discussed below). Here we briefly describe some main features the FSW model which are common to the model employed here. A more detailed description of the FSW model can be found in Ballard, Fullerton, Shoven, and Whalley (1985).

First, we describe the producer side of the model. In any single period, there are 19 profit-maximizing producer good industries. They produce output by combining capital, labor, and the outputs of other industries. Capital and labor are combined according to constant elasticity of substitution (CES) value added functions. Value added is combined with intermediate inputs according to a fixed coefficient technology. Tax rates on labor for each industry are derived by taking payroll taxes and other contributions as a proportion of labor income. The tax rates on capital for each industry are derived by taking corporate income and corporate franchise taxes, and property taxes as a proportion of capital income. Each of the 19 producer goods is used directly by the government sector, for export, and for investment. The producer goods are used indirectly to create 15 consumption goods, through a matrix of fixed coefficients. This transition is necessary because the goods classification of the consumer expenditure data is different from the classification of the 19 production sectors. Producers are only concerned with present prices.

The government sector collects taxes on labor, capital, outputs, intermediate goods purchases, incomes, and consumer purchases. The revenue is used to purchase producer goods and factors (based on the assumption of constant expenditure shares), to make transfer payments to consumers, and to subsidize government enterprises. (We model government enterprises, such as the U.S. Postal Service and the Tennessee Valley Authority, as one of the 19 industries.) The government is constrained to run a balanced budget in every period. An "equal yield" feature enables us to analyze the effects of policy changes while maintaining a constant level of government activity. When this feature is employed, revenues which were collected in every period of a base case sequence (before the policy change) must also be collected in the corresponding period of the revised case sequence (after the policy change). If a tax policy change would ordinarily lead to a decrease in revenues, the lost revenue must be recouped. To make up the necessary revenues, we increment consumers' marginal income tax rates.

Fullerton, Shoven, and Whalley specify their model with data from 1973 because this is the most recent year during which the Department of Labor conducted a Consumer Expenditure Survey. In addition to this survey, four other major sources provide the data for the model. These are the July 1976 <u>Survey of Current Business</u>, the Bureau of Economic

Analysis (BEA) input-output tables for 1972, unpublished worksheets of
BEA's National Income Division, and the U.S. Treasury Department's Merged
Tax File. In order to use all of these data together, a number of consistency adjustments must be made and certain model parameters must be
selected. [See Fullerton, King, Shoven, and Whalley (1981) for some
details, or Ballard, Fullerton, Shoven and Whalley (1985) for a very
detailed treatment of these procedures.]

3.2 Welfare Comparisons

After all the consistency adjustments and parameter selections
have been made, we are able to perform policy simulations with our model.
In this study, we are especially interested in comparing the welfare
consequences of alternative specifications about consumer foresight. To
make useful comparisons, we perform a "base case" simulation which can be
used as a common standard for welfare comparisons. As indicated in Section
2, our base case simulation generates steady-state growth with prices
unchanging and equal to one. The specification of consumer foresight makes
no difference in the base case: when prices are constant over time, the
expected prices under static expectations and under various degrees of
foresight are identical.

Against the steady-state, base-case simulation we compare
results of "revised case" simulations under which a consumption tax policy
is adopted. These revised case simulations will differ according to the
specified number of years of foresight.

Since consumer groups are regarded as infinitely-lived, to make
welfare assessments it is necessary to calculate the utility derived from
an infinite stream of consumption of goods and leisure. However, because
of the steady-state properties of the model, it is possible to approximate
the contribution to discounted utility of these infinite streams using
results from simulations over a finite time interval. Under a revised
case simulation, the economy departs from its initial steady-state path
immediately following the policy change; however, the growth path of the
economy converges to a new steady-state path and generally comes very close
to the new steady state within about 30 years. We generally perform
simulations which calculate equilibria over a period of 80 years, which is
a long enough interval to allow one to observe the features of the new
steady state. With this information, we can calculate to a very close
approximation the welfare value of the infinite stream of consumption and
leisure in the new steady state. We combine this information with results

obtained for the transition period to come up with an overall welfare
measure.

To assess the welfare change implied by the adoption of a
consumption tax, we employ a welfare measure which is a dynamic analog of
the Hicksian compensating variation. Let $\tilde{V}$ represent the indirect utility
function corresponding to the (direct) lifetime utility function, $\tilde{U}$. Then
the equivalence between $\tilde{V}$ and $\tilde{U}$ is expressed by

$$\tilde{U}(\underset{\sim}{C}, \underset{\sim}{H}) = \tilde{V}(\underset{\sim}{P}, W_1, X)$$

where $\underset{\sim}{P}$ represents all prices (over all time), W_1 is initial wealth, and X
denotes exogenous parameters. If we let the subscript B denote the status
quo or base case policy regime and R the new or revised case policy regime,
then our compensating variation measure is the change in initial wealth, Δ,
such that

$$\tilde{V}(\underset{\sim}{P}_R, W_{1B} + \Delta, X_R) = \tilde{V}(\underset{\sim}{P}_B, W_{1B}, X_B) \tag{26}$$

When consumers are taken to have perfect foresight, this
calculation is relatively straightforward. Since $\tilde{V}(P_B, W_{1B}, X_B)$ is known
as are $\underset{\sim}{P}_R$ and X_R, determining Δ is simply a matter of calculating the
consumer's expected lifetime utility as it is expected from period 1, using
$\underset{\sim}{P}_R$ and X_{1B}, and finding the Δ which generates the lifetime utility level
$\tilde{V}(P_B, W_{1B}, X_B)$. Since consumers have perfect foresight, ex ante and
ex post utility are the same.

In scenarios where consumers do not have perfect foresight,
the welfare calculation can be a bit more complex. The question arises:
what should be the definition of a compensating variation when expectations
change over time? Several interpretations are possible, but we think the
most sensible specification is as follows.

Let E_t represent the set of expectations held by a given
consumer at time t about future prices. (E_t can be represented by a vector
of finite length, since in this model there is always some future date T
such that consumers do not expect prices to change beyond that date).
Each policy scenario involves a specific sequence of expectations, given
by E_1, E_2, E_3, etc. We define the compensating variation in terms of the
ex post lifetime utility which the consumer would attain given the same

parameters, the same realized prices, <u>and the same sequence of price expectations</u> as occurred in the revised case. This obliges us to calculate recursively the instantaneous utility (or felicity) of each successive period. In period 1, instantaneous utility is

$$U_1(\widetilde{C}_1, \widetilde{H}_1)$$

where $\widetilde{C}_1$ and $\widetilde{H}_1$ represent the optimal levels of period 1 consumption and hours worked, as functions of E_{1R}, $W_{1B} + \underset{\sim}{\Delta}$, P_R and X_R. In period 2, instantaneous utility is

$$U_2(\widetilde{C}_2, \widetilde{H}_2)$$

where $\widetilde{C}_2$ and $\widetilde{H}_2$ are optimal consumption and hours as functions of E_{2R}, $W_2(\widetilde{C}_1)$, $\underset{\sim}{P}_R$, and X_R. Note that wealth in period 2, W_2, depends on $\widetilde{C}_1$ which in turn depends on $W_{1B} + \Delta$. More generally, for $t \geq 2$, we have

$$\widetilde{C}_t = \widetilde{C}_t[E_{tR}, W_t(W_{t-1}, \widetilde{C}_{t-1,R}), \underset{\sim}{P}_R, X_R]$$
$$\widetilde{H}_t = \widetilde{H}_t[E_{tR}, W_t W_{t-1}, \widetilde{C}_{t-1,R}), \underset{\sim}{P}_R, X_R]$$

Thus we have a system which can be solved recursively for the $\widetilde{C}$ and $\widetilde{H}$ of every period. The compensating variation is thus the change in initial wealth which generates <u>ex post</u> lifetime utility

$$\widetilde{U}(\widetilde{C}_1, \widetilde{H}_1; \widetilde{C}_2, \widetilde{H}_2; \widetilde{C}_3 \widetilde{H}_3; \ldots)$$

equal to $\widetilde{V}(\underset{\sim}{P}_B, W_{1B}, X_B)$.

4 SIMULATION RESULTS

In this section, we present the results from simulating the adoption of a consumption tax policy in the U.S. The simulations differ with regard to the amount of foresight possessed by consumers. Our purpose is to examine the degree to which the effects of this tax alternative depend on the amount of foresight.

The "base case" sequence of equilibria is the standard against which each of the alternative tax policies is measured. As discussed in Section 3, the economy achieves steady-state growth in the base case.

Our base case sequences are parameterized on the basis of data
from the Flow of Funds accounts, which indicate that, in 1973, about 30
percent of savings were sheltered from tax by flowing through such investment vehicles as Individual Retirement Accounts, Keogh Plans, etc. We
model this as a subsidy which accrues to consumers when they purchase the
"saving good," which is a fixed coefficient composite of the producer goods
which are used for investment. The subsidy applies at the rate of 30 percent times the consumer's marginal income tax rate. The Flow of Funds data
also indicate that 20 percent of saving are sheltered from tax because they
are invested in residential real estate. Therefore, an increase from 30
percent to 80 percent in the protection afforded to saving which flows
through financial instruments would effectively shelter all saving from
tax. Consequently, we model the move to a consumption tax as an increase
in financial saving deductions from 30 percent to 80 percent. This is the
capital deepening policy on which we will focus.

In Table 3 we present the effects of the consumption tax policy
on the price of capital relative to labor (the numeraire) under various
foresight specifications. These prices may be compared with the base case,
where all prices are equal to one.

Table 3. Changes in the Relative Price of Capital Resulting
From the Adoption of a Consumption Tax*

Year	Years of Correct Foresight (Consumption Tax)					
	0	2	4	6	10	20
1973	1.012	1.009	1.007	1.006	1.004	1.003
1983	.843	.864	.878	.889	.903	.922
1993	.827	.833	.841	.848	.859	.879
2003	.827	.828	.830	.834	.841	.855
2013	.827	.827	.828	.829	.833	.842
2023	.827	.827	.827	.827	.829	.835
2033	.827	.827	.827	.827	.828	.832
2043	.827	.827	.827	.827	.827	.829**

*Results are from simulations in which equilibrium
calculations are performed every two years beginning
in 1973, the benchmark year.
**This price reaches the steady state value .827 in year 2073.

In the first equilibrium period (1973), the capital stock is
the same in both the base case sequence and the revised sequence. The

model is structured so that changes in the level of saving do not translate
into changes in the stock of capital goods until the next period.

The policy change leads to a higher savings rate, so that,
after the first period, the capital stock increases at a faster rate than
the effective labor endowment. This capital deepening causes the relative
price of capital to drop. Under static expectations, for example, the
price of capital falls from 1.012 in 1973 to .827 by the year 2043. In the
other simulations, where consumers have foresight, the price of capital
also declines over time and eventually reaches the same steady-state value
of .827.

The path of capital prices changes in a systematic way with
changes in the specified number of years of foresight. With greater
foresight, the decline in capital prices proceeds more slowly over time,
and the new steady state is reached more slowly. These results stem from
the effect of foresight on saving behavior. The greater the degree of
foresight, the more consumers can anticipate future declines in the price
of capital and the associated reductions in the rate of return to saving.
Consequently, a greater degree of foresight leads to lower saving by
consumers, as indicated in Table 4. With lower saving, capital deepening
proceeds at a slower pace, and the price of capital falls less quickly
over time.

Table 4.   Household Saving (Consumption Tax Case
Compared with Base Case)

Year	Base Case	Years of Foresight (Consumption Tax)			
		0	2	6	20
1973	105.4	223.0	195.9	171.0	145.0
1983	140.0	190.4	197.5	196.2	185.3
1993	185.9	226.8	232.8	238.7	237.8
2003	246.9	299.6	301.3	305.6	309.0
2013	327.9	397.8	398.1	400.5	405.5
2023	435.4	528.2	528.1	529.5	533.0
2033	578.2	701.5	702.3	701.8	706.8
2043	767.9	931.5	932.1	930.7	934.7

*In billions of 1973 dollars. These results are for
simulations in which the equilibria are spaced two
years apart.

In Table 5 we present the welfare gains under different foresight scenarios, from adopting the consumption tax policy. The measures of
the welfare gain, as discussed in Section 3, is the change in (discounted)
lifetime resources necessary to generate base case utility, given revise
case prices and expectations.

Table 5. Welfare Gains from Adoption of a Consumption Tax*

Number of Years of Correct Foresight	Welfare Gain
0	2.07
2	2.04
4	2.03
6	1.96
10	1.91
20	1.89

*The welfare gain is defined here as the percentage reduction
in the present value of lifetime resources necessary to
generate base case utility under the revise case policy
regime, given revise case prices and expectations.

In all simulations in the table, equilibria are calculated at two-year
intervals.

Before we consider how these welfare gains change with changes
in foresight, we shall comment briefly on the general order of magnitude
of these gains. The gains, in the vicinity of 1.9 percent to 2.2 percent
of wealth, are somewhat larger than the gains simulated with the FSW
model, which cluster in the vicinity of one percent of wealth. Because
the method of calculating lifetime utility and of obtaining a compensating
variation is quite different in the FSW model from the method employed
here, it is difficult to make meaningful comparisons of the welfare gains
of the different models. However, one factor contributing to the larger
welfare gain obtained in the present study appears to be a higher responsiveness of saving with respect to changes in the rate of return. The
consumption tax leads to welfare gains because it encourages saving in a
world where (because of taxes on capital) the marginal social benefit to
saving exceeds its marginal social cost.

Such a tax policy will have a greater potential payoff (up to
a point), the greater the responsiveness of savings to changes in rates
of return. In our model, it is possible to solve analytically for the
elasticity of saving with respect to the rate of return. This elasticity

represents the ratio of the proportionate change in saving to the proportionate change in the rate of return, when the change in the rate of return
is expected to be permanent. In our new model, this elasticity is 1.46;
in the FSW model, the corresponding interest elasticity is lower--0.4.

Differences in the interest elasticity of saving also help
explain the differences between our results and those of Auerbach,
Kotlikoff, and Skinner (1983). These authors obtain higher welfare gains
from the consumption tax, but their model exhibits more responsiveness of
saving to changes in the rate of return.

It appears that the saving responses generated by our model
are fairly large: in most cases, the saving rate in the first period of a
consumption tax simulation is at least twice as great as the saving rate
in the base case. These responses are considerably lower than those found
in Auerbach and Kotlikoff (1983), but much higher than those reported in
FSW (1983). An important feature of our model is that it distinguishes
between discretionary and nondiscretionary (or "required") consumption;
incorporating the nondiscretionary element of consumption reduces the level
of intertemporal substitutability and thereby helps to avoid the unrealistically high saving responsiveness that would otherwise occur.[3]

An important result from Table 5 is that additional foresight
weakens the beneficial effect of the policy change. The largest welfare
gains occurs under static expectations; and such gains diminish with the
amount of consumer foresight. Why do the welfare gains from a consumption
tax decline with foresight? The explanation has to do with the effect of
foresight on saving behavior. We have seen that consumers save less when
they have more foresight: they are better at anticipating future reductions in rates of return. In a world with capital taxes the social return
from a unit of savings exceeds the private return, or, equivalently, the
marginal social value of saving exceeds the marginal social value of
current consumption. This is due in part to taxes at the firm level (like
the corporate income tax), which reduce the rental price of capital below
its marginal productivity; it also is a consequence of the double taxation
of saving under an income tax system. Moving from an income tax to a
consumption tax system eliminates the double taxation of saving, but the
social return to saving still exceeds the private return because of capital
taxes at the firm level. Under these conditions greater foresight implies
lower welfare because it leads to less saving.

Thus, in a second-best world where, at the margin, the social value of saving exceeds the social value of consumption, additional foresight (possessed by all consumers) may have negative welfare consequences. Under policy changes which reduce the price of capital over time, consumers with a great deal of foresight are quite good at anticipating these lower prices; they expect a lower return to their saving and thus they save less. Consumers with little foresight, on the other hand, overestimate future capital prices and the rate of return to saving, and they save more. Myopia thus produces a better outcome than perfect foresight; the saving behavior of an economy in which consumers are myopic is closer to the social optimum. By overestimating the private return to saving, myopic consumers act as if they were concerned with the social return.

This result might seem to conflict with the result of Chamley (1981), who finds that the welfare gain from abolition of capital income taxation is smaller when the private sector does not have perfect foresight than when it does have perfect foresight. However, we should stress that Chamley studies the replacement of capital taxes by lump sum taxes in an economy in which no other taxes are present. Consequently, the second-best issue which we have discussed cannot arise in Chamley's model.

These results conform to those of our previous study, which employed a more restrictive model of consumer behavior. In this study and in the previous one, greater foresight implies reduced saving, a smaller initial impact on the price of capital, and a longer period of transition to the new steady state. In addition, in both studies greater foresight reduces the potential welfare gains from the consumption tax.

5   SENSITIVITY ANALYSIS

In this section we briefly describe results from consumption tax simulations under alternative specifications for parameter values. We vary the following parameters:

CRATIO: specified ratio of required consumption to total (required plus discretionary) consumption in the benchmark. Since total benchmark consumption (C_1) is observed, a different value for CRATIO implies a different benchmark value for benchmark required consumption, C_1^*.

HRATIO: specified ratio of total labor time (hours of work
         plus leisure time) to hours of work. Since benchmark
         hours of work (H_1) is observed, a different value for
         HRATIO implies a different value for benchmark total
         labor time, H_1^*.

δ :   (Inverse of intertemporal elasticity of substitution.)
         As discussed in subsection 2C, the requirement that
         the model replicate the observed benchmark equilibrium
         implies a relationship between the parameters δ and ρ
         (time preference). Higher values of δ imply lower
         values of ρ.

The model results under different parameter values are summarized in Table 6. Lower values for CRATIO imply greater responsiveness of
consumption or saving to policy changes. With a lower value of CRATIO,
the consumption tax generates more saving, and the transition to the new
steady state is more rapid. Welfare gains are larger, since the distortions caused by the income tax are greater when behavior is more elastic.

Higher values for HRATIO also imply more responsive behavior,
this time in regard to the labor/leisure choice. The consumption tax
lowers the price of future bundles of consumption and leisure relative to
current bundles. When HRATIO is larger, households have a greater tendency
to substitute future bundles of consumption and leisure; hence they save
more, and the transition is more rapid. Welfare gains, however, are larger
under lower values for HRATIO--perhaps because the consumption tax generates greater distortions regarding the labor/leisure choice when HRATIO
is larger.

A lower value of δ (a higher intertemporal elasticity of substitution) yields a greater savings response, faster transition, and larger
welfare gain. This occurs despite the fact that a lower δ implies a higher
ρ, which tends to have an offsetting effect. (A δ of 0.8 implies a value
of .0199 for ρ; a δ of 1.4 implies a value of .0027 for ρ.)

The overall result emerging from Table 6 is that the welfare
results from the consumption tax appear to be robust across alternative
parameter specifications; the welfare gains range from 1.76 percent to
2.28 percent of lifetime resources.

Table 6. Model Results under Alternative Parameter Values*

	Price of Capital				Household Saving			Welfare Gain
	1973	1975	1979	Steady State	1973	1975	1979	
BASE CASE (with "standard" parameter values**)	1.000	1.000	1.000	1.000	105.4	111.6	125.0	
CONSUMPTION TAX CASES standard parameter values**	1.012	.951	.875	.827	223.0	218.1	200.3	2.07
CRATIO = 0.7	.996	.925	.854	.830	257.6	237.3	191.7	2.28
CRATIO = 0.9	1.026	.978	.907	.321	189.5	193.5	197.4	1.76
HRATIO = 1.1	.991	.949	.892	.831	194.8	197.9	199.3	2.25
HRATIO = 1.3	1.034	.950	.858	.824	252.6	235.6	192.7	1.93
δ = 0.8	1.018	.931	.846	.827	270.3	245.4	184.5	2.14
δ = 1.4	1.009	.962	.896	.827	196.8	198.7	198.8	2.00

*All simulations involve myopic expectations.
**Standard values are 0.8 for CRATIO, 1.2 for HRATIO, and 1.1 for δ.

6 CONCLUSION

In this paper we employ a computational general equilibrium model to assess how the appeal of adopting a consumption tax depends on the level of foresight possessed by consumers.

One of our main findings is that the social value of additional foresight can be negative: more foresight can lead to lower welfare. This occurs under policies like a consumption tax which lead to capital deepening and a declining price of capital over time. To the extent that consumers have more foresight, they become better able to anticipate these declines in capital prices and they lower their estimation of the rate of return to capital. Consequently, they save less and--given the existence of taxes on capital and the discrepancy between the social and private return to capital--the reduction in saving leads to lower welfare. Myopia, on the other hand, can be of social value if, under such circumstances, consumers tend to overestimate the private return to capital and act as if they were concerned with the social return.

The level of foresight attributed to consumers can affect sig-nificantly the welfare gain or loss afforded by alternative tax policies, although policy changes which produce welfare gains under the assumption of myopic behavior also show gains under perfect foresight. We find that the welfare gain from adopting a consumption tax is reduced by about ten percent when we move from myopia to a great deal of foresight.

These results are qualitatively similar to those which we generated in our earlier investigation. However, we feel that the present model has a much more satisfactory intertemporal structure than the earlier model, and therefore has advantages for examining issues related to expectations.

There are many other important issues associated with dynamic tax reform which the model presented seems well suited to address. These include the announcement effects of tax policies as well as the effects of policies involving changing tax rates over time. In addition, an important area which relatively few numerical general equilibrium models have entered thus far is the analysis of government debt. Since it is widely believed the structure of expectations about future tax liabilities can have a large effect when government bonds are issued, a model like this one can be very useful in evaluating alternative tax and deficit plans.

Footnotes

1 Because of space limitations, we have not included in this paper a formal proof demonstrating that as the specified number of years of foresight increases, the model's results asymptotically approach the results of a perfect foresight equilibrium. Such a proof is provided in Ballard and Goulder (1984).

2 Our initially specified expectations are the equilibrium prices which are generated in simulations with myopic behavior.

3 Starrett (1982) indicates that the inclusion of a consumption floor (that is, non-discretionary consumption) helps prevent an excessive degree of substitution across periods:

> The introduction of a consumption floor has a more important implication than simply that of changing the intertemporal elasticity of substitution; it introduces an element of complementarity across time which is otherwise totally absent in additive separable models of this kind. Without complementarity, substitution effects "compound" across time; the rate at which a consumer can trade consumption many periods hence for consumption now is very sensitive to the rate of interest and (in the absence of complementarity) all consumers will engage in a lot of substitution (unless δ is very large).

References

Auerbach, Alan J., Laurence J. Kotlikoff, and Jonathan Skinner (1983).
The Efficiency Gains from Dynamic Tax Reform. International
Economic Review, 24, 83-100.

Auerbach, Alan J., and Laurence J. Kotlikoff (1983). National Savings,
Economic Welfare, and the Structure of Taxation. In Behavioral
Simulation Methods in Tax Policy Analysis, ed. Martin Feldstein.
Chicago: University of Chicago Press.

Ballard, Charles L. (1983). Evaluation of the Consumption Tax with Dynamic
General Equilibrium Models. Ph.D. dissertation, Stanford
University.

Ballard, Charles L., and Lawrence H. Goulder (1982). Tax Policy and
Consumer Foresight: A General Equilibrium Simulation Study.
Harvard Institute of Economic Research Discussion Paper No.
940, Harvard University, December.

Ballard, Charles L., and Lawrence H. Goulder (1984). Convergence to the
Perfect Foresight Equilibrium. Harvard University. Mimeo,
July.

Ballard, Charles L., Don Fullerton, John B. Shoven, and John Whalley (1985).
A General Equilibrium Model for Tax Policy Evaluation.
Chicago: University of Chicago Press for the National Bureau
of Economic Research.

Borges, Antonio M., and Lawrence H. Goulder (1984). Decomposing the Impact
of Higher Energy Prices on Long-Term Growth. In Applied
General Equilibrium Analysis, eds. Herbert E. Scarf and John
Shoven, pp. 319-362. Cambridge: Cambridge University Press.

Chamley, Christophe (1981). The Welfare Cost of Capital Income Taxation
in a Growing Economy. Journal of Political Economy, 89, June,
468-96.

Chao, Hung-po (1982). Resource Exhaustion, Economic Growth and Income
Distribution, A Comparison of an Optimization and a Competitive
Equilibrium Model. Journal of Policy Modeling, IV, no. 2,
191-209.

Davies, James B. (1981). Uncertain Lifetime, Consumption, and Dissaving
in Retirement. Journal of Political Economy, 89, no. 3,
561-77.

Dervis, K., J. de Melo and S. Robinson (1982). General Equilibrium Models
for Development Policy. New York: Cambridge University Press.

Fullerton, Don, A. Thomas King, John B. Shoven, and John Whalley (1981).
Corporate Tax Integration in the United States: A General
Equilibrium Approach. American Economic Review, 71, September,
677-91.

Fullerton, Don, John B. Shoven, and John Whalley (1983). Replacing the
U.S. Income Tax with a Progressive Consumption Tax: A Sequenced
General Equilibrium Approach. Journal of Public Economics, 20,
no. 1, 3-24.

Hansen, Lars P., and Kenneth J. Singleton (1982). Generalized Instrumental
Variables Estimation of Nonlinear Rational Expectation Models.
Econometrica, 50, no. 5.

Hudson, E. A., and D. W. Jorgensen (1978). Energy Policy and U.S. Economic
Growth. American Economic Review, 68, no. 2, 118-123.

Kimbell, J. J., and G. W. Harrison (1983). On the Solution of General
Equilibrium Models. University of Western Ontario. Draft
manuscript, January.

Lucas, Robert E. (1976). Econometric Policy Evaluation: A Critique. In
    The Phillips Curve and Labor Markets, eds. K. Brunner and
    Allan H. Meltzer, eds., pp. 19-46. Pittsburgh: Carnegie-
    Rochester Series on Public Policy.
Manne, A. S., and P. V. Preckel (1983). A Three-Region Intertemporal Model
    of Energy, International Trade and Capital Flows. Department
    of Operations Research, Stanford University. Mimeo, January.
Starrett, David A. (1982). Long Run Savings Elasticities in the Life Cycle
    Model. Factor Markets Workshop Research Paper No. 24, Stanford
    University.
Strotz, Robert H. (1955-1956). Myopia and Inconsistency in Dynamic Utility
    Maximization. Review of Economic Studies, 23, 165-80.
Summers, Lawrence H. (1981). Capital Taxation and Accumulation in a Life
    Cycle Growth Model. American Economic Review, 71, September,
    533-44.

SPECIAL PURPOSE VERSIONS OF A GENERAL PURPOSE MULTISECTORAL
MODEL : TAX ISSUES AND THE AUSTRALIAN WINE INDUSTRY*

G.A. Meagher, B.R. Parmenter and R.J. Rimmer
Department of Economics, La Trobe University, Bundoora,
Vic. 3083, Australia

K. W. Clements
Department of Economics, University of Western Australia,
Nedlands, W.A. 6009, Australia

1 *INTRODUCTION : THE STRATEGY OF SPECIAL PURPOSE MODIFICATIONS*

ORANI is a very detailed multisectoral model of the
Australian economy in the tradition pioneered by Johansen (1960). The
model has been implemented using Australian data which distinguish 113
domestic industries, 115 commodity categories and 9 occupational categories of labour. A facility has been included for the disaggregation
(via a tops-down method) of economy-wide projections from the model to
the 6-State level. A complete description can be found in Dixon et al.
(1982).

This level of detail was necessary to support the primary
role for which the model was constructed, namely, its role as a vehicle
for policy analysis in a wide range of public-sector institutions.
Despite its versatility, the standard version of ORANI has not always
proved to contain sufficient detail about particular sectors of the
economy to satisfy the requirements of users with special interests.
The approach which has been taken in cases such as this has been the
creation of special purpose versions of ORANI in each of which a more
detailed model of the sector of special interest is embedded, replacing
the simpler specification of the standard version but retaining the
linkages between the sector and the rest of the economy. The modifications might extend to the theoretical specification of the sector of
special interest as well as to its data.

An example of a modification of the more ambitious type is
the treatment of the agricultural sector. In the first version of

* The assistance of the South Australian Department of Agriculture and
of the New South Wales Drug and Alcohol Authority in providing financial
support for parts of the research reported in this paper is gratefully
acknowledged. A more detailed earlier version of the paper is available
on request from the authors.

283

ORANI, agriculture was specified as composed of single-product
industries in accordance with input-output conventions. This specification has now been replaced with one which models explicitly the multi-
product nature of most Australian agriculture and the regional
differences in production technology which characterize it. Because of
the importance of agricultural commodities in total Australian exports,
the performance of the agricultural sector is usually crucial for trade-
related policy questions. For this reason, the respecification of the
agricultural sector was considered to be of sufficient importance to
warrant its permanent incorporation in the standard version of the model
(see Dixon et al. subsection 28.2.1). Other examples are described in
IAC (1983) and Higgs et al. (1983).

In the rest of this paper we illustrate the methodology for
building special-purpose versions of ORANI by describing the construction and application of ORANI-WINE, a version of ORANI specifically designed for analysing policy questions bearing upon the alcoholic
beverages sector of the Australian economy and thus on associated agricultural activities, especially viticulture. The most important such
policy issue is the question of the indirect tax treatment afforded to
different commodities produced in the sector. At present, heavy
indirect taxes are levied on beer and spirits, and on imported wine.
Domestically produced wine is exempt from tax. The removal of this form
of assistance from the wine industry is often canvassed. ORANI-WINE
allows us to analyse the effects of the imposition of indirect taxes on
domestically produced wine and the effects of changes to the tax rates
applied to other alcoholic beverages.

2   SPECIFICATION AND IMPLEMENTATION OF ORANI-WINE

2.1   Input-output structure

The standard ORANI data base distinguishes only two
alcoholic beverages, namely *Beer and malt* and *Alcoholic beverages nec*.
The latter includes both spirits and wine. The standard version of the
model is therefore unable to deal explicitly with the tax differential
which exists between domestically produced wine and other alcoholic
beverages, imported and domestically produced. Nor is it able to focus
specifically on the grape-growing industry, support of which is the main
justification for continuation of the current indirect-tax exemption for

domestically produced wine. The reason is that grape growing is aggregated into the model's *Other farming, import competing* activity.

In ORANI-WINE a specialist grape-growing industry is distinguished and there are three industries which manufacture alcoholic beverages : the *Wine and brandy* industry, the *Beer and malt* industry, and a specialist producer of alcoholic beverages other than wine, brandy and beer (*Alcoholic beverages nec*). Four separate commodities are produced by these industries. They are *Grapes, Wine, Beer and malt* and *Alcoholic beverages nec*. The last of these is a composite commodity including mainly brandy and other potable spirits. The make matrix for the sector is shown in Table 1.

A number of data sources were used to compile data on the sales patterns of grapes and of wine, and on the cost structures of the *Grapes* and the *Wine and brandy* industries. These data were then used to split the corresponding commodity rows and industry columns of the standard ORANI data base.

2.2 *Consumption specification*

The household consumption side of the standard version of ORANI is based on the assumption of additive preferences. This is more likely to be appropriate when applied to broad aggregates, which do not interact in the utility function a great deal. However, the specification of preferences must be more flexible when dealing with more disaggregated commodity groups such as beer, wine and spirits.

Table 1 Commodity and Industry Structure of the Grapes and Alcoholic Beverages Sectors of the ORANI-WINE Data Base : Basic Value of Output by Commodity and Industry ($1974/5 m.)

Industry / Commodity	Grapes	Wine and brandy	Alcoholic beverages nec	Beer and malt	Output by commodity
Grapes	97.4				97.4
Wine		176.5			176.5
Alcoholic beverages, nec		19.6	12.5		32.1
Beer and malt				468.7	468.7
Output by industry	97.4	196.1	12.5	468.7	774.7

In ORANI-WINE the utility function for the representative household takes the form

$$U = U_A(q_1, q_2, q_3) + \sum_{i=4}^{n} U_i(q_i) \quad , \tag{1}$$

where q_i $(i=1,\ldots,n)$ denotes the quantity consumed of each of n commodities and the subscript A denotes an alcoholic beverages sub-group comprising ORANI-WINE's three alcoholic beverages (beer, wine and spirits) labelled for convenience as commodities 1 - 3. The sub-utility function $U_A(\ )$ is not additive.

To implement the consumption specification based on (1), formally all that is required is a revised set of expenditure and own- and cross-price elasticities of demand. The new conditional demand parameters required to support within-alcoholic-beverages-group demand equations implied by constrained maximization of (1) are given in Table 2. For full details see Clements & Smith (1983).

2.3 *A facility for tax analysis*

In the ORANI model, commodity tax rates are formulated as a weighted sum of a real tax rate (defined in terms of the Consumer Price Index), a specific rate and an ad valorem rate. This formulation is designed to allow the user a full range of options for modelling the tax structure via suitable choice of the weights. The tax facility implements the required option and computes the changes in the relevant composite variables that result from given rate changes. The computer

Table 2 Conditional Demand Parameters for Alcoholic Beverages, 1955/6 - 1976/7

Beverage	Conditional marginal share θ_i	Conditional Slutsky coefficients		
		π_{i1}^{A} × 100	π_{i2}^{A} × 100	π_{i3}^{A} × 100
Beer	.590	-.390	.150	.240
Wine	.099		-.293	.144
Spirits	.311			-.384

Source: Clements & Johnson (1982, Table 5).

programs that perform these functions are not fully integrated with the
ORANI programs, but exist as side calculations with a limited number of
interfaces to the main system. This strategy results in some loss of
computational efficiency and requires iterative solution of the model
for changes expressed in nominal, specific or ad valorem terms.
However, it also obviates the necessity for the user to be familiar with
details of the long and difficult ORANI code, an advantage without which
user-initiated special purpose applications like ORANI-WINE would
probably not be feasible.

3 RESULTS : AN ANALYSIS OF THE EFFECTS OF IMPOSING AN INDIRECT TAX ON WINE

3.1 The specification of the tax shock

Using ORANI's 1974/5 data as a base (see Table 3) our
purpose is to investigate the effects of bringing the tax on wine more
into line with that on other alcoholic beverages.

We have chosen to impose a specific tax of $1.37 per unit of
consumption, the unit being the physical quantity that could be
purchased for one dollar at basic values in 1974/5. (For imported wine
this required the imposition of a tax of $1.25 per unit in addition to
the base-period levy.) That is, the tax is imposed at the average rate
of commodity tax on the commodity *Beer and malt* in the base period.
This is sufficient to increase the purchasers' price of wine by approximately 58 per cent.

Table 3 Household Consumption of Alcoholic Beverages in the ORANI-WINE
Data Base

Commodity	(1) Consumption at basic values ($1974/5 m)	(2) Commodity tax revenue ($1974/5 m)	(3) Implied tax rate ((2)/(1))
Wine			
- domestic	133.52	0.0	0.0
- imported	7.53	0.93	0.12
Alcoholic beverages nec	53.61	155.08	2.89
Beer and malt	350.82	480.10	1.37

3.2 *Macro results*

At the level of the macroeconomy, the wine tax exerts its influence via a change in domestic relative to world prices. In our simulation the nominal exchange rate is exogenous, hence the relevant relative price change is measured by the change in a domestic price index, say the Consumer Price Index (CPI). The weight of wine in the CPI is about 0.9 per cent; therefore in the absence of any economic adjustment to the change, the tax would increase the CPI by approximately 0.5 per cent. However wages (as paid by producers) are assumed fully indexed to the CPI. By the time the implied wage-price spiral is exhausted the CPI has risen by a total of 1.67 per cent.

Exporters are assumed to face fairly elastic demand for their products in foreign markets and can pass on cost increases only at the expense of rapidly declining sales. Hence they become caught in a cost-price squeeze as money wages rise. Import competing industries likewise find their competitiveness being eroded. Consequently exports fall (1.69 per cent), imports rise (0.49 per cent) and the balance of trade moves towards deficit by an additional 0.33 per cent of base-period GDP. The nontraded sector on the other hand is relatively unaffected, since aggregate domestic final demand is assumed to remain constant in real terms. However it does suffer some reduction in intermediate demand for its output because of the contraction in the traded sectors. The projected fall in aggregate employment is 0.65 per cent.

3.3 *The alcoholic beverages sector*

The output changes (by industry and commodity) in the alcoholic beverages sector are set out in Table 4. For all three commodities produced in the sector, the share of sales to household consumption is large. Hence, the changes in commodity outputs can be understood in terms of the effect of the wine tax on the pattern of consumption demand.

In the ORANI model, substitution in consumption can occur between commodities of different types (e.g., wine and beer) and between commodities of the same type from different sources (e.g., domestic and imported wine). Substitution of the first kind is governed by demand equations of the following form :

$$x_i = \varepsilon_i c + \sum_{k=1}^{115} n_{ik} p_k \quad , \qquad (i=1,\ldots,115) \quad , \qquad (2)$$

where x_i is the percentage change in the quantity of commodity of type
i consumed by households, p_i is the percentage change in the
purchasers' price of the commodity, and c is the percentage change in
total consumption expenditure. The parameters ε_i and n_{ik}
(k=1,...,115) are the expenditure and own- and cross-price
elasticities.

By assumption, real aggregate household expenditure remains
constant when the wine tax is imposed. Hence the percentage change in
nominal expenditure is equal to the percentage change in the CPI, i.e.,
c = 1.67. Given also the relevant changes in purchasers' prices,
the changes in consumption of the various alcoholic beverages can be
decomposed into expenditure and price effects, as set out in Table 5.
Note that the price changes shown are projected price changes from
ORANI. Hence, the final percentage change in the purchasers price of
wine (55.13 per cent) differs from the percentage change (58 per cent)
generated as an impact effect of the tax increase (see section 3). To
complete Table 5 we have shown how the changes in household consumption
are allocated between domestic and imported supplies. As can be seen,
substitution between the two sources of supply is not a crucial feature
of our results.

The most surprising result in Table 5 is that the net effect
of an increase in the purchasers' price of *Wine* is to decrease slightly

Table 4 The Projected Percentage Effects of a Wine Tax on Industry
and Commodity Outputs in the Domestic Alcoholic Beverages Sector

Commodity \ Industry	Wine and brandy	Alcoholic beverages nec	Beer and malt	Total commodity outputs
Wine	-18.05			-18.05
Alcoholic beverages nec	2.52	0.81		1.85
Beer and malt			-0.76	-0.76
Total industry outputs	-16.00	0.81	-0.76	

Table 5   Projected Effects of a Wine Tax on Household Consumption

Category	Symbol	Commodity		
		Wine	Alcoholic beverages nec	Beer and malt
Commodity number	i	11	12	32
Expenditure elasticity	ε_i	0.725	1.843	0.771
Price elasticities	$n_{i,11}$	-0.375	0.058	-0.021
	$n_{i,12}$	0.058	-0.756	-0.547
	$n_{i,32}$	-0.104	-0.373	-0.372
Percentage change in price	p_i	55.13	1.38	1.29
Percentage change in consumption (price and expenditure effects)				
due to change in expenditure	$\varepsilon_i c$	1.21	3.07	1.29
due to change in price of *Wine*	$n_{i,11}p_{11}$	-20.67	3.20	-1.17
due to change in price of *Alcoholic beverages nec*	$n_{i,12}p_{12}$	0.08	-1.05	-0.76
due to change in price of *Beer and malt*	$n_{i,32}p_{32}$	-0.13	-0.48	-0.48
due to changes in all other prices	$\sum_{\substack{j=1 \\ j \neq 11,12,32}}^{115} n_{ij}\, p_j$	-0.35	-0.87	0.31
total	x_i	<u>-19.86</u>	<u>3.87</u>	<u>-0.81</u>
Percentage change in consumption by source of supply				
domestic commodity	$x_{(i1)}$	-20.05	3.42	-0.81
imported commodity	$x_{(i2)}$	-16.52	4.13	-0.45
total	x_i	<u>-19.86</u>	<u>3.87</u>	<u>-0.81</u>

the consumption of *Beer and malt*. The parameters described in section 2
imply that, within the alcoholic beverages group, *Wine* and *Beer and
malt* are substitutes (see Table 2). However, the wine tax increases the
price of the composite alcoholic-beverages commodity and thus induces a
fall in the consumption of alcoholic beverages as a whole. For *Beer and
malt* (but not for *Alcoholic beverages nec*) the within-group substitution
effect is insufficient to outweigh the shift in the pattern of consumption away from the alcoholic beverages group.

Returning now to Table 4, it is clear that the changes in
output of the commodities *Wine* and *Beer and malt* are closely explained
by the changes in consumption demand (domestic commodities) reported in
Table 5. The increase in the output of the commodity *Alcoholic
beverages nec* falls somewhat below the increase in its consumption
demand. While the output of the commodity *Alcoholic beverages nec*
increases by 1.85 per cent, the output of the specialist industry
Alcoholic beverages nec increases only by 0.81 per cent. The difference
is taken up by the increase of 2.52 per cent in the production of this
commodity by the *Wine and brandy* industry. The output mix of the *Wine
and brandy* industry is governed by a CET (constant elasticity of transformation) function. To a limited extent, therefore, the *Wine and brandy*
industry is able to offset the effects of the wine tax by shifting its
output mix in favour of *Alcoholic beverages nec*.

Finally, the grape-growing industry (not included in the
tables) is projected to suffer an 8.6 per cent reduction in output.
About 50 per cent of its total output is sold to the *Wine and brandy*
industry.

4 CONCLUSION

We have described modifications to the data and implemented
theory of ORANI which have enabled us to use the model to analyse the
effects of changing indirect taxes on the products of the alcoholic
beverages sector. This strategy of constructing special-purpose
versions of a general-purpose multisectoral model has proved useful in a
number of contexts. In each case detailed projections were required for
some sector (industrial or regional) of the economy, accounting also for
the interdependence of the sector with the rest of the economy. Even
though ORANI is among the most detailed of the current generation of
multisectoral models, users of the model often require more detail on
particular sectors than is available in the standard version.

A number of features of our modelling methodology are important in allowing us to construct special-purpose versions at tolerable cost. The first and most crucial is our computing method. Following Johansen (1960), ORANI is solved by linear approximations. Minor changes to the model's theoretical structure, the addition of new equations and variables, etc., can therefore be implemented without extensive reprogramming (see Dixon et al., chapter 5). Secondly, many parts of the ORANI theory are specified at a more general level than is implemented in the standard version of the model. For example, in the theory, multi-product technology is allowed for all industrial sectors although it is implemented at present only for the agricultural sector. We took advantage of this, and of the generality of the consumption specification, in constructing ORANI-WINE. The consequence is that substantive changes to the implemented theory of ORANI formally require only changes to the data base. A third methodological feature which renders ORANI amenable to modification is the widespread use of nested utility and production functions. This allows us to introduce more sophisticated theory about individual arguments at one level of the nesting with minimum disruption elsewhere. In ORANI-WINE, for example, we specified the alcoholic-beverages composite as a commodity entering the first (additive) level of the nested utility function, with specific substitution effects between beer, wine and spirits accommodated in a second-level (non-additive) nest.

REFERENCES
Clements, K.W. & Johnson, L.W. (1983). The demand for beer, wine and spirits: a system-wide analysis. Journal of Business 56, 273-304.
Clements, K.W. & Smith, M.D. (1983). Extending the consumption side of the ORANI model. IMPACT Project Preliminary Working Paper no.OP-38, IMPACT Research Centre, Melbourne.
Dixon, P.B., Parmenter, B.R., Sutton, J. & Vincent, D.P. (1982). ORANI: A Multisectoral Model of the Australian Economy. Amsterdam: North-Holland Publishing Company.
Higgs, P.J., Parmenter, B.R. & Rimmer, R.J. (1983). Modelling the effects of economy-wide shocks on a state economy in a federal system, IMPACT Project Preliminary Working Paper, no.OP-37, IMPACT Research Centre, Melbourne.
Industries Assistance Commission (1983). Certain iron and steel products and certain alloy steel products, Draft Report, Canberra.
Johansen, L. (1960). A Multisectoral Study of Economic Growth. Amsterdam: North-Holland Publishing Company.

GENERAL EQUILIBRIUM ANALYSIS OF ECONOMIC POLICY

Dale W. Jorgenson
Harvard University, Cambridge, Massachusetts 02138

Daniel T. Slesnick
University of Texas, Austin, Texas 78712

1   INTRODUCTION

The purpose of this paper is to present a new approach to the general equilibrium analysis of economic policy. Our objective is to provide an ordering of alternative economic policies. The most desirable economic policy is the policy yielding the highest level of social welfare. This principle can be used to evaluate a specific policy change or to select the optimal policy from a set of alternatives.

Dupuit (1969) originated the appraisal of alternative economic policies on the basis of their impact on consumer welfare. He proposed to measure individual welfare on the basis of preferences revealed by consumer behavior. The prices faced by the consumer and the corresponding quantities demanded were used to obtain estimates of consumer's surplus. (Dupuit's approach to welfare economics has generated a voluminous literature. Key references include Harberger (1971), Hicks (1942), Hotelling (1938), and Marshall (1920).)

Hicks (1942) introduced measures of consumer's surplus based on compensating and equivalent variations in income or total expenditure. The intuition underlying Hicks's approach to welfare economics is straightforward. Levels of welfare before and after a change in economic policy can be ordered by comparing the required levels of total expenditure. For Hicks's compensating variation the difference in total expenditure is evaluated at prices prevailing after the change in policy. For the equivalent variation the difference is evaluated at prices before the policy change.

Chipman and Moore (1980) have shown that a necessary and

sufficient condition for Hicks's compensating variation to provide an
appropriate ordering of economic policies is that individual preferences
are homothetic. Chipman and Moore recommend Hicks's equivalent variation,
since homothetic preferences are inconsistent with well established regularities in the behavior of individual consumers, such as those reviewed
by Houthakker (1957). (Evidence on the nonhomotheticity of preferences is
presented by Houthakker (1957), Leser (1963), Muellbauer (1976), Pollak
and Wales (1978), and Prais and Houthakker (1971).)

The individual expenditure function introduced by McKenzie
(1957) provides the simplest approach for implementing Hicks's measures
of welfare. The expenditure function gives the minimum level of total
expenditure required to attain a stipulated level of utility as a function of the prices faced by the consumer. This level of expenditure can
be derived from the indirect utility function, which gives the maximum
attainable utility level as a function of prices and total expenditure.

The approach to welfare measurement originated by Dupuit is
limited to individual welfare. Under the Pareto principle a change in
economic policy can be recommended if all consuming units are at least as
well off under the policy change and at least one consuming unit is
better off. This principle provides a partial ordering of economic policies. To obtain a complete ordering we require the concept of a social
welfare function originated by Bergson (1938) and discussed by Samuelson
(1947, 1982).

A social welfare function gives the level of social welfare
as a function of the distribution of individual welfare over the population of consumers. The social welfare function incorporates the effects
of changes in economic policy on the welfare of individual consumers. A
requirement often imposed on social welfare functions is that they must
obey the Pareto principle. A social welfare function also includes the
impacts of policy changes on horizontal and vertical equity among consumers.

Since the pioneering work of Atkinson (1970) and Kolm (1969),
the measurement of social welfare has been based on explicit social welfare functions. However, the social welfare functions introduced by
Atkinson and Kolm are defined on the distribution of income rather than
the distribution of individual welfare. Muellbauer (1974b) and Roberts
(1980c) have shown that measures of social welfare based on income coincide with measures based on individual welfare if and only if preferences

are identical and homothetic for all consumers. (See, for example, Muellbauer (1974b), p. 498.)

Identical preferences are inconsistent with empirical findings on consumer behavior, such as those of Prais and Houthakker (1971), showing that expenditure patterns depend on the demographic characteristics on individual consuming units. (Evidence on the impact of demographic characteristics on expenditure allocation is given by Lau et al. (1978), Muellbauer (1977), Parks and Barten (1973), Pollak and Wales (1980, 1981), and Ray (1982).) Muellbauer (1974) has defined social welfare functions on the distribution of Hicks's equivalent variation or money metric individual welfare. This approach has also been employed by Deaton and Muellbauer (1980), King (1983a, 1983b), and McKenzie (1982).

Roberts (1980c) has derived restrictions on preferences under which measures of social welfare based on the distribution of money metric individual welfare coincide with measures based on the distribution of individual welfare. In the absence of restrictions on social welfare functions, individuals must have identical homothetic preferences. Roberts (1980c) also considers possible restrictions on the class of social welfare functions. With no restrictions on individual preferences, the social welfare functions must be dictatorial in the sense of Arrow (1963) and Roberts (1980a).

Our approach to policy evaluation is based on an econometric model of aggregate consumer behavior. The novel feature of this model is that systems of individual demand functions can be recovered uniquely from the system of aggregate demand functions. By requiring that the individual demand functions are integrable, we can also recover indirect utility functions and individual expenditure functions for all consumers. Finally, we can define measures of individual welfare in terms of these indirect utility and individual expenditure functions.

In Section 2 we outline an econometric methodology for developing a model of aggregate consumer behavior. In this model systems of individual demand functions depend on the prices faced by all households. These systems also depend on total expenditures and attributes such as demographic characteristics that vary among households. We obtain aggregate demand functions by summing over individual demand functions. The resulting system of aggregate demand functions depends on summary statistics of the joint distribution of total expenditures and attributes among all households.

In Section 3 we implement our econometric model of aggregate consumer behavior for the United States. For this purpose we employ cross section data on individual expenditure patterns. We combine these data with time series data on aggregate expenditure patterns and prices for all commodities. We also employ time series data on the distribution of total expenditures among households.

In Section 4 we present methods for evaluating the impact of alternative economic policies on the distribution of individual welfare. We illustrate these methods by comparing alternative regulatory and tax policies for petroleum production in the United States. For this purpose we require projections of prices and total expenditure under each policy. We obtain these projections from the Dynamic General Equilibrium Model (DGEM) of the U.S. economy, constructed by Hudson and Jorgenson (1974, 1976, 1978a, 1978b). This model is based on a breakdown of the U.S. economy into nine industrial sectors, including five energy sectors and four aggregates of the nonenergy sectors.

Our approach to the measurement of individual welfare is based on the indirect utility function and the individual expenditure function for each consuming unit. The indirect utility function can be used to generate measures of individual welfare. The individual expenditure function can then be employed to translate these measures of individual welfare into money metric individual welfare. Money metric individual welfare provides a monotone increasing transformation of individual welfare that is not full comparable among consuming units. This measure can be used in evaluating economic policies by constructing partial orderings of these policies on the basis of the Pareto principle.

In Section 5 we introduce a class of social welfare functions capable of expressing a variety of ethical judgements. This class is based on the distribution of individual welfare over the population of consuming units. In measuring social welfare we employ cardinal measures of individual welfare that are fully comparable among units. To translate comparisons among economic policies into money measures of social welfare, we introduce the social expenditure function in Section 6. This function gives the minimum level of aggregate expenditure required to attain a stipulated level of social welfare as a function of the prices faced by all consumers.

The social expenditure function can be used to translate changes in social welfare based on a social welfare function into money

metric social welfare. The concept of money metric social welfare can be
used in comparing alternative economic policies on the basis of the
aggregate expenditure required for each policy. As a measure of efficiency we introduce the maximum level of social welfare that can be
attained by lump sum redistributions of aggregate expenditure among consuming units. Using this measure, we can decompose money metric social
welfare into the sum of money metric equity and money metric efficiency.

In Section 7 we present an evaluation of alternative regulatory and fiscal policies for petroleum production in the United States,
based on projections of prices and the distribution of total expenditure
from the DGEM model of the U.S. economy. On the basis of these projections we first construct the distribution of measures of individual welfare for each policy. We then evaluate the corresponding level of social
welfare and translate the differences in levels of social welfare among
policies into money measures of changes in efficiency and changes in
equity. Section 8 of the paper provides a summary and conclusion.

2 AGGREGATE CONSUMER BEHAVIOR

In this Section we develop an econometric model of aggregate consumer behavior based on the theory of exact aggregation, following Jorgenson, Lau, and Stoker (1980, 1981, 1982). Our model incorporates time series data on prices and aggregate quantities consumed. We also include cross section data on individual quantities consumed, individual total expenditure, and attributes of individual households such as demographic characteristics.

To represent preferences for all individuals in a form suitable for measuring individual welfare, we take households as consuming units. We assume that expenditures on individual commodities are allocated so as to maximize a household welfare function. As a consequence, the household behaves in the same way as an individual maximizing a utility function, as demonstrated by Samuelson (1956) and Pollak (1981). By assuming that each household maximizes a household welfare function, we can focus on the distribution of welfare among households rather than the distribution among individuals within households.

To construct an econometric model based on exact aggregation we first represent individual preferences by means of an indirect utility function for each consuming unit, using the following notation:

p_n -- price of the nth commodity, assumed to be the same for all consuming units.

$p = (p_1, p_2 \cdots p_N)$ -- the vector of prices of all commodities.

x_{nk} -- the quantity of the nth commodity group consumed by the kth consuming unit ($n = 1, 2 \ldots N$; $k = 1, 2 \ldots K$).

$M_k = \sum_{n=1}^{N} p_n x_{nk}$ -- total expenditure of the kth consuming unit ($k = 1, 2 \ldots K$).

$w_{nk} = p_n x_{nk} / M_k$ -- expenditure share of the nth commodity group in the budget of the kth consuming unit ($n = 1, 2 \ldots N$; $k = 1, 2 \ldots K$).

$w_k = (w_{1k}, w_{2k} \cdots w_{Nk})$ -- vector of expenditure shares for the kth consuming unit ($k = 1, 2 \ldots K$).

$\ln \dfrac{p}{M_k} = (\ln \dfrac{p_1}{M_k}, \ln \dfrac{p_2}{M_k} \cdots \ln \dfrac{p_N}{M_k})$ -- vector of logarithms of ratios of prices to expenditure by the kth consuming unit ($k = 1, 2 \ldots K$).

$\ln p = (\ln p_1, \ln p_2 \cdots \ln p_N)$ -- vector of logarithms of prices.

A_k -- vector of attributes of the kth consuming unit (k = 1, 2 ... K).

We assume that the kth consuming unit allocates expenditures in accord with the transcendental logarithmic or translog indirect utility function, say V_k, where:

(2.1) $\ln V_k = G(\ln\frac{p}{M_k}'\alpha_p + \frac{1}{2} \ln\frac{p}{M_k}'B_{pp}\ln\frac{p}{M_k} + \ln\frac{p}{M_k}'B_{pA}A_k, \ A_k),$

(k = 1, 2 . . . K).

In this representation the function G is a monotone increasing function of the variable $\ln\frac{p}{M_k}'\alpha_p + \frac{1}{2} \ln\frac{p}{M_k}'B_{pp}\ln\frac{p}{M_k} + \ln\frac{p}{M_k}'B_{pA}A_k$. In addition, the function G depends directly on the attribute vector A_k. The vector α_p and the matrices B_{pp} and B_{pA} are constant parameters that are the same for all consuming units.

(The translog indirect utility function was introduced by Christensen, Jorgenson, and Lau (1975) and extended to encompass determinants of expenditure allocation other than prices and total expenditure by Jorgenson and Lau (1975). Alternative approaches to the representation of the effects of prices and total expenditure on expenditure allocation are summarized by Barten (1977), Deaton and Muellbauer (1980), pp. 60-85, and Lau (1977a). Alternative approaches to the representation of household characteristics in expenditure allocation are presented by Barten (1964), Gorman (1976), and Prais and Houthakker (1971). A review of the literature is presented by Deaton and Muellbauer (1980), pp. 191-213.)

The expenditure shares of the kth consuming unit can be derived by the logarithmic form of Roy's (1943) Identity. (The specification of a system of individual demand functions by means of Roy's Identity was first employed in econometric modeling of consumer behavior by Houthakker (1960). A detailed review of econometric models based on Roy's Identity is given by Lau (1977a)).

(2.2) $w_{nk} = \dfrac{\partial \ln V_k}{\partial \ln (p_n/M_k)} \ / \ \displaystyle\sum_{n=1}^{N} \dfrac{\partial \ln V_k}{\partial \ln (p_n/M_k)}$,

$$(n = 1, 2 \ldots N; \ k = 1, 2 \ \cdots \ K).$$

Applying this Identity to the translog indirect utility function (2.1), we obtain the system of individual expenditure shares:

(2.3) $\quad w_k = \dfrac{1}{D_k(p)} \ (\alpha_p + B_{pp} \ln \dfrac{p}{M_k} + B_{pA} A_k)$, $(k = 1, 2 \ \cdots \ K)$,

where the denominators $\{D_k\}$ take the form:

(2.4) $\quad D_k = i' \alpha_p + i' B_{pp} \ln \dfrac{p}{M_k} + i' B_{pA} A_k$, $(k = 1, 2 \ \cdots \ K)$.

The individual expenditure shares are homogeneous of degree zero in the unknown parameters -- α_p, B_{pp}, B_{pA}. By multiplying a given set of these parameters by a constant we obtain another set of parameters that generates the same system of individual budget shares. Accordingly, we can choose a normalization for the parameters without affecting observed patterns of individual expenditure allocation. We find it convenient to employ the normalization:

$$i' \alpha_p = -1 .$$

Under this restriction any change in the set of unknown parameters will be reflected in changes in individual expenditure patterns.

The conditions for exact aggregation are that the individual expenditure shares are linear in functions of the attributes $\{A_k\}$ and total expenditures $\{M_k\}$ for all consuming units. (For further discussion, see Lau (1977b, 1982) and Jorgenson, Lau, and Stoker (1980, 1981, 1982).) These conditions will be satisfied if and only if the terms involving the attributes and expenditures do not appear in the denominators of the expressions given above for the individual expenditure shares, so that:

$$i' B_{pp} i = 0 ,$$

$$i'B_{pA} = 0 .$$

The exact aggregation restrictions imply that the denominators $\{D_k\}$ reduce to:

$$D = -1 + i'B_{pp}\ln p,$$

where the subscript k is no longer required, since the denominator is the same for all consuming units. Under these restrictions the individual expenditure shares can be written:

$$(2.5) \quad w_k = \frac{1}{D(p)} (\alpha_p + B_{pp}\ln p - B_{pp} i \cdot \ln M_k + B_{pA}A_k),$$

$$(k = 1, 2, \ . \ . \ . \ K).$$

The individual expenditure shares are linear in the logarithms of expenditures $\{\ln M_k\}$ and in the attributes $\{A_k\}$, as required by exact aggregation.

Under exact aggregation the indirect utility function for each consuming unit can be represented in the form:

$$(2.6) \quad \ln V_k = F(A_k) + \ln p'(\alpha_p + \frac{1}{2} B_{pp}\ln p + B_{pA}A_k) - D(p) \ln M_k,$$

$$(k = 1, 2, \ . \ . \ . \ K).$$

In this representation the indirect utility function is linear in the logarithm of total expenditure $\ln M_k$ with a coefficient that depends on the prices p (k = 1, 2 ... K). This property is invariant with respect to positive affine transformations, but is not preserved by arbitrary monotone increasing transformations. We conclude that the indirect utility function (2.6) provides a cardinal measure of utility for each consuming unit.

If a system of individual expenditure shares (2.3) can be generated from an indirect utility function of the form (2.1) we say that the system is <u>integrable</u>. A complete set of conditions for integrability (discussed by Jorgenson and Lau (1979) and Jorgenson, Lau, and Stoker

(1982)) is the following:

    1. Homogeneity. The individual expenditure shares are homo-
geneous of degree zero in prices and total expenditure.

    We can write the individual expenditure shares in the form:

(2.7) $\beta_{pM} = B_{pp} i.$

Given the exact aggregation restrictions, there are N-1 restrictions
implied by homogeneity.

    2. Summability. The sum of the individual expenditure
shares over all commodity groups is equal to unity:

    $i' w_k = 1,$ $(k = 1, 2 \cdots K).$

    We can write the denominator D(p) in (2.4) in the form:

    $D = -1 + \beta_{Mp} \ln p,$

where the vector of parameters β_{Mp} is constant and the same for all commodity groups and all consuming units. Summability implies that this
vector must satisfy the restrictions:

(2.8) $\beta_{Mp} = i' B_{pp}.$

Given the exact aggregation restrictions, there are N-1 restrictions
implied by summability.

    3. Symmetry. The matrix of compensated own- and cross-price
substitution effects must be symmetric.

    If the system of individual expenditure shares can be gen-
erated from an indirect utility function of the form (2.1), a necessary
and sufficient condition for symmetry is that the matrix B_{pp} must be symmetric. Without imposing this condition, we can write the individual

expenditure shares in the form:

$$w_k = \frac{1}{D(p)} (\alpha_p + B_{pp} \ln \frac{p}{M_k} + B_{pA} A_k), \qquad (k = 1, 2 \cdots K).$$

Symmetry implies that the matrix of parameters B_{pp} must satisfy the restrictions:

(2.9) $B_{pp} = B_{pp}'$.

The total number of symmetry restrictions is $\frac{1}{2} N(N-1)$.

    4. Nonnegativity. The individual expenditure shares must be nonnegative.

        By summability the individual expenditure shares sum to unity, so that we can write:

$$w_k \geq 0, \qquad (k = 1, 2 \cdots K),$$

where $w_k \geq 0$ implies $w_{nk} \geq 0$, $(n = 1, 2 \ldots N)$, and $w_k \neq 0$.

        Since the translog indirect utility function is quadratic in the logarithms of prices, we can always choose the prices so that the individual expenditure shares violate the nonnegativity conditions. Accordingly, we cannot impose restrictions on the parameters of the translog indirect utility functions that would imply nonnegativity of the individual expenditure shares. Instead we consider restrictions on the parameters that imply monotonicity of the system of individual demand functions for all nonnegative expenditure shares.

        5. Monotonicity. The matrix of compensated own- and cross-price substitution effects must be nonpositive definite.

        We introduce the definition due to Martos (1969) of a strictly merely positive subdefinite matrix, namely, a real symmetric matrix S such that:

    xSx <0

implies $Sx > 0$ or $Sx < 0$. A necessary and sufficient condition for monotonicity is either that the translog indirect utility function is
homothetic or that B_{pp}^{-1} exists and is strictly merely positive subdefinite. (For further discussion see Jorgenson, Lau, and Stoker (1982), esp.
pp. 175-186.)

To provide a basis for evaluating the impact of transfers
among households on social welfare, we find it useful to represent household preferences by means of a utility function that is the same for all
consuming units. For this purpose, we assume that the kth consuming unit
maximizes its utility, say U_k, where:

$$(2.10) \quad U_k = U[\frac{x_{1k}}{m_1(A_k)}, \frac{x_{2k}}{m_2(A_k)} \cdots \frac{x_{Nk}}{m_N(A_k)}], \quad (k = 1, 2 \cdots K),$$

subject to the budget constraint:

$$M_k = \sum_{n=1}^{N} p_n x_{nk}, \quad (k = 1, 2 \cdots K).$$

In this representation of consumer preferences the quantities
$\{x_{nk}/m_n(A_k)\}$ can be regarded as __effective quantities consumed__, as proposed by Barten (1964). The crucial assumption embodied in this
representation is that differences in preferences among consumers enter
the utility function U only through differences in the commodity specific
household equivalence scales $\{m_n(A_k)\}$. (Household equivalence scales are
discussed by Barten (1964), van der Gaag and Smolensky (1982), Kakwani
(1977), Lazear and Michael (1980), Muellbauer (1974a, 1977, 1980), and
Prais and Houthakker (1971), among others. Alternative approaches are
summarized by Deaton and Muellbauer (1980).)

Consumer equilibrium implies the existence of an indirect
utility function, say V, that is the same for all consuming units. The
level of utility for the kth consuming unit, say V_k, depends on the
prices of individual commodities, the household equivalence scales, and
the level of total expenditure:

$$(2.11) \quad V_k = V[\frac{p_1 m_1(A_k)}{M_k}, \frac{p_2 m_2(A_k)}{M_k} \cdots \frac{p_N m_N(A_k)}{M_k}],$$

$$(k = 1, 2 \cdot \cdot \cdot K).$$

In this representation the prices $\{p_n \, m_n(A_k)\}$ can be regarded as **effective prices**. Differences in preferences among consuming units enter this indirect utility function only through the household equivalence scales $\{m_n(A_k)\}$ $(k = 1, 2 \cdot \cdot \cdot K)$.

To represent the translog indirect utility function (2.1) in terms of household equivalence scales, we require some additional notation:

$\ln \dfrac{p \, m(A_k)}{M_k}$ — vector of logarithms of ratios of effective prices

$\{p_n \, m_n(A_k)\}$ to total expenditure M_k of the kth consuming unit $(k = 1, 2 \ldots K)$.

$\ln m(A_k) = (\ln m_1(A_k), \ln m_2(A_k) \cdot \cdot \cdot \ln m_N(A_k))$ — vector of logarithms of the household equivalence scales of the kth consuming unit $(k = 1, 2 \ldots K)$.

We assume, as before, that the kth consuming unit allocates its expenditures in accord with the translog indirect utility function (2.1). However, we also assume that this function, expressed in terms of the effective prices $\{p_n \, m_n(A_k)\}$ and total expenditure M_k, is the same for all consuming units. The indirect utility function takes the form:

$$(2.12) \quad \ln V_k = \ln \frac{p \, m(A_k)}{M_k}' \, \alpha_p + \frac{1}{2} \ln \frac{p \, m(A_k)}{M_k}' B_{pp} \ln \frac{p \, m(A_k)}{M_k} ,$$

$$(k = 1, 2 \cdot \cdot \cdot K).$$

Taking logarithms of the effective prices $\{p_n \, m_n(A_k)\}$, we can rewrite the indirect utility function (2.12) in the form:

$$(2.13) \quad \ln V_k = \ln m(A_k)' \alpha_p + \frac{1}{2} \ln m(A_k)' B_{pp} \ln m(A_k) + \ln \frac{p}{M_k}' \alpha_p + \frac{1}{2} \ln \frac{p}{M_k}' B_{pp} \ln \frac{p}{M_k}$$

$$+ \ln \frac{p}{M_k}' B_{pp} \ln m(A_k), \qquad (k = 1, 2 \cdot \cdot \cdot K).$$

Comparing the representation (2.13) with the representation
(2.6), we see that the term involving only the household equivalent
scales must take the form:

$$(2.14) \quad F(A_k) = \ln m(A_k)' \, \alpha_p + \frac{1}{2} \ln m(A_k)' \, B_{pp} \, \ln m(A_k),$$

$$(k = 1, 2 \ldots K).$$

Second, the term involving ratios of prices to total expenditure and the
household equivalence scales must satisfy:

$$(2.15) \quad \ln \frac{p}{M_k}' \, B_{pA} \, A_k = \ln \frac{p}{M_k}' \, B_{pp} \ln m(A_k), \qquad (k = 1, 2 \ldots K),$$

for all prices and total expenditure.

The household equivalence scales $\{m_n(A_k)\}$ defined by (2.15)
must satisfy the equation:

$$(2.16) \quad B_{pA} A_k = B_{pp} \ln m(A_k), \qquad (k = 1, 2 \ldots K).$$

Under monotonicity of the individual expenditure shares the matrix B_{pp}
has an inverse, so that we can express the household equivalence scales
in terms of the parameters of the translog indirect utility function --
B_{pp}, B_{pA} -- and the attributes $\{A_k\}$:

$$(2.17) \quad \ln m(A_k) = B_{pp}^{-1} \, B_{pA} \, A_k, \qquad (k = 1, 2 \ldots K).$$

We can refer to these scales as the **commodity specific translog household
equivalence scales**.

Substituting the commodity specific equivalence scales (2.16)
into the indirect utility function (2.13) we obtain a representation of
the indirect utility function in terms of the attributes $\{A_k\}$:

(2.18) $\ln V_k = A_k' B_{pA}' B_{pp}^{-1} \alpha_p + \frac{1}{2} A_k' B_{pA}' B_{pp}^{-1} B_{pA} A_k$

$\qquad + \ln p' (\alpha_p + \frac{1}{2} B_{pp} \ln p + B_{pA} A_k) - D(p) \ln M_k,$

$\qquad\qquad\qquad\qquad\qquad (k = 1, 2 \ldots K).$

This form of the translog indirect utility function is equivalent to the form (2.1) in that both generate the same system of individual demand functions. By requiring that the attributes A_k enter only through the commodity specific household equivalence scales, we have provided a specific form for the function $F(A_k)$ in (2.6).

Given the indirect utility function (2.18) for each consuming unit, we can express total expenditure as a function of prices, consumer attributes, and the level of utility:

(2.19) $\ln M_k = \frac{1}{D(p)} [A_k' B_{pA}' B_{pp}^{-1} \alpha_p + \frac{1}{2} A_k' B_{pA}' B_{pp}^{-1} B_{pA} A_k$

$\qquad + \ln p'(\alpha_p + \frac{1}{2} B_{pp} \ln p + B_{pA} A_k) - \ln V_k],$

$\qquad\qquad\qquad\qquad\qquad (k = 1, 2 \ldots K).$

We can refer to this function as the _translog expenditure function_. The translog expenditure function gives the minimum expenditure required for the kth consuming unit to achieve the utility level V_k, given prices p (k = 1, 2 ... K).

We find it useful to introduce household equivalence scales that are not specific to a given commodity. (The use of household equivalence scales in evaluating transfers among individuals has been advocated by Deaton and Muellbauer (1980), esp. pp. 205-212, and by Muellbauer (1974a). Pollak and Wales (1979) have presented arguments against the use of household equivalence scales for this purpose.) Following Muellbauer (1974a), we define a general household equivalence scale, say m_0, as follows:

$$(2.20) \quad m_0 = \frac{M_k[p\, m(A_k),\, V_k^0]}{M_0(p,\, V_k^0)}, \qquad\qquad (k = 1, 2 \ \ldots \ K),$$

where M_k is the expenditure function for the kth household, M_0 is the expenditure function for a reference household with commodity specific equivalence scales equal to unity for all commodities, and $p\, m(A_k)$ is a vector of effective prices $\{p_n\, m_n(A_k)\}$.

The general household equivalence scale m_0 is the ratio between total expenditures required by the kth household and by the reference household required for the same level of utility V_k^0 (k = 1, 2 $\ \ldots \ $ K). This scale can be interpreted as the number of household equivalent members. The number of members depends on the attributes A_k of the consuming unit and on the prices p.

If each household has a translog indirect utility function, then the general household equivalence scale for the kth household takes the form:

$$(2.21) \quad \ln m_0 = \ln M_k - \ln M_0,$$

$$= \frac{1}{D(p)}\, [\ln m(A_k)'\alpha_p + \frac{1}{2} \ln m(A_k)'B_{pp}\ln m(A_k) + \ln m(A_k)'B_{pp}\ln p],$$

$$(k = 1, 2 \ \ldots \ K).$$

We can refer to this scale as the general translog household equivalence scale. The translog equivalence scale depends on the attributes A_k of the kth household and the prices p of all commodities, but is independent of the level of utility V_k^0.

Given the general translog equivalence scale, we can rewrite the indirect utility function (2.18) in the form:

$$(2.22) \quad \ln V_k = \ln p'\alpha_p + \frac{1}{2} \ln p'B_{pp}\ln p - D(p) \ln [M_k/m_0(p, A_k)],$$

$$(k = 1, 2 \ \ldots \ K).$$

The level of utility for the kth consuming unit depends on prices p and

total expenditure per household equivalent member
$M_k/m_0(p, A_k)$ $(k = 1, 2 \ldots K)$. Similarly, we can rewrite the expenditure function (2.19) in the form:

$$(2.23) \quad \ln M_k = \frac{1}{D(p)}[\ln p'(\alpha_p + \frac{1}{2} B_{pp}\ln p) - \ln V_k] + \ln m_0(p, A_k),$$

$$(k = 1, 2 \ldots K).$$

Total expenditure required by the kth consuming unit to attain the level of utility V_k depends on prices p and the number of household equivalent members $m_0(p, A_k)$ $(k = 1, 2 \ldots K)$.

To construct an econometric model of aggregate consumer behavior based on exact aggregation we obtain aggregate expenditure shares, say w, by multiplying individual expenditure shares (2.5) by expenditure for each consuming unit, adding over all consuming units, and dividing by aggregate expenditure, $M = \sum\limits_{k=1}^{K} M_k$:

$$(2.24) \quad w = \frac{\sum M_k w_k}{M}.$$

The aggregate expenditure shares can be written:

$$(2.25) \quad w = \frac{1}{D(p)} (\alpha_p + B_{pp} \ln p - B_{pp}i \frac{\sum M_k \ln M_k}{M} + B_{pA} \frac{\sum M_k A_k}{M}).$$

The aggregate expenditure patterns depend on the distribution of expenditure over all consuming units through summary statistics of the joint distribution of expenditures and attributes --
$\sum M_k \ln M_k / M$ and $\{\sum M_k A_k / M\}$. Systems of individual expenditure shares (2.5) for consuming units with identical demographic characteristics can be recovered in one and only one way from the system of aggregate expenditure shares (2.25).

The first step in analyzing inequality in the distribution of individual welfare is to select a representation of the individual

welfare function. We assume that individual welfare for the kth consuming unit, say W_k (k = 1, 2 ... K), is equal to the logarithm of the
translog indirect utility function (2.22):

(2.26) $W_k = \ln V_k$,

$$= \ln p'\alpha_p + \frac{1}{2}\ln p'B_{pp}\ln p - D(p) \ln [M_k/m_0(p, A_k)],$$

$$(k = 1, 2 \ . \ . \ . \ K).$$

(Deaton and Muellbauer (1980), pp. 227-239, King (1983a,
1983b), McKenzie (1982), and Muellbauer (1974b, 1974c) present approaches
to welfare measurement based on the distribution of "real expenditure."
Measures of "real expenditure" could be derived from the individual
expenditure function (2.23) by varying the level of utility V_k for a
fixed set of prices p (k = 1, 2 ... K). Restrictions on preferences
under which measures of social welfare defined on the distribution of
real expenditure coincide with measures defined on the distribution of
individual welfare are given by Roberts (1980c).)

To summarize: For our econometric model a system of individual expenditure shares (2.5) can be recovered in one and only one way
from the system of aggregate expenditure shares (2.25). Given a system
of individual expenditure shares (2.5) that is integrable, we can recover
the translog indirect utility function (2.22). This indirect utility
function provides a cardinal measure of utility. We obtain a cardinal
measure of individual welfare for each consuming unit (2.26) by setting
this measure equal to the logarithm of the indirect utility function.

3   ECONOMETRIC MODEL

In this Section we present the empirical results of implementing the econometric model of consumer behavior described in Section
2. We divide consumer expenditures among five commodity groups:

1. Energy: Expenditures on electricity, natural gas, heating
oil, and gasoline.

2. Food: Expenditures on all food products, including
tobacco and alcohol.

3. Consumer Goods: Expenditures on all other nondurable
goods included in consumer expenditures.

4. Capital Services: The service flow from consumer durables
and the service flow from housing.

5. Consumer Services: Expenditures on consumer services,
such as car repairs, medical services, entertainment, and so
on.

We employ the following demographic characteristics as attributes of individual households:

1. Family size: 1, 2, 3, 4, 5, 6, and 7 or more persons.

2. Age of head: 16-24, 25-34, 35-44, 45-54, 55-64, 65 and
over.

3. Region of residence: Northeast, North Central, South, and
West.

4. Race: White, nonwhite.

5. Type of residence: Urban, rural.

Our cross section observations on individual expenditures for
each commodity group and on demographic characteristics of individual
households are for the year 1972 from the 1972-3 Survey of Consumer
Expenditures (CES). (The 1972-3 Survey of Consumer Expenditures is discussed by Carlson (1974).) Our time series observations are based on data
on personal consumption expenditures from the United States National
Income and Product Accounts (NIPA) for the years 1958 to 1974. (We employ
data on the flow of services from durable goods rather than purchases of
durable goods. Personal consumption expenditures in the U.S. National
Income and Product Accounts are based on purchases of durable goods.)
Prices for each commodity group are defined in terms of translog price
indexes computed from detailed prices included in NIPA for each year. We
employ time series data on the distribution of expenditures over all
households and among demographic groups based on Current Population

Reports. (This series is published annually by the U.S. Bureau of the
Census.)

In our application we treat the expenditure shares for five
commodity groups as endogenous variables, so that we estimate four equations. As unknown parameters we have four elements of the vector α_p,
four expenditure coefficients of the vector $B_{pp}i$, sixteen attribute coefficients for each of the four equations in the matrix B_{pA}, and ten price
coefficients in the matrix B_{pp}, which is constrained to be symmetric.
The expenditure coefficients are sums of price coefficients in the
corresponding equation, so that we have a total of eighty-two unknown
parameters. We estimate the complete model, subject to inequality restrictions implied by monotonicity of the individual expenditure shares,
by pooling time series and cross section data. (A detailed discussion of
the stochastic specification of our model and of econometric methods for
pooling time series and cross section data is presented by Jorgenson, Lau
and Stoker (1982), Section 6. This stochastic specification implies that
time series data must be adjusted for heteroscedasticity by multiplying
each observation by the statistic:

$$\rho = \frac{(\sum M_k)^2}{\sum M_k^2} \quad . \quad)$$

The results are given in Table 1.

The impacts of changes in total expenditures and in demographic characteristics of the individual household are estimated very
precisely. This reflects the fact that estimates of the expenditure and
demographic effects incorporate a relatively large number of cross section observations. The impacts of prices enter through the denominator
of the equations for expenditure shares; these price coefficients are
estimated very precisely since they also incorporate cross section data.
Finally, the price impacts also enter through the numerators of equations
for the expenditure shares. These parameters are estimated somewhat less
precisely, since they are based on a much smaller number of time series
observations on prices.

To summarize: We have implemented an econometric model of
aggregate consumer behavior by combining time series and cross section
data for the United States. This model allocates personal consumption
expenditures among five commodity groups -- energy, food, other consumer

TABLE 1

POOLED ESTIMATION RESULTS

Notation:

CONST	=	constant term.
ln PEN	=	coefficient of log of price of energy.
ln PF	=	coefficient of log of price of food.
ln PCG	=	coefficient of log of price of consumer goods.
ln PK	=	coefficient of log of price of capital services.
ln PCS	=	coefficient of log of price of consumer services.
ln M	=	coefficient of log of total expenditure.
S2	=	coefficient of dummy for family of size 2.
S3	=	coefficient of dummy for family of size 3.
S4	=	coefficient of dummy for family of size 4.
S5	=	coefficient of dummy for family of size 5.
S6	=	coefficient of dummy for family of size 6.
S7+	=	coefficient of dummy for family of size 7 or more.
A25 - 34	=	coefficient of dummy for age between 25 and 34.
A35 - 44	=	coefficient of dummy for age between 35 and 44.
A45 - 54	=	coefficient of dummy for age between 45 and 54.
A55 - 64	=	coefficient of dummy for age between 55 and 64.
A65+	=	coefficient of dummy for age of 65 and over.
RNC	=	coefficient of dummy for family living in Northcentral.
RS	=	coefficient of dummy for family living in South.
RW	=	coefficient of dummy for family living in West.
NW	=	coefficient of dummy for nonwhite family.
RUR	=	coefficient of dummy for family living in rural area.

$$D(p) = -1 - .007900 \ln PEN - .06479 \ln PF + .02752 \ln PC$$
$$- .005559 \ln PK + .05023 \ln PCS$$

TABLE 1 (CONTINUED)   POOLED ESTIMATION RESULTS

Parameter	Energy Estimate	Standard Error
CONST	-.1418	.0106
ln PEN	.04021	.00374
ln PF	-.06449	.0106
ln PCG	.03769	.0112
ln PK	.03041	.00817
ln PCS	-.05172	.00651
ln M	.007900	.00116
S2	-.01448	.00147
S3	-.01686	.00174
S4	-.01669	.00185
S5	-.01519	.00217
S6	-.01265	.00270
S7+	-.01080	.00283
A25 - 34	-.002054	.00203
A35 - 44	-.005095	.00220
A45 - 54	-.008143	.00208
A55 - 64	-.01364	.00208
A65+	-.009532	.00207
RNC	-.008130	.00137
RS	-.008457	.00137
RW	.007488	.00148
NW	.002603	.00171
RUR	-.03145	.00138

TABLE 1   (CONTINUED)   POOLED ESTIMATION RESULTS

Parameter	Food Estimate	Standard Error
CONST	-.7138	.0235
ln PEN	-.06449	.0106
ln PF	.1354	.0418
ln PCG	-.1229	.0434
ln PK	-.02709	.0296
ln PCS	.01479	.0198
ln M	.06429	.00258
S2	-.03419	.00324
S3	-.04442	.00383
S4	-.06991	.00408
S5	-.07268	.00480
S6	-.1040	.00596
S7+	-.1194	.00623
A25 - 34	-.04683	.00447
A35 - 44	-.09233	.00484
A45 - 54	-.09846	.00459
A55 - 64	-.1011	.00458
A65+	-.09010	.00455
RNC	.01461	.00303
RS	.004641	.00301
RW	.01406	.00325
NW	-.006326	.00377
RUR	.009619	.00304

TABLE 1   (CONTINUED)   POOLED ESTIMATION RESULTS

Parameter	Food Estimate	Standard Error
CONST	-.7138	.0235
ln PEN	-.06449	.0106
ln PF	.1354	.0418
ln PCG	-.1229	.0434
ln PK	-.02709	.0296
ln PCS	.01479	.0198
ln M	.06429	.00258
S2	-.03419	.00324
S3	-.04442	.00383
S4	-.06991	.00408
S5	-.07268	.00480
S6	-.1040	.00596
S7+	-.1194	.00623
A25 - 34	-.04683	.00447
A35 - 44	-.09233	.00484
A45 - 54	-.09846	.00459
A55 - 64	-.1011	.00458
A65+	-.09010	.00455
RNC	.01461	.00303
RS	.004641	.00301
RW	.01406	.00325
NW	-.006326	.00377
RUR	.009619	.00304

TABLE 1 (CONTINUED)   POOLED ESTIMATION RESULTS

Parameter	Consumer Goods Estimate	Standard Error
CONST	.1015	.0137
ln PEN	.03769	.0112
ln PF	−.1229	.0434
ln PCG	.2761	.0512
ln PK	−.1909	.0336
ln PCS	.02753	.0191
ln M	−.02752	.00149
S2	.002259	.00186
S3	−.005487	.00220
S4	−.007615	.00234
S5	−.007393	.00275
S6	−.008864	.00342
S7+	−.006818	.00358
A25 − 34	−.003208	.00257
A35 − 44	−.00008580	.00278
A45 − 54	.006572	.00263
A55 − 64	.007436	.00263
A65+	.002513	.00261
RNC	.001349	.00174
RS	−.001261	.00173
RW	.003393	.00186
NW	−.01331	.00216
RUR	.006909	.00174

TABLE 1 (CONTINUED)   POOLED ESTIMATION RESULTS

Parameter	Capital Services Estimate	Standard Error
CONST	−.5354	.0264
ln PEN	.03041	.00817
ln PF	−.02709	:0296
ln PCG	−.1909	.0336
ln PK	.3618	.0271
ln PCS	−.1798	.0184
ln M	.005559	.00293
S2	.03686	.00368
S3	.04804	.00436
S4	.06821	.00464
S5	.06445	.00546
S6	.08742	.00678
S7+	.09841	.00709
A25 − 34	.04087	.00509
A35 − 44	.08380	.00551
A45 − 54	.1074	.00523
A55 − 64	.1286	.00521
A65+	.1433	.00518
RNC	.0009652	.00345
RS	.02319	.00342
RW	−.009788	.00370
NW	.02840	.00429
RUR	.02125	.00346

TABLE 1 (CONCLUDED)   POOLED ESTIMATION RESULTS

Parameter	Consumer Services Estimates	Standard Error
CONST	.2895	.0197
ln PEN	−.05172	.00651
ln PF	.01479	.0198
ln PCG	.02753	.0191
ln PK	−.1798	.0184
ln PCS	.2394	.0260
ln M	−.05023	.00216
S2	.009544	.00269
S3	.01873	.00319
S4	.02600	.00339
S5	.03081	.00399
S6	.03810	.00496
S7+	.03859	.00518
A25 − 34	.01122	.00372
A35 − 44	.01371	.00402
A45 − 54	−.007396	.00382
A55 − 64	−.02128	.00381
A65+	−.04615	.00378
RNC	−.008790	.00252
RS	−.01811	.00250
RW	−.01515	.00270
NW	−.01137	.00314
RUR	−.006330	.00253

Cross Section SSR = 38059.56   Convergence after 149 iterations.
Aggregate   SSR = 2165.14

goods, capital services, and other consumer services. Households are
classified by five sets of demographic characteristics -- family size,
age of head, region of residence, race, and urban versus rural residence.

4   MONEY METRIC INDIVIDUAL WELFARE.

   The translog indirect utility function (2.22) and the translog individual expenditure function (2.23) can be employed in assessing
the impacts of alternative economic policies on individual welfare. To
analyze the impact of economic policy on the welfare of the kth household, we first evaluate the indirect utility function after the change in
policy has taken place. Suppose that prices are p^1 and expenditure for
the kth household is M_k^1 (k = 1, 2 . . . K). The level of individual
welfare for the kth consuming unit after the policy change W_k^1 is given
by:

(4.1) $W_k^1 = \ln V_k^1$,

$$= \ln p^{1'}(\alpha_p + \frac{1}{2} B_{pp} \ln p^1) - D(p^1) \ln [M_k^1/m_0(p^1, A_k)],$$

$$(k = 1, 2 \; . \; . \; . \; K).$$

   To evaluate the impact of alternative economic policies we
must compare the total expenditure required to attain the individual welfare resulting from each policy at prices prevailing before any change,
say p^0. For this purpose we can define money metric individual welfare
for the kth household, say N_k , as the difference between the total
expenditure required to attain W_k^1 and the expenditure required to attain
W_k^0, the level before the policy change. Both are evaluated at prices p^0:

(4.2) $N_k = M_k(p^0, W_k^1, A_k) - M_k(p^0, W_k^0, A_k)$,

$$= M_k(p^0, W_k^1, A_k) - M_k^0,$$

$$(k = 1, 2 \; . \; . \; . \; K),$$

where M_k^0 is total expenditure before the policy change. If money metric
individual welfare is positive, the welfare of the consuming unit is
increased; otherwise, the welfare of the consuming unit is decreased or
left unaffected.

   (This concept of money metric individual welfare coincides
with the concept of net equivalent variation employed by Jorgenson, Lau,

and Stoker (1982). Measures of equivalent variations based on the translog indirect utility function were introduced by Jorgenson, Lau, and
Stoker (1981). The corresponding measures of compensating variations
were introduced by Jorgenson, Lau, and Stoker (1980). The concepts of
equivalent and compensating variations are due to Hicks (1942) and have
been discussed by Chipman and Moore (1980), Deaton and Muellbauer
(1980b), pp. 184-190, Diamond and McFadden (1974), Hausman (1981), and
Hurwicz and Uzawa (1971), among others. An individual ordering based on
money metric individual welfare is identical to that based on Samuelson's
(1974) concept of money metric utility.)

    We illustrate the concept of money metric individual welfare
geometrically in Diagram 1. This diagram represents the indifference map
for a consuming unit with indirect utility function (2.22). For simplicity we consider the case of two commodities ($N = 2$). Consumer equilibrium before the policy change is represented by the point A. The
corresponding level of total expenditure $M_k^0(p^0, W_k^0)$, divided by the price
of the second commodity p_2^0, is given on the vertical axis. This axis
gives total expenditure in units of the second commodity.

    Similarly, consumer equilibrium after the policy change is
represented by the point C. To translate the corresponding level of welfare into total expenditure at the prices before the change, we evaluate
the expenditure function (2.23) at this level of welfare and at the
prices p^0. The resulting level of total expenditure $M_k(p^0, W_k^1, A_k)$
corresponds to consumer equilibrium at the point B. Money metric individual welfare is the difference between the levels of total expenditure
$M_k(p^0, W_k^1, A_k)$ and M_k^0.

    To illustrate the measurement of individual welfare we under-
take a comparison of alternative policies for regulation of petroleum
prices and taxation of petroleum production in the United States. These
policies have been analyzed by the Office of Policy, Planning, and
Analysis of the U.S. Department of Energy (DOE). Our reference case for
policy analysis is the policy of petroleum price decontrol instituted in
January 1981. Under this policy price controls were eliminated on all
petroleum products, but petroleum production is taxed under the provisions of the windfall profits tax. Our base case for policy analysis is
the behavior of the U.S. economy under these policies with the regime of
low world petroleum prices.

    Alternatives to current regulatory and fiscal policies for

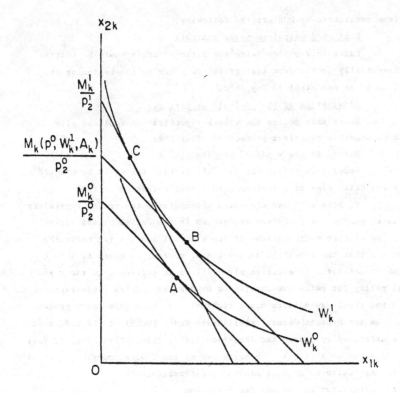

Diagram 1.   Money Metric Individual Welfare.

petroleum considered by DOE are the following:

Continued petroleum price controls.

Under this policy petroleum price controls would be continued, essentially in the form that prevailed prior to the beginning of
petroleum price decontrol in May 1980.

Elimination of the windfall profits tax.

Under this policy the windfall profits tax would be eliminated on domestic petroleum production after 1980.

Reform of the windfall profits tax.

Under this policy the windfall profits tax would be reduced
on certain categories of petroleum production, beginning in 1983.

We have analyzed the three alternatives to current regulatory
and fiscal policy for petroleum production in the United States listed
above. We analyze modifications of the windfall profits tax under the
assumption that the shortfall in government revenue is added to the
government deficit. To evaluate alternatives to current regulatory and
fiscal policy for petroleum considered by DOE, we require projections of
prices and total expenditure under each policy. We obtain these projections from the Dynamic General Equilibrium Model (DGEM) of the U.S. economy, constructed by Hudson and Jorgenson (1974, 1976, 1978a, 1978b). This
model is based on a nine sector breakdown of the U.S. economy:

1. Agriculture, Nonfuel Mining, Construction.

2. Manufacturing, except for Petroleum.

3. Transportation.

4. Communications, Trade, and Services.

5. Coal Mining.

6. Crude Petroleum and Gas Extraction.

7. Refined Petroleum Products.

8. Electric Utilities.

9. Gas Utilities.

The first step in analyzing alternative policies for
petroleum price regulation and taxation is to establish projections of
prices and total expenditure for all consuming units under current policy. To simulate the impact of alternatives to current regulatory and
fiscal policy, projections of the resulting changes in prices of
petroleum to the individual industrial sectors and to final demand are
incorporated into DGEM. Financial flows resulting from the alternatives
to current policy are also projected and incorporated into the model.

Changes in demand for petroleum by manufacturing industries and by electric utilities are projected and incorporated into DGEM, while changes in demand by the other sectors of the economy are determined endogenously within the model. The response of domestic petroleum supply to changes in regulatory and fiscal policy are specified exogenously. Total domestic supply is required to be equal to total domestic demand plus losses in transportation, plus the petroleum demands of petroleum producers, and less imports.

Projections of prices for each of the five commodities included in our model of aggregate consumer behavior -- energy, food, consumer goods, capital services, and consumer services -- are presented in Table 2 for the reference case corresponding to current regulatory and fiscal policy and for alternative policies. (These price projections are based on the projections of the U.S. economy under alternative regulatory and fiscal policies for petroleum production by Goettle and Hudson (1983)). Table 2 presents projections of total expenditure per household for the U.S. economy for each of the alternative regulatory and fiscal policies that we consider. The projections of prices and total expenditure cover the period 1980-1995. It is important to note that the prices given in Table 2 are purchasers' prices for the five commodity groups. Price projections from DGEM are given in terms of producers' prices and must be transformed by incorporating trade and transportation margins to obtain purchasers' prices.

Under continued petroleum price controls we find that the price of energy is lower than under the current policy of petroleum price decontrol. However, the prices of all nonenergy commodities are higher under continued controls than under current policy. We also find that total expenditure per household is higher under a policy of continued controls than under current policy. It is not obvious whether individual welfare is higher or lower under continued controls than under the reference case.

To evaluate the change in individual welfare for typical households, we employ prices in the reference case as a basis for calculating money metric individual welfare (4.2). We make the simplifying assumption that total expenditure changes in the same proportion for all consuming units. Changes in relative levels of individual welfare are the result of differential impacts of price changes associated with changes in regulatory and fiscal policy.

TABLE 2

PROJECTIONS OF PRICES AND TOTAL EXPENDITURES

PRICES

(Equal to 1.000 in 1972)

	Current Policy					Continued Controls				
Year	Energy	Food	Consumer Goods	Capital Services	Consumer Services	Energy	Food	Consumer Goods	Capital Services	Consumer Services
1980	2.0019	1.6798	1.6646	1.8775	1.6356	1.9387	1.7183	1.7025	1.9322	1.6686
1981	2.2669	1.8198	1.8022	2.0811	1.7721	2.1202	1.8872	1.8689	2.1934	1.8304
1982	2.4852	1.9376	1.9182	2.2236	1.8924	2.3417	2.0183	1.9981	2.3731	1.9641
1983	2.6410	2.0497	2.0269	2.4174	1.9901	2.5448	2.1408	2.1170	2.6035	2.0728
1984	2.8150	2.1510	2.1252	2.6214	2.0816	2.7290	2.2492	2.2222	2.8407	2.1714
1985	3.0286	2.2851	2.2549	2.8160	2.1995	2.9448	2.3913	2.3598	3.0680	2.2965
1986	3.2194	2.4129	2.3788	2.9718	2.3169	3.1356	2.5259	2.4903	3.2521	2.4205
1987	3.4299	2.5222	2.4830	3.1971	2.4051	3.3428	2.6414	2.6004	3.5116	2.5135
1988	3.6352	2.6279	2.5842	3.4167	2.4951	3.5379	2.7509	2.7053	3.7589	2.6063
1989	3.8746	2.7779	2.7279	3.6420	2.6212	3.7709	2.9073	2.8551	4.0159	2.7375
1990	4.0730	2.9013	2.8456	3.7904	2.7270	3.9585	3.0357	2.9775	4.1878	2.8472
1991	4.2992	3.0299	2.9665	4.0128	2.8273	4.1747	3.1681	3.1020	4.4377	2.9500
1992	4.5396	3.1525	3.0830	4.2405	2.9354	4.3967	3.2912	3.2189	4.6785	3.0578
1993	4.7774	3.2901	3.2123	4.4543	3.0468	4.6247	3.4329	3.3519	4.9127	3.1719
1994	5.0559	3.4799	3.3897	4.5830	3.1929	4.8879	3.6321	3.5381	5.0613	3.3249
1995	5.2784	3.6089	3.5086	4.7954	3.2895	5.1040	3.7651	3.6608	5.2964	3.4241

TABLE 2 (CONTINUED)

PROJECTIONS OF PRICES AND TOTAL EXPENDITURES

PRICES
(Equal to 1.000 in 1972)

Year	No Windfall Profits Tax					Reformed Windfall Profits Tax				
	Energy	Food	Consumer Goods	Capital Services	Consumer Services	Energy	Food	Consumer Goods	Capital Services	Consumer Services
1980	1.9865	1.6744	1.6593	1.8753	1.6304	2.0019	1.6798	1.6646	1.8775	1.6356
1981	2.2499	1.8114	1.7939	2.0802	1.7641	2.2669	1.8198	1.8022	2.0811	1.7721
1982	2.4670	1.9274	1.9080	2.2239	1.8825	2.4852	1.9376	1.9182	2.2236	1.8924
1983	2.6152	2.0401	2.0173	2.4226	1.9806	2.6392	2.0492	2.0264	2.4170	1.9896
1984	2.7934	2.1429	2.1171	2.6335	2.0736	2.8123	2.1499	2.1241	2.6207	2.0805
1985	3.0100	2.2785	2.2484	2.8347	2.1931	3.0209	2.2830	2.2529	2.8141	2.1974
1986	3.2098	2.4088	2.3746	2.9983	2.3130	3.2148	2.4109	2.3768	2.9701	2.3149
1987	3.4271	2.5208	2.4815	3.2330	2.4039	3.4253	2.5201	2.4809	3.1954	2.4030
1988	3.6371	2.6290	2.5852	3.4626	2.4963	3.6273	2.6252	2.5816	3.4144	2.4924
1989	3.8823	2.7816	2.7314	3.6975	2.6248	3.8665	2.7749	2.7251	3.6396	2.6183
1990	4.0824	2.8070	2.8510	3.8528	2.7324	4.0645	2.8984	2.8428	3.7881	2.7240
1991	4.3183	3.0387	2.9749	4.0842	2.8359	4.2939	3.0275	2.9642	4.0114	2.8250
1992	4.5605	3.1636	3.0937	4.3192	2.9461	4.5332	3.1505	3.0810	4.2396	2.9333
1993	4.8045	3.3034	3.2251	4.5388	3.0595	4.7744	3.2887	3.2109	4.4544	3.0454
1994	5.0851	3.4948	3.4040	4.6702	3.2070	5.0521	3.4786	3.3884	4.5834	3.1915
1995	5.3105	3.6248	3.5240	4.8855	3.3046	5.2782	3.6080	3.5078	4.7966	3.2887

TABLE 2 (CONCLUDED)

PROJECTIONS OF PRICES AND TOTAL EXPENDITURES

| | TOTAL EXPENDITURE PER HOUSEHOLD | | | |
| | (Current Prices) | | | |
Year	Current Policy	Continued Controls	No Tax	Reformed Tax
1980	20895.20	21656.03	20820.57	20895.20
1981	22913.16	23945.35	22948.26	22913.16
1982	24554.57	25509.16	24638.97	24554.57
1983	26096.65	26989.83	26246.48	26094.74
1984	28004.82	28805.27	28219.38	27996.21
1985	29672.51	30410.93	29925.72	29649.17
1986	31123.50	31811.41	31422.85	31113.34
1987	32759.69	33459.28	33106.60	32752.48
1988	34776.13	35453.27	35160.68	34760.77
1989	36835.98	37526.38	37245.01	36823.05
1990	38341.84	39040.83	38740.92	38332.59
1991	40331.78	41031.39	40730.46	40336.98
1992	43361.01	43983.71	43725.01	43363.93
1993	45861.79	46513.24	46207.58	45875.05
1994	48075.13	48839.90	48400.22	48080.81
1995	50414.99	51237.25	50734.36	50430.82

The dollar value of changes in individual welfare under a
policy of continued controls is given for typical households in Table 3.
We present results for families of size five, with age of head 35-44,
living in the Northeast region of the United States, and with average
total expenditure in each year. Under continued controls all types of
households gain during the period 1980 and 1981 and rural households continue to gain in 1982. However, all types of families lose under continued controls beginning 1983. For example, a white urban family living in
the Northeast loses $236.03 in 1983. This loss rises to $745.09 by 1992.
The time pattern of losses for a nonwhite urban household living in the
Northeast is similar to that for a white family.

With elimination of the windfall profits tax we find that the

price of energy is lower through 1987 and higher for the remaining period
1988-1995. Elimination of the tax reduces prices of nonenergy commodities at the beginning of the period of our study. However, prices of
these commodities rise more rapidly with elimination of the tax. We also
find that total expenditure per household is lower in 1980 and higher for
all subsequent years. Again, it is not obvious whether individual welfare is higher or lower with elimination of the tax than under the reference case. As before, we employ prices of the reference case as a basis
for calculating money metric individual welfare (4.2).

The dollar value of changes in welfare under a policy of
eliminating the windfall profits tax is given for various types of households in Table 3. Under elimination of the tax all households experience
a slight decline in welfare in 1980 and substantial gains in welfare for
the period 1981-1993; urban households in 1994 and 1995 undergo a slight
decline in welfare for those years. As before, the time pattern of gains
and losses in welfare is similar for urban and rural households and for
white and nonwhite households living in the Northeast.

The final alternative to current regulatory and fiscal policy
that we consider is reform of the windfall profits tax beginning in 1983.
This policy results in slightly lower energy prices for the period 1983-
1995. The changes in prices of nonenergy commodities are relatively
small under reform of the windfall profits tax. Total expenditure per
household is lower under this policy than under current policy through
1990. For the remainder of the period 1991-1995 total expenditure per
household is higher. The dollar value of the change in welfare for various types of households is nonnegative for the entire period of our
study. However, the gains in welfare are small by comparison with those
for eliminating the windfall profits tax after 1983.

To summarize: Most of the households we have considered
would be better off with elimination of the windfall profits tax than
under current policy. Continued controls would result in welfare losses
for most households, while reform of the windfall profits tax would produce welfare gains that are positive but smaller in magnitude than elimination of the tax. However, these comparisons do not hold uniformly for
all households and all years.

TABLE 3

MONEY METRIC INDIVIDUAL WELFARE

(Current Prices; Northeast Region)

Year	Continued Controls				No Windfall Profits Tax			
	Urban		Rural		Urban		Rural	
	White	Nonwhite	White	Nonwhite	White	Nonwhite	White	Nonwhite
1980	338.99	340.32	378.54	379.86	-12.33	-11.36	-8.47	-7.50
1981	248.39	253.60	324.65	329.93	109.06	111.47	112.77	115.18
1982	-22.86	-13.06	54.41	64.30	156.27	159.56	159.78	163.06
1983	-236.03	-222.10	-169.49	-155.41	190.85	195.06	197.06	201.29
1984	-406.19	-389.74	-340.17	-323.49	206.99	212.47	213.20	218.70
1985	-518.20	-499.65	-452.06	-433.26	199.28	205.53	205.53	211.80
1986	-599.82	-579.39	-533.27	-512.58	187.54	194.87	192.87	199.83
1987	-629.25	-607.57	-561.47	-539.45	179.79	187.63	184.96	192.82
1988	-665.92	-643.48	-595.77	-572.92	168.05	176.82	173.62	182.41
1989	-684.77	-661.19	-613.58	-589.56	146.18	155.45	151.80	161.10
1990	-696.44	-671.71	-623.54	-598.36	115.76	125.18	121.85	131.29
1991	-705.12	-679.71	-630.94	-605.03	83.20	92.81	88.72	98.34
1992	-745.09	-719.94	-668.28	-642.59	41.69	51.39	47.79	57.52
1993	-743.30	-717.77	-665.33	-639.23	12.38	21.96	18.17	27.78
1994	-723.81	-697.18	-643.95	-616.80	-11.87	-2.60	-6.04	3.24
1995	-712.22	-685.06	-631.65	-603.93	-21.79	-12.72	-16.17	-7.09

TABLE 3 (CONCLUDED)

MONEY METRIC INDIVIDUAL WELFARE

(Current Prices; Northeast Region)

	Reformed Windfall Profits Tax			
	Urban		Rural	
Year	White	Nonwhite	White	Nonwhite
1980	0.00	0.00	0.00	0.00
1981	0.00	0.00	0.00	0.00
1982	0.00	0.00	0.00	0.00
1983	3.89	3.93	4.22	4.26
1984	4.19	4.32	4.57	4.70
1985	4.31	4.39	5.50	5.59
1986	10.40	10.58	10.92	11.10
1987	12.64	12.87	13.10	13.33
1988	12.85	13.09	13.77	14.02
1989	15.00	15.27	15.85	16.13
1990	16.54	16.83	17.42	17.72
1991	18.44	18.80	18.92	19.27
1992	15.32	15.68	16.04	16.40
1993	14.73	15.13	15.06	15.46
1994	10.03	10.38	10.47	10.83
1995	10.30	10.69	10.35	10.74

5. ## SOCIAL WELFARE FUNCTIONS

Under the Pareto principle an economic policy can be recommended if all consuming units are as well off as under any alternative policy and at least one unit is better off. The Pareto principle provides a partial ordering of economic policies. This ordering is invariant with respect to monotone increasing transformations of individual welfare that differ among consuming units. Only welfare comparisons that are ordinal and not comparable among consuming units are required.

Money metric individual welfare (5.2) is a monotone increasing transformation of the measure of individual welfare (2.26). This transformation depends on the prices faced by all consuming units and on the attributes of the individual consuming unit. Considered as a measure of individual welfare in its own right, money metric individual welfare provides all the information about consumer preferences required for application of the Pareto principle. To obtain a complete ordering of economic policies we next introduce a social welfare function.

We consider the set of all possible social orderings over the set of social states, say X, and the set of all possible real-valued individual welfare functions, say W_k (k = 1, 2 ... K). A social ordering, say R, is a complete, reflexive, and transitive ordering of social states. A social state is described by the quantities consumed of N commodity groups by K individuals. The individual welfare function for the kth individual W_k (k = 1, 2 ... K) is defined on the set of social states X and gives the level of individual welfare for that individual in each state.

To describe social orderings in greater detail we find it useful to introduce the following notation:

x -- a matrix with elements $\{x_{nk}\}$ describing the social state.

u = $(W_1, W_2 \cdots W_K)$ -- a vector of individual welfare functions of all K individuals.

Following Sen (1970, 1977) and Hammond (1976) we define a social welfare functional, say f, as a mapping from the set of individual welfare functions to the set of social orderings, such that f(u') = f(u) implies R' = R, where:

$$u = [W_1(x), W_2(x) \cdots W_K(x)],$$

$$u' = [W_1'(x), W_2'(x) \cdots W_k'(x)],$$

for all $x \in X$. Similarly, we define L_k $(k = 1, 2 \ldots K)$ as the set of admissible individual welfare functions for the kth individual and L as the Cartesian product $\prod\limits_{k=1}^{K} L_k$. Finally, let $\underline{L}$ be the partition of L such that all elements of $\underline{L}$ yield the same social ordering.

We can describe a social ordering in terms of the following properties of a social welfare functional:

1. **Unrestricted Domain**

The social welfare functional f is defined for all possible vectors of individual welfare functions u.

2. **Independence of Irrelevant Alternatives**

For any subset A contained in X, if $u(x) = u'(x)$ for all $x \in A$, then $R:A = R':A$, where $R = f(u)$ and $R' = f(u')$ and $R:A$ is the social ordering over the subset A.

3. **Positive Association**

For any vectors of individual welfare functions u and u', if for all y in X-x, such that:

$$W_k'(y) = W_k(y),$$

$$W_k'(x) > W_k(x), \qquad\qquad (k = 1, 2 \cdots K),$$

then xPy implies xP'y and yP'x implies yPx, where P is a strict ordering of social states.

4. **Nonimposition**

For all x, y in X there exist u, u' such that xPy and yP'x.

5. **Cardinal Full Comparability**

The set of admissible individual welfare functions that yield the same social ordering $\underline{L}$ is defined by:

$$\underline{L} = \{u': W_k'(x) = \alpha + \beta W_k(x), \ \beta > 0, \ k = 1, 2 \cdots K\},$$

and $f(u') = f(u)$ for all $u' \; \varepsilon \; \underline{L}$.

Cardinal full comparability implies that social orderings are invariant with respect to any positive affine transformation of the individual welfare functions $\{W_k\}$ that is the same for all individuals. Arrow (1977, p. 225) has defended noncomparability in the following terms:

> ...the autonomy of individuals, an element of mutual incommensurability among people seems denied by the possibility of interpersonal comparisons.

He requires ordinal noncomparability, which implies that social orderings are invariant with respect to monotone increasing transformations of the individual welfare functions that may differ among individuals:

5'. Ordinal Noncomparability.

The set of individual welfare functions that yield the same social ordering $\underline{L}$ is defined by:

$$\underline{L} = \{u': W_k'(x) = \rho_k[W_k(x)], \; \rho_k \text{ increasing}, \; k = 1, 2 \; \cdots \; K\},$$

and $f(u') = f(u)$ for all u' in $\underline{L}$.

The properties of a social welfare functional corresponding to unrestricted domain and independence of irrelevant alternatives are used by Arrow in proving the impossibility of a nondictatorial social ordering:

4'. Nondictatorship.

There is no individual k such that for all x, $y \; \varepsilon \; X$, $W_k(x) > W_k(y)$ implies xPy.

Under ordinal noncomparability the assumptions of positive association and nonimposition employed by Arrow imply the weak Pareto principle:

3'. Pareto Principle.

For any x, $y \; \varepsilon \; X$, if $W_k(x) > W_k(y)$ for all individuals ($k = 1, 2 \ldots K$), then xPy.

If a social welfare functional f has the properties of unrestricted domain, independence of irrelevant alternatives, the weak Pareto principle, and ordinal noncomparability, then no nondictatorial social

ordering is possible. This result is Arrow's impossibility theorem.
Since it is obvious that the class of dictatorial social orderings is too
narrow to provide an adequate basis for expressing the implications of
alternative ethical judgements, we propose to generate a class of social
welfare functions suitable for the evaluation of alternative economic
policies by weakening Arrow's assumptions.

We first consider weakening the assumption of ordinal noncomparability of individual welfare functions. Sen (1970) has shown that
Arrow's conclusion that no nondictatorial social ordering is possible is
preserved by replacing ordinal noncomparability by cardinal noncomparability. This implies that social orderings are invariant with respect to
positive affine transformations of the individual welfare functions that
may differ among individuals:

5''. Cardinal Noncomparability.

The set of individual welfare functions that yield the same
social ordering $\underline{L}$ is defined by:

$$\underline{L} = \{u': W_k'(x) = \alpha_k + \beta_k W_k(x), \ \beta_k > 0, \ k = 1, 2 \ \cdot \ \cdot \ \cdot \ K\},$$

and $f(u') = f(u)$ for all u' in $\underline{L}$.

However, d'Aspremont and Gevers (1977), Deschamps and Gevers
(1978), Maskin (1978), and Roberts (1980b) have shown that we obtain an
interesting class of nondictatorial social orderings by requiring cardinal unit comparability of individual welfare functions, which implies
that social orderings are invariant with respect to positive affine
transformations with units that are the same for all individuals:

5'''. Cardinal Unit Comparability.

The set of individual welfare functions that yield the same
social ordering $\underline{L}$ is defined by:

$$\underline{L} = \{u': W_k'(x) = \alpha_k + \beta W_k(x), \ \beta > 0, \ k = 1, 2 \ \cdot \ \cdot \ \cdot \ K\},$$

and $f(u') = f(u)$ for all u' in $\underline{L}$.

If a social welfare functional f has the properties of unrestricted domain, independence of irrelevant alternatives, the weak Pareto
principle, and cardinal unit comparability, there exist social orderings

and a continuous real-valued social welfare function, say W, such that if
$W[u(x)] > W[u(y)]$, then xPy. Furthermore, the social welfare function
can be represented in the form:

(5.1) $W[u(x)] = \sum_{k=1}^{K} a_k W_k(x).$

If we add the assumption that the social welfare function has
the property of anonymity, that is, no individual is given greater weight
than any other individual in determining the level of social welfare,
then the social welfare function W in (5.1) must be symmetric in the
individual welfare functions $\{W_k\}$. The property of anonymity incorporates a notion of horizontal equity into the representation of social
orderings.

Under anonymity the function W in (5.1) reduces to the sum of
individual welfare functions and takes the form of a utilitarian social
welfare function. Utilitarian social welfare functions have been
employed extensively in applications of welfare economics, especially in
the measurement of inequality by methods originated by Atkinson (1970)
and Kolm (1969, 1976a, 1976b), in the design of optimal income tax
schedules along the lines pioneered by Mirrlees (1971), and in the
evaluation of alternative economic policies by Arrow and Kalt (1979).

The approach to the measurement of social welfare based on a
utilitarian social welfare function provides a worthwhile starting point
for applications. Harsanyi (1976) and Ng (1975) have pointed out that
distributional considerations can be incorporated into a utilitarian
social welfare function through the representation of individual welfare
functions. However, Sen (1973, p. 18) has argued that a utilitarian
social welfare function does not take appropriate account of the distribution of welfare among individuals:

> The distribution of welfare between persons is a relevant
> aspect of any problem of income distribution, and our evalua-
> tion of inequality will obviously depend on whether we are
> concerned only with the loss of the sum of individual utili-
> ties through a bad distribution of income, or also with the
> inequality of welfare levels of different individuals.

To broaden the range of possible social orderings we can
require cardinal full comparability of individual welfare functions, as
defined above. Roberts (1980b) has shown that a social welfare functional f with the properties of unrestricted domain, independence of
irrelevant alternatives, the weak Pareto principle, and cardinal full
comparability implies the existence of a social welfare function that
takes the form:

(5.2) $W[u(x)] = \overline{W}(x) + g[u(x) - \overline{W}(x) \; i],$

where i is a vector of ones, the function $\overline{W}(x)$ corresponds to average
individual welfare:

$$\overline{W}(x) = \sum_{k=1}^{K} a_k \; W_k(x),$$

and g(x) is a linear homogeneous function of deviations of levels of
individual welfare from the average. (It is important to note that the
social welfare function in (5.2) represents a social ordering over all
possible individual orderings and exemplifies the multiple profile
approach to social choice of Arrow (1963) rather than the single profile
approach employed by Bergson (1938) and Samuelson (1947). The literature
on the existence of single profile social welfare functions is discussed
by Roberts (1980d), Samuelson (1982), and Sen (1979b).)

If the function g(x) in the representation (5.2) of the
social welfare function is identically equal to zero, then the social
welfare function reduces to the form (5.1). If the function g(x) is not
identically zero, then the social welfare function incorporates both a
measure of average individual welfare and a measure of inequality in the
distribution of individual welfare. We conclude that the class of possible social welfare functions (5.2) includes utilitarian welfare functions, but also includes functions that are not subject to the objections
that can be made to utilitarianism.

Although Roberts (1980b) has succeeded in broadening the
class of possible social welfare functions beyond those consistent with
utilitarianism, the social welfare functions (5.2) are subject to an

objection raised by Sen (1973). (See Sen (1977, 1979b) for further discussion.) Information about alternative social states enters only through
the individual welfare functions $\{W_k\}$. Sen refers to this property of a
social welfare functional f as _welfarism_. Welfarism rules out characteristics of a social state that are conceivably relevant for social orderings, but that cannot be incorporated into the social welfare function
through the individual welfare functions.

Roberts (1980b) has suggested the possibility of further
weakening Arrow's assumptions in order to incorporate nonwelfare characteristics of social states. (See Roberts (1980b), esp. pp. 434-436.) For
this purpose we can replace the weak Pareto principle by positive association and nonimposition, as defined above. We retain the assumptions of
unrestricted domain, independence of irrelevant alternatives, and cardinal full comparability of measures of individual welfare. We can partition the set of social states X into subsets, such that all states within
each subset have the same nonwelfare characteristics. For each subset
there exists a social ordering that can be represented by a social welfare function of the form (5.2).

Under the assumptions we have outlined there exists a social
ordering for the set of all social states that can be represented by a
social welfare function of the form:

$$(5.3) \quad W(u,x) = F\{\overline{W}(x) + g[x, u(x) - \overline{W}(x)\, i], x\},$$

where the function $\overline{W}(x)$ corresponds to average individual welfare:

$$\overline{W}(x) = \sum_{k=1}^{K} a_k(x)\, W_k(x).$$

As before, the function g is a linear homogeneous function of deviations
of levels of individual welfare from average welfare.

The class of social welfare functions (5.3) incorporates
nonwelfare characteristics of social states through the weights $\{a_k(x)\}$
in average individual welfare $\overline{W}(x)$, through the function $g(x)$, which
depends directly on the social state x as well as on deviations of levels
of individual welfare from the average welfare, and through the function

F, which depends directly on the social state x and on the sum of the
functions W(x) and g(x). This class includes social welfare functions
that are not subject to the objections that can be made to welfarism.

At this point we have generated a class of possible social
welfare functions capable of expressing the implications of a variety of
different ethical judgements. In order to choose a specific social welfare function, we must narrow the range of possible ethical judgements by
imposing further requirements on the class of possible social welfare
functions. First, we must limit the dependence of the function F(x) in
(5.3) on the characteristics of alternative social states. Second, we
must select a form for the function g(x) in (5.3), which depends on deviations of levels of individual welfare from average welfare W(x).
Finally, we must choose representations of the individual welfare functions $\{W_k(x)\}$ that provide cardinal full comparability.

We first rule out the dependence of the function F(x) in
(5.3) on characteristics of social states that do not enter through the
functions W(x) and g(x). This restriction reduces F to a function of a
single variable W + g. We obtain an ordinal measure of social welfare by
permitting the function F to be any monotone increasing transformation.
To obtain a cardinal measure of social welfare we observe that the function W(x) + g is homogeneous of degree one in the individual welfare
functions $\{W_k(x)\}$. All representations of the social welfare function
that preserve this property can be written in the form:

(5.4) $W(u,x) = \beta[\overline{W}(x) + g(x)], \quad \beta > 0.$

We conclude that only positive, homogeneous, affine transformations are
permitted.

The restrictions embodied in the class of social welfare
functions (5.4) do not reduce social welfare to a function of the individual welfare functions $\{W_k(x)\}$ alone, since the weights $\{a_k(x)\}$ in average individual welfare W(x) and the function g(x) depend on nonwelfare
characteristics of the social state x. However, these social welfare
functions are homogeneous of degree one in levels of individual welfare.
This implies that doubling the welfare of each individual will double
social welfare, holding nonwelfare characteristics of the social state
constant. Blackorby and Donaldson (1982) refer to this class of social

welfare functions as __distributionally__ __homothetic__. (The implications of
distributional homotheticity are discussed by Kolm (1976b) and Blackorby
and Donaldson (1978).)

We impose a second set of requirements on the class of social
welfare functions (5.3) by selecting an appropriate form for the function
$g(x)$. In particular, we require that this function is additive in _devia_-
tions of individual welfare functions $\{W_k(x)\}$ from average welfare $W(x)$.
Since the function $g(x)$ is homogeneous of degree one, it must be a mean
value function of order $\rho(x)$:

$$(5.5) \quad g[x, u(x) - \overline{W}(x) \, i] = -\gamma(x)[\sum_{k=1}^{K} b_k(x) \, |W_k - \overline{W}|^{-\rho(x)}]^{-\frac{1}{\rho(x)}},$$

where:

$$\gamma(x) > 0, \; \rho(x) \leq -1, \; \sum_{k=1}^{K} b_k(x) = 1, \; 0 < b_k(x) < 1,$$

$$(k = 1, 2 \; \cdots \; K).$$

Under these restrictions the function $g(x)$ is negative, except at the
point of perfect equality $W_k = \overline{W}$ $(k = 1, 2 \; \cdots \; K)$, where it is zero.
(Mean value functions were introduced into economics by Bergson (1936)
and have been employed, for example, by Arrow, Chenery, Minhas, and Solow
(1961) and Atkinson (1970). Properties of mean value functions are discussed by Hardy, Littlewood, and Polya (1959).)

The function $\rho(x)$ in the representation (5.5) determines the
curvature of the social welfare function in the individual welfare functions $\{W_k(x)\}$. We can refer to this function as the __degree__ __of__ __aversion__
__to__ __inequality__. We assume that this function is constant, so that the
corresponding social welfare function $W(u, x)$ is characterized by a constant degree of aversion to inequality. To complete the selection of an
appropriate form for the social welfare function we must choose appropri-
ate weights $\{a_k(x)\}$ for average individual welfare $\overline{W}(x)$ and $\{b_k(x)\}$ for
the measure of equality $g(x)$. We find it natural to require that the two
sets of weights are the same.

To incorporate a notion of horizontal equity into the social
welfare functions (5.5) we can impose a weak form of the property of
anonymity. In particular, we require that no individual is given greater
weight in the social welfare function than any other individual with an
identical individual welfare function. This implies that the social welfare function is symmetric in the levels of individual welfare for identical individuals. The weights $\{a_k(x)\}$ in average welfare $W(x)$ and the
measure of equality $g(x)$ must be the same for identical individuals.

Under the restrictions presented up to this point the social
welfare function W takes the form:

$$(5.6) \quad W(u,x) = \overline{W} - \gamma(x) \ [\sum_{k=1}^{K} a_k(x) |W_k - \overline{W}|^{-\rho}]^{-\frac{1}{\rho}}$$

where:

$$\overline{W}(x) = \sum_{k=1}^{K} a_k(x) \ W_k(x).$$

The condition of positive association requires that an
increase in all levels of individual welfare must increase social wel-
fare._ This condition implies that the average level of individual welfare W must increase by more than the function $g(x)$, whatever the initial
distribution of individual welfare. We assume that the function $\gamma(x)$ in
(5.6) must take the maximum value consistent with positive association,
so that:

$$(5.7) \quad \gamma(x) = \{1 + [\frac{\sum_{k=1}^{K} a_k(x)}{a_j(x)}]^{-(\rho+1)}\}^{\frac{1}{\rho}},$$

where:

$$a_j(x) = \min_{k} a_k(x), \qquad\qquad (k = 1, 2 \ \cdots \ K),$$

for the social state x.

To complete the selection of a social welfare function $W(u,x)$ we require that the individual welfare functions $\{W_k\}$ in (5.3) must be invariant with respect to any positive affine transformation that is the same for all households. (This assumption implies that individual welfare increases with total expenditure at a rate that is inversely proportional to total expenditure. This is also implied by the utilitarian social welfare function employed by Arrow and Kalt (1979).) Under this assumption the logarithm of the translog indirect utility function is a cardinal measure of individual welfare with full comparability among households. The social welfare function takes the form:

(5.8) $W(u,x) = \ln \bar{V} - \gamma(x) \; [\sum\limits_{k=1}^{K} a_k(x) |\ln V_k - \ln \bar{V}|^{-\rho}]^{-\frac{1}{\rho}}.$

where:

$$\ln \bar{V} = \sum\limits_{k=1}^{K} a_k(x) \; \ln V_k [\frac{p \; m(A_k)}{M_k}] \; .$$

We can complete the specification of a social welfare function $W(u,x)$ by choosing a set of weights $\{a_k(x)\}$ for the levels of individual welfare $\{\ln V_k [\frac{p \; m(A_k)}{M_k}]\}$ in (5.8). For this purpose we must appeal to a notion of vertical equity. Following Hammond (1977), we define a distribution of total expenditure $\{M_k\}$ as more equitable than another distribution $\{M_k'\}$ if:

(i) $M_i + M_j = M_i' + M_j'$,

(ii) $M_k = M_k'$ for $k \neq i, j$,

(iii) $\ln V_i [\frac{p \; m(A_i)}{M_i'}] > \ln V_i [\frac{p \; m(A_i)}{M_i}] >$

$$\ln V_j[\frac{p \; m(A_j)}{M_j}] \; > \; \ln V_j[\frac{p \; m(A_j)}{M'_j}],$$

We say that a social welfare function $W(u,x)$ is _equity-regarding_ if it is larger for a more equitable distribution of total expenditure.

We require that the social welfare functions (5.8) must be equity-regarding. This amounts to imposing a version of Dalton's (1920) principle of transfers. This principle requires that a transfer of total expenditures from a rich household to a poor household that does not reverse their relative positions in the distribution of total expenditure must increase the level of social welfare.

If the social welfare functions (5.8) are required to be equity-regarding, then the weights $\{a_k(x)\}$ associated with the individual welfare functions $\{\ln V_k[\frac{p \; m(A_k)}{M_k}]\}$ must take the form:

(5.9) $$a_k(x) = \frac{m_0(p,A_k)}{\sum\limits_{k=1}^{K} m_0(p,A_k)}, \qquad (k = 1, 2 \; \cdots \; K).$$

We conclude that an equity-regarding social welfare function of the class (5.8) must take the form:

(5.10) $$W(u,x) = \ln \overline{V} - \gamma(x) \; [\frac{\sum\limits_{k=1}^{K} m_0(p,A_k)|\ln V_k - \ln \overline{V}|^{-\rho} \; \frac{1}{K}}{\sum\limits_{k=1}^{K} m_0(p,A_k)}]^{\frac{1}{\rho}},$$

where:

$$\ln \overline{V} = \frac{\sum\limits_{k=1}^{K} m_0(p,A_k) \; \ln V_k[\frac{p \; m(A_k)}{M_k}]}{\sum\limits_{k=1}^{K} m_0(p,A_k)},$$

$$= \ln p' \; (a_p + \frac{1}{2} B_{pp} \ln p) - D(p) \; \frac{\sum\limits_{k=1}^{K} m_0(p,A_k) \; \ln [M_k/m_0(p,A_k)]}{\sum\limits_{k=1}^{K} m_0(p,A_k)}.$$

Furthermore, the condition of positive association implies
that the function $\gamma(x)$ in (5.8) must take the form:

$$(5.11) \qquad \gamma(x) = \{1 + [\frac{\sum\limits_{k=1}^{K} m_0(p,A_k)}{m_0(p,A_j)}]^{-(\rho+1)}\}^{-\frac{1}{\rho}},$$

where:

$$m_0(p,A_j) = \min_k m_0(p,A_k), \qquad\qquad (k = 1, 2 \cdots K).$$

To summarize: We have generated a class of social welfare
functions (5.3) that has the properties of unrestricted domain, independence of irrelevant alternatives, positive association, nonimposition,
and cardinal full comparability. By imposing the additional assumption
that the degree of aversion to inequality is constant and requiring the
social welfare function to satisfy requirements of horizontal and vertical equity, we obtain the social welfare functions (5.10).

6   MONEY METRIC SOCIAL WELFARE

In assessing the impact of changes in economic policy on levels of individual welfare for each consuming unit, we have found it useful to express the change in welfare in terms of the change in total
expenditure. Similarly, to provide a basis for comparisons among social
states $\{x_{nk}\}$ we propose to formulate a money measure of social welfare.
(Alternative money measures of social welfare are discussed by Arrow and
Kalt (1979), Bergson (1980), Deaton and Muellbauer (1980), pp. 214-239,
Roberts (1980c), and Sen (1976). A survey of the literature is presented
by Sen (1979a).) Following Pollak (1981), we can define the social expenditure function as the minimum level of total expenditure $M = \sum_{k=1}^{K} M_k$
required to attain a given level of social welfare, say W, at a specified
price system p. More formally, the social expenditure function M(p, W)
is defined by:

$$(6.1) \quad M(p,W) = \min\{M: W(u,x) \geq W; M = \sum_{k=1}^{K} M_k\}.$$

The social expenditure function (6.1) is precisely analogous
to the individual expenditure function (2.23). The individual expenditure function gives the minimum level of expenditure required to attain a
stipulated level of individual welfare; the social expenditure function
gives the minimum level of aggregate expenditure required to attain a
stipulated level of social welfare. The individual expenditure function
and the indirect utility function can be employed in assessing the impact
of alternative economic policies on individual welfare. Similarly, the
social expenditure function and the social welfare function can be
employed in assessing the impacts of alternative policies on social welfare.

We can translate any level of social welfare into monetary
terms by evaluating the social expenditure function at that level of welfare for a given price system p. Two different levels of social welfare
can be compared with reference to a single price system by determining
the minimum level of aggregate expenditure required to attain each level
of social welfare for the reference prices. In addition, changes in
social welfare can be decomposed into changes in efficiency and changes
in equity. Money measures of both components of the change in social

welfare can be defined in terms of the social expenditure function and
the social welfare function.

In order to determine the form of the social expenditure
function $M(p,W)$ in (6.1), we can maximize the social welfare function
(5.10) for a fixed level of aggregate total expenditure by equalizing
total expenditure per household equivalent member $\{M_k/m_0(p,A_k)\}$ for all
consuming units. If aggregate total expenditure is distributed so as to
equalize total expenditure per household equivalent member, the level of
individual welfare is the same for all consuming units. For this distribution of total expenditure the social welfare function reduces to the
average level of individual welfare $\ln V$.

For the translog indirect utility function the maximum value
of social welfare for a given level of aggregate expenditure takes the
form:

(6.2) $W(x,u) = \ln \overline{V}$.

$$= \ln p'(a_p + \frac{1}{2} B_{pp} \ln p) - D(p) \ln [M/\sum_{k=1}^{K} m_0(p, A_k)].$$

This maximum value of social welfare reduces to average individual welfare. The average is obtained by evaluating the translog indirect utility function (2.22) at total expenditure per household equivalent member
$M/\sum_{k=1}^{K} m_0(p,A_k)$ for the economy as a whole.

We can solve for aggregate expenditure as a function of the
level of social welfare and prices:

(6.3) $\ln M(p, W) = \frac{1}{D(p)} [\ln p'(a_p + \frac{1}{2} B_{pp} \ln p) - W] + \ln [\sum_{k=1}^{K} m_0(p,A_k)]$.

We can refer to this function as the <u>translog social expenditure func-
tion</u>. The value of aggregate expenditure is obtained by evaluating the
translog individual expenditure function (2.23) at the level of social
welfare W and the number of household equivalent members $\sum_{k=1}^{K} m_0(p,A_k)$ for
the economy as a whole.

To obtain a money measure of social welfare we first evaluate the social welfare function (5.10) at prices p^0 and distribution of total expenditure $\{M_k^0\}$ prevailing before any change in policy. We can express the level of social welfare before any change in policy, say W^0, in terms of the social expenditure function:

$$(6.4) \quad \ln M(p^0, W^0) = \frac{1}{D(p^0)}[\ln p^{0'}(\alpha_p + \frac{1}{2} B_{pp} \ln p^0) - W^0] + \ln[\sum_{k=1}^{K} m_0(p^0, A_k)].$$

Second, we can decompose our money measure of social welfare into money measures of efficiency and equity. (Alternative money measures of efficiency and equity are discussed by Arrow and Kalt (1979), Bergson (1980), and Sen (1976, 1979a).) For this purpose we evaluate the social welfare function at the maximum level, say W^2, that can be attained through lump sum redistributions of aggregate expenditure $M^0 = \sum_{k=1}^{K} M_k^0$. Total expenditure per household equivalent member must be equalized for all consuming units, so that the social welfare function (5.10) reduces to average individual welfare (6.2). This is the maximum level of social welfare that is potentially available and can be taken as a measure of efficiency. Evaluating the social expenditure function at the potential level of welfare, say W^2, we obtain:

$$(6.5) \quad M(p^0, W^2) = M^0,$$

so that aggregate total expenditure M^0 is the resulting money measure of efficiency.

Given a money measure of efficiency, we can define the corresponding money measure of equity as the difference between the money measure of actual social welfare $M(p^0, W^0)$ and the money measure of potential social welfare M^0. This measure of equity is nonpositive and equal to zero only for perfect equality in the distribution of individual welfare. Under perfect equality total expenditure per household equivalent member is equalized among all consuming units. Using the social expenditure function, we can express our money measure of social welfare $M(p^0, W^0)$ as the sum of a money measure of efficiency M^0 and a money measure of equity $M(p^0, W^0) - M^0$:

(6.7) $M(p^0,W^0) = M^0 + [M(p^0,W^0) - M^0]$.

The critical feature of this decomposition is that all three money measures are expressed in terms of the same set of prices p^0.

        Finally, to analyze the impact of a change in economic policy
on social welfare, we can evaluate the social welfare function (5.10) at
prices p^1 and distribution of total expenditure $\{M_k^1\}$ after the change in
policy has taken place. In order to evaluate the impact of a change in
economic policy on social welfare, we must compare the levels of aggregate total expenditure required to attain the actual levels of social
welfare before and after the policy change at prices prevailing before
the change. For this purpose we define money metric social welfare, say
M_A, as the difference between the total expenditure required to attain
the actual level of welfare after the policy change, say W^1, and the
expenditure required to attain the actual level of welfare before the
policy change W^0 at prices prevailing before the policy change p^0:

(6.8) $M_A(p^0,W^0,W^1) = M(p^0,W^1) - M(p^0,W^0)$.

If money metric social welfare is positive, the level of social welfare
is increased by the policy change; otherwise, social welfare is decreased
or left unaffected.

        We can decompose our money measure of social welfare after
the change in economic policy into money measures of efficiency and
equity. For this purpose we first determine the maximum level of welfare, say W^3, that can be attained through lump sum redistributions of
aggregate total expenditure $M^1 = \sum_{k=1}^{K} M_k^1$. As before, aggregate expenditure must be distributed so as to equalize individual expenditure per
household equivalent member, so that the social welfare function (5.10)
reduces to average individual welfare (6.2). This is the maximum level
of social welfare that is potentially available after the change in
economic policy and can be taken as a measure of efficiency.

        To preserve comparability between money measures of actual
social welfare W^1 and potential welfare W^3 after the change in economic

policy, we can evaluate the measure of potential welfare at prices prevailing before the change in policy p^0, using the social expenditure
function:

$$(6.9) \quad \ln M(p^0,W^3) = \frac{1}{D(p^0)} \; [\ln p^{0'}(\alpha_p + \frac{1}{2} \, B_{pp} \; \ln p^0) - W^3] + \ln[\sum_{k=1}^{K} m_0(p^0,A_k)].$$

The corresponding money measure of equity in terms of prices prevailing
before the change in policy is given by the difference between the money
measure of actual social welfare after the policy change $M(p^0,W^1)$ and the
money measure of potential social welfare after the policy change
$M(p^0,W^3)$. Our money measure of actual social welfare $M(p^0,W^1)$ is the sum
of money measures of efficiency and equity. All three measures are
evaluated at prices prevailing before the change in policy p^0:

$$(6.10) \quad M(p^0,W^1) = M(p^0,W^3) + [M(p^0,W^1) - M(p^0,W^3)].$$

Finally, we can decompose money metric social welfare (6.8)
into the sum of money metric efficiency and money metric equity. _Money
metric efficiency_, say M_p, can be defined as the difference between the
total expenditure required to attain the potential level of welfare after
the policy change W^3 and the expenditure required to attain the potential
level of welfare before the policy change W^2. Both are evaluated at
prices prevailing before the policy change p^0:

$$(6.11) \quad M_p(p^0,W^2,W^3) = M(p^0,W^3) - M^0.$$

Similarly, _money metric equity_, say M_E, can be defined as the
difference between money measures of equity before and after the policy
change, evaluated at prices before the change p^0:

$$(6.12) \quad M_E(p^0,W^0,W^1,W^2,W^3) = [M(p^0,W^1) - M(p^0,W^3)] - [M(p^0,W^0) - M^0].$$

Money metric social welfare is the sum of money metric efficiency and money metric equity:

$$(6.13) \quad M_A(p^0,W^0,W^1) = M_P(p^0,W^2,W^3) + M_E(p^0,W^0,W^1,W^2,W^3),$$

All three money measures of social welfare in this decomposition are expressed in terms of the same set of prices p^0.

To illustrate the measurement of social welfare we can represent the concept of money metric social welfare geometrically, as in Diagram 2. In this diagram we have depicted a representative consumer with indirect utility function given by the average level of utility $\ln \bar{V}$ in (6.2). As before, we consider the case of two commodities ($N = 2$) for simplicity. Consumer equilibrium at the actual level of social welfare W^0 before the policy change is represented by the point A. The corresponding level of aggregate expenditure $M(p^0, W^0)$, divided by the price of the second commodity p_2^0, is given on the vertical axis. This axis provides a representation of aggregate expenditure in terms of units of the second commodity.

Aggregate expenditure M^0 is the value of the social expenditure function at the potential level of welfare W^1. This is the maximum level of welfare that can be obtained by lump sum redistributions of aggregate expenditure. The corresponding consumer equilibrium is represented by the point B. A money measure of efficiency, expressed in terms of units of the second commodity, is given by the level of aggregate expenditure M^0/p_2^0. The corresponding money measure of equity is provided by the distance along the x_2-axis between aggregate expenditure M^0/p_2^0 and the value of the social expenditure function $M(p^0, W^0)/p_2^0$; each is divided by the price of the second commodity. The money measure of social welfare at A is the sum of money measures of efficiency and equity.

As before, consumer equilibrium at the level of social welfare W^1 after the policy change is represented by the point C. In (6.8) we have determined this level of welfare by evaluating the social welfare function (5.10) at the prices p^1 and the distribution of total expenditure $\{M_k^1\}$ after the change in policy has taken place. To translate the level of social welfare W^1 into aggregate expenditure at the prices prevailing before the policy change, we evaluate the social expenditure function (6.3) at this level of social welfare and the prices before the

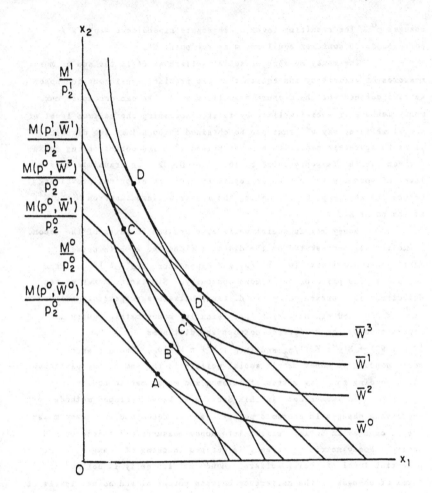

Diagram 2. Money Metric Social Welfare.

changes p^0. The resulting level of aggregate expenditure $M(p^0, W^1)$ corresponds to consumer equilibrium at the point C'.

The money measure of social welfare at C' is the sum of money measures of efficiency and equity that are precisely analogous to those we have defined for the measure of welfare at A. We can decompose our money measure of social welfare by first determining the maximum level of social welfare, say W^3, that can be obtained through lump sum distributions to aggregate expenditure M^1 at prices p^1. The corresponding consumer equilibrium is represented by the point D. We can translate this level of social welfare into aggregate expenditure at prices prevailing before the change p^0 by evaluating the social welfare function $M(p^0, W^3)$ at the point D'.

Money metric social welfare, expressed in units of the second commodity, is represented by the distance along the x_2-axis between aggregate expenditure $M(p^0, W^1)/p_2$ and expenditure $M(p^0, W^0)/p_2$, each divided by the price of the second commodity. Similarly, money metric efficiency is represented by the distance between aggregate expenditure $M(p^0, W^3)/p_2$ and expenditure M^0/p_2. Finally, money metric equity is represented by the difference between the distances $[M(p^0, W^1) - M(p^0, W_3)]/p_2$ and $[M(p^0, W^0) - M^0]/p_2$. The distance corresponding to money metric social welfare is the sum of the distances corresponding to money metric efficiency and money metric equity.

To summarize: In this Section we have developed methods for expressing changes in economic policy. We can decompose our money measure of changes in social welfare into money measures of efficiency and equity. Money metric efficiency is defined in terms of changes in the potential level of social welfare. Money metric equity is defined in terms of changes in the difference between potential and actual levels of social welfare.

7   EFFICIENCY VERSUS EQUITY

Given methods for measuring social welfare, we are in a position to evaluate alternative policies for petroleum price regulation and
taxation of petroleum production in the United States. As a basis for
comparison of levels of social welfare associated with alternative policies, we take current policy as a reference case. Under this policy
petroleum price controls were eliminated in January 1981; a windfall profits tax is levied on petroleum production. We employ the behavior of
the U.S. economy under these policies with a regime of low oil prices as
a base case for policy analysis.

The value of social welfare depends on prices for each of the
five commodities included in our model of aggregate consumer behavior --
energy, food, consumer goods, capital services, and consumer services.
In addition, it depends on total expenditure for the U.S. economy as a
whole. As before, we make the simplifying assumption that total expenditure changes in the same proportion for all consuming units. We employ
the projections of prices and total expenditure based on the Dynamic General Equilibrium Model (DGEM) of the U.S. economy given in Table 2.

We can translate our evaluation of alternative policies for
petroleum price regulation into money measures of social welfare by
employing the social expenditure function introduced in Section 6. In
Table 4 we present money metric social welfare for the three alternatives
to current policy described in Section 4 above. Although the magnitude of
money metric social welfare depends on the degree of aversion to inequality, we find that the qualitative features of comparisons among alternative policies for different values of this parameter are almost identical. We present money metric social welfare for all three alternatives
to the base case for the degree of aversion to inequality ρ equal to one.

Under continued controls money metric social welfare is positive for the years 1980, 1981, and 1982, and becomes negative for the
rest of the period. Money metric social welfare under elimination of the
windfall profits tax is slightly negative for the year 1980. For all
subsequent years included in our study money metric social welfare is
positive, reaching a maximum of $10.524 billion dollars in 1984. Reform-
ing the windfall profits tax has no impact on social welfare during 1980,
1981, and 1982, since the reform does not take effect until 1983.

TABLE 4

MONEY METRIC SOCIAL WELFARE

(Millions of Current Dollars)

Year	Continued Controls	No Tax	Reformed Tax
1980	17359.914	-412.867	0.000
1981	14289.919	5509.200	0.000
1982	1732.022	7836.263	0.000
1983	-8386.252	9642.212	198.001
1984	-16326.843	10524.042	221.431
1985	-21510.685	10224.960	244.202
1986	-25253.311	9699.709	526.232
1987	-26531.095	9404.192	636.930
1988	-28165.957	8933.008	660.231
1989	-28953.384	7932.562	764.214
1990	-29377.805	6501.736	840.548
1991	-29711.136	4943.447	926.703
1992	-31584.172	2977.254	783.785
1993	-31444.095	1554.040	748.735
1994	-30377.851	367.070	522.893
1995	-29766.946	-131.788	528.650

Beginning in 1983 a reformed windfall profits tax produces a gain in social welfare, relative to the base case, but produces lower social welfare levels than elimination of the windfall profits tax for this entire period. Our analysis of current regulatory and fiscal policy for petroleum and the three alternative policies appears to justify change in policy to eliminate the windfall profits tax. This policy is superior to current policy and to a policy of continued price controls. It is also superior to a reformed windfall profits tax.

Money metric social welfare is the sum of money metric efficiency and money metric equity. Money metric efficiency corresponds to the gain in potential social welfare associated with a change in

regulatory and fiscal policy and is independent of the degree of aversion
to inequality ρ. We present money metric efficiency for all three alternatives to the base case in Table 5.

Under continued controls money metric efficiency is positive
for 1980-1982 and negative for the rest of the period 1983-1995. Money
metric efficiency under elimination of the windfall profits tax is
slightly negative for the year 1980. For the period 1981-1993 money
metric social welfare is positive, reaching a maximum of $18.530 billion
dollars in 1987. Reforming the windfall profits tax produces no gains in
efficiency for the years 1980, 1981, and 1982, but produces relative modest efficiency gains for the period 1983-1995. Money metric efficiency
is higher for elimination of the windfall profits tax than for reform of
this tax for the period 1981-1993.

Gains in potential welfare under a policy of eliminating the
windfall profits tax are greater than under continued controls or under
reform of the windfall profits tax for the period 1982-1994. Current
policy results in lower efficiency than a policy of elimination of the
windfall profits tax, except for 1980. A common practice in welfare
economics is to recommend the policy with the greatest efficiency. On
these grounds the policy of elimination of the windfall profits tax would
be judged superior to current policy and to continued controls and reform
of the windfall profits tax.

We next consider money measures of equity for all three
alternatives to current regulatory policy. Money metric equity is
defined as the difference between actual and potential gains in social
welfare resulting from a change in regulatory and fiscal policy. Money
metric equity, unlike money metric efficiency, depends on the degree of
aversion to inequality ρ. We have found, as before, that the qualitative
features of comparisons among alternative policies are almost identical
for different values of this parameter, so that we present money metric

TABLE 5

MONEY METRIC EFFICIENCY

(Millions of Current Dollars)

Year	Continued Controls	No Tax	Reformed Tax
1980	30705.080	-951.504	0.000
1981	23801.790	9734.482	0.000
1982	311.309	13904.026	0.000
1983	-18387.854	17047.828	350.182
1984	-33176.097	18529.671	381.874
1985	-42890.709	17903.877	409.799
1986	-49954.218	16892.739	932.365
1987	-52461.101	16263.804	1130.191
1988	-55596.050	15296.033	1161.109
1989	-57190.454	13411.956	1349.977
1990	-58134.560	10767.518	1487.271
1991	-58857.002	7910.025	1648.278
1992	-62325.187	4284.953	1380.887
1993	-62143.559	1698.934	1321.890
1994	-60361.396	-442.609	909.944
1995	-59323.376	-1330.389	926.484

equity for the three alternatives to current regulatory policy in Table 6 for degree of aversion to inequality ρ equal to one.

Money metric equity for a policy of continued petroleum price controls is negative for 1980 and 1981 and positive for the remainder of the period 1982-1995, reaching a level of $30.741 billion dollars in 1995. By contrast a policy of eliminating the windfall profits tax improves equity in 1980 and after 1992, but worsens equity for the period 1981-1993. A policy of reforming the windfall profits taxes worsens equity through the period covered by our study.

Finally, by comparing the results presented in Tables 4 and 5 we can see that money metric efficiency and equity can move in the same

TABLE 6

MONEY METRIC EQUITY

(Millions of Current Dollars)

Year	Continued Controls	No Tax	Reformed Tax
1980	-13345.166	538.637	0.000
1981	-9511.871	-4225.283	0.000
1982	1420.713	-6067.762	0.000
1983	10001.602	-7405.616	-152.181
1984	16849.254	-8005.630	-160.443
1985	21380.025	-7678.917	-165.597
1986	24700.906	-7193.029	-406.133
1987	25930.005	-6859.612	-493.261
1988	27430.094	-6363.025	-500.878
1989	28237.070	-5479.394	-585.763
1990	28756.755	-4265.782	-646.723
1991	29145.867	-2966.579	-721.575
1992	30741.014	-1307.699	-597.101
1993	30699.465	-144.894	-573.155
1994	29983.545	809.679	-387.051
1995	29556.429	1198.601	-397.834

direction or in opposite directions. For example, a policy of eliminating the windfall profits tax is preferred to all other policies for the period 1982-1993. During the period 1982-1993 money metric efficiency under elimination of the windfall profits tax dominates that for the alternative policies. However, money metric equity under elimination of the tax is lower than that for current policy, for continued controls and for reform of the tax for the period 1982-1992.

To summarize: We have translated comparisons among alternative policies for petroleum price regulation and taxation into money measures of social welfare. Money metric social welfare for a policy of eliminating the windfall profits tax is higher than for any of the

alternative policies we have considered. Finally, we have decomposed
money metric social welfare into money metric equity and money metric
efficiency. We have found that money metric equity and money metric
efficiency are both essential to the determination of money metric social
welfare.

8   SUMMARY AND CONCLUSION

We can summarize our approach to the general equilibrium
analysis of economic policy as follows: First we introduce a measure of
individual welfare based on the indirect utility function for each consuming unit. We assume that individual welfare is equal to the logarithm
of the translog indirect utility function (2.22). The indirect utility
function enables us to express individual welfare in terms of the price
system and the level of total expenditure.

In Section 2 we show how the translog indirect utility function can be determined from a system of individual expenditure shares
(2.5) that is integrable. We also demonstrate how the individual expenditure shares (2.5) can be recovered uniquely from the system of aggregate expenditure shares (2.25). In Section 3 we fit an econometric model
of aggregate consumer behavior that incorporates the restrictions implied
by integrability of the individual expenditure shares.

In Section 4 we employ the translog individual expenditure
function (2.23) to translate changes in individual welfare into money
metric individual welfare. Money metric individual welfare provides a
monotone increasing transformation of individual welfare that is not fully
comparable among consuming units. This measure can be used in evaluating
economic policies by constructing partial orderings of these policies
based on the Pareto principle. We illustrate the application of money
metric individual welfare by analyzing the impact of alternative policies
for regulation and taxation of domestic petroleum production in the
United States.

A complete ordering of economic policies requires a social
welfare function. In Section 5 we have introduced a class of social welfare functions capable of expressing a variety of ethical judgements.
This class is based on the distribution of individual welfare over the
population of consuming units. In measuring social welfare we require
cardinal measures of individual welfare that are fully comparable among
units. For this purpose we employ translog indirect utility functions
for all units.

In Section 6 we introduce a social expenditure function.
This function can be used to translate changes in social welfare into
money metric social welfare. The concept of money metric social welfare
can be used in comparing alternative economic policies on the basis of
the aggregate expenditure required for each policy. In addition, we

introduce the maximum level of social welfare that can be attained by lump sum redistributions of aggregate expenditure among consuming units as a measure of efficiency. Using this measure, we can decompose money metric social welfare into the sum of money metric equity and money metric efficiency.

In Section 7 we compare the impact of alternative policies for regulation and taxation of domestic petroleum production in the United States on social welfare. We find that continued controls would produce gains in equity, but that these would be offset by losses in efficiency, resulting in a loss in social welfare. By contrast dropping the windfall profits tax would produce gains in efficiency that outweigh losses in equity, resulting in a gain in social welfare.

The approach to general equilibrium analysis of economic policy we have presented has been fruitful in generating interesting and useful applications. However, a great deal of important and worthwhile research remains to be done. Completion of this line of research promises to restore normative economics to its rightful place -- as an equal partner of positive economics in the general equilibrium analysis of economic policies.

REFERENCES

Arrow, K.J. (1963), Social Choice and Individual Values, New Haven, Yale
University Press, 2nd ed.

_____ (1977), "Extended Sympathy and the Possibility of Social Choice,"
American Economic Review, Vol. 67, No. 1, February, pp. 219-
225.

Arrow, K.J., H.B. Chenery, B.S. Minhas, and R.M. Solow (1961), "Capital-
Labor Substitution and Economic Efficiency, Review of Economics and Statistics, Vol. 43, No. 3, August, pp. 225-250.

Arrow, K.J. and J.P. Kalt (1979), Petroleum Price Regulation: Should We
Decontrol, Washington, American Enterprise Institute.

d'Aspremont, C. and L. Gevers (1977), "Equity and the Informational Basis
of Collective Choice," Review of Economic Studies, Vol. 44,
No. 137, June, pp. 199-209.

Atkinson, A.B. (1970), "On Measurement of Inequality," Journal of
Economic Theory, Vol. 2, No. 3, September, pp. 244-263.

Barten, A.P. (1964), "Family Composition, Prices, and Expenditure Patterns," in P. Hart, G. Mills, and J.K. Whitaker (eds.),
Econometric Analysis for National Economic Planning: 16th
Symposium of the Colston Society, London, Butterworth, pp.
277-292.

_____ (1977), "The Systems of Consumer Demand Functions Approach: A
Review," in M.D. Intriligator (ed.), Frontiers of Quantitative Economics, Vol. IIIA, Amsterdam, North-Holland, pp. 23-
58.

Bergson, A. (1936), "Real Income, Expenditure Proportionality, and
Frisch's 'New Methods of Measuring Marginal Utility'," Review
of Economic Studies, Vol. 4, No. 1, October 1936, pp. 33-52.

_____ (1938), "A Reformulation of Certain Aspects of Welfare Economics," Quarterly Journal of Economics, Vol. 52, No. 2, February, pp. 310-334.

_____ (1980), "Consumer's Surplus and Income Redistribution," Journal of Public Economics, Vol. 14, No. 1, August, pp. 31-47.

Blackorby, C. and D. Donaldson (1978), "Measures of Relative Equality and their Meaning in Terms of Social Welfare," Journal of Economic Theory, Vol. 18, No. 1, June, p. 651-75.

_____, and _____ (1982), "Ratio-Scale and Translation-Scale Full Interpersonal Comparability without Domain Restrictions: Admissible Social-Evaluation Functions," International Economic Review, Vol. 23, No. 2, June, pp. 249-268.

Bureau of the Census (various annual issues), Current Population Reports, Consumer Income, Series P-60, Washington, D.C., U.S. Department of Commerce.

Carlson, M.D. (1974), "The 1972-73 Consumer Expenditure Survey," Monthly Labor Review, Vol. 97, No. 12, December, pp. 16-23.

Chipman, J.S., and J.C. Moore (1980), "Compensating Variation, Consumer's Surplus, and Welfare," American Economic Review, Vol. 70, No. 5, December 1980, pp. 933-949.

Christensen, L.R., D.W. Jorgenson, and L.J. Lau (1975), "Transcendental Logarithmic Utility Functions," American Economic Review, Vol. 65, No. 3, June, pp. 367-383.

Dalton, H. (1920), "The Measurement of Inequality of Income," Economic Journal, Vol. 30, No. 119, September, pp. 361-84.

Deaton, A. and J. Muellbauer (1980), Economics and Consumer Behavior, Cambridge, Cambridge University Press.

Deschamps, R. and L. Gevers (1978), "Leximin and Utilitarian Rules: A

Joint Characterization," _Journal of Economic Theory_, Vol. 17,
No. 2, April, pp. 143-63.

van der Gaag, J. and E. Smolensky (1982), "True Household Equivalence
Scales and Characteristics of the Poor in the United States,"
Review of Income and Wealth, Series 28, No. 1, March, pp.
17-28.

Diamond, P.A. and D. McFadden (1974), "Some Uses of the Expenditure Function in Public Finance," _Journal of Public Economics_, Vol. 3,
No. 1, February, pp. 3-21.

Dupuit, J. (1969), "On the Measurement of the Utility of Public Works,"
in K.J. Arrow and T. Scitovsky, eds., _Readings in Welfare
Economics_, Homewood, Richard D. Irwin, pp. 255-283 (originally published in French in 1844).

Goettle, R.J., IV, and E.A. Hudson (1983), "The Macroeconomic Consequences of Oil Price and Tax Policies," Dale W. Jorgenson
Associates, Cambridge.

Gorman, W.M. (1976), "Tricks with Utility Functions," in M.J. Artis and
A.R. Nobay (eds.), _Essays in Economic Analysis_: _Proceedings
of the 1975 AUTE Conference_, Cambridge, Cambridge University
Press, pp. 211-243.

Hammond, P.J. (1976), "Equity, Arrow's Conditions and Rawl's Difference
Principle," _Econometrica_, Vol. 44, No. 4, July, pp. 793-804.

_____ (1977), "Dual Interpersonal Comparisons of Utility and the Welfare
Economics of Income Distribution," _Journal of Public Econom-
ics_, Vol. 7, No. 1, February, pp. 51-71.

Harberger, A.C. (1971), "Three Basic Postulates for Applied Welfare
Economics: An Interpretive Essay," _Journal of Economic
Literature_, Vol. 9, No. 3, September, pp. 785-797.

Hardy, G.H., J.E. Littlewood, and G. Polya (1959), _Inequalities_,

Cambridge, Cambridge University Press, 2nd ed.

Harsanyi, J.C. (1976), Essays on Ethics, Social Behavior and Scientific Explanation, Dordrecht, D. Reidel.

Hausman, J.A. (1981), "Exact Consumer's Surplus and Deadweight Loss," American Economic Review, Vol. 71, No. 4, September, pp. 662-676.

Hicks, J.R. (1942). "Consumers' Surplus and Index-Numbers," Review of Economic Studies, Vol. 9, No. 2, Summer, pp. 126-137.

Hotelling, H. (1938), "The General Welfare in Relation to Problems of Taxation and of Railway and Utility Rates," Econometrica, Vol. 6, No. 3, July, pp. 242-269.

Houthakker, H.S. (1957), "An International Comparison of Household Expenditure Patterns Commemorating the Centenary of Engel's Law," Econometrica, Vol. 25, No. 4, October, pp. 532-551.

_____ (1960), "Additive Preferences," Econometrica, Vol. 28, No. 2, April, pp. 244-257.

Hudson, E.A. and, Jorgenson, D.W. (1974). "U.S. Energy Policy and Economic Growth, 1975-2000," Bell Journal of Economics and Management Science, Vol. 5, No. 2, Autumn, pp. 461-514.

_____ (1976). "U.S. Tax Policy and Energy Conservation." In D. Jorgenson (ed.), Econometric Studies of U.S. Energy Policy, Amsterdam, North-Holland, pp. 7-94.

_____ (1978a). "Energy Prices and the U.S. Economy, 1972-1976," Natural Resources Journal, Vol. 18, No. 4, pp. 877-897.

_____ (1978b). "The Economic Impact of Policies to Reduce U.S. Energy Growth," Resources and Energy, Vol. 1, No. 3, November, pp. 205-230.

Hurwicz, L. and H. Uzawa (1971), "On the Integrability of Demand Func-
    tions," in J.S. Chipman, et. al. (eds.), Preferences, Utility
    and Demand, New York, Harcourt Brace, pp. 114-48.

Jorgenson, D.W. and L.J. Lau (1975), "The Structure of Consumer Prefer-
    ences," Annals of Economic and Social Measurement, Vol. 4,
    No. 1, January, pp. 49-101.

_____, and _____ (1979), "The Integrability of Consumer Demand Func-
    tions," European Economic Review, Vol. 12, No. 2, April, pp.
    115-147.

Jorgenson, D.W., L.J. Lau, and T.M. Stoker (1980), "Welfare Comparison
    Under Exact Aggregation," American Economic Review, Vol. 70,
    No. 2, May, pp. 268-272.

_____, _____, and _____ (1981), "Aggregate Consumer Behavior and Indivi-
    dual Welfare," in D. Currie, R. Nobay, and D. Peel (eds.),
    Macroeconomic Analysis, London, Croom-Helm, pp. 35-61.

_____, _____, and _____ (1982), "The Transcendental Logarithmic Model of
    Aggregate Consumer Behavior," in R.L. Basmann and G.F.
    Rhodes, Jr. (eds.), Advances in Econometrics, Vol. 1,
    Greenwich, JAI Press, pp. 97-238.

Kakwani, N.C. (1977), "On the Estimation of Consumer Unit Scales," Review
    of Econmics and Statistics, Vol. 59, No. 4, November, pp.
    507-510.

King, M.A. (1983a), "An Index of Inequality: With Applications to Hor-
    izontal Equity and Social Mobility," Econometrica, Vol. 51,
    No. 1, January, pp. 99-115.

_____ (1983b), "Welfare Analysis of Tax Reforms Using Household Data,"
    Journal of Public Economics, forthcoming.

Kolm, S.C. (1969), "The Optimal Production of Social Justice," in J. Mar-
    golis and H. Guitton (eds.), Public Economics, London:

Macmillan, pp. 145-200.

_____ (1976a and 1976b), "Unequal Inequalities I and II," Journal of Economic Theory, Vol. 12, No. 3, June, pp. 416-42, and Vol. 13, No. 1, August, pp. 82-111.

Lau, L.J. (1977a), "Complete Systems of Consumer Demand Functions through Duality," in M.D. Intriligator (ed.), Frontiers of Quantitative Economics, Vol. IIIA, Amsterdam, North-Holland, pp. 59-86.

_____ (1977b), "Existence Conditions for Aggregate Demand Functions," Technical Report No. 248, Institute for Mathematical Studies in the Social Sciences, Stanford University, Stanford (revised 1980 and 1982).

_____ (1982), "A Note on the Fundamental Theorem of Exact Aggregation," Economics Letters, Vol. 9, No. 2, pp. 119-126.

Lau, L.J., W.L. Lin, and P.A. Yotopoulos (1978), "The Linear Logarithmic Expenditure System: An Application to Consumption-Leisure Choice," Econometrica, Vol. 46, No. 4, July, pp. 843-868.

Lazear, E.P. and R.T. Michael (1980), "Family Size and The Distribution of Real Per Capita Income," American Economic Review, Vol. 70, No. 1, March, pp. 91-107.

Leser, C.E.V. (1963), "Forms of Engel Functions," Econometrica, Vol. 31, No. 4, October, pp. 694-703.

Marshall, Alfred (1920), Principles of Economics, 8th ed., London, Macmillan.

Martos, B. (1969), "Subdefinite Matrices and Quadratic Forms," SIAM Journal of Applied Mathematics, Vol. 17, pp. 1215-1223.

Maskin, E. (1978), "A Theorem on Utilitarianism," Review of Economic Studies, Vol. 42, No. 139, February, pp. 93-96.

McKenzie, G.W. (1982), _Measuring Economic Welfare_: New _Methods_, Cambridge, Cambridge University Press.

McKenzie, L.W. (1957), "Demand Theory without a Utility Index," _Review of Economic Studies_, Vol. 24(3), No. 65, June, pp. 185-189.

Mirrlees, J.A. (1971), "An Exploration in the Theory of Optimal Income Taxation," _Review of Economic Studies_, Vol. 38, No. 114, April, pp. 175-208.

Muellbauer, J. (1974a), "Household Composition, Engel Curves and Welfare Comparisons between Households: A Duality Approach," _European Economic Review_, Vol. 5, No. 2, August, pp. 103-22.

_____ (1974b), "Inequality Measures, Prices and Household Composition," _Review of Economic Studies_, Vol. 41(4), No. 128, October, pp. 493-504.

_____ (1974c), "Prices and Inequality: The United Kingdom Experience," _Economic Journal_, Vol. 84, No. 333, March, pp. 32-55.

_____ (1976), "Economics and the Representative Consumer," in L. Solari and J.N. Du Pasqueir (eds.), _Private and Enlarged Consumption_, Amsterdam, North-Holland, pp. 29-54.

_____ (1977), "Testing the Barten Model of Household Composition Effects and the Cost of Children," _Economic Journal_, Vol. 87, No. 347, September, pp. 460-487.

_____ (1980), "The Estimation of the Prais-Houthakker Model of Equivalence Scales," _Econometrica_, Vol. 48, No. 1, January, pp. 153-176.

Ng, Y.K. (1975), "Bentham or Bergson? Finite Sensibility, Utility Functions and Social Welfare Functions," _Review of Economic Studies_, Vol. 42, No. 4, October, pp. 545-569.

Parks, R.W. and A.P. Barten (1973), "A Cross Country Comparison of the

Effects of Prices, Income, and Population Composition on Consumption Patterns," Economic Journal, Vol. 83, No. 331, September, pp. 834-852.

Pollak, R.A. (1981), "The Social Cost of Living Index," Journal of Public Economics, Vol. 15, No. 3, June, pp. 311-336.

Pollak, R.A. and T.J. Wales (1978), "Estimation of Complete Demand Systems from Household Budget Data: The Linear and Quadratic Expenditure Systems," American Economic Review, Vol. 68, No. 3, June, pp. 348-359.

_____, and _____ (1979), "Welfare Comparisons and Equivalent Scales," American Economic Review, Vol. 69, No. 2, May, pp. 216-21.

_____, and _____ (1980), "Comparisons of the Quadratic Expenditure System and Translog Demand Systems with Alternative Specifications of Demographic Effects," Econometrica, Vol. 48, No. 3, April, pp. 595-612.

_____, and _____ (1981), "Demographic Variables in Demand Analysis," Econometrica, Vol. 49, No. 6, November, pp. 1533-1552.

Prais, S.J. and H.S. Houthakker (1971), The Analysis of Family Budgets, Cambridge, Cambridge University Press, 2nd ed.

Ray, R. (1982), "The Testing and Estimation of Complete Demand Systems on Household Budget Surveys: An Application of AIDS," European Economic Review, Vol. 17, No. 3, March 1982, pp. 349-370.

Roberts, K.W.S. (1980a), "Possibility Theorems with Interpersonally Comparable Welfare Levels," Review of Economic Studies, Vol. 47, No. 147, January, pp. 409-20.

_____ (1980b), "Interpersonal Comparability and Social Choice Theory," Review of Economic Studies, Vol. 47, No. 147, January, pp. 421-439.

_____ (1980c), "Price-Independent Welfare Prescriptions," _Journal of Public Economics_, Vol. 13, No. 3, June, pp. 277-298.

_____ (1980d), "Social Choice Theory: The Single-profile and Multi-profile Approaches," _Review of Economic Studies_, Vol. 47, No. 147, January, pp. 441-450.

Roy, R. (1943), _De l'Utilite: Contributions a la Theorie des Choix_, Paris, Herman.

Samuelson, P.A. (1947), _Foundations of Economic Analysis_, Cambridge, Harvard University Press.

_____ (1956), "Social Indifference Curves," _Quarterly Journal of Economics_, Vol. 70, No. 1, February, pp. 1-22.

_____ (1974), "Complementarity -- An Essay on the 40th Anniversary of the Hicks-Allen Revolution in Demand Theory," _Journal of Economic Literature_, Vol. 12, No. 4, December, pp. 1255-1289.

_____ (1982), "Bergsonian Welfare Economics," in S. Rosefielde (ed.), _Economic Welfare and the Economics of Soviet Socialism: Essays in Honor of Abram Bergson_, Cambridge, Cambridge University Press, pp. 223-266.

Sen, A.K. (1970), _Collective Choice and Social Welfare_, Edinburgh, Oliver and Boyd.

_____ (1973), _On Economic Inequality_, Oxford, Clarendon Press.

_____ (1976), "Real National Income," _Review of Economic Studies_, Vol. 43, No. 133, February, pp. 19-40.

_____ (1977), "On Weights and Measures: Informational Constraints in Social Welfare Analysis," _Econometrica_, Vol. 45, No. 7, October, pp. 1539-72.

_____ (1979a), "The Welfare Basis of Real Income Comparisons: A Survey,"

Journal of Economic Literature, Vol. 17, No. 1, March, pp. 1-45.

_____ (1979b), "Personal Utilities and Public Judgements: Or What's Wrong with Welfare Economics," _Economic Journal_, Vol. 89, No. 763, September, pp. 537-558.

THE WELFARE COST OF INTEREST RATE CEILINGS IN DEVELOPING
COUNTRIES: A GENERAL EQUILIBRIUM APPROACH

M. Hasan Imam
Brock University, St. Catharines, Ontario, Canada

I. INTRODUCTION

The purpose of this study is to evaluate the welfare cost
of statutory ceilings on the rate of interest in many of the less
developed countries (LDC). While a typical LDC is invariably scarce in
capital reflected by its low capital-labor ratio and high rate of
return to investment, the real rate of return to savings is maintained
at a very low level, presumably, with a view to lowering the cost of
investment. If the ceiling on the rate of return to savings is a
binding constraint, it necessarily distorts the intertemporal
consumption by raising the cost of future consumption in terms of
current consumption. This obviously results in smaller savings due to
both income and substitution effects and thereby generates a smaller
investable surplus. Since savings in any period increments capital
stock of the next period, and since capital formation is a necessary
condition for economic growth, a repressive interest rate policy
results in a suboptimal growth. Such a repressive policy has been
coined in the literature as 'financial repression' (See Shaw (1973),
McKinnon (1974)). Moreover, if the rate of interest faced by borrowers
is lower than the rate of return to capital as well, an excess demand
for investment funds is created. This in turn results in rent seeking
behaviour which devotes real resources to obtain permits for
investments. This itself affects both economic efficiency and income
distribution.

The objective of this paper is, therefore, to evaluate the
degree of economic inefficiency arising out of distortion of savings
behavior due to the ceiling on the rate of return to savings. The
quantitative evaluation of the social cost involved in such a policy is
performed within a framework of computable general equilibrium model.
The numerical exercise is carried out for India.

371

Since savings, investment and the resulting economic growth
are essentially intertemporal issues, the analyses of interest rates
policies in LDCs should be carried out in an intertemporal framework.
Therefore, an intertemporal general equilibrium model is developed.
This model is similar to Fullerton-Shoven-Whalley (FSW) (1978, 1981,
1983) which analyse the welfare consequences of replacing the income
tax by an equivalent consumption tax. While the distortionary tax rate
on savings is exogeneously determined in FSW, the degree of interest
rate repression is endogenously determined in this paper. The welfare
consequences of liberalizing interest rates are evaluated by comparing
optimal with sub-optimal growths in terms of (i) national income, the
(ii) consumption, and (iii) dynamic analogs of compensating variation
equivalent variation developed by FWS (1978).

If interest rate is liberalized, the results indicate, the
national income and consumption in Indian economy would increase by nce
about 10%, for a reasonable set of values for key parameters of model
developed in this paper.

The plan of the paper is as follows: Section II presents
the analytical framework while Section III contains the methodology and
results of numerical evaluations for India. A final section contains
some concluding remarks and suggestions for possible extensions.

II. AN INTERTEMPORAL GENERAL EQUILIBRIUM MODEL
WITH A CEILING ON INTEREST RATES

Since interest rates determine saving and investment which,
in turn, determine growth rate of an economy the effects of a ceiling
on interest rate can be adequately analysed only in an intertemporal
framework. I therefore develop an intertemporal general equilibrium
model for evaluating the welfare cost of ceilings on the rate of return
to saving. Although an interest rate policy can be analyzed in terms
of a highly aggregative growth model of a single commodity, a
disaggregative model with several goods and consumer groups is required
for capturing the effects of differential preference structures and
production technologies usually seen in an actual economy. If, for
example, individuals have differences in their intertemporal preference
structures, the aggregate savings will be affected differently by a

given change in the interest rate. Further, if their preferences on contemporaneous consumer goods are also different, the changes in interest rates will affect the structure of demands for contemporaneous commodities. Such a change in demands will affect factor prices and factor incomes if the production technologies are different for different commodities.

In order to evaluate the welfare cost of restrictive interest rate policy in a disaggregative model, I follow the Lindahl-Hicks "temporary equilibria" approach which has also been used by FSW (1978, 1980, 1983) to evaluate the welfare gain from replacing the U.S. income tax with consumption tax. Under this approach, (See Grandmont (1982) trade takes place sequentially over time and at each date. Unlike Arrow-Debreu's perfect foresight model, the future is unknown at any point in time. In order to make a decision at any time period, each economic agent must forecast the future state of the economy. However, forecasts made today may not be necessarily realized when the actual time period occurs, and most likely, is not realized as no auctioneer coordinates these forecasts across economic agents.

In temporary "equibria approach", therefore, expectations play an important role. The expectation about future states are formed by an agent on the basis of his information available today. I assume that economic agents are myopic and expect the current state of the economy to prevail at future dates. For any vector z, his forecast is given as follows:

$$z_0 = z_t \text{ for all } t. \tag{1}$$

z may contain factor or commodity prices, or even quantities or any institutional constraint of the economy. Zero subscript of vector z stands for current period.

By using a "temporary equilibria" approach, a sequence of competitive equilibria is computed over time which mimics an equilibrium growth path. For example, at a given point in time, t_0, the stock of capital, labor, consumer preferences and production technologies generate a competitive equilibrium as consumers maximize utility and producers maximize profit. In such an equilibrium, the quantity of investment goods is determined along with all other quantities and prices. The investment good purchased in the current period increments the capital stock in the next period (t_1). The new

capital stock, along with given preferences and technologies of that
period similarly generates an equilibrium quantity of investment good
which increments capital stock of the following period (t_2). A
sequence of equilibria so generated over time, yields a growth path.
Different interest rate policies give rise to different growth paths.
The welfare impacts of policy changes are then evaluated by comparing
these alternative growth paths with and without ceilings on the rate of
return to savings.

Consumption

Since savings increment the capital stock through
investment and since savings are generated from intertemporal utility
maximization, consumption behavior occupies the central position in our
model. The ceiling on interest rate is assumed only to distort
consumption decisions; and whatever savings are mobilized are assumed
to be efficiently allocated through market forces.

For the sake of notational clarity, we avoid using a
subscript j in the following pages, although the description holds for
any typical consumer j, j=1, ...,m. We consider a typical consumer
faces two optimization problems which he solves sequentially. The
first is the allocation of his current income between consumption
expenditure and savings. The second is the allocation of current
consumption expenditure among different consumer goods. Assuming the
savings to be fully invested, his savings are viewed as current
"spending" made to enhance his consumption in the future. Thus, if the
consumer wants to provide himself with future consumption, C_t, in
period t, t=1, ...,T, from savings out of his current income, his
intertemporal utility function may be written as:

$$U = U(C_0, \ldots, C_t) \tag{2}$$

where C_0 is his <u>total</u> amount of consumption in period 0. Given the
definition of C_t above, it is quite possible for any consumer to have
$C_t < 0$ for any or all t. If $C_t < 0$ for all t, the consumer is
necessarily dissaving in the current period. However, all consumers
can not dissave together in any period since the aggregate demand for
current consumption in the economy is constrained by the aggregate
current income. This is due to the requirement of competitive
(temporary) equilibrium in each period.

Let us assume that the utility function (2) can be written as a separable function

$$U = U(C_0, H) \tag{3}$$

where H is a linear homogeneous function of C_t, t=1,...,T. Without the loss of generality, such an assumption allows us to express C_t, for all t, as a Hicksian composite commodity provided the rates of return to savings, δ_t, are constant. Let us define ϕ as:

$$\phi_t = \frac{1}{\prod\limits_{t=1}^{t}(1 + \delta_t)^t} \tag{4}$$

As shown by Liviatan (1965), ϕ_t can be interpreted as the "price" of C_t in terms of current consumption. If rates of return to savings in all future periods are constant, not necessarily identical, we can write a composite commodity of future consumption, C_f, as

$$C_f = \frac{\sum\limits_{t=1}^{T}\phi_t C_t}{D_f} \tag{5}$$

where D_f is the price of composite commodity and is defined as

$$D_f = \sum\limits_{t=1}^{T}\phi_t \tag{6}$$

Since the consumer forms expectations about future rates of return to savings and make his saving decisions today on that basis, and since the consumer is assumed to be myopic, we can write (3) as:

$$V = V(C_0, C_f) \tag{7}$$

It should be noted from (5) that $D_f C_f = \sum \phi_t C_t$ is the present value of his future consumption. Since C_t is financed with saving, $D_f C_f$ must be equal to his current "spending" on investment goods. If P_I and I are respectively the acquisition price and quantity of investment good,

$$D_f C_f = P_I I \tag{8}$$

Thus, $P_I I$ is the total saving or, as noted earlier, the current "spending" on investment good to enchance future consumption.

The budget constraint of a consumer can, therefore, be written as,

$$Y = P_0 C_0 + P_I I \tag{9}$$

or, by substituting from (8),

$$Y = P_0 C_0 + D_f C_f \tag{9'}$$

where P_0 is the price of current consumption and is a linear homogeneous function of prices of all consumer goods in period 0. Y is his income in period 0 which is defined as

$$Y = P_k' K + W'L + R \tag{10}$$

where P_k' and W' are (net of tax) rental price of capital services and wage rate, respectively, R is the transfer received from all sources including the government. Endowments of capital services and labour in the current period are given by K and L respectively.

Given the expectations defined by (1), we have $\delta_0 = \delta_t = \delta$. for all t. Assuming the consumer to have an infinite time horizon, we can write (6) as

$$D_f = \frac{1}{\delta} \tag{11}$$

implying that the price of future consumption is inversely related to the current rate of return to saving. In terms of the acquisition price of investment good, P_I, and rental price of capital services, P_k', rate of return to savings can be written as:

$$\delta = \frac{\lambda P_k'}{P_0 P_I} \tag{12}$$

here λ the units of capital services per unit of physical capital. P_0 appears in the denominator of (12) to express the return to savings in terms of consumption in period 0. From (12) it can be easily seen that the rate of return to savings can be regulated by affecting P_k' or P_I. Consider, for example, that the government imposes a ceiling on the rate of return to savings such that

$$\delta = \text{Min. } (\bar{\delta}, r) \tag{13}$$

where $\bar{\delta}$ is the rate of return to savings set by the government and r is the rate of return to investment determined by free market forces.

Using (12), $\bar{\delta}$ can be defined by imposing a minimum price for acquisition of investment good,

$$\bar{\delta} = \frac{\lambda P_k'}{P_0 \bar{P}_I} \tag{14}$$

where $\bar{P}_I$ is the appropriately set acquisition price of investment good.

Similarly, the rate of return to investment determined by the free
market forces is given by

$$r = \frac{\lambda \, P_k'}{P_0 \, P_I'} \tag{15}$$

where P_I' is the producer price of investment good and λ, Pk and P_0 are
the same as in relations (12) and (15). Utilizing (14) and (15), we
can express a ceiling on δ as:

$$P_I = \text{Max} \, (\bar{P}_I, \, P_I') \tag{16}$$

which implies that ceiling on the rate of return to savings is
equivalent to a floor on the acquisition price of investment good. The
exact relationship between P_I P_I' can be given as:

$$P_I = \left(\tfrac{r}{\delta}\right) P_I' \tag{17}$$

This implies that a wedge between rates of return to savings and
investment can be maintained if savers and investors are separated by
some intermediation so that different prices can be changed for the
same investment good. Financial institutions in LDCs carry out such a
task largely because of underdeveloped capital market, indivisibility
of investment projects, institutional arrangements and infrastructure
of less developed economies.

The capital market is very rudimentary, if it exists at
all, in a typical less developed country. Savings of an individual are
also too meagre to finance a worthwhile project. Consequently, deposit
accounts with financial institutions and government bonds are the two
most important instruments of savings. The nominal rates of return to
these forms of savings are regulated by the government and are fixed at
a low level, resulting in a very low, if not zero, real rate of return
to savings due to inflation rate.

As regards the ownership of financial institutions, these
are either nationalized by the government or privately owned with an
implicit cartel market structure. As shown below, it is anlytically
identical whether the financial institutions are privately owned or
nationalized by the government where it redistributes the excess
revenue of nationalized financial sector to consumers in the lump sum
form.

Let us consider for the sake of simplicity that financial institutions themselves make the actual investment. If $r > \delta$, financial institutions generate a surplus of $(\frac{r - \delta}{\delta}) P'_I$ for each unit of investment good. If privately owned, it creates an additional income for shareholders; if nationalized, government makes additional income which is transferred to the public. In our budget constraint, R contains this additional income. For simplicity, we consider no other transfer income. Consequently, R for the jth consumer is defined as:

$$R_j = w_j \left(\frac{r - \delta}{\delta}\right) I \ P'_I \tag{18}$$

where ω_j is the share of excess income received by the jth consumer due to the presence of ceilings on rate of return to savings; and $\sum\limits_{j}^{m} \omega_j = 1$ implying that total surplus is distributed back to consumers. In our analysis, we assume that the financial sector is nationalized and the consumer receives a transfer in proportion to their savings. Therefore, ceilings on the rate of return to savings create a substitution effect only.

Given the above discussions of the budget constraint and the intertemporal utility function, we can derive demand functions for investment and consumer goods.

I assume that the intertemporal utility function in (7) can be written in C.E.S. form, by suppressing the subscript j for jth consumer, as:

$$V = [\beta C_0^{\frac{\sigma-1}{\sigma}} + (1-\beta) C_f^{\frac{\sigma-1}{\sigma}}]^{\frac{\sigma-1}{\sigma}} \tag{19}$$

where σ is the elasticity of substitution between current and future consumptions and is determined primarily by interest elasticity of savings. For each of the consumers, both β and σ are different indicating the differences of their preference functions.

Maximizing (19) subject to (9'), we have

$$C_0 = \frac{Y^{\sigma}}{P_0^{\sigma} \Pi} \tag{20}$$

and

$$C_f = \frac{Y (1-\beta)^{\sigma}}{D_f^{\sigma} \Pi} \tag{21}$$

where $\Pi = [\beta^{\sigma} P_0^{(1-\sigma)} + (1-\beta)^{\sigma} D_f^{(1-\sigma)}]$. $\qquad\qquad$ (22)

Utilizing the conditions that $D_f C_f = P_I I$, we have

$$I = \frac{Y (1-\beta)^{\sigma}}{P_I D_f^{\sigma-1} \Pi} \qquad\qquad (23)$$

Substituting for D_f we can write (23) as

$$I = \frac{Y (1-\beta)^{\sigma}}{P_I (\frac{P_0}{\lambda P_k})^{\sigma-1} \Pi} \qquad\qquad (24)$$

Since P_I is the acquisition price of investment good from a consumer's point of view, his income allocated to current consumption expenditure is given by $(Y - P_I I)$. However, the consumer receives a lump sum transfer from the government which the latter accumulates through the administration of minimum price for investment good. Assuming the lump sum transfer to be proportional to the purchase of investment good, the jth consumer receives a transfer equal to $P_I - P_I')I_j$, where I_j is his purchase of investment good, his constraint on current consumption expenditure is given, by omitting j subscript, as:

$$P_0 C_0 = (Y - P_I I) + (P_I - P_I') \cdot I$$
$$= Y - P_I' I \qquad\qquad (25)$$

where C_0 and P_0 are composite quantity and price of his current consumption. Once the consumer determines how much to spend on current consumption, his next optimization problem is the allocation of this expenditure on different consumer goods of the same period. The preference over consumer goods in period 0 is assumed to be described by Cobb-Douglas type utility function,

$$C_0 = X_1^{\Theta_1} X_2^{\Theta_2} \cdots X_n^{\Theta_n} \qquad\qquad (26)$$

where X_i, $i = 1, \ldots n$, is ith consumer good in period 0, Θ_i is the weight on ith commodity and $\Sigma \Theta_i = 1$.

Maximizing (26) subject to (25), demand for X_i is given as:

$$X_i = \frac{\Theta_i (Y - P_I' I)}{P_i}, \quad i=1,\ldots,n \qquad\qquad (27)$$

where P_i is the consumer price of ith commodity. P_0 in (25) is a linear homogeneous function of these P_i and is determined by the exact functional form of the contemporaneous utility function, such as (26).

Production

The production of each of the consumer goods, X_i, and investment good, I, is characterized by a continuous, differentiable and constant return to scale production function using labour and capital services as primary factors of production. In addition, outputs of other industries are also used as inputs where the inter-industry transaction is described by a fixed coefficient input-out matrix. The decision to supply a commodity is determined by cost minimizing behavior of firms where the producer price of a commodity is equal to the unit cost of production. The unit cost function for the ith industry is given by,

$$\phi_i(W, P_k) = W\, b_i(W, P_k) + P_k v_i(W, P_k) + \Psi_i(W, P_k) \qquad (28)$$

where W and P_k are wage rate and price of capital services gross of factor taxes respectively. $b_i(W, P_k)$ and $v_i(W, P_k)$ are requirements of labor and capital services, respectively, per unit of output. These are determined by cost minimization subject to production functions. These are obviously functions of factor prices reflecting the substitution between the primary factors of production. The term $\Psi_i(W, P_k)$ represents the cost of intermediate inputs used to produce a unit of the commodity and is determined by the sum of the product of intermediate inputs and their respective prices. Since the price of each of the commodities is a function of factor prices, Ψ_i depends on factor prices also. From the profit maximization condition of the firm we have,

$$W\, b_i(W, P_k) + P_k v_i(W, P_k) + \Psi_i(W, P_k) \geqslant P_i' \qquad (29)$$
$$\text{for } i=1, n \text{ and } i=I$$

where P_i' is the producer of the ith commodity. From zero profit condition, the relation (29) must hold with equality for a positive supply of ith commodity.

General Equilibrium

A competitive general equilibrium is achieved when no excess demand exists in any market at a given period and thus satisfies the condition of a temporary competitive equilibrium. This is guaranteed by satisfying Walrus Law. It has been shown by Imam and Whalley (1982) that a competitive equilibrium exists without any rationing rule even when some of the economic agents face ceilings or floors on some prices. As shown earlier, consumers face a floor price for the acquisition of an investment good, the floor being determined

by the real rates of return to investment and savings. Proof of
existence of a competitive equilibrium in this case follows from Imam-
Whalley (1982). Such an equilibrium is computable by following their
technique.

The Imam-Whalley technique is essentially a modified Scarf
(1973, 1982) algorithm. From an arbitrarily chosen vector of factor
prices, producer prices for all consumer and investment foods are
determined by utilizing relation (28). For each set of producer prices
we can determine consumer prices of all consumer goods and the
acquisition price of investment good, P_I, given by (17). Given
consumer prices so determined and the consumer income for a given
factor prices, quantities of I and X_i are determined by (24) and (27)
respectively. These quantities along with intermediate inputs
determine the aggregate demand for labour and capital as follows:

$$D_L = \sum_{i=1}^{n} X'_i \, b_i (W, P_k) + I' \, b_I (W, P_k) \qquad (30)$$

$$D_K = \sum_{i=1}^{n} X'_i \, v_i (W, P_k) + I' \, v_I (W, P_k) \qquad (31)$$

where X'_i = sum of final and intermediate demands for ith good.

I' = sum of final and intermediate demands for investment
good. Thus, D_L and D_K give the aggregate demands for labour and
capital services, respectively, for the chosen vector of factor prices.
D_L and D_K so determined may or may not be equal to endowments of these
two factors; if not, we do not have a competitive equilibrium and a new
vector of factor prices are chosen and all of the above steps are
performed until an equilibrium in factor markets is reached.

Once a competitive general equilibrium is reached through
above procedure, equilibrium quantity of investment good, I, along with
all other equilibrium quantities of consumer goods are determined. The
investment good so determined enhances the capital endowment of the
next period by λI, where λ is defined as the units of capital services
per unit of physical capital. When this enhanced capital is utilized
with labour of that period, a new set of equilibrium quantities are
determined which may or may not fully realize the expectations of
economic agents formed in the previous period. A sequence of
equilibria is computed until a new steady state is reached when growth
rate of capital is equal to that of labour. Once such a stage is

reached, relative prices do not change in the subsequent periods. Consequently, expectations of all agents are fully realized in the future periods.

The welfare is evaluated by comparing two sequences of equilibria, one with the ceiling on the rate of return to savings and the other without it. Three alternative criteria are used to compare these sequences of equilibria. These criteria are: (a) real national income, (b) real consumption, and (c) present value of consumption. The third criteria is essentially similar to dynamic analogs of compensating variation (DACV) and equivalent variations (DAEV) developed by FSW (1978, 1983), which utilize the consumers' preference function.

The comparison of real national income gives an aggregate picture of efficiency without any consideration to distributional effects. This measure is, of course, in line with the concern of the aggregate growth models. Similarly, the comparison of real consumption at the terminal period gives an aggregate result with the exception that consumption which is the ultimate objective of economic growth is the basis for comparison; a similar concern expressed in the "golden rule" literature. The present value of consumption also gives an aggregate result with the exception that consumption of all the periods are taken into account for a welfare judgement. Moreover, in this criteria, utility functions of consumers are taken into account instead of just comparing the real consumption of the terminal year.

III. A NUMERICAL EVALUATION FOR INDIA

The financial sector in India was nationalized in 1967. Since then it has been under direct control of the government. Before nationalization, financial sector had a structure similar to cartel which had been regulated by the government in regard to nominal interest rates on savings deposits, proportion of assets to be held in government bonds and other securities sponsored by the government, rates of interest on loans and so on. In either institutional set up the government has regulated nominal interest rates on saving deposits around 10%. The nominal return to government bonds has also been maintained at a very low level, presumably to lower its costs of borrowing. Since bank deposits and government bonds are the two most

important financial instruments, if not the only, for mobilizing the
savings in India and since the double digit inflation rate has been
typical for India, real rates of return to savings have been
effectively controlled by the government at about 1% or less. However,
real rate of return to investments in India has been estimated by
several authors (Chakravanty (1964), Harberger (1964), Lal (1977),
Mydral (1967), Shah (1980), Shaw (1973)) to be in the range of 10-27%.
These estimates are quite consistent with similar estimates for other
less developed countries. All these factors suggest a kind of ceiling
on real rate of return to savings in India.

I attempt here to evaluate the welfare loss due to ceilings
on the rate of return savings in India by using the framework developed
in section II above. I divide consumers into four groups and
commodities in three categories for the numerical exercise. These
consumer groups are: urban poor, urban rich, rural poor and rural
rich. Such a classification of consumer groups reasonably
characterizes the dualistic feature of Indian economy, besides
distinguishing consumer groups in terms of income. By poor I mean the
groups of consumers who have an annual income of Rs. 3000.00 or less.
It appears from data that both urban and rural poor dissave in India.
The commodities we consider are food (X_1), all non-food consumer goods
(X_2) and investment good (I).

<u>Data</u>

The computable general equilibrium analysis requires quite
a comprehensive and disaggregative data set which are difficult to
collect even in many developed economies. These difficulties are
further aggravated by scarcity of basic reliable data in many of LDCs.
For India, however, data bases and their qualities are somewhat better
than most of LDCs, but falls short of requirements for a numerical
general equilibrium analysis. We have, therefore, drawn raw data from
different diverse published sources, sometimes with inconsistencies for
the same data.

Major sources of raw data for this paper are:
(i) Household Income, Saving and Consumption Survey 1967-68 - an all
India survey conducted by the National Council of Applied Economic
Research, (ii) National Accounts Statistics, 1960-61 to 1973-74,

(iii) Statistical Yearbook of India, 1973-74, and (iv) Input-Output
Table 1970-71, compiled by M.R. Saluja.

I choose 1970-71 as the base year when the economy has been
free from such abrupt shocks as:

(i)   War with Pakistan (1965)

(ii) Devaluation of Indian Rupee (1968)

(iii) Instability of government (1965-1967)

(iv) Influx of a million Bangladesh refugees (1971-72) and

(v)   Oil crisis and world-wide depression (1973-74).

In order to construct a benchmark equilibrium data set for 1970-71, I
have updated the Household Income, Saving and Expenditure Survey
1967-68, by taking into account the growth rate of the Indian economy
during the said period. The I-0 table for 144 commodities had been
aggregated to arrive at our 3x3 I-0 table.

Production

The production technology in each of the industries is
considered to be described by a C.E.S. production function using labour
(L) and capital services (K) as primary inputs. Thus,

$$Q_i = \gamma_i \left[\alpha_i L_i^{-\rho_i} + (1-\alpha_i) K_i^{-\rho_i} \right]^{-\frac{1}{\rho_i}}, \quad i = 1, 2 \text{ and } I. \quad (32)$$

where Q_i is the level of output in the ith sector, ρ_i and α_i are
substitution and distributional parameters respectively. The
minimization of cost subject to the above production function
determines labour and capital requirements, respectively, per unit of
output as:

$$b_i(W, P_k) = \left[(1-\alpha_i) \left(\frac{\alpha_i P_k}{(1-\alpha_i)W} \right)^{\frac{\rho_i}{\rho_i + 1}} + \alpha_i \right]^{\frac{1}{\rho_i}} \gamma_i^{-1} \quad (33)$$

$$v_i(W, P_k) = \left[\alpha_i \left(\frac{(1-\alpha_i)W}{\alpha_i P_k} \right)^{\frac{\rho_i}{\rho_i + 1}} + (1-\alpha_i) \right]^{\frac{1}{\rho_i}} \gamma_i^{-1} \quad (34)$$

where W and P_k are wage rate and rental price of capital; $\frac{1}{1+\rho_i}$ is the
elasticity of substitution, (S_i), between labour and capital in the ith
sector.

In order to determine the production function parameters,
α_i, γ_i and ρ_i, we use the extraneous estimates for S_i from Sankar(1970)

saving, $\eta_s = \frac{\partial I}{\partial \delta} \frac{\delta}{I}$, as

$$\eta_s = 1 - \beta_i (1-\sigma_i) P_{0_i}^{1-\sigma_i} \Pi_i$$

By taking extraneous estimates for η_s, we can solve for β_i and σ_i. The magnitudes for β_i and σ_i are therefore dependent on pre-assigned magnitude of η_s, the estimates of which are very scarce in general and particularly rare for LDCs. For India, only Gupta (1970) has estimated a saving function with interest rate as one of the arguments. When η_s is derived from that estimated function, it appears to be around 0.3, which is comparable to the interest elasticity of saving estimates for the U.S.A. by Boskin (1978), Summers (1980) and Evans (1983). Gupta (1971) has estimated the interest elasticity of the growth of bank deposits in India to be around 20. This may also shed some light on the interest elasticity of savings since bank deposit is the single most important component of private savings in India. The contemporaneous utility function defined over current period consumer's goods is described by a Cobb-Douglas type of function similar to (26). The parameters for the Cobb-Douglas utility function are determined by the shares of expenditure on each of the current commodities in the benchmark period.

Results

In our central case, we consider the rate of return to investment to be 10 per cent. This is the lowest of the range of estimates for it (see Chakravarty (1964), Harberger (1964), Lal (1977), Myrdal (1967), Shah (1980) and Shaw (1973)). The effective real rate of return to savings, defined as the difference between the statutorily determined nominal interest rate on saving deposits and the inflation rate, is taken to be 2 per cent. Given the double digit inflation rate and the nominal rate of interest fixed at about 10 per cent, a 2 per cent real rate of return to saving may appear to be over-estimated. In fact, McKinnon and Shaw (McKinnon (1974), Shaw (1973)) argue that the rate of return to savings is zero, if not negative, in most of the LDCs. It may be argued, however, that a part of savings in LDCs including India may find its way to self-financed project which may have a lower return than the national average but higher than what is offered by the banking sector. Moreover, some forms of financial savings such as post office savings banks, defence certificates and the like have some tax incentives. Taking all these factors into account,

and Banerja (1973) for non-food and saving goods and from Rao (1965)
for food. The non-food and investment goods are considered to be
manufacturing sectors and food as the agriculture sector. Besides
the primary inputs, the use of intermediate inputs is determined by
1970-71 I-0 table for India aggregated over our three commodities.

Consumption

The intertemporal utility function for each of consumer
groups with positive savings is described by the C.E.S. utility
function similar to (19) above, where β and σ are different for each of
the consumer groups. In order to capture the possibility of negative
savings by any consumer group at any period, their intertemporal
preferences are described by linear expenditure functions. The
resulting demand functions for current consumption expenduture and
savings are given by (20) and (24) which are reproduced below, by
substituting for $\dfrac{\lambda P_k'}{P_I P_0} = \delta$, the rate of return to saving, as:

$$C_{0_i} = \frac{\beta_i Y_i}{P_{0_i}^{\sigma_i} \Pi_i} \qquad i=1,\ldots,4$$

$$I_i = \frac{Y_i (1-\beta_i)}{P_I \delta^{(1-\sigma)} \Pi_i} \qquad i=1,\ldots,4 \tag{36}$$

In order to determine C and I for a consumer group, one
needs to know σ_i and β_i which are derived as follows. From (35) and
(36) we have

$$\beta_i = \frac{C_{0_i}^{\frac{1}{\sigma_i}} P_{0_i}}{(P_I I_i)^{\frac{1}{\sigma_i}} \delta^{\frac{1-\sigma_i}{\sigma_i}} + C_{0_i}^{\frac{1}{\sigma_i}}} \tag{37}$$

which has two unknowns, β_i and σ_i. In order to solve for σ_i and β_i,
therefore, I generate another equation in terms of β_i and σ_i. Since
the saving is fully invested, this is achieved by differentiating (36)
with respect to δ and expressing it in terms of interest elasticity of

liberalization of interest rate, per capita availability of capital
(K/L) continues to increase until a new steady state with higher K/L is
reached. As K/L increases, the rate of return to capital, defined in
terms of the marginal product of capital, declines which in turn
increasingly favours consumption over saving due to the substitution
effect. The endowment of capital at the terminal period T_n, is about
11% higher in a new steady state than in the initial steady state. In
terms of the discounted present value of real consumption, which is
similar to the dynamic analog of compensating variation developed by
Fullerton-Shoven-Whalley, it increases by more than 6%. Such a welfare
gain is quite significant for a change in policy even when we take the
lowest magnitudes for the important parameters.

As has been shown above, the interest elasticity of savings
(η_s) affects the elasticity of substitution between current and future
consumption (σ) directly and the distribution parameter (α) indirectly
in the C.E.S. utility function. Since we are to take an extraneous
estimate for η_s, it is quite desirable to perform a sensitivity
analysis for this extraneous parameter. The result of this simulation
is presented in Table II.

The Welfare consequences seems to be significantly
influenced by the magnitude of η_s. In Table II we find that both
income and consumption are increasingly responsive to the interest
elasticity of saving. Such a responsiveness is quite consistent with
the economic intuition. The higher interest elasticity of savings
leads to a higher rate of saving for a given change in the interest
rate due to the substitution in favour of future consumption. Since
the saving is considered to be fully invested, the higher saving
elasticity result in a higher rate of capital formation, which, in
turn, increases growth rate of national income. This eventually
results in a higher rate of steady state consumption.

The degree of repression of interest rate in India or any
other less developed country is obviously a debatable issue,
particularly for the policy makers in those countries. While McKinnon
and Shaw argue that the interest rate is severely repressed in LDCs,
sometime to the extent of 20%, others may have more moderate views.
We, however, present the consequence of varying degrees of interest
rate repression on income, consumption and welfare in Table III. This
at least shows sensitivity of welfare gain with respect to the
plausible degrees of interest rate repression.

we consider it reasonable to take 2% as the real rate of return to
savings. As regards the interest elasticity of savings, we take 0.3,
probably the lowest of its range of estimates.

The results of the central case are presented in Table I
where we compare new steady state (revised case) with that of initial
steady state (base case). In the period T_0, consumption in the initial
steady state exceeds that of the revised equilibrium. Such a decline
is consistent with economic intuitions: with the liberalization of
interest rates, price of current consumption in terms of future
consumption increases resulting a substitution against current
consumption. In the terminal period, T_n (n=60), consumption in the new

Table I

Comparison of Growth Patterns With and Without Ceiling
on Interest Rate in a General Equilibrium Framework
(with interest elasticity of saving η_s = .3,
rate of return to capital λ = .10, and
rate of return to saving δ = .02)

(Figures are in billions of Indian Currency, Rs)

	BASE CASE Steady State Eqm.)		REVISED CASE		% Change of Values of revised case over base case in T_n period.
	Initial Period (T_0)	End Period (T_n)	Initial Period (T_n)	End Period (T_n)	
Consumption	382.94	486.86	380.22	536.25	10.14
National Income	408.58	519.42	408.58	568.58	9.46
Endowment of Capital Services	135.24	171.93	135.24	188.21	10.95
Present Value of Consumption	18,816.00		19,981.57		6.2

steady state increases by more than 10 percent over the initial steady
state. Such an increase in consumption can be attributed to both
income and substitution effects: the higher growth rate in capital
stock due to the liberated interest rate generates higher growth rate
of income which obviously contributes to greater consumption potential.
Moreover, as the growth rate of capital exceeds that of labour with

Table II

Sensitivity Analysis of Interest Elasticity of Saving

(with rate of return to capital, r = 10%, rate of return to saving, δ = 2%)

(Figures are in billions of Rupees, Indian Currency)

Interest Elasticity of Saving	Consumption at Period T_n			National Income in Period T_n			Present Value of Consumption		
	BASE CASE	REVISED CASE	%	BASE STEADY STATE	REVISED STEADY STATE	%	BASE CASE	REVISED CASE	%
η = .3	486.86	536.25	10.0	519.42	568.58	9.5	18,816.05	19,981.57	6.2
η = .5	486.86	635.46	30.5	519.42	670.39	29.0	18,816.07	22,339.79	18.7
η = .75	486.86	769.13	58.0	519.42	908.55	55.6	18,816.07	27,628.09	46.8

Table III

Sensitivity Analysis of The Wedge Between Rates of Return to Investments (r) and Savings (δ)

(δ is taken to 2% while η = .5 in all cases)

(Figures are in billion of Rupees, Indian currency)

Rate of return to investment	Consumption at Period T_n			National Income in Period T_n			Present Value of Consumption		
	BASE CASE STEADY STATE (A)	REVISED CASE STEADY STATE (B)	B/A %	BASE CASE STEADY STATE (A)	REVISED CASE STEADY STATE (B)	B/A %	BASE CASE	REVISED CASE	%
r = .08	485.72	606.09	24.0	520.51	644.14	23.5	28,786.32	21,616.60	15.0
r = .10	486.86	635.46	30.0	519.42	670.39	29.2	18,816.07	22,339.79	18.0
r = .12	487.62	665.75	36.0	518.72	694.53	35.0	18,835.83	22,987.79	22.0
r = .15	488.37	703.94	42.0	518.04	727.46	41.0	18,885.50	23,850.46	26.0

IV. CONCLUSIONS AND POSSIBLE EXTENSIONS

In this paper I have shown that a ceiling on rates of return to savings is an important form of distortion in a less developed country like India where the scarcity of capital is an important bottleneck towards attaining a desirable economic growth. If interest rates are allowed to be determined by market forces, India - or any other LDC with interest rate ceiling - would be able to attain a significantly higher level of income, consumption, and as such, welfare, under varying circumstances. Therefore, this paper provides some empirical support to the McKinnon-Shaw thesis that repressive interest rate policy in LDCs is one of the most important reasons for their shower economic growth. This paper may also provide an explanation for the significant growth rates experienced by South Korea and Taiwan after their reforms of interest rates. In terms of methodological developments, this paper provides a technique for evaluating welfare in a computable general equilibrium model when some of the prices are rigid due to institutional factors.

While this paper probably unveiled a part of the puzzle why an LDC suffers from low level stagnation, it may not have answered all the questions raised by itself. For example, if the rate of return to investment is so high in India why does the stock market mobilize only about 1% of industrial finance; why does the internal savings of the industrial houses and corporations play only a nominal role in industrial finance (see Gupta (1969)). Moreover, if the rate of return to investment is so high in LDCs compared to developed nations, why international mobility of capital does not equate, net of risk premiums, rates of return to investment across the national boundaries and thus enhance the welfare of the world as a whole. The answers to all these equations may be sought in the socio-economic and political structure of these countries which I have not attempted in this paper.

Moreover, I have made a lot of simplifying assumptions in this paper. With the high rate of return to savings after liberalization, it is quite possible that savings in the form of low yield physical assets, such as expensive housing, or in financial asset, such as gold and jewelry, would decline giving way to savings in high yielding financial instruments. Such a possible change in asset

structure has not been considered in this paper. On the demand side of
investment, I have considered that whatever saving is mobilized is also
efficiently invested. Such a competitive allocation of investment
funds is not quite common in LDCs. In fact, the government plays a
very important role in allocating the saving in these countries. Such
a governmental allocation sometimes leads investment to low yield
projects. Further, if the government resorts to some rationing
mechanism to meet the excess demand for investment funds, there is
always a possibility of profitable rent-seeking which itself drains out
scarce resources. Incorporation of these factors would simply
compound the loss of welfare in these countries.

However, the future research works in this area may evaluate
the extent of welfare loss when one relaxes some of the simplifying
assumptions of this paper.

Acknowledgement

Presented to the conference on Policy Use of Numerical Micro-Models:
Issues, Applications, and New Developments held in Canberra, Australia,
August 22-24, 1983. Kenneth Clements, Erwin Diewert, Glenn Harrison,
Larry Kimbell, Joel Slemrod, and other participants of the conference
had made valuable comments on an earlier draft of this paper. I am
grateful to Professor John Whalley for his continuous help throughout
the preparation of this manuscript and to professor Ake Blomqvist for
his thorough comments on the first draft of this paper. The results of
this paper had also been discussed at seminars at Brock, Carleton,
Simon Fraser and Victoria. I am grateful to the participants of these
seminars for their comments and to Wilfrid Laurier University for
financial assistance. I am, however, fully responsible for any error
or omissions in this paper.

References

Banejee, A. (1973), "Capital-labour Substitution in Selected Indian Industries," In, Sankhya.

Bacharach, M. (1970), Bi-Proportional Matrices and Input-Output Changes, Cambridge University Press.

Boskin, M.J. (1978), "Taxation, Saving and the Rate of Interest," In, Journal of Political Economy, Supplement of NBER Conference.

Chakravarty, S. (1964), The Use of Shadow Prices in Program Evaluation," Rosenstein-Rodan (ed.), Capital Formation and Economic Development, M.I.T. Press.

Chandavarkar, A. (1971), "Some Aspects of Interest Rate Policy in Less Developed Countries, The Experience of Selected Asian Countries," In, I.M.F. Staff Paper.

_____(1976), "Interest Rates as a Means of Mobilizing Personal Savings in Less Developed Countries," Paper presented to International Workshop on Policies and Techniques for Mobilizing Personal Savings in Developing Countries, Santa Marta, Colombia, February 18-27, 1976.

Evans, O. (1983), "Tax Policy, The Interest Elasticity of Savings and Capital Accumulation: Numerical Analysis of Theoretical Models," In, American Economic Review.

Fry, M. (1978), "Money and Capital or Financial Deepening in Economnic Development," In, Journal of Money, Credit and Banking.

Fullerton, D., Shoven, J., Whalley, J. (1978), "A General Equilibrium Analysis of U.S. Taxation Policy," U.S. Treasury Department, Office of Tax Analysis.

____, ____, ____ (1980), "How Long is the Long Run: A Study State Model with Temporary Equilibria in Transition," Office of Tax Analysis, U.S. Treasury Department, Research Report No. 13.

____, ____, ____ (1981), "Corporate Tax Integration in the U.S.: A General Equilibrium Approach", In, American Economic Review.

____, ____, ____ (1983), "Replacing the U.S. Income Tax with Progressive Consumption Tax: A Sequenced General Equilibrium Approach," In, Journal of Public Economics.

Grandmond, J.M. (1982): "On Temporary Equilibria" in K.J. Arrow and M.D. Intriligator (eds), Handbook of Mathematical Economics, North-Holland Publishing Co.

Gupta, K.L. (1970), "Personal Savings in Developing Countries: Further Evidences," In, Economic Record.

Gupta, L.C. (1969) The Changing Structure of Industrial Finance in India, Oxford University Press. England.

Gupta, G.S. (1971), "Interest Sensitiveness of Deposits in India," In, Economic and Political Weekly.

Lal, D. (1977), "Distributional Weights, Shadow Wages and Accounting Rate of Interest: Estimates for India," In, Indian Economic Review.

Imam, H., and Whalley, J. (1982), "General Equilibrium with Price Intervention Policies: A Computational Approach," Journal of Public Economics.

_____, _____ (1983), "Incidence Analysis of a Sector-Specific Minimum Wage in a Two-Sector Harris-Todaro Model," In, Quarterly Journal of Economics (forthcoming).

Leontief, W. (1958), "Theoretical Note on Time Preference, Productivity of Capital, Stagnation and Economic Growth," In, American Economic Review.

Liviatan, N. (1966), "Multiperiod Future Consumption as an Aggregate," In, American Economic Review.

Harberger, A.C. (1974), Project Evaluation: Collected Papers, Markham Publishing Co., Chicago.

McKinnon, R. (1974), Money and Capital in Economic Development, Brookings Institute, Washington.

Myrdal, G. (1968), Asian Drama, An Inquiry into the Poverty of Nationa, Vol. III, Penguin Books.

Rao, H. (1965), Agricultural Production Function, Cost and Returns in India.
Samuelson, P.A. (1947), Foundations of Economic Analysis, Cambridge, Mass.

Scarf, H. (1967), "On the Computation of Equilibrium Prices," in W.M. Fellner (ed.) Ten Essays in Honour of Irving Fisher, Wiley, New York.

_____ (1973), With collaboration of T. Hansen, The Computation of Economic Equilibria, Yale University Press.

_____ (1982), "The Computation of Equilibrium Prices: An Exposition," in K.J. Arrow and M.D. Intriligator (eds.), Handbook of Mathematical Economics, North-Holland Publishing Co.

Shaw, E. (1973), Financial Deepening in Economic Development, Oxford.

Shoven, J., and Whalley, J. (1973), "General Equilibrium with Taxes: Computational Procedure and Existence Proof," Review of Economic Studies.

Sankar, U. (1970), "Elasticities of Substitution and Returns to Scale in Indian Manufacturing Industries," International Economic Review.

Sinha, C. (1978), "Financial Intermediation and Rural Development," The Indian Economic Journal, Special Conference Issue, Part III.

Summers, L. (1981), "Capital Taxation and Accumulation in a Life Cycle Growth Model," American Economic Review.

Wai, U.T. (1972), Financial Intermediaries and National Savings in Developing Countries, Praeger Publishers, New York.

Williamson (1968), "Personal Saving in Developing Nations: An Intertemporal Cross Section from Asia," Economic Record.

GENERAL EQUILIBRIUM WITH PRICE RIGIDITIES

T.T. Nguyen[1]

Department of Economics
University of Waterloo
Waterloo, Ontario, Canada
N2L 3G1

This paper presents a framework to study the issue of resource allocation under price controls from a computational general equilibrium viewpoint. Under a regime of comprehensive price controls[2], prices are exogenously fixed by government decrees at levels which would preclude the traditional Walrasian market clearing process. In such a situation agents on the long side of any market would have to make an effort to obtain trades (e.g., search, queue, waiting, excessive shopping, black markets, and bribery). These activities are closely related to recent non-traditional types of market distortions such as Krueger's [1974] rent seeking, Ruys' [1982] equilibrium effort, and Postlewaite's [1979] endowment manipulation. Our central thesis is that under price controls attempts by agents to obtain trades do use up real resources and thereby give rise to a dual price system with actual buying prices higher than controlled prices and actual selling prices lower than controlled prices. More severe price controls imply more pressures on agents on the long side of the market, greater wedges between controlled prices and buying or selling prices, and higher efficiency loss. The dual price system serves as an alternative equilibrating mechanism with which resource costs are endogenously determined both at individual and market levels so as to simultaneously clear several markets under government controls. This contrasts with the partial equilibrium literature (e.g., Barzel [1974] and Cheung [1974]) which focuses on nonprice rationing and waiting time in only one market under price controls.

This paper differs from the recent literature on fixed price equilibria generated by Drèze [1975] and Benassy [1975] which has been largely concerned with general equilibrium models with downward price rigidities as theoretical foundations for Keynesian macroeconomics. Less common in this literature, however, are models with fixed prices created by government policies (instead of just being sticky). This is surprising since arguments against wage and price controls are often made in terms of inefficiency or resource misallocation. We are concerned with welfare issues of these price distortion policies. Our eventual aim is to provide a numerical assessment of the welfare costs of recent wage and price controls.

The plan of the paper is as follows: section 1 sets out the basic theoretical framework of an economy under comprehensive price controls. Section 2 provides a numerical example to illustrate the equilibrium concept and the welfare costs of price controls. Section 3 concludes the paper with some remarks on possible extensions of the model and its potential policy applications.

1. BASIC THEORETICAL FRAMEWORK

For simplicity in exposition we consider a pure exchange economy with m agents $(i = 1,...,m)$ and n goods $(j = 1,...,n)$. Each agent i is characterized by a consumption set X^i which is nonempty convex compact in the nonnegative orthant of the n-dimensional euclidean space, a preference ordering which can be represented by a continuous quasiconcave utility function U^i defined on X^i, and initial endowment vector w^i in the interior of X^i.

All prices are exogenously fixed by government decrees at positive non-market clearing levels $p = (p_1,...,p_n) > 0$. All trades take place at these controlled prices. Agents on the long side of the market, however, would have to make an effort to obtain trades. These efforts represent the extra resource costs borne by the long side of the market under price controls. They thus raise the issue of how far the presumed benefits from government price controls are dissipated in real resources used in rent seeking activities. Agents now face two implicit price vectors $p^b >= p$ and $p^s <= p$ instead of one single price vector as in the traditional Arrow–Debreu theory of competitive markets. For each good $j = 1,...,n$ any discrepancy $(p_j^b - p_j) >= 0$ represents the per unit resource cost on the buying side while any discrepancy $(p_j - p_j^s) >= 0$ represents the per unit resource cost on the selling side. This is similar to the tax wedge in tax incidence theory except that the tax wedge does not involve the destruction of real resources.

Taking the dual price system (p^b, p^s) and initial endowments as given, each agent i determines individual excess demand correspondence $Z^i (p^b, p^s)$ from the choice problem[3]: maximize $U^i (x^i)$ subject to

$$x^i \in X^i,$$
$$z^i = x^i - w^i,$$
$$p^b.\max(z^i,0) + p^s.\min(z^i,0) <= 0. \tag{1}$$

Agents are aware of potential resource costs under price controls and modify their choice decisions accordingly. In effect, they are still rational in the usual sense of constraint utility maximization except that the budget constraint (1) now includes resource costs under price controls as expressed by the dual system of buying and selling prices instead of the usual single price system. Two equivalent forms of the budget constraint (1) are

$$p.(z^i + g^i) <= 0, \tag{1'}$$
$$p.x^i <= p.(w^i - g^i) \tag{1''}$$

where the vector $g^i = (g_1^i,...,g_n^i)$ of individual resource costs under price controls is defined by

$$g_j^i = ((p_j^b/p_j) - 1) \max(z_j^i,0) + ((p_j^s/p_j) - 1) \min(z_j^i,0) \tag{2}$$

for $j = 1,...,n$. Clearly g_j^i is nonnegative, continuous in p_j^b, p_j^s, z_j^i and convex in z_j^i. The formulation in (2) is quite general in the sense that resource costs are expressed in terms of all goods $j = 1,...,n$. While this is intuitively reasonable in some cases (e.g., losing gasoline in search for gasoline), it is much less appealing in other cases (e.g., losing apples in search for apples). A possible alternative formulation is to express resource costs in terms of one specific good (e.g., money, labor, leisure time, or the numeraire).

A parable for resource costs g^i is that under effective price rigidities agents on the constrained side of the market would have to search for agents on the unconstrained side of the market in order to make transactions. For example, motorists drive around town in search for gas stations during a gasoline shortage (search costs are gasoline itself) or workers visit firms after firms in search for jobs during unemployment (search costs are labor or leisure time). The search process can be explicitly introduced into the model as Bernoulli trials where the expected number of attempts before the agent succeeds in finding a suitable trading partner is endogenously determined. The price wedges $(p^b - p)$ and $(p - p^S)$ then can be derived from this primitive concept of number of trials.[4]

Resource costs g^i are endogenously determined by both individual decisions z^i and the extent to which prices are controlled as measured by the divergence between (p^b, p^S) and p. These terms will vanish in the event that agents are on the unconstrained side of the market or prices happen to be fixed at market clearing levels such that $p^b = p^S = p$. This contrasts with the literature on general equilibrium with transactions costs where fixed transactions technology exists like friction, regardless of states of the economy.

Three versions $(1,1',1'')$ of the budget constraint are mathematically equivalent but have different economic interpretations:

o   (1) is the budget constraint evaluated at two different price vectors p^b and p^S which account for the resource costs per unit of goods bought or sold by agents at fixed prices. Agents with different trading plans thus face different vectors of buying and selling prices as contrast to the traditional Arrow-Debreu theory with one single price vector for all agents in the economy.[5]

o   (1') is the budget constraint evaluated at fixed prices p with the vector of net
     excess demands $z^i + g^i$ defined by

$$z_j^i + g_j^i = (p_j^b/p_j)) \max(z_j^i, 0) + (p_j^s/p_j)) \min(z_j^i, 0)$$

for $j = 1, ..., n$. The first half of the right-hand side (RHS) represents individual
demand for good j gross of resource costs on the buying side as agents would
have to buy more than $\max(z_j^i, 0)$ to compensate for the amount of resource
lost during the buying process. Similarly, the second half of the RHS represents individual demand for good j net of resource costs on the selling side as
agents would actually sell less than $\min(z_j^i, 0)$ due to resources being destroyed
during the selling process. Both halves together then represent individual
excess demand net of resources costs on buying or selling side. The definitions
of g^i and $z^i + g^i$ depend heavily on price vectors p^b, p^s, p and thus suggest a
more significant role for absolute prices than the usual general equilibrium
model with relative prices. This should not be surprising as the entire analysis
centers around the exogenous fixed price vector p set by the goverment.

o   (1") is the budget constraint evaluated at fixed price p with resource costs g^i
     now appearing in the form of the new endowment distribution $w^i - g^i$. The
     formulation thus naturally leads to the important issue of how the welfare
     burden of price controls is distributed among agents in the economy.[6]

Resource costs under price rigidities thus affect individual choice decisions in one
way or another as agents are forced to modify trading plans to accommodate the
additional constraints induced by price and market distortions.

    Walras law is obtained by summing the budget constraint (1') over all
agents: $p.(z + g) <= 0$ where aggregate excess demands and resource costs are
$z = \Sigma z^i$ and $g = \Sigma g^i$. That is, the value of aggregate excess demands net of
resource losses, evaluated at fixed prices p, must be nonpositive. This is true for
any arbitrary dual price system (p^b, p^s). In the degenerate case of no resource losses, the vector g vanishes implying the traditional Walras law $p.z <= 0$.

An equilibrium concept under price rigidities can now be described as follows: at the individual level all agents behave rationally in the sense of constrained utility maximization with respect to the dual price system (p^b, p^s). On the other hand, at the aggregate level all markets clear in the sense that aggregate demands <u>net</u> of resource losses must not exceed aggregate endowments. In addition, there is an interesting asymmetry in the burden of resource losses under price rigidities. As prices can be fixed either above or below market clearing levels (but not both), agents can be either on the long side or the short side of the market (but not both). Resource losses are consequently borne by only one side of the market. This is similar to Drèze's [1975] condition that quantity rationing may be either on the demand side or the supply side (but not both).

Definition. Given fixed prices p and initial endowments w^i (i = 1,...,m) an equilibrium consists of the dual price system (p^{b*}, p^{s*}) and individual excess demands z^{i*} (i = 1,...,m) such that

$$z^{i*} \ \epsilon \ Z^i \, (p^{b*}, p^{s*}) \text{ for } i = 1,...,m, \tag{3a}$$

$$z^* + g^* \ <= \ 0, \tag{3b}$$

$$\text{either } p_j^{b*} > p_j \text{ and } p_j^{s*} = p_j$$

$$\text{or} \quad p_j^{b*} = p_j \text{ and } p_j^{s*} < p_j \text{ for } j = 1,...,n \tag{3c}$$

where equilibrium aggregate excess demands and resource losses are $z^* = \Sigma \, z^{i*}$ and $g^* = \Sigma \, g^{i*}$.

Condition (3a) requires rational behavior of all individual agents while condition (3b) clears all markets <u>net</u> of resource losses under price rigidities. Condition (3c) places the burden of resource losses on only one side of the market: either the demand side bears resource losses when $p_j^{b*} > p_j = p_j^{s*}$ or the supply side bears resource losses when $p_j^{s*} < p_j = p_j^{b*}$. In no case do both sides of the market bear resource losses under price rigidities. This one side of market condition is an interesting and nontrivial extension of the traditional Arrow-Debreu theory of competitive markets.

Figure 1: EQUILIBRIUM UNDER PRICE RIGIDITIES

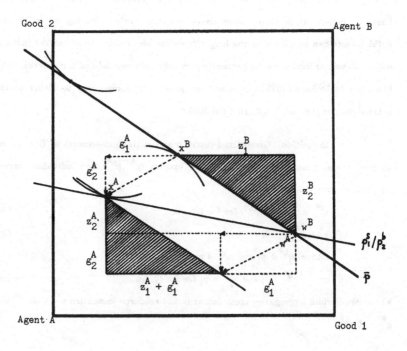

Figure 2: THE SHRINKING EDGEWORTH BOX

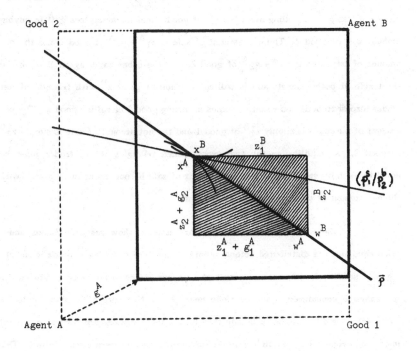

The equilibrium concept is graphically illustrated in Figure 1 for the 2x2 case. Fixed prices p result in an Edgeworth box with an excess supply of good 1 and an excess demand for good 2. Agent A is on the long side of both markets with effective price line $(p_1{}^s/p_2{}^b)$ below the fixed price line (p_1/p_2). The budget set of agent A is thus smaller than the traditional triangular budget set defined by p. Agent A is willing to trade at point x^A with triangle of net trades (crosshatched): incurring loss $g_1{}^A$ in selling amount $z_1{}^A$ of good 1 and incurring loss $g_2{}^A$ in buying amount $z_2{}^A$ of good 2. The net amount of sale is $z_1{}^A + g_1{}^A$ of good 1 and the net amount of purchase is $z_2{}^A + g_2{}^A$ of good 2. On the other hand, agent B is on the short side of both markets and is willing to trade at point x^B with triangle of net trades (crosshatched): no resource losses in buying good 1 or selling good 2. The net amount of purchase is simply $z_1{}^B$ of good 1 and the net amount of sale is simply $z_2{}^B$ of good 2. At equilibrium the two crosshatched triangles of net trades must be equal to each other. That is, the net amount of sale by one agent must match with the net amount of purchase by the other agent.

Figure 2 illustrates the welfare issue of how resource losses under price rigidities are distributed among agents A and B. The Edgeworth box is shrinking to a smaller dimension as a result of resource losses under price rigidities. In the example considered, agent A alone bears the entire burden of resource losses under price rigidities. The shrinkage thus moves the southwestern corner to a point inside the original Edgeworth box while leaving the northeastern corner intact. This is a result of condition (3c): only one side of any market is constrained under price rigidities (the selling side of good 1 and the buying side of good 2). Under no circumstances will both sides of the same market be constrained.

Figure 2 also shows that at equilibrium the two indifference curves have different tangent lines. That is, the marginal rates of substitution of the two agents are not equal to each other. The usual marginal conditions for Pareto optimality thus do not hold. This implies that the efficiency loss associated with price rigidities has two components, namely, the shrinkage of the Edgeworth box due to resource losses and the absence of Pareto optimality of the equilibrium achieved.

2. A NUMERICAL EXAMPLE

This section provides a numerical example to illustrate the equilibrium concept and the welfare effects of price rigidities. The example is a pure exchange economy abstracted from the benchmark equilibrium data set compiled by St. Hilaire & Whalley [1980, Table 11] for the 1972 Canadian economy. There are ten consumer income groups and eight commodities.

Income Groups		Commodities	
1.	Under $4727	1.	Food
2.	$4728 - $5909	2.	Housing
3.	$5910 - $7091	3.	Furniture, Equipment
4.	$7092 - $8273	4.	Clothing
5.	$8274 - $9455	5.	Personal Care, Health
6.	$9456 - $10637	6.	Transportation
7.	$10638 - $11819	7.	Tobacco, Alcoholic Beverage
8.	$11820 - $13001	8.	Personal, Financial, Misc. Services
9.	$13002 - $14183		
10.	Over $14184.		

Cobb-Douglas consumer preference parameters of all income groups were obtained by the calibration technique (Mansur & Whalley [1983]) commonly used in applied general equilibrium analysis. The technique basically assumes that the economy is already in an equilibrium state at unity prices (or the barycenter of the unit price simplex) and works backwards to solve for consumer preference parameters.

The existence proof of equilibrium can be briefly outlined as follows: the basic idea is to define the dual price system (p^b, p^s) in terms of elements of a unit simplex such that the one side of market condition (3c) is automatically satisfied. Specifically we normalize p to the interior of an (n-1) dimensional unit simplex S and define $p^b = \max(p,s) >= p$ and $p^s = \min(p,s) <= p$ for s ε S. This construction satisfies the equilibrium condition (3c) immediately. The existence of equilibrium is then proved by a standard fixed point argument using a variant of Gale–Nikaido mapping (see Nguyen [1981]).

The variable dimension restart algorithm by van der Laan & Talman [1980] then can be applied to compute Brouwer fixed point of the Gale–Nikaido mapping. The computer code was written in standard Pascal and implemented on a CDC Cyber 170 computer. Competitive equilibrium prices were first calculated as a recheck of the calibration procedure. They were found to be 0.125 for all eight commodities (i.e., at the barycenter of the unit price simplex) thereby confirming the calibration procedure. Table 1 presents computational results for the case prices are fixed below competitive equilibrium levels for the first four commodities and above competitive equilibrium levels for the last four commodities.

For the first four commodities, resource losses are borne by the buying side alone as equilibrium buying prices are above fixed prices. On the other hand, for the last four commodities, resource losses are borne by the selling side alone as equilibrium selling prices are below fixed prices. The one side of market condition (3c) thus holds. Market excess demands net of resource losses are all less than 0.08 in absolute values for a grid size of 100,000. Computational costs in terms of cpu seconds are small.

Welfare losses from price controls as measured in terms of compensating variations (C.V.) and equivalent variations (E.V.) are 34.83% and 35.51% of national income.[7] These large welfare costs reflect the sizable amounts of resource costs in fixing all prices at non-market clearing levels. On the average, the Edgeworth box shrinks by one third in each dimension (vector g as % of total endowments in Table 1). The shrinkage ranges from almost half of the original dimension for good 1 to about 3% of the original dimension for good 3.

Table 1: COMPUTATIONAL RESULTS

(a) Equilibrium Under Price Rigidities

	p	p^b	p^s	g (% total endowment)		
Good 1	.1000	.1880	.1000	46.80	on buyers	only
Good 2	.1000	.1613	.1000	37.99	on buyers	only
Good 3	.1000	.1034	.1000	3.32	on buyers	only
Good 4	.1000	.1473	.1000	33.33	on buyers	only
Good 5	.1500	.1500	.1000	33.33	on sellers	only
Good 6	.1500	.1500	.1000	33.33	on sellers	only
Good 7	.1500	.1500	.1000	33.33	on sellers	only
Good 8	.1500	.1500	.1000	33.33	on sellers	only

(b) Distribution of Welfare Costs Among Income Groups

	C.V. (%)	E.V. (%)
Group 1	12.64	12.96
Group 2	4.96	5.00
Group 3	6.23	6.24
Group 4	8.13	8.12
Group 5	8.26	8.26
Group 6	8.71	8.68
Group 7	7.95	7.94
Group 8	6.74	6.73
Group 9	6.24	6.21
Group 10	30.13	29.85

The distribution of these welfare losses among ten income groups is also shown in Table 1. Income groups at both ends of the distribution curve seems to bear highest proportions of the total welfare loss associated with price controls. In fact, the top income bracket (group 10) bears about 30% of the welfare loss while to bottom income bracket (group 1) bears about 13% of the total welfare loss. Each of the remaining income brackets bear about 7% of the total welfare loss. While these might not be the most accurate results for the actual Canadian economy under price controls, they provide interesting insights to the issue of distributional effects of price control policies. The calculation thus seems to suggest that the order of magnitude for the welfare effects of price controls may be substantially larger than commonly expected.

3. CONCLUSION

This paper provides a general equilibrium framework to evaluate the welfare effects of price rigidities. The central idea is that under price rigidities only one side of any market is constrained to bear real resource costs. As a result, there are two vectors of buying and selling prices giving rise to excess demands <u>net</u> of resource costs and hence, the shrinking Edgeworth box. The analysis is readily applicable to a numerical evaluation of the welfare costs of economy-wide wage and price controls in a comparative static "controls on, controls off" setting. The framework can be easily extended to a production economy. The paper thus contributes to the increasing applicability of computational general equilibrium analysis in policy issues.

NOTES

1. Helpful comments by the referee are gratefully acknowledged. Cory Bur-
    gener of the Department of Computer Services, University of Waterloo has
    given tremendous help on the word processing package SCRIPT/GML and the
    laser printer Xerox 2700. The author assumes sole responsibility for any
    shortcoming of the paper.

2. Price controls have been known to exist since early times in history. They
    have been used by governments everywhere in the world and through all
    times - war as well peace. One well-known case is the ambitious plan to
    control 900 commodities, 130 different grades of labor, and 41 types of
    freight rates in 301 A.D. by the Roman emperor Diocletian. During World
    War II the U.S. Office of Price Administration commanded a staff of 68,000
    employees plus 400,000 volunteers "price watchers" to administer and
    enforce over 600 price regulations concerning more than eight million prod-
    ucts and twenty categories of rationing schemes. The British Ministry of
    Food used a staff of 46,000 employees to make about 3000 prosecutions per
    month. See Schuettinger & Buttler [1979] for an amusing account of forty
    centuries of wage and price controls.

3. Vector notations for $a = (a_1,...,a_n)$ and $b = (b_1,...,b_n)$:
    dot product $a.b = \Sigma \; a_i b_i$,
    componentwise product $ab = ((a_1 b_1),...,(a_n b_n))$,
    componentwise quotient $a/b = ((a_1/b_1),...,(a_n/b_n))$ with nonzero $b_1,...,b_n$,
    maximum vector $\max (a,b) = (\max(a_1,b_1),...,\max(a_n,b_n))$,
    minimum vector $\min (a,b) = (\min(a_1,b_1),...,\min(a_n,b_n))$.

4. This is discussed in Nguyen [1981].

5. For example, the relevant price vector is $(p_1{}^s, p_2{}^b)$ for an agent who sells
    good 1 and buys good 2.
    On the other hand, the relevant price vector is $(p_1{}^b, p_2{}^s)$ for an agent who
    buys good 1 and sells good 2.
    In the traditional Arrow-Debreu theory, both agents would face the same
    price vector (p_1, p_2).

6. It is possible to give g^i an alternative interpretation other than resource
    losses under price rigidities. In fact, bribery or transfers also commonly
    occur as means of circumventing price controls. See Nguyen [1981] for an
    alternative formulation in which g^i are endogenously determined commodity
    tax (or subsidy) rates, without any loss of real resources. The welfare issues
    considered then are who gains and who loses under price controls instead of
    how the burden of price controls is distributed among agents (i.e., who loses
    and who does not lose).

7. National income is defined as the value of aggregate endowments at com-
    petitive equilibrium prices.

REFERENCES

1.   Barzel, Y. (1974). A Theory of Rationing by Waiting. Journal of Law and
        Economics, 17, 73-95.

2.   Benassy, J.P. (1975). Neo-Keynesian Disequilibrium Theory in a Monetary
        Economy. Review of Economic Studies, 42, 503-23.

3.   Cheung, S.N. (1974). A Theory of Price Control. Journal of Law and Eco-
        nomics, 17, 53-71.

4.   Dreze, J.H. (1975). Existence of an Exchange Equilibrium Under Price Rig-
        idities. International Economic Review, 16, 301-20.

5.   Krueger, A.O. (1974). The Political Economy of the Rent-Seeking Economy.
        American Economic Review, 64, 291-303.

6.   Mansur. A. & Whalley, J. (1983), Numerical Specification of Applied General
        Equilibrium Models: Estimation, Calibration and Data. In Applied General
        Equilibrium Analysis, ed. H. Scarf & J.B. Shoven. Cambridge: Cambridge
        University Press.

7.   Nguyen, T.T. (1981). General Equilibrium Under Price Controls. Unpub-
        lished doctoral dissertation, University of Western Ontario.

8.   Postlewaite, A. (1979). Manipulation via Endowments. Review of Economic
        Studies, 46, 255-62.

9.   Ruys, P.H.M. (1982). Disequilibrium Characterized by Implicit Prices in
        Terms of Effort. In Econometric Modelling in Theory and Practice, ed. J.
        Plasman. The Hague: Matinus Nijhoff.

10.   Schuettinger, R.L. & Butler, E.F. (1979). Forty Centuries of Wage and
        Price Controls. Washington, D.C.: The Heritage Foundation.

11.   St. Hilaire, F. & Whalley, J. (1980). A Micro-consistent Equilibrium Data
        Set for Canada for Use in Tax Policy Analysis. Unpublished paper, Univer-
        sity of Western Ontario.

12.   van der Laan, G. (1980). Simplicial Fixed Point Algorithms. Amsterdam:
        Vrije Universiteit Amsterdam.

SHORT-RUN* MACROECONOMIC CLOSURE IN APPLIED

GENERAL EQUILIBRIUM MODELLING :

Experience from ORANI and Agenda for Further Research

by

R.J. Cooper
Macquarie University, Sydney, Australia
K.R. McLaren
Monash University, Melbourne, Australia
A.A. Powell
University of Melbourne, Melbourne, Australia

1. INTRODUCTION

Perhaps most important among the contentious issues remaining
in applied general equilibrium modelling is the role (if any) of
conventional macroeconomics. Models in the Walrasian tradition are
comparative static in nature; they are not well suited, therefore, to
the analysis of transitory phenomena such as the stage of the business
cycle. When our policy-analytic models are focussed at one or two years
into the hypothetical future, however, it may be impossible to ignore
transients and remain convincing. In other words, we may be required to
tell a story which is part Walrasian and part macroeconomic. How can
such an unlikely hybrid be seeded?

1.1 The extended Walrasian paradigm

Several approaches are possible. The cleanest, of course,
involves a Walrasian take-over bid for macroeconomics. In such an
extended Walrasian paradigm demand and supply functions for money and
perhaps other financial assets are added to the real system (Patinkin
(1958); Feltenstein (1981); Vincent (1983))[1]. This introduces at
least one additional agent (the supplier of money, usually the
government), and the opportunity to endogenize such important
macroeconomic variables as the price level and the money supply.

In terms of applied work, it is early days yet for the
extended Walrasian paradigm. If eventually it turns out that transients
with expected lives of (say) less than a year cannot really be modelled
successfully using the tools of economic analysis, then the limitations
inherent in the comparative static nature of the extended Walrasian
method may come to be accepted as the state of the art for the analysis

of short-run issues. In the meantime there is a large profession engaged in applied macrodynamic analysis who claim otherwise. Taking their claim (provisionally) at its face value, is there a method of incorporating macrodynamic insights within a Walrasian framework?

1.2   The IMPACT paradigm

The institutional environment within which the IMPACT project was set up provided a strong incentive to find an affirmative answer to the preceding question.   While necessarily we were required to concentrate on the real economy and relative prices because of our principal backer's (the Industries Assistance Commission, IAC's) interest in international trade and industry protection, and while also we were required to build a model which would produce sectoral policy recommendations in harmony with the thrust of the government's macroeconomic policy, under no circumstances were we to build our own macro models.   The latter interdiction was motivated by two considerations: one survival oriented, the second more honourable. The former could be paraphrased as "Keep off the Treasury's turf, or you know what!", while the latter simply recognized that the community had already made a very large investment in macrodynamic analysis, especially at the Reserve Bank and at the Treasury. Macroeconomic insights, if such were available, were to be harvested from the work of others. In due course these motivations led to the development of the IMPACT paradigm. The latter allows a macrodynamic model to determine all of the major monetary, financial and macroeconomic aggregates simultaneously with the determination by a computable general equilibrium (CGE) model of relative prices and the commodity and factor composition of the economy along strictly Walrasian lines.

2.   MACROECONOMIC CLOSURE OF A CGE: BASIC CONCEPTS

2.1   Basic closure

The term 'closure' is used in various ways, and with varying degrees of precision, in our literature. At the most basic level we say that a model is 'closed' if we have sufficient information to compute a solution. It will suffice here to restrict attention to linear models. Let M,

$$M: \quad Ax = 0 \qquad\qquad (1.1)$$

be a linear model containing m consistent, linearly independent equations in k variables (k $\geqslant$ m). Then a closure of M, in the basic sense referred to above, consists of

(a)   a declaration that a certain subset x_2 of x containing (k-m) variables is exogenous

and

(b)   an assignment of a set of values (say $\bar{x}_2$) to these exogenous variables.

Sometimes the term 'closure' is used loosely to describe (a) alone. In that case, closure means that we could, if we were to make an assignment (b), solve the model. Since the variables x_2 are exogenous, their assignment can be completely arbitrary, and hence these two primitive notions of closure boil down to the same thing.

2.2   Closure with respect to a subset of variables

A second notion of closure is defined relative to some subset of the model's variables. We say that M is closed with respect to the variables x^m ($x^m \subset x$) provided the variables x^m are endogenized by the model in the context of the basic closure selected. Thus M is closed with respect to x^m if the x_2 chosen in (a) is such that x^m and x_2 have no elements in common. 'Macroeconomic closure' is of this second type. In this case the components of x^m will include the real values of major aggregates (consumption, investment) plus a range of monetary and financial variables (the exact list will depend upon the application). Macroeconomic closure is then achieved by ensuring that M has sufficient equations to endogenize these variables in the context of a suitable partition of the variables x into the endogenous and exogenous categories. Here 'suitable' has two implications:

(i)   in partitioning x into $[x_1, x_2]$ (where $x^m \subset x_1$) so that

$$Ax = 0$$

becomes

$$A_1 x_1 + A_2 x_2 = 0,$$

the choice made must result in A_1 having full rank;

and

(ii)   no variable (outside the set x^m) which the model is required
       to explain may be assigned to the exogenous set x_2 .

Condition (i) is required in order to obtain a unique solution of
M ($x_1 = -A_1^{-1} A_2 x_2$), while condition (ii) ensures that macroeconomic
closure is not obtained at the expense of other purposes for which the
model was built.

2.3   Short versus long-run closure

The first crucial difference between short and long-run
modelling is in the choice of variables to be included in the model.
While transients may play important roles in short-run modelling, by
definition they have no place in the long run. If transient variables
are included in a model to be used in a long-run closure, they should
appear on the exogenous list where they should be assigned neutral
values. Alternatively, it should be a property of the model's structure
that such transient variables can be guaranteed endogenously to take on
neutral values in a long solution. If the focus is on the long run, then
in keeping with the long-run neutrality of money, variables included in
x^m (and therefore within x_1 in a macroeconomically closed model) should
be real stocks or flows, or relative prices.

In the standard version of IMPACT's CGE model, ORANI (Dixon,
Parmenter, Sutton and Vincent (1982) - hereafter DPSV (1982)) provision
is made for the user to select his own basic closure (DPSV (1982),
Ch.7)). The choice of endogenous and exogenous sets x_1 and x_2 (along
with some choices about the values of behavioural parameters) crucially
affects the interpretation of the comparative static time frame.   In
ORANI's standard (or neo-classical) short-run closure, the elapsed time
between the base-period and the attainment of the new solution is assumed
to be sufficiently short to allow one to ignore the impact of the shock
under analysis on capital stocks in use in each industry, but
sufficiently long for relative prices, consumption, investment demands
and production of every commodity to have reached a new equilibrium
configuration. (As will be seen below, such a short-run concept might
well correspond in calendar time to about two years.) With capital
stocks fixed, rates of return in the different industries are
endogenous. If we reverse the roles of these two sets of variables -
i.e., we take industry rates of return as exogenous and endogenize the

vector of capital stocks - then, clearly, a longer time-frame must be involved. In fact this is what is done in long-run closures of ORANI, where it is assumed that, relative to the world capital market, Australia is a small country. Given that any initial deviations in Australian industries' relative and absolute rates of return from the competitive world-wide values of these variables are eliminated, in the long run, by accumulation or decumulation of capital, what are the sources of such capital?

2.4   ORANI's lack of long-run macroeconomic closure

It is at this point that ORANI's lack of long-run macroeconomic closure becomes evident. The standard version of ORANI focusses heavily on commodity markets, and on the demand side of the labour market, but does not deal with financial or capital markets. To provide long-run macroeconomic closure it is necessary to add additional equations in order to endogenize the real flow of foreign capital. Inter alia this involves also endogenizing real saving and consumption (not usually endogenous in closures of the standard version of ORANI). The basic approach for such an extension of ORANI has been developed by Dixon, Parmenter and Rimmer (1984).

2.5   ORANI's lack of short-run macroeconomic closure

In a standard short-run closure of the standard version of ORANI, the following variables of macroeconomic interest are routinely assigned to the exogenous set x_2:

(i)   one of the price level or the exchange rate (as numeraire),

(ii)   one of the real wage or the aggregate level of employment,

(iii) one of real absorption (C+I+G) or the balance of trade surplus (X-M).

These three choices are forced on users of ORANI (in stand-alone mode) because there are no mechanisms in the model suitable for determining

(I)   the extent to which induced changes in the real exchange rate will be realized as changes in the domestic inflation rate relative to the foreign rate or as changes in the nominal exchange rate;

(II)   the extent to which induced changes in the buoyancy of the
         labour market will be realized as changes in real wages or as
         changes in employment;

(III)   the extent to which induced changes in national income will be
         realized as changes in aggregate absorption or as changes in
         the balance of trade.

Thus at the outset three important macro variables must be exogenized in
stand-alone applications of ORANI.   But there are further macro
variables, such as interest rates, the money stock, the stock of bonds
held by the non-bank sector and the level of foreign reserves, which do
not appear in ORANI at all.   If these are to be included in x^m, then
additional equations are needed for short-run macroeconomic closure.

3.   THE IMPACT APPROACH TO SHORT-RUN MACROECONOMIC CLOSURE[2]

         The IMPACT paradigm is based on the following, strong,
maintained hypothesis: in the short run
"... financial and money markets, as well as fiscal actions, are only
important for individual industries insofar as they exert a real effect
on the big components of national income: namely, private consumption,
private capital formation, and government spending" (Powell (1981),
p.242).
Under this paradigm the absence of monetary and financial variables in
ORANI is no embarrassment since the economy is visualized as being
separable between its macro (including financial and monetary) components
on the one hand, and its micro (especially sectoral, and relative price)
components on the other.   Indeed there are some virtues in carrying out
simulations with ORANI in an exogenous macroeconomic environment: there
are, after all, a set of macro instruments available to sterilize any
unwanted macro consequences of sectoral and relative price shocks.
Nevertheless we have found that policy advisers are preoccupied with
these macro consequences (probably because their potential sizes have
been seriously overestimated, especially in the case of tariff-related
shocks).   Thus the problem has required serious attention.

3.1   The nature of an ORANI solution
         The comparative static method can be used in two essentially
different ways.   In the first, two equilibria which are supposed to occur

at different points in time are compared. In the second, the differentials between two equilibria occurring at the <u>same</u> notional period of time are calculated. The difference between the values Y^A and Y^B of a given endogenous variable Y at a given point of time in two equilibrium solutions is then attributed to differing scenarios A and B which vary with respect to the settings of the exogenous variables. Thus the computed value (Y^A-Y^B) answers the question:

> By how much would Y differ at time τ as the result of making the assumptions A about the exogenous variables rather than the assumptions B?

Here the assumptions B define <u>ceteris paribus</u> and generate the control values Y^B of the endogenous variables. In ORANI simulations this second method (contemporaneous differential comparative statics - <u>cdcs</u> for short) will almost always be the relevant approach. While all pretence of forecasting is eschewed in <u>cdcs</u>, the policy questions addressed come into sharper focus.

3.2   Problems of the interface

Our approach is to use a small macrodynamic model, MACRO, to close ORANI in short-run simulations. MACRO is a slightly revised mid 1979 version of the Reserve Bank of Australia's RBII model (Jonson and Trevor (1981) - see also Cooper (1983), p.28). This attempt to interface a comparative static model with a macrodynamic model threw up some substantial theoretical challenges. Among the more notable ones are:

  (i)   the lack of an explicit dynamics in ORANI,
 (ii)   temporal aggregation problems,
(iii)   the presence of variables which are endogenous to both models,
 (iv)   differing definitions in the two models of essentially the same variables,
  (v)   the presence in MACRO of macrorelations which cannot be derived as explicit aggregates of microrelations in ORANI (e.g., the production function),
 (vi)   the difficulty of preserving homogeneity properties in the interfaced system.

The interfacing method developed by Cooper and McLaren (1980, 1982, 1983) seems to resolve the first four of these simultaneously. The

difficulties posed by (v) and (vi) seem to be irreducible liabilities of
the method. In particular one cannot expect a separately developed macro
model to be formulated in terms of perfect aggregates (where such exist)
of the variables appearing in a given CGE model, nor could one expect the
interfaced system to display excess supply functions for commodities
which are homogeneous of first degree in the monetary stock and in
nominal prices (see Weintraub (1974), p.51). On these two points of
theoretical consistency the extended Walrasian paradigm offers better
prospects.

Some of these problems were minimized by the particular macro
model chosen. MACRO is a Bergstrom-Wymer model formulated in continuous
time (see Bergstrom and Wymer (1976)). This continuous time formulation
made solution of the temporal aggregation problem much easier. The
relatively extensive coverage of money and financial markets, both of
which are totally lacking in ORANI, was an advantage, as was the small
size of MACRO (26 equations) and the consequent relatively infrequent
occurrence of double endogeneities. Indeed, as we will see below, the
double endogeneities were actually turned to advantage in the development
of the interfacing methodology. This was possible because these
variables provide a link between ORANI solutions and realizations of
observable variables in real time.

3.3   Basic approach

The cdcs interpretation of ORANI solutions gels nicely with
the macrodynamic method: in both cases attention is focussed on
deviations from control. In the case of MACRO, such deviations can be
computed for all instants of continuous time after the injection of a
shock. A short-run solution of ORANI, on the other hand, only projects a
single deviation from control at a single point of time after this
shock. The interfacing methodology is based on attempting to identify an
instant after an exogenous shock which reconciles these two stories. The
elapsed time then provides an estimate of the ORANI short run t*.

For the moment take it as given that some method of supplying
feedbacks to ORANI from MACRO can be found. (With only a minor over-
simplification, for the moment we ignore feedbacks from ORANI to
MACRO.) Call the resulting system ORANI-MACRO (O-M). The response of
this system will be shown below to be a function of the unknown length t*
of the ORANI short run (and of certain other parameters). The response

of ORANI within O-M is a <u>cdcs</u> point solution which varies parametrically
with t*. In Figure 1 we concentrate on a doubly endogenous variable,
Y. The deviation-from-control of this variable, according to the MACRO
equations in O-M, has a path in real time shown by the broken line. The
points marked with a cross, on the other hand, do not form a path in real
time. Rather, they indicate a point solution for the deviation-from-
control of Y as endogenized by ORANI within O-M <u>conditional</u> on the
assumption that the length of the ORANI short run is the elapsed time on
the horizontal axis. Thus we can select an ORANI short run t* which
makes the MACRO solution for Y at t* in real time as close as possible to
the ORANI solution conditional on a short run of t*. Such a procedure

Figure 1. A shock is injected at t=0. The deviation-from-
control in a doubly endogenous variable Y, $y_M(t)$, as
endogenized as a function of real time by MACRO, is shown as
the broken line - - -.   Within ORANI-MACRO, the ORANI
contemporaneous differential comparative static solutions for
the same variable at t (where t is the assumed length of the
ORANI short run), are shown as x x x.   At t* the MACRO and
ORANI stories are reconciled.

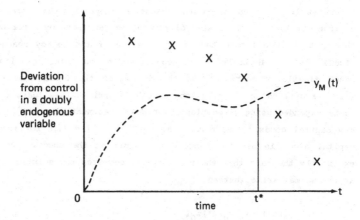

simultaneously provides an indirect real time validation of ORANI via
MACRO and as well furnishes an estimate of the calendar period
corresponding to the ORANI short run. The only complications to this
story in practice are due to the vector nature of Y, and the need to
choose t* simultaneously with other parameters of the interface.

4.   THE TWO MODEL TYPES

(a)   ORANI   ORANI (DPSV (1982)) is a CGE model of the Johansen
(1960) class. As we have seen in Section 3.1, under a typical allocation
of variables to the endogenous and exogenous categories, a cdcs solution
to ORANI can be written

$$y_0 = C_0 z_0 \qquad\qquad (4.1)$$

where the subscript 0 denotes ORANI variables and parameters; y_0
represents a vector of proportional changes (relative to control) in
ORANI endogenous variables; z_0 represents a vector of sustained
proportional changes (relative to control) in ORANI exogenous variables,
and C_0 is the matrix of ORANI elasticities.[3] The following quotation
illustrates the way in which results generated by (4.1) may be
interpreted: "given a policy change A, then in the macro-economic
environment B, variable C will differ in the short-run by x per cent from
the value it would have had in the absence of the policy change" (DPSV
(1982) p.63). Implicit in the construction and interpretation of the
ORANI elasticity matrix C_0 is the notion of the ORANI short-run, t*,
which is defined as a period long enough for prices to adjust, for output
to be expanded using given plant, for new investment plans to be made and
new capital goods to be purchased, but not long enough for the size of
capital stock in use to change as a result of the shock. To indicate
explicitly the fact that the result (4.1) compares two solutions of ORANI
at t*, we may write instead

$$y_0(t^*) = C_0(t^*)z_0. \qquad\qquad (4.2)$$

Thus y_0 is the proportional difference between two equilibria at t*.
This difference is conditional on the maintenance of the exogenous
macroeconomic environment. Variables embodying this environment are
represented in z_0 where they are assigned zero values. However the

original shock (i.e., the non-zero elements of z_0) may also cause changes in variables outside ORANI (i.e., in MACRO).   Some of the latter variables appear among the elements of z_0 which are set to zero in stand-alone applications of ORANI using (4.2).   Thus when (4.2) is used alone the implicit assumption is that the induced differentials in the macroeconomic environment are sterilized by offsetting use of fiscal and/or monetary instruments.

   (b)   __MACRO__   Our MACRO model, MACRO81, is an adaptation (see Cooper (1983)) of the Reserve Bank's RBII model as documented in the appendix to Jonson and Trevor (1981).   Underlying it is a first-order stochastic differential equation system which may be written

$$d\,Y_M(t) \;=\; A_M\,Y_M(t)dt + B_M\,Z_M(t)dt + dv(t) \tag{4.3}$$

where the subscript M indicates MACRO variables and coefficients, Y and Z respectively are vectors of logarithms of endogenous and exogenous variables respectively, and dv(t) is a Gaussian vector process.   The solution of this system may be written

$$Y_M(t) \;=\; e^{A_M t}\Big\{Y_M(0) + \int_0^t e^{-A_M \tau}\,B_M Z_M(\tau)d\tau\Big\} \tag{4.4}$$

$$+ \, e^{A_M t}\int_0^t e^{-A_M \tau}\,dv(\tau),$$

where $e^{A_M \tau}$ is defined by $Pe^{\Lambda \tau}P^{-1}$, in which P is the matrix containing the characteristic vectors of A_M, and Λ is the diagonal matrix containing the characteristic roots of A_M.   The matrix $e^{\Lambda \tau}$ has typical element $e^{\lambda_i \tau}$, in which λ_i is the ith characteristic root of A_M.   Let $\Delta^*(\cdot)$ be the operator taking the differential between $(\cdot)$ when the exogeneous variables follow the shocked path $\{Z_M(\tau) + z_M;\ \tau \in (0,t]\}$ and its value at the same point of time when they follow the control path $\{Z_M(\tau);\ \tau \in (0,t]\}$.   Since $\Delta^*(Z_M(\tau) + z_M) \equiv z_M$ for all relevant τ, we have

$$\Delta^* y_M(t) = \left[e^{A_M t} \int_0^t e^{-A_M \tau} B_M d\tau \right] z_M, \tag{4.5}$$

or

$$y_M(t) = C_M(t) z_M \quad \text{(say)}, \tag{4.6}$$

where

$$C_M(t) = A_M^{-1} \left[e^{A_M t} - I \right] B_M. \tag{4.7}$$

The notation on the left of (4.5) emphasises that the differentials involved are deviations from control at t. However the notation (4.6) is more convenient and is adopted from hereon. The stochastic term on the right of (4.4) disappears in (4.5) because the introduction of the shock z_M into $\{Z_M(\tau); \tau \in (0,t]\}$ does not affect the realization of $v(t)$. Thus Δ^* differences alternative realizations of the same sample which differ only in their systematic part.

5.   TEMPORAL AGGREGATION

Equation (4.6) demonstrates that, for arbitrary t, the MACRO model can be written in a Johansen-like form. It is tempting to combine (4.2) and (4.6) into one system. Before this can be accomplished successfully, however, it is necessary to take account of the difference between the time profile of shocks z_0 suitable for input into ORANI and the evolving nature of outputs $y_M(t)$ (t $\in$ (0,t*]) from MACRO.

In Figure 2a are shown a sustained proportional shock z in a doubly exogenous variable Z and the response $y_M^0(t)$ in time of a variable Y_M^0 which is endogenous to MACRO but exogenous to ORANI. (In typical short-run ORANI configurations, the real wage is such a variable.) Considered as an exogenous input to ORANI, z in Figure 2a is a suitable shock; however $y_M^0(t)$ is not. Notionally $y_M^0(t)$ can be split up into a (large) number of step functions; this is shown in Figure 2b. We are interested in the ORANI response at t* to the combined stimuli of z maintained throughout (0,t*] and the series of step shocks in Y_M^0, which are maintained for successively shorter and shorter periods as we move from 0 to t*. To be able to evaluate the impact of these shocks whose duration is less than t* it is necessary to endow ORANI with a within-short-period dynamics. The so augmented model will be referred to as ORANI+.

Figure 2a. The shock z in a doubly exogenous variable Z is injected into MACRO at t=0. t* is the length of the ORANI short run. The proportional response in the MACRO endogenous variable Y_M is $y_M^0(t)$. ORANI will accept shocks in the step-function form displayed by z; it cannot accept an arbitrarily evolving shock such as that displayed by $y_M^0(t)$.

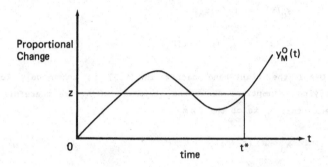

Figure 2b. The log differential $y_M^0(t)$ is endogenous to MACRO but appears also as an exogenous input into ORANI. The continuously varying shock $y_M^0(t)$ can be represented as a sequence of discrete step-function shocks as shown.

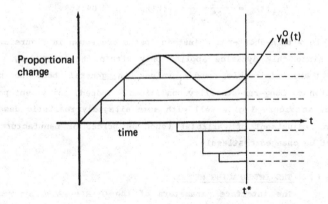

The dynamics in ORANI+ is kept as simple as possible. For each of a small, but exhaustive, number of classes of endogenous variables in ORANI+, it is assumed that the within-short-run response belongs to a one parameter family. Given (4.7) it is natural to assume (by analogy with MACRO) that the ORANI+ endogenous responses at s, $s \in (0, t*]$, take the form

$$y_0(s) = C_0(s)z_0, \qquad (5.1)$$

where

$$C_0(s) = A_0^{-1}\left[e^{A_0 s} - I\right]B_0. \qquad (5.2)$$

From ORANI the right-hand matrix in (5.2) is known only for $s=t*$. Simplifying assumptions about the structure of A_0 are therefore needed. We assume that A_0 is of the form

$$A_0 = (\ell n \; \hat{\beta})I, \qquad (5.3)$$

where $(\ell n \; \hat{\beta})$ is a diagonal matrix which, in the application reported below, has only six distinct elements. Let $(\ell n \; \beta_i)$ be the ith such distinct value, and let $y_{0j}(\tau)$ be the cdcs solution for the jth ORANI endogenous variable, which is assigned the within-short-run adjustment parameter β_i. Then our assumptions imply

$$y_{0j}(\tau) = \frac{\beta_i^{\tau} - 1}{\beta_i^{t*} - 1} y_{0j}(t*), \qquad 0 < \tau < t*. \qquad (5.4)$$

Possible within-short-run adjustment paths are shown in Figure 3. Notice that since this dynamics applies only within the short-run, values of $\beta_i > 1$ are admissible, and β_i values in general bear no necessary relation to long-run-stability conditions. Indeed, adjustment paths such as (e) in Figure 3 gibe well with some allegedly realistic descriptions of the adjustment of variables (such as prices of manufactures) which cannot be changed costlessly.

6.   THE INTERFACING METHOD

The interface parameters of the ORANI+ MACRO system are the length of the ORANI short run, $t*$, and the adjustment parameters β_i. The two models are to be interfaced with these parameters set initially to arbitrary values. A search procedure is then used to optimize their values. In what follows the various coefficient matrices in the system are all known up to an arbitrary specification of t* and the vector of β values. We start with the assumption that the system is recursive; that is, while we allow ORANI to be driven by variables that are endogenized in MACRO, we assume initially that there are no MACRO exogenous variables endogenized by ORANI.

Consider again the evolution of $y_M^0(t)$ in Figure 2b. Suppose now that this is the path of just one of many such variables; i.e., redefine $y_M^0(t)$ to be <u>vector</u> of exogenous inputs into ORANI which are endogenized in MACRO. In order to take an infinitesimal rather than a discrete step-function decomposition of $y_M^0(t)$, write it as the integral of its own derivatives:

Figure 3.   Within short-run dynamics in ORANI.   t* is the ORANI short run.   The within-short-period dynamics in ORANI+ for an endogenous variable with adjustment coefficient β_i is shown for different values of β_i.   The point A is the short run contemporaneous differential comparative static solution for ORANI at t*.   The adjustment paths in (0,t*] imply nothing about long run dynamics.

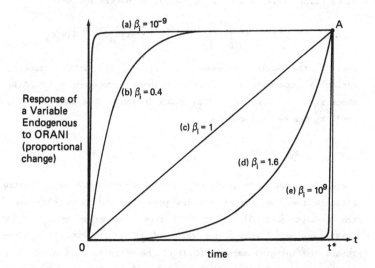

Response of a Variable Endogenous to ORANI (proportional change)

(a) $\beta_i = 10^{-9}$

(b) $\beta_i = 0.4$

(c) $\beta_i = 1$

(d) $\beta_i = 1.6$

(e) $\beta_i = 10^9$

A

0   time   t*   t

$$y_M^0(t) = \int_0^t \frac{dy_M^0(\tau)}{d\tau} \, d\tau. \tag{6.1}$$

Each of these derivatives may be interpreted as an infinitesimal shock to ORANI sustained over the interval $[\tau,t]$. Let L be the linear operator which, when operating on $y_M^0(t)$, produces a vector conformable with z_0, having as its elements the values of the appropriate elements of $y_M^0(t)$ in positions corresponding to ORANI exogenous variables endogenized by MACRO, and zeros elsewhere. Then $d[Ly_M^0(\tau)] \equiv Ld[y_M^0(\tau)]$ is a shock in a form suitable for acceptance by ORANI+. Inject these instantaneous shocks for $\tau \in (0,s]$ into ORANI+ via (5.1); given the linearity of the model, the accumulated response at $s, s \in (0,t^*]$, is obtained by summation:

$$y_0(s) = \int_0^s C_0(s-\tau) L dy_M^0(\tau) . \tag{6.2}$$

$$= \int_0^s C_0(s-\tau) LQ dy_M(\tau) ,$$

where Q is the linear operator that selects the subset $y_M^0(\tau)$ from $y_M(\tau)$. Using (4.6), (4.7) and (5.2) in (6.2), we obtain for $s=t^*$

$$y_0(t^*) = \int_0^{t^*} A_0^{-1} \left[e^{A_0(t^*-\tau)} -I \right] B_0 LQ e^{A_M \tau} d\tau B_M z_M . \tag{6.3}$$

This is the ORANI+ response at t^* (i.e., the ORANI response) to the variables exogenous to it which respond endogenously in MACRO to the shock z_M. If z is the initial shock in the double exogeneities, then in (6.3) z_M can be replaced by

$$z_M = Rz , \tag{6.4}$$

where the operator R produces a vector conformable to z_M having as its elements the elements of z where possible, and zeros elsewhere. Given the assumption (5.3) on A_0, and given the value of $C_0 (\equiv C_0(t^*))$ from ORANI, for any β vector and value of t^* we can compute B_0 from (5.2). Thence the integral term in (6.3) can be computed (see Cooper and McLaren (1980) p.26 and (1982) p.16 for the details). Let its computed value be

$$\int_0^{t^*} A^{-1} \left[e^{A_0(t^*-\tau)} -I \right] B_0 LQ e^{A_M \tau} d\tau = H \quad (\text{say}) . \tag{6.5}$$

Then (6.3) can be written more simply as

$$y_0(t^*) = HB_M z_M .$$ (6.6)

The right-hand side of (6.6) can be expressed in terms of $y_M(t^*)$ by the following argument:

$$y_0(t^*) = H \left[e^{A_M t^*} - I \right]^{-1} A_M A_M^{-1} \left[e^{A_M t^*} - I \right] B_M z_M .$$ (6.7)

Thus from (4.6) and (4.7)

$$y_0(t^*) \equiv H \left[e^{A_M t^*} - I \right]^{-1} A_M y_M(t^*)$$

$$= G y_M(t^*) \quad (\text{say}) .$$ (6.8)

The coefficient matrix G in (6.8) gives the effects at t^* on the ORANI endogenous variables of the shocks endogenized by MACRO as evaluated at t^*. G can be thought of as an operator which corrects the timing of these MACRO variables to make them suitable inputs to ORANI and then performs the required multiplication.

Let S be a selection operator analogous to R in (6.4) such that putting

$$z_0 = Sz$$ (6.9)

produces an ORANI shock vector containing zeros except for the doubly exogenous shocks which take on their values as in z. The initial doubly exogenous shock z produces in ORANI a direct effect $C_0 Sz$ and an indirect effect $G y_M(t^*) = G C_M(t^*) Rz$. The total ORANI response is obtained by adding these:

$$y_0(t^*) = C_0 Sz + G C_M(t^*) Rz .$$ (6.10)

In the case where the initial shock is not confined to double exogeneities (but in which the shocks z_0 and z_M contain no contradictions), (6.10) generalizes to

$$y_0(t^*) = C_0 z_0 + G C_M(t^*) z_M .$$ (6.11)

In the recursive case developed above in which there are no reverse linkages from ORANI to MACRO, the complete ORANI-MACRO system consists of (6.11) and the MACRO solution

$$y_M(t^*) = C_M(t^*)z_M .$$

(6.12)

In this system certain variables will be endogenized both in y_M and in y_O. The interfacing method consists of choosing the within-short-run-adjustment coefficients vector β and the length of the ORANI short run t^* which minimize the inconsistencies between the MACRO and ORANI sides of the model.

In the case where there exist variables driving MACRO which are endogenous to ORANI - this occurs in fact (see below) - the same principles are used to interface the models: that is, ORANI is endowed with a within-short-run dynamics conditional on the unknown values of the interface parameters, which are then chosen to minimize inconsistencies in the double endogeneities at t^*. The formalities of this procedure are set out in Cooper and McLaren (1982).

7.   CALIBRATION OF THE INTERFACE PARAMETERS

In sections 5 and 6 we have described an interfacing method that is specific to some injected shock or shocks. Possible approaches to making the procedure operational are:

(i)   the construction of a new interface for each simulation conducted on the O-M system;

(ii)   the selection of interface parameters which optimize a criterion function defined over a nominated set containing a variety of shocks;

(iii)   the selection of a set of interface parameters from a single standard simulation.

We have chosen (iii). In keeping with the literature on the comparative analysis of macrodynamic models (see, e.g. De Bever et al. (1979)), we have chosen an exogenous increase in government spending as the standard simulation.

In considering the interplay between ORANI and MACRO variables it is not necessary to carry the complete (and impossibly long) list of

ORANI variables.   Only macroeconomic variables are involved at the
interface.   A listing of ORANI variables relevant to the interface is
given in Table 1.   Table 2 shows a similar partial listing of MACRO
variables.

From the listings of ORANI and MACRO variables in Tables 1 and
2 respectively it is evident that the following variables are endogenous
to both models:

<u>Double Endogeneities</u>

$\log y_g$	Output
$\log P$	Prices
$\log L_h$	Employment
$\log i$	Imports

A set of variables of particular interest in view of the role
of MACRO in endogenizing the macroeconomic environment of ORANI is the
following group of ORANI exogenous variables:

<u>MACRO to ORANI Feedbacks (ORANI Definitions)</u>

$\log E$	Exchange Rate
$\log (W/P)$	Real Wages
$\log C_R$	Real Household Expenditure
$\log I_R$	Real Gross Private Investment
	(including investment in dwellings)
$\log K(0)$	Initial Capital Stocks

Variables exogenous to MACRO and endogenized by ORANI are:

<u>ORANI to MACRO Feedbacks</u>

$\log P_{wl}$	Price of Wool
$\log x$	Quantity of Exports
$\log P_x$	Price of exports

In practice matters are complicated by the need to select various
combinations of MACRO endogenous variables to correspond to the
definitions of certain ORANI exogenous variables (for details, see Cooper
(1983), pp.12-13).

TABLE 1
A PARTIAL LISTING OF VARIABLES APPEARING IN ORANI78

Variables Endogenous to ORANI: The Vector Y_0

1.	$\log y_g$	Real Gross Domestic Product
2.	$\log P$	Price Deflator for Aggregate Production ($A)
3.	$\log L_h$	Aggregate Employment Demand (labour-hours)
4.	$\log i$	Real Imports
5.	$\log P_{wl}$	Price of Wool ($A)
6.	$\log x$	Real Exports
7.	$\log P_x$	Price of Exports ($US)
8.	$\log (x\, P_x)$	Foreign Currency Value of Exports ($US)

Variables Exogenous to ORANI: The Vector Z_0

1.	$\log E$	Exchange Rate ($A/$US)
2.	$\log (W/P)$	Real Wages
3.	$\log C_R$	Real Household Expenditure
4.	$\log I_R$	Real Private Investment
5.	$\log K(0)$	Initial Capital Stocks
6.	$\log g_1$	Government Expenditure
7.	$\log t_3$	Average Level of Tariffs

Source: Cooper (1983)

TABLE 2
A PARTIAL LISTING OF VARIABLES APPEARING IN MACRO81

Variables Endogenous to MACRO81 (A Subset of Y_M)

1.	$\log y_g$	Real Gross Domestic Product
2.	$\log P$	Price Deflator for Aggregate Production ($A)
3.	$\log L_h$	Aggregate Employment Demand (labour-hours)
4.	$\log i$	Real Imports
5.	$\log E$	Exchange Rate ($A/$US)
6.	$\log W$	Nominal Wages (average weekly earnings, $A)
7.	$\log d$	Aggregate Real Household Expenditure (including investment in dwellings)
8.	k	Proportional Change in New Investment (=DK/K)
9.	$\log K$	Business Fixed Capital Stock

Variables Exogenous to MACRO81 (A Subset of Z_M)

1.	$\log P_{wl}$	Price of Wool ($US)
2.	$\log x$	Real Exports
3.	$\log P_x$	Price of Exports ($A)
4.	$\log g_1$	Government Expenditure
5.	$\log (1+t_3)$	Power of Tariff
6.	$\log P_i$	Price of Imports ($US)
7.	$\log P_w$	World Prices ($US)

Source: Cooper (1983)

The standard simulation consisted of a 10 per cent increase in real government spending. Other than the average tariff rate, this is the only double exogeneity. The main interface parameters to be estimated are:

(i)   the speeds of adjustment (i.e., the elements of the matrix A_0). For parsimony of parameterisation this matrix is chosen to be diagonal. This has the advantage of assigning at most one adjustment speed parameter to each ORANI equation. Since usually only the aggregate versions of ORANI equations are used explicitly in the interfaced system, this provides a simple identification of an adjustment speed which may subsequently be applied to some subset of the general ORANI disaggregated families of equations. For the model specification given above the matrix A_0 is of dimension 8 and the respective adjustment speeds relate to the following variables:

ORANI Variable		Adjustment Speed
1. Y_g	Real Gross Domestic Product	β_1
2. P	Price Deflator for Aggregate Production	β_2
3. L_h	Aggregate Employment Demand (labour-hours)	β_3
4. i	Real imports	β_4
5. P_{wl}	Price of Wool	β_5
6. x	Real Exports	β_6
7. P_x	Price of Exports ($US)	β_6
8. $x\,P_x$	Foreign currency Value of Exports	β_6

Since variable 8 must be assigned an adjustment speed which is consistent with variables 6 and 7, these are constrained to a common adjustment speed (β_6). The remaining five adjustment speeds are freely chosen. The parameterisation is in fact made upon e^{A_0}, so that the field of search is the six-dimensional positive orthant.

(ii)   the ORANI "short run", t*: the length of time during which the effects calculated from an ORANI stand-alone experiment would be expected to be working themselves out. A priori this interval was expected to be in the range 6 to 8 quarters and an intensive search over 5 to 12 quarters was carried out.

The criterion for choice of the interface parameters was the minimization of the (unweighted) sum of squared deviations of the double endogeneities when evaluated at t*. An intensive search over an eight-dimensional space[4] led to the parameter values shown in column I of Table 3.

Besides the estimates of the main interface parameters, this table also shows the values, at these parameter settings, of the doubly endogenous variables. These figures correspond to a shock of 10.0 to log g_1, government expenditure, and may be interpreted as percentage responses to a 10 per cent shock. The method has been successful in finding a setting for the interface parameters which eliminates inconsistency between ORANI and MACRO under a shock in government spending.

8.   RESULTS FOR A TARIFF SHOCK

Using the above parameter values, this experiment shocked t_3, the average tariff variable in ORANI, by 25 per cent. A search over t_3 to determine the appropriate corresponding shock to $(1 + t_3)$, the power of the tariff variable in MACRO, subject to the criterion of minimizing the squared difference between the ORANI and MACRO projections of the output double endogeneity, led to the following results:

Shock to $(1 + t_3)$:   3.434%

Implied Value of t_3 :   15.923%

Value of real output (y_g) as
computed by both the MACRO and
ORANI components of the
interfaced system   :   -0.089%

This implied value of t_3 (approximately 16 per cent) is of broadly comparable size to more direct estimates by the Industries Assistance Commission (1980, Table 2.1). Using weights based on the unassisted value of domestic production of commodities, the average tariff levels on manufactured products were estimated by the Commission to be 24 per cent in 1968-69, and 15 per cent in 1977-78.

TABLE 3
ESTIMATED VALUES OF MAIN INTERFACE PARAMETERS

ORANI Variables		Adjustment Speeds (Diagonal elements of e^{A_0}) (I)	Solution Values at t* of the Double Endogeneities** (II)
y_g	Output	$\beta_1 = 4.39$	1.073
P	Domestic Prices	$\beta_2 = 74.4$	1.358
L_h	Employment	$\beta_3 = 9.8$	1.557
i	Imports	$\beta_4 = 5.9$	1.854
P_{wl}	Price of Wool	$\beta_5 = 10$	n.a.
$x, P_x, (x\, P_x)$	Export Sector	$\beta_6 = .5$	n.a.

ORANI Response Interval : t* = 7.94 quarters

** Result shown in column II applies to both the ORANI and MACRO projections of the doubly endogenous variable within the interfaced ORANI-MACRO system. At the given parameter settings, the two projections are in fact identical to the fourth decimal place. Further details are available in Appendix 3 of Powell, Cooper and McLaren (1983), where a comparison is given with solution values for t* set at 7.93 and 7.95 quarters.

n.a. Not applicable (variable is not doubly endogenous).

Source: Cooper (1983).

The principal results of the tariff experiment are given in Table 4. The main feature to note is the strong similarity between columns I and II, and the extent of the divergence between them and column III.

Column II shows the 'macroeconomically compensated' values of the responses of the major macroeconomic aggregates to a 25 per cent increase in tariffs. This is the standard ORANI, stand-alone, story. Column I shows how the ORANI story must be modified to allow for the impact of the tariff shock on the macroeconomic environment. These results in column I are based on the interface parameters shown in Table 3. The overwhelming impression gained by comparison of columns I and II is that the change in the macroeconomic environment induced by the tariff shock has only second order consequences to major macroeconomic aggregates.

Comparison of columns I and III of Table 4 reveals that MACRO and ORANI want to tell somewhat different stories about the impact of the tariff rise. By construction, their output responses were made identical (-0.089%) by selection of a suitable value of t_3 (the average tariff level). It will be noted that the MACRO responses in employment and output are equal, whereas ORANI shows the standard neo-classical short run result in which the employment response is a multiple (namely, 1.9) of the output response. Imports decline according to both sides of the interfaced model; the MACRO response, however, is 2 to 3 times larger in absolute value. The key to this is the behaviour of the price level in MACRO, which is the glaring inconsistency. It seems here difficult to accept the MACRO result that a 25 per cent increase in tariffs could be deflationary at a two year lag. Given this result, however, the consequent increase in the competitiveness of the domestic economy leads in MACRO to a substantial decline in imports. It may be expected that, in the presence of an experiment involving a highly non-neutral shock, the model which has been built more specifically for analysis of the type of shock in question would give the more reasonable results. In the above case it is not surprising that the ORANI results for a tariff shock would be the more reasonable.

9.   CONCLUSION AND PROSPECT FOR FURTHER RESEARCH

The ORANI model is an example of a large CGE model used routinely for policy analysis. It is not macroeconomically closed.

TABLE 4
PRINCIPAL RESULTS OF A 25 PER CENT TARIFF INCREASE IN THE ORANI-MACRO SYSTEM*

	Endogenous Variable	ORANI Response within the Intefaced System (I)	Standard ORANI Response (II)	MACRO Response within the Interfaced System (III)
y_g	Output	-0.089	-0.123	-0.089
P	Prices	1.862	1.805	-0.374
L_h	Employment	-0.167	-0.205	-0.082
i	Imports	-1.322	-1.528	-3.625
$(x\ p_x)$	Value of Exports ($US)	-2.824	-2.523	n.a.
E	Exchange Rate ($A/$US)	n.a.	n.a.	-0.237
W/P	Real Wages	n.a.	n.a.	0.104
k	Rate of Net Investment	n.a.	n.a.	0.003
K	Capital Stock	n.a.	n.a.	0.112
d	Household Expenditure	n.a.	n.a.	-0.053

*   Based on the interface parameters shown in Table 3 and $t_3 = 0.15923$. For further details, see Cooper (1983). Figures in the table are percentage deviations from control at 7.94 quarters after the tariff shock.

n.a. not applicable

Source: Cooper (1983).

Monetary and other transient phenomena are involved in short-run economic analysis. Essentially two options are available for the short-run macro-closure of ORANI: (i) the extended Walrasian paradigm and (ii) the IMPACT paradigm. (A third option, currently on the back-burner because of the probably insurmountable data problems inherent in the estimation of its additional parameters, endows every ORANI micro-variable with its own adjustment path - see FitzGerald (1979)). During the last four years work at IMPACT has concentrated on (ii). This work has resulted in an operational method for interfacing a small macrodynamic model in the Bergstrom-Wymer (1976) class with a large CGE model in the Johansen (1960) class (Cooper and McLaren (1980), (1982), (1983); Cooper (1983)). It is hoped that other researchers will extend the range of simulations made with the interfaced system; above we have reported only the (aggregate) results for a shock in government spending (used to calibrate the interface) and for a uniform tariff change. In 1984 we have initiated work on the extended Walrasian paradigm with a view to comparative analysis of its performance against that of the IMPACT paradigm.

NOTES

* Aspects of the long-run macroeconomic closure of ORANI are discussed by Dixon, Parmenter and Rimmer (1984), by Powell, Cooper and McLaren (1983), Section3, and by Horridge and Powell (1984).

1. In his later work, Walras himself took the initial steps in extending his framework to include a monetary asset. For a critique of this attempt, see Patinkin (1965), pp.541-572. An important initial step in the extension of the Walrasian paradigm in applied work was the 'helicopter drop' assumption made by Clements (1980) who treated domestic credit expansion as an exogenous variable, but one entailing real monetary effects in the short run. Kehoe (1981) also adds government debt (but not money) to the Walrasian real system. Another group of authors (e.g., Piggott (1981)) explore the real effects which an exogenous inflation produces via the failure, in varying degrees, of the different elements of the tax system to be fully and instantaneously indexed to the general price level.

2. In this section we draw feely on Cooper and McLaren (1980), (1982), (1983), and on Cooper (1983).

3. The table of elasticities - the derivatives of elements of Y_0 with respect to elements of Z_0 (the matrix C_0) - is given in Appendix 2 of Powell, Cooper and McLaren (1983). The numerical values of these elasticities correspond to the underlying numerical data base and parameter values of ORANI78 used in the tariff experiment reported in DPSV (1982), Chapter 7. The split of variables into endogenous and exogenous sets corresponds to the standard short-run neoclassical mode with a slack labour market. The table of elasticities is therefore a subset of a standard basic solution of ORANI78. It may be noted that the numeraire of the model is the exchange rate and, with respect to this variable, the model is homogenous of degree zero in reals and one in nominals.

4. MACRO endogenizes the number of persons employed, whereas ORANI endogenizes total labour hours. This led to the addition to the system of the equation

$$d \log L_h = d \log L + \eta (d \log y - d \log y^*),$$

where L_h is labour hours, L is persons employed, y is output and y^* is the output level corresponding to "standard hours". η was treated as an interface parameter; its estimated value, 0.45, was determined jointly with the seven other interface parameter estimates reported in Table 3. For further details, see Cooper (1983), pp.8-9.

REFERENCES

Bergstrom, A.R., and Wymer, C.R. (1976). A model of disequilibrium neoclassical growth and its application to the United Kingdom. In Statistical Inference in Continuous Time Econometric Models, ed. A.R. Bergstrom. Amsterdam: North-Holland.

Boadway, R. & Treddenick, J. (1978). A general equilibrium computation of the effects of the Canadian tariff structure. Canadian Journal of Economics, XI, 424-46.

Bureau Of Industry Economics (1981). The long run impact of technological changes in the structure of Australian industry 1990-91. Research Report No. 7, Canberra.

Clements, K.W. (1980). A general equilibrium econometric model of the open economy. International Economic Review, 21, 469-88.

Cooper, R.J. (1983). A tariff experiment on the interfaced ORANI-MACRO system. IMPACT Project Preliminary Working Paper No. IP-18, University of Melbourne, pp.29.

Cooper, R.J. & McLaren, K.R. (1983). The ORANI-MACRO interface; an illustrative exposition. Economic Record, 59, 166-79.

_____ and _____ (1982). An approach to the macroeconomic closure of general equilibrium models. IMPACT Project Preliminary Working Paper No. IP-15, University of Melbourne, pp.28.

_____ and _____ (1980). The ORANI-MACRO interface. IMPACT Project Preliminary Working Paper No. IP-10, University of Melbourne, pp.83.

De Bever, L., Foot, D.K., Helliwell, J.F., Jump, G.V., Maxwell, T., Sawyer, J.A. & Waslander, H.E.L. (1979). Dynamic properties of four Canandian macroeconomic models. Canadian Journal of Economics, XII, 133-94.

Dixon, P.B., Parmenter, B.R. & Rimmer, R.J. (1984). Extending the ORANI model of the Australian economy: adding foreign investment to a miniature version. In Applied General Equilibrium Analysis, ed. H.E. Scarf & J.B. Shoven. New York: Cambridge University Press, 485-533.

Dixon, P.B., Powell, A.A. & Parmenter, B.R. (1979). Structural Adaptation in an Ailing Macroeconomy, Melbourne: Melbourne University Press.

Dixon, P.B., Parmenter, B.R., Sutton, J. & Vincent, D.P. (1982). ORANI: A Multisectoral Model of the Australian Economy, Amsterdam: North-Holland.

Feltenstein, A. (1981). A general equilibrium approach to the analysis of monetary and fiscal policy. IMF Staff Papers, 27, 653-81.

FitzGerald, V.W. (1979). A variant of the ORANI model for the analysis of short-period responses. IMPACT Project Preliminary Working Paper No. OP-23, University of Melbourne, pp.63.

Horridge, M. & Powell, A.A. (1984). Long-run closure of 'ORANI': a proposal. IMPACT Project Preliminary Working Paper No. OP-46, University of Melbourne, pp.109.

Industries Assistance Commission (1980). Trends in the Structure of Assistance to Manufacturing, Approaches to General Reductions in Protection. Information Paper No. 1, Canberra.

Jonson, P.D. & Trevor, R.G. (1981). Monetary rules: A preliminary analysis. Economic Record, 57, 150-67.

Johansen, L. (1960). A Multi-Sectoral Study of Economic Growth. Amsterdam: North-Holland.

Kehoe, T.J. (1981). Discretionary fiscal policy in a general equilibrium model. Massachusetts Institute of Technology, Cambridge (mimeo), pp.41.

Patinkin, D. (1965). Money, Interest and Prices, 2nd edn. New York: Harper and Row.

Patinkin, D. (1958). Liquidity preference and loanable funds. Economica, XXV, 308-14.

Piggott, J. (1981). The microeconomic effects of tax inflation interactions: general equilibrium investigations of the Australian case. Australian National University, Canberra, paper presented to the Centre for Economic Policy Research Conference on the Effects of Inflation in Australia (mimeo), pp.61 + 6.

Powell, A.A. (1981). The major streams of economy-wide modelling: Is rapprochement possible?. In Large-Scale Macro-Econometric Models, eds. J. Kmenta & J.B. Ramsey, Ch.9. North-Holland: Amsterdam, 219-64.

Powell, A.A., Cooper, R.J. & McLaren, K.R. (1983). Macroeconomic closure in applied general equilibrium modelling: Experience from ORANI and agenda for further research. IMPACT Project Preliminary Working Paper No. IP-19, pp.iii + 60. University of Melbourne.

Vincent, D.P. (1983). Exchange rate devaluation, monetary policy and wages: A general equilibrium analysis for Chile. Kiel Institute of World Economics, draft working paper (mimeo), pp.36.

Weintraub, E. R. (1974). General Equilibrium Theory. London: Macmillan.

Wright, J. & Cowan, P. (1980). Comparative short run behaviour of ORANI77 in neo-classical and neo-Keynesian modes. IMPACT Project Working Paper No. O-29, University of Melbourne, pp.42.

NEW DEVELOPMENTS IN THE APPLICATION OF GENERAL EQUILIBRIUM
MODELS TO ECONOMIC HISTORY

J. A. James
University of Virginia
Charlottesville, Virginia, U.S.A.

Rather than strictly "new" developments in the application
of general equilibrium models to economic history, I would like to
consider instead developments in the application of general equilibrium
models in the New Economic History. This allows me to extend the
perspective back twenty or so years, to span the duration of the New
Economic History. By that term I mean the discipline which emphasizes
the application of formal neoclassical economic theory and quantitative
techniques to historical problems. One of the distinctive
characteristics of the New Economic History has been the use of explicit
counterfactual analysis, the posing of alternative states of the world
and comparing them with the actual one in order to identify the effects
of a particular factor, institution, or course of action. First and
perhaps most provocatively employed by Robert Fogel (1964) in analyzing
the contribution of the railroad to American economic growth by posing a
counterfactual world of what the United States would have been like in
1890 without the railroad, it has become a staple in the economic
historian's garden of techniques.

The formulation of counterfactual states of nature or
examination of how the economy would have performed under alternative
historical conditions clearly in principle demand a general equilibrium
approach. Moreover, since economic historians are often interested in
the impact of large changes in variables or institutions in which
interaction or reallocation effects may be significant, partial
equilibrium analysis may be inappropriate in many cases. Economic
history then would seem to represent an area in which the use of general
equilibrium models would be natural and very useful. In 1971, for

441

example, Peter Temin argued for the greater use of general equilibrium
models in economic history to deal with increasingly complex problems of
resource allocation and growth to which partial equilibrium analysis was
unsuited. However, in spite of the fact that the New Economic History
has been potentially such a fertile field for the application of general
equilibrium modelling, such techniques have not been as widely adopted
and had as much influence as may have been supposed. To be sure, the
rate of diffusion of a new technology is almost invariably rather slow
initially, but the application of computable general equilibrium (CGE)
modelling techniques in economic history does face some special
problems.

   I would first like to identify some reasons that CGE
modelling techniques have perhaps not been used to their full potential
in the New Economic History and then in Section II to discuss briefly
some important applications of general equilibrium modelling in order to
illustrate some of the problems involved. This, needless to say, will
not be an exhaustive chronicle of CGE models used in economic history.
Finally in Section III, I would like to identify some general areas that
are particularly amenable to the CGE modelling approach. Previous work
in the area as well as potentially fruitful topics for future
applications will be considered.

   I.

   One factor inhibiting the widespread acceptance of general
equilibrium analysis is the lack of intuition in evaluating results. On
the one hand, we may be able to take into account complicated
interactions neglected by partial equilibrium analysis; but on the other
hand, once we obtain a result it may be quite difficult to puzzle out
why it turned out as it did. In other words, one may have considerable
difficulty in determining what forces are driving the results. These
conflicting considerations of realism, or complexity, in modelling and
loss of insight are certainly not unique to GE modelling in economic
history however, and sensitivity analysis can be used to identify the
crucial assumptions or parameters in a particular problem. As a result,
I shall not linger here on such difficulties and shall consider instead
some problems more specific to economic history.

   Lack of data may, of course, be a constraint on applications of CGE modelling in many fields, but it is particularly serious in economic history. In the United States, for example, the Census Bureau did in fact collect remarkably detailed information about population, manufacturing, and agriculture in the mid and late nineteenth century and that data base has been supplemented by the works of Kuznets, Gallman, Easterlin, and Lebergott. Nevertheless, the Census comes only every ten years, so that Williamson (1974) in his general equilibrium model of late nineteenth century American development is forced to interpolate between Census years to develop series for some parameters. Furthermore, there are also significant gaps in data necessary for a complete CGE model - little information on services, an important component of total output, exists, for example, and data on patterns of consumer demand are limited to the budget studies by Carroll Wright of Massachusetts workers in 1875 and of workers' households from nine protected industries in 1889-90 (Williamson, 1967; Haines, 1979). For the earlier part of the century, even the Census data on agriculture and manufactures become too sketchy to be completely reliable.

One consequence of the limited empirical base is that CGE models which are feasible to construct are in some cases too simple for the tasks at hand. As I shall argue later, some CGE models used have not been detailed or complex enough to deal with some of the interesting questions in economic history. Moreover, data limitations make the ever-present problems of correct model specification more serious here. Disputes over proper functional specification, of which there are several, cannot at times easily be resolved empirically. Sensitivity analysis may be used to put bounds on the effects of alternative specifications and thereby mitigate some of the problems of data deficiencies. However, in at least some cases the range of these bounds could be quite wide.

A related specification problem, although not the result of data problems, is that general equilibrium analysis may have difficulty in properly modelling many interesting questions in economic history. Economic historians are especially concerned with questions involving economic growth and development, dynamic problems in other words. Comparative static counterfactual analysis may ignore, for example, the effects of changes in the tariff or in the stock of land on, say, the rate of capital formation or technological progress, but CGE models have

not yet been particularly successful in capturing the dynamics of
economic growth. In his late nineteenth century CGE model Williamson
(1974) does try to compare the dynamic effects of various counterfactual
specifications but the dynamic framework is relatively simple with many
sources of growth being exogenous.

The class of simple general equilibrium models suggested by
Ron Jones (1965) and Johansen (1960), essentially systems of linear
equations in changes in the variables, does allow change over time to be
modeled explicitly quite easily. In addition, they are quite moderate
in their data and parameterization requirements and can be solved more
readily and rapidly than nonlinear models. Not surprisingly, such
characteristics have made this type of model especially appealing to
economic historians (e.g., Pope (1972), Hueckel (1973), Lewis (1979),
Williamson & Lindert (1980), Darity (1982)). While their simple linear
structure is certainly a great advantage, a significant disadvantage,
the fact that they produce only approximate solutions, has perhaps been
insufficiently recognized. These models are based on local linear
approximations of supply and demand fucntions, so the errors should be
small for small changes in exogenous variables from the observed
equilibrium. Economic historians though are more often than not
interested in the effects of large changes - what if institutions had
developed differently? What would have happened if the tariff had been
abolished? In those circumstances the local linearity assumptions may
not be appropriate, and the results of such Jones-style CGE models
should be viewed with caution. New solution methods however are
available which divide the large change into a sequence of smaller
changes for which the local linearity assumptions would hold
approximately (Dixon, et al., pp. 199-251). The advantages of a simple
linear structure which can be readily solved thus can be retained, even
for large overall parameter shifts.

II.

One of the first and more controversial applications of a
simple general equilibrium model in the New Economic History was to the
question of relative labor scarcity and technical efficiency in American
and British manufacturing in the nineteenth century. Many British
visitors to the United States, such as the celebrated groups of

engineers in the 1850's, noted with great surprise the sophistication of
the machinery in so rude a country. The problem as posed by Habakkuk
was, "Why should mechanisation, standardisation, and mass production
have appeared before 1850 and to an extent which surprised reasonably
dispassionate English observers?" (1962, p. 5) The answer, assuming the
same technology between the U.S. and U.K., seemed to lie in relative
factor endowments, and in the American abundance of land in
particular. A high ratio of land to labor in agriculture was thought to
lead in turn to a high ratio of capital to labor in manufacturing, so
that abundant land made U.S. industry more capital-intensive than
British industry. In a two good, three factor general equilibrium model
which was solved analytically, Peter Temin (1966) showed that such a
result holds - abundant land attracts labor but not capital from
manufacturing so that the capital-labor ratio is higher in manufacturing
in the relatively land-abundant country, i.e., the U.S. However, under
these assumptions the capital-labor ratio is inversely related to the
interest rate. The U.S. interest rate was higher than the British, so
the U.S. capital-labor ratio in manufacturing must have been lower.
Rather than being labor scarce in manufacturing, as had been widely
believed, Temin concluded that the U.S. must have been relatively labor
abundant as compared with Britain.

This surprising conclusion provoked considerable criticism
directed primarily at the simplicity of the model in which only labor
and land were used to produce agricultural goods and only labor and
capital for manufactured goods. Other writers (e.g., Fogel, 1967)
suggested more general specifications of the production functions, such
as capital entering in the production of agricultural goods or
agricultural goods entering in the production of manufactured goods, in
order to reverse the conclusion. Summers & Clarke (1980) in turn
developed and solved analytically a model assuming Cobb-Douglas
production functions which could restore the traditional labor-scarcity
result if the rather questionable empirical assumption is made that
there was perfect international capital mobility in the antebellum
period.

The sectoral interrelationships in the problem require a
general equilibrium approach, a fact recognized by the protagonists in
the debate, and by structuring it in such a framework the points at

issue have been greatly clarified. A consensus has not developed
however, because there has not been widespread agreement on the proper
specification of the model. The debate has centered primarily on
developing theoretical models such that labor scarcity is or is not a
necessary result. The focus has shifted from the original historical
question identified by Rothbarth and Habakkuk to one of whether there is
necessarily a general link between land abundance and labor scarcity.
Remarkably little effort in this long controversy has been devoted to
developing relevant empirical evidence, but data are available on which
to base a well-specified model. In a recent paper James & Skinner
(1983) develop a CGE model, based on empirically estimated parameters
and factor endowments for the mid-nineteenth century United States and
Britain, which is capable of reproducing and reconciling the major
empirical stylized facts - that U.S. manufacturing was relatively labor
scarce only in some industries, that both real and nominal wages and
capital costs were higher in the U.S. than in Britain in the antebellum
period. They identify the crucial factor in U.S. labor scarcity as the
relative complementarity between capital and natural resources in
skilled manufacturing, a point emphasized earlier by David (1975) albeit
without empirical support. The course of this controversy is strong
evidence, I believe, of the value of numerical methods in economic
history and of the importance of developing relevant data for them.

Now I shall turn to some of the works of Jeffrey G.
Williamson who has been the pathbreaking figure in the application of
general equilibrium models to economic history over the last decade.
That questions may be raised about some points in his innovative and
imaginative works should be taken as evidence of the complexities
involved in using general equilibrium techniques to analyze historical
problems. I shall not consider here his general equilibrium modelling
of development in Meiji Japan, done with Kelley and Cheatham, in which
they finesse the problem of data deficiencies for late nineteenth-
century Japan by using parameters calculated from contemporary data from
Asian underdeveloped countries (Kelley et al., 1972; Kelley &
Williamson, 1974). Instead I shall focus on Williamson's enormously
ambitious counterfactual general equilibrium model of the postbellum
United States in his book Late Nineteenth-Century American Development
(1974). In it he attempts to address almost all of the major topics in

postbellum economic history: the impact of capital market
imperfections, changes in transport costs, variation in the terms of
trade, rates of land settlement, and immigration on economic growth,
causes of agrarian discontent, causes of the "Great Depression," and so
on.

        The two region, three sector, three factor neoclassical
growth model contains 72 equations. It is essentially a supply-oriented
long-term growth model with no cycles, no variations in aggregate demand
(demand functions only influence the volume of international and
interregional trade), and no deviations from full employment.
Agricultural goods and manufactures are produced in the Midwest, while
only manufactured goods are made in the East. Neither the South nor the
service sector is included, so the model encompasses only 36 percent of
the 1870 labor force. The model is a disequilibrium one in the sense
that there exist barriers to factor mobility across regions. Labor and
capital adjust to interregional differences in returns but not
completely in every period. The United States is taken as a small open
economy with relative prices fixed in world markets in the East, which
in turn translate into fixed Midwestern prices after adjusting by
exogenous transport costs.

        In brief, the retardation in American growth during the
psotbellum period is viewed as an adjustment to the economic impact of
the Civil War. The war, according to Williamson, was the principal
source of disequilibrium in the nineteenth-century U.S. economy, with
the savings rate, for example, almost doubling by late in the century.
The model quite successfully captures the slowing of growth due to a
rise in the capital-output and capital-labor ratios and a fall in the
rate of capital accumulation. Most of the sources of growth, however,
are exogenous - technical change, labor force growth, the rate of land
settlement. The capital stock is endogenous, but the savings rate is
exogenous. Less restrictive specifications are offered in later
chapters, such as making the savings rate and immigration flow
endogenous. Nevertheless, the model perhaps should be viewed primarily
as determining factor incomes and interregional and interindustry flows
of products and factors.

        The model ignores monetary factors and still successfully
reproduces the decline in the real interest rate over the late

nineteenth century. However, it misses the turning point in 1896 and
the subsequent acceleration in GNP and rises in real interest rates
rather badly (p. 118). The period of secular retardation is tracked
quite well, but the post-1896 revival remains a mystery here. Perhaps
the neglected monetary sector may have had some influence. Indeed, the
question arises as to how appropriate a CGE model with the fairly
standard characteristics of being in real terms with no monetary
influences, fully employed resources, and perfect competition is to the
late nineteenth century, a period encompassing substantial deviations
from full employment, a period of substantial change in industrial
structure and monetary turmoil, even if it is a long-run growth model.

Nevertheless, the accomplishments of the model in analyzing
questions of historical interest in late nineteenth-century American
development are far-reaching and impressive. The range of topics
addressed in fact is much too extensive to be discussed here, so I shall
limit myself to considering only a few areas. However, the multitude of
applications of the CGE model and profusion of results should be
noted. For example, Williamson tackles the long-standing question of
the impact of trade on growth and the influence of American agricultural
exports on the rate of U.S. industrialization in particular. He finds,
quite strikingly, that if the world market conditions for farm exports
had not deteriorated after 1870, i.e. if the terms of trade had remained
constant, industrialization in the U.S. would not have proceeded (pp.
214-215). While the direction of the terms of trade effect may be clear
from trade theory in this case (no interactions lead to counterintuitive
results), using a CGE model allows us to measure its quantitative
impact. Similarly, he finds that if the immigration restrictions of the
1920's had been imposed in 1870, real GNP per head would have been only
1 percent higher by 1910 (p. 249).

Was the decline in the rate of growth in the U.S. the result
of the closing or disappearance of the frontier? In this case the
Frederick Jackson Turner thesis is examined in terms of quantifying the
effects of an exogenous decrease in the growth rate of the stock of
land. Williamson finds that if the land stock had continued to growth
at the 4 percent per annum rate of the early 1870's through the period
1870-1905 the average annual growth rate of per capita income would have
been a negligible .1 percentage points higher than the actual rate (p.

174). However, Kahn finds an effect of essentially the same magnitude from a simple sources-of-growth, pencil-and-paper calculation, neglecting any induced changes in growth rates of other factors or induced changes in total factor productivity growth because of shifts in the composition of output (1981, pp. 9-11). The interaction or reallocation effects in the GE problem do not appear to be important here. Does this mean that CGE analysis is not appropriate or successful in such a problem? I would suggest that the answer to this question is no. A priori, the effects of reallocating factors across sectors in response to increased land growth may have seemed significant. Only after simulating the CGE model are we able to say that such effects were in fact small. Being able to quantify these effects, rather than neglecting or assuming them away, does represent progress in historical analysis.

Williamson's model seems appropriate for answering the question of the effects of the disappearance of the frontier on U.S. economic growth at the end of the nineteenth century, but can it be used to study the more general question of the influence of land abundance on American development? The answer here I believe is no, because the model is too simple for such a complex question. For one thing, the model neglects the possible influence of land or natural resources on technical choice and induced technical change (David, 1975), which we have seen is an important theme in American economic history. Also, allowing agricultural production only in the Midwest with only one output makes it difficult to capture the gains from regional specialization, which may have been significant (Fisher & Temin, 1970). Such considerations need to be specified more precisely before coming to any judgments about the influence of land on long-term U.S. growth.

The impact of the railroad on economic growth is another major theme in economic history. Robert Fogel (1964) attempted to quantify this by calculating the social saving (or increase in GNP) generated by the railroad as compared with a world with traditional transportation technologies (canals and wagons). His approach was comparative statics - comparing the actual 1890 United States with the railroad with the counterfactual U.S. without it. Fogel allows adjustments to the new (i.e., old) technology in the counterfactual

world, such as by letting land infeasible for commercial agriculture go
out of production. However, his solution is still basically a partial
equilibrium one. The pattern of final demands, for example, is held
constant in the comparisons. Other studies of the impact of railroads
(Fishlow, 1965; references cited in Fogel, 1979) all share this partial
equilibrium character as well.

This is clearly a general equilibrium problem. A
multisector model is needed to examine the effects of transport
improvements and Williamson approaches the question in such a
framework. His focus, however, is rather different from Fogel's. By
"social saving" Williamson means the effects on GNP of the fall in
transport costs due to changes in railroad rates over time rather than
from the substitution of the railroad for alternative methods of
transportation. He also, quite properly, tries to take the dynamic
effects of the railroad into account, that is, its impact on the pattern
and levels of savings and investment. In contrast to Fogel, he finds
the social saving generated by railroads to have been very
significant. If no interregional improvements in transportation had
taken place between 1871 and 1890, GNP would have been 21 percent lower
than it actually was (pp. 184-201).

The specification of Williamson's model however weakens the
force of this conclusion. The sector providing transportation services
is not specified, so that they are taken essentially as a free good.
The supply of transport services can be increased without diverting
resources from other sectors. Kahn, reworking Williamson's model, with
the crude assumption that transportation is produced entirely by
industrial labor and no capital, finds the estimate of social savings
generated over the 1871-1890 period falls by more than one-third (1981,
pp. 23-26). The dynamic effects on capital need to be considered more
carefully as well. If transportation innovations had not taken place
over the late nineteenth century, capital investment in railroads,
representing almost 20 percent of gross domestic investment between 1850
and 1880, would have been freed. Would it have moved into other
sectors? How much would the rates of savings and investment have
declined in the absence of the railroad? Even though in Williamson's
words, "net foreign capital imports formed an insignificant share of
gross domestic investment in post-Civil War America" (Williamson, 1974,

p. 33), foreign capital may well have represented a major portion of
railroad investment. For example, during the railroad construction boom
of 1871-74, 40 percent of new U.S. railroad bonds were issued in London
(Williamson, 1964, p. 131). In the absence of railroads would this
capital have been lost to the United States? The foreign sector and
foreign capital flows need to be specified more carefully and integrated
into the model to simulate the dynamic impact of the railroad.

      Another of Williamson's more interesting results is that
declining interregional transport costs had a substantial negative
influence on U.S. industrialization, particularly in the Midwest. The
Midwest industrial employment share would have been .427 in 1890 rather
than the actual .273 in the absence of a fall in transport costs. This
is primarily due to the fact that Williamson's transport costs for
agricultural goods falls rapidly over the period while those for
manufactured goods remain roughly stable. This conclusion that
railroads inhibited industrialization is all the more remarkable in view
of the fact that railroads have usually been ascribed a central role in
accounting for the growth of the manufacturing sector and of large
industrial firms after the Civil War. Both Alfred Chandler (1977) and
Oliver Williamson (1981) emphasize the expansion of the railroads,
making a system of mass distribution possible, in promoting the
development of the modern large, vertically integrated corporation.

      The impact of the railroads on manufacturing is much too
complex a topic to be analyzed within the framework of Williamson's
model. For one thing, even though it models changes in railroad rates
between West and East, it doesn't capture the geographical expansion of
the market through the expansion of the rail network within regions.
Even if rates had remained constant, the substitution of railroads for
wagons (following Fogel) must have had an impact on the size of the
potential market. In turn, Williamson's constant returns to scale
production functions do not allow the possibility of exploiting
increased economies of scale in response to the expansion of the
market. However, even in a CGE model with more sophisticated production
functions it would still be very difficult to analyze the impact of
railroad expansion on distribution. The railroad enabled manufacturers
to expand their market, but as they did so, it became increasingly
difficult to monitor the activities of local distributors closely at

greater and greater distances away. As a result, according to Oliver
Williamson, manufactures of products in which there was a possibility of
unintended quality debasement by distributors had a strong incentive to
integrate forward. Even though the effects of the railroads are
conceptually a general equilibrium problem, they may be very difficult
to deal with in a feasible CGE model.

The last aspect of Williamson's model that I would like to
consider here is that of financial markets. Capital market
disequilibrium is taken to have been due to the existence of
transactions costs in the interregional transfer of funds, and they are
assumed constant. The model successfully reproduces the observed
pattern of regional interest rates viewed as evidence of the evolution
of a national capital market - in the 1870's the Midwestern interest
rate is substantially higher than the Eastern one, but the differential
narrows dramatically over time. Williamson, however, rather than
focusing on structural changes within the capital market to account for
this narrowing, as earlier writers had done, instead emphasized economy-
wide conditions exogenous to the financial system. In particular, after
the Civil War there was strong investment demand in the Midwest,
primarily from railroads and to a lesser extent from mechanization in
agriculture and industrialization, forcing interest rates up. As
investment demand declined relatively over time, the gap between
Midwestern and Eastern interest rates narrowed (pp. 130-134). This
picture of national interest rate convergence over this period however
is rather misleading, because the model is not fully specified. In this
case the South was omitted from the model. Interest rates were quite
high after the Civil War in the South (and West) as well as in the
Midwest, but in the South it would seem implausible that it was due to
strong investment demand. The differential between Southern and Eastern
interest rates narrows over time as well but more slowly (James,
1978a). A more general explanation appears to be called for. Focusing
only on the Midwest and East in the CGE model and assuming perfect
competition does not lead to a convincing explanation for capital market
integration over the period.

Nevertheless, a fully elaborated CGE appears to be the only
satisfactory way to resolve finally the issue of the forces promoting
capital market integration - to identify explicitly the influences of

factors exogenous to the market from those resulting from structural change internal to the market. Rather paradoxically, the Williamson model is both too complex and too simple to address successfully such issues as the effects of the railroads on manufacturing growth or the determinants of capital market integration. Williamson tried to develop a large CGE model that could deal with most of the major issues of postbellum American economic history. The model is perhaps too complicated for a number of specific problems in the sense that many of the 72 equations may be extraneous to a given issue. However, at the same time, as we have seen, the specification is too simple to resolve these same questions convincingly. This would suggest that different CGE models need to be developed to study particular issues, holding constant factors not relevant to the problem. The ambitious attempt to construct a "true" or general or mega-CGE model to solve all the economic questions of the period has not been entirely successful.

The work of Williamson & Lindert on income distribution illustrate that a full-scale, "mega" model is not always necessary to take interactions into account. In their book American Inequality (1980) they investigate the sources or determinants of American wage inequality, as measured by the skilled-unskilled labor wage ratio. To explain changes in the skilled wage premium between 1839 and 1909 (omitting the Civil War decade) they develop a three output, four factor (land, capital, skilled, and unskilled labor) CGE model in the Jones tradition. Changes in prices and final outputs are determined endogenously with rates of growth of factor supplies and rates of factor-augmenting technical change specified exogenously. The exogeneity of the capital stock is initially troubling in view of the result that the rate of capital formation was by far the most important influence on changes in wage inequality (capital and skilled labor are taken to be relative complements), but in a later chapter the rates of savings and investment are made endogenous in a simultaneous equations system.

Strictly speaking, this is not a full general equilibrium system because there is no direct feedback between the endogenous savings-investment rate determined in the simultaneous equations and the exogenous rate of increase of the capital stock in the Jones-style model, or between the endogenously determined factor incomes in the

Jones model and the exogenous shift in the savings rate due to changes
in relative factor shares. Nevertheless, they draw strong conclusions
from such a structure by specifying upper bounds to the magnitude of
such feedback effects. They calculate the maximum shift in the savings
function that could have resulted from the increasing inequality of
factor income distribution over the period, making the extreme
assumption that saving is only out of property (human and nonhuman)
income. This in turn is shown to account for only a small part of the
observed increase in the savings-investment rate, allowing them to
conclude that even though inequality may have been a "by product" of
economic growth, it was not a necessary condition. In this case the CGE
model is kept to a quite tractable linear one, avoiding the difficulties
of specifying and solving a fully-endogenized model incorporating
savings and investment, while at the same time allowing strong
conclusions about the growth-inequality relationship to be drawn.

        One final area in which general equilibrium modelling has
been applied in economic history has been the welfare and distributional
effects of the tariff in the antebellum United States. The tariff was
most probably the major economic issue in the period before the Civil
War, having been strongly opposed by the South, the producer of the
principal exportable good, cotton. Metzler raised the possibility that
if the U.S. had had monopoly power in the cotton trade and demand was
relatively inelastic, the standard effects of tariffs on factor incomes
may have been reversed. Was the Southern diagnosis of their position as
victims of the tariff correct? If so, by how much were Southern incomes
reduced? The question of the incidence and magnitudes of the
redistributional effects of the tariff is one which demands general
equilibrium analysis. Clayne Pope (1972) in one of the first CGE models
applied to economic history considered this problem in the framework of
a simple Jones-style model. As we have noted however, such models are
not appropriate for analyzing the effects of large changes in variables
because they rely on local linear approximations of the underlying
functions, and the structure of the model was relatively inflexible as
well. For example, a composite factor of slaves and Southern land could
only be used in cotton production; capital in agriculture and
manufacturing are separate entities and no transfers across sectors were
permitted. Therefore, it was suitable for measuring only essentially

the short-run impact of relatively small changes in the tariff.

Using a fixed-point solution method, James (1978b) later developed a more general model of tariff impact. Such a formulation did not have to rely on linear approximations of supply and demand curves, and thus was suitable for examining the effects of large changes in the tariffs, such as its abolition. He finds in 1859 that if the tariff had been abolished, real income in the United States would have declined by somewhat more than 1 percent. Free laborers were the principal beneficiaries of the tariff, and, as they suspected, slaveholders were injured the most. Slaveholder income would have been over 10 percent higher in 1859 if the tariff had been abolished. In a second paper James (1981) calculates the optimal tariff for the 1859 United States. By computing a succession of equilibria under different tariff rates, he could identify the welfare maximizing tariff. As it turns out, the antebellum U.S. possessed unexploited monopoly power in world trade, with the optimal tariff in 1859 being around 35 percent as compared with the actual level of about 20 percent.

These papers use a relative approach to produce a rather persuasive result to a limited comparative statics exercise. They answer the question: What would have happened if the tariff had been abolished in 1859? However, the model is not dynamic. The model makes no attempt to consider any effects of the tariff on savings and investment and hence to characterize what the 1859 U.S. would have been like if it had always followed a free trade policy. It can answer static questions of tariff incidence, but not dynamic questions of its impact on the growth. On the other hand, such a question would be very difficult to handle with any precision because data on the savings propensities of different factor income classes at the time are not available.

III.

Historical problems therefore may present difficulties for the application of general equilibrium modelling, because of their complexity, data deficiencies, and problems of proper specification. Furthermore, it may be the case that, as Paul David argues, historical change is more correctly viewed as an unstable process, characterized by disequilibrium due to the influences of factors such as pervasive

economies of scale or learning-by-doing effects. In such an event, the
"Newtonian" conception of historically stable equilibria should be of
limited value in analyzing the past (David, 1975, pp. 1-16).
Nevertheless, I would like to suggest that general equilibrium modelling
has great strengths for studying some classes of historical problems and
that it can and should be used increasingly as a powerful analytical
technique in economic history. A CGE model allows detailed and explicit
counterfactuals to be posed and solved, an essential part of analyzing
the historical influence of a given event or factor. Alternative
policies, institutions, or regimes may be better compared and evaluated
in a CGE framework than in any other approach. For progress to be made
on complex historical issues involving global changes, for instance, CGE
techniques will have to be used increasingly. Only in an explicit model
can interdependence effects be assessed empirically to form a basis for
serious debate. The alternatives--vaguely formulated hypotheses with no
model or partial equilibrium analysis--simply are not satisfactory.
Better data and more sophisticated models should lead to CGE models
having more influence in the future in economic history.

 Although Jeffrey Williamson has touched on virtually every
general equilibrium problem for the late nineteenth-century United
States, let me outline briefly a few classes of problems that might be
profitably studied using general equilibrium techniques. This does not
imply however that implementation will necessarily be easy.

 The first class of general equilibrium problems that appear
in economic history are multi-regional, multi-country trade or
allocation problems. Williamson's model of late nineteenth-century
American development is, of course, primarily an interregional trade and
growth model. Mark Thomas (1983c) in a recent paper studies the
regional impact on income and employment of the British rearmament
program in the 1930's using a social accounting matrix (or SAM), an
input-output based multisectoral model. The SAM allows substantial
disaggregation, while Thomas argues that, because of the substantial
amounts of unemployed resources in Britain of the 1930's, the fixed
prices assumption is not inappropriate.

 One rather complicated multi-country trade problem is
determining the effects of the Atlantic slave trade, which followed
essentially a triangular pattern involving Africa, the American

colonies, and Britain. In the traditional depiction, Britain exported
finished goods to Africa for slaves, which were exported to the colonies
to produce raw materials, which were in turn exported to Britain for
use, directly or indirectly, in manufactured goods production. Darity
(1982) constructs a three-sector Jones-style model to test the
hypotheses of the "Caribbean School", that the Atlantic slave trade
played a central role in the industrialization of Europe, while at the
same time leading to the underdevelopment of Africa. Rather
interestingly, the neoclassical model does lend some support to this
Marxist theory of European development. For example, the European
growth rate turns out to be inversely related to the growth rate of the
African capital stock (p. 313). However, it is not clear how much
credence should be put in the results of this model, since there are no
balance of payments constraints imposed. The Jones-type model does
conserve on data, but still the parameter specifications are in many
cases quite arbitrary, and the results of the model are often quite
sensitive to them. If the labor share in colonial production of raw
materials (set at .8) had been 10 percent lower, not an implausible
range, for example, real income growth per capita in Europe would have
been 264 percent higher and in the colonies it would have been 175.7
percent lower (pp. 314-317). Another important multisector problem that
invites or rather demands a general equilibrium approach is analyzing
the economic effects of political unification. The cases of Germany and
Italy in the nineteenth century (or for that matter, the United States
in the eighteenth) would be very interesting but data problems may well
be severe.

        One final particularly hotly-contested sectoral allocation
problem is that of the retardation in economic growth in Victorian
Britain. In those well-known (actually McCloskey's) words, did
Victorian Britain fail? The slowing of economic growth in Britain and
the consequent loss of industrial leadership in the half century before
1914 had widely been taken as evidence of economic failure. The
British, it is said, remained committed to old, relatively stagnant
industries and failed to take sufficient advantage of new technologies
in expanding sectors, such as electricity, electrical engineering,
automobile manufacture, chemicals, and so on, as the Americans and
Germans had done. McCloskey, however, argues that such a critique is

basically hindsight and fails to consider seriously the profitability of the existing economic structure relative to alternatives at that time. Moreover, since the British economy came as close to the laissez-faire ideal as any, any profitable opportunities would surely have been seized (McCloskey, 1970).

Nevertheless, the notion that the British must have been doing something wrong dies hard. William Kennedy (1982) has calculated that if the expanding sectors in Britain between 1870 and 1914 had been the same relative size as their American counterparts (with the other sectors shrinking by that proportion) the British growth rate would have been 50 percent higher than the actual rate. This computation, however, is only illustrative of the possible effects of sectoral reallocations rather than necessarily a feasible alternative because it does not take resource constraints explicitly into account, although the feasibility of such a reallocation might be tested in a SAM (Thomas, 1983a).

Ultimately the question of whether the British economy could have grown faster with an alternative sectoral structure, and if so, by what magnitude, must be addressed in a CGE model, one which can deal satisfactorily with investment decisions in the presence of market imperfections. Edelstein (1982, pp. 62-71) in examining risk-return relatinships in the British capital market does find a "weak and unstable" preference for foreign issues between 1870 and 1889. However, more work first needs to be done on a precise specification of entrepreneurial failure. Kennedy, for example, argues that the capital market was biased toward foreign investment because insufficient information about British domestic companies was available to outside investors, an information asymmetry akin to a market for "lemons" (pp. 112-114). Constructing such a CGE model, to capture this picture of the Victorian economy, with entrepreneurial failure and the existence of unexploited profit opportunities due to informational problems, should be challenging.

Another area in which general equilibrium modelling has been influential has been that of tax incidence. Mark Thomas (1983b) is also examining the effects of the Liberal tax reforms in Edwardian England in the framework of a social accounting matrix. In the nineteenth century however taxes usually meant tariffs, and notwithstanding the studies of the antebellum tariff in the U.S. there are a number of other long-

standing issues that bear investigation in a CGE framework. One of the
most well-known problems would be to identify and quantify the effects
on welfare and income distribution of the repeal of the Corn laws in the
1840's and the move of Great Britain toward free trade. Using some
simple calculations McCloskey (1980) suggested that the move toward free
trade actually reduced British national income, although the final word
awaits a well-specified CGE model of the nineteenth-century British
economy.

Even though general equilibrium analysis has been used
primarily to study the welfare effects of tariffs, it can also be used
to study interindustry production or resource allocation effects of
protection. Such effects have usually been studied using effective
protection rates. Calculations of rates of effective protection are
based on a Leontief fixed-coefficient production technology, such as
those for the late nineteenth-century U.S. done by Hawke (1974) or for
1930's Britain by Capie (1978). This approach however ignores any
effects resulting from relative price changes resulting from tariffs
imposed on final or intermediate goods. It neglects demand and supply
elasticities, as well as the potential for input substitution and
subsequent factor reallocations across industries. Clearly the ultimate
resource allocation effects of a tariff must be assessed within the
framework of a CGE model. Taylor and Black (1974) find considerable
differences between partial and general equilibrium estimates of
resource pulls under tariffs. The measures based on effective
protection rates are seriously distorted relative to the full general
equilibrium result.

The relationship between tariffs and growth is also a topic
deserving exploration. The postbellum United States which had quite
high tariffs also experienced quite rapid economic growth. To make it
more interesting, there were two different international payments
regimes as well, floating exchange rates up to 1879 and fixed exchange
rates (the gold standard) thereafter. The macroeconomic impact of the
tariff in such a situation would be an interesting question to pursue.
Eichengreen (1981) has shown that a tariff under floating exchange rates
can have expansionary effects, at least in the short run. The impact of
the tariff could also be studied in a CGE model of the postbellum United
States under alternate international regimes - tariff effects do not

appear explicitly in Williamson's 1974 model. Another interesting case
of tariff macroeconomic effects might be the tariff increase in Britain
after leaving the gold standard during the interwar period.

Somewhat related to the general topic of tariffs is the
issue of the impact of the 1807-1809 U.S. embargo against Great
Britain. It has widely been described as being one of Mr. Jefferson's
most unfortunate decisions, having produced disastrous economic effects
domestically, but the magnitude of these consequences has never been
measured. Frankel (1982) concludes the embargo was in fact effective
from an examination of relative price movements, but does attempt to
quantify the effects. Although data are not abundant for this period in
American history, it may be possible to construct a simple CGE model in
which to quantify the economic impact of the embargo on the United
States.

A CGE framework is particularly suitable for topics in
income distribution because it captures the interactions between
production, distribution, and the pattern of demand. Similarly, it
enables the relationship between growth and inequality to be analyzed
because both distribution and accumulation can be made endogenous in the
model. Williamson & Lindert (1980), as we have seen, in studying the
relationship between economic growth in the United States and the
skilled-unskilled wage differential have examined the connection between
capital accumulation and inequality, as measured by differences in
factor incomes (also, Williamson, 1979). For the nineteenth-century
United States data are not available for any categories more detailed
than factor income. In particular, the data are not available to
examine directly the effects of growth on inequality by income class, or
for that matter on the other side of the coin, it is not possible to
study directly the influence of income inequality on savings and
economic growth. Under such circumstances, it may be possible to use a
CGE model with plausible parameters to simulate the possible effects of
economic growth on income inequality by class and vice versa for the
nineteenth century U.S. The CGE approach may be especially valuable in
view of the lack of direct evidence, so that data deficiencies in this
case would be an impetus rather than an impediment to the use of general
equilibrium models. Simulations appear to be the only way in which the
topic of income inequality by class over this period may be studied.

Probably the most controversial (or at least the longest controversy) income distribution issue in economic history has been the impact of the Industrial Revolution on workers' living standards in the period before 1840. Did workers share in the growth of real income per capita caused by industrialization, and if so by how much? These questions have been especially difficult to resolve because of the problems of disentangling the influences of industrialization from those of the wars with France which lasted essentially from 1793 to 1815. Virtually a quarter century of warfare must have had a considerable impact on the performance of the British economy. The effects of the early part of the Industrial Revolution can not be determined without allowing for the domestic impact of the Revolutionary and Napoleonic wars. Indeed, wars and their effects are certainly one of the major themes through economic history, but New Economic historians have devoted relatively little attention to them, with the possible exception of the American Civil War. In part this might be due to the complexity of modelling the impact of war. CGE analysis is well suited to capturing the complicated interactions that might result from wartime shifts in demands and supplies, as well as institutional changes. In general, it should be especially valuable in examining or factoring out the influences of exogenous shocks on the economy.

CGE models should be of great value in analyzing the effects of war in economic history but at the same time the difficulties in doing so should not be underestimated. The impact of the Napoleonic Wars in Britain has been examined in a Jones-style CGE model by Hueckel (1973) and by Williamson (1983). The first question which arises is whether such a model, based on linear approximations, is adequate to the task of simulating what would have happened if an event the magnitude of the Napoleonic Wars had not occurred. In this case, the new solution methods now allow the effects of large changes to be approximated fairly accurately in linear models, so even though such an objection may be raised to previous applications it does not hold in principle to using CGE's to quantify the effects of wars. However, regardless of whether the model is linear or nonlinear, there are other specification problems to be faced. In particular, the multiplicity of possible alternative scenarios to wartime make the specification of an appropriate counterfactual particularly difficult - for example, how would British

trade patterns have changed in the absence of the Napoleonic Wars?
Finally, there is the more fundamental objection that the structure of a
neoclassical CGE model is not appropriate for the British economy over
this time period. Patrick O'Brien (1983) has argued recently that the
British economy in the late eighteenth century was characterized by
reserves of underemployed labor and underutilized pools of savings, so
that the adverse effects of the war on factor supplies may have been
less than had been supposed. Here again data problems may make it
difficult to resolve this revived debate about proper specification and
hence to settle on a CGE model in which to assess the War's impact.

       In summary, I have argued that general equilibrium analysis
is a technique which can and should be of great value in economic
hsitory, where in evaluating the effects of particular policies,
institutions, or events interaction or interdependency considerations
may often be significant. However, thus far it has perhaps not had as
much influence as it should in part because of difficulties of finding
sufficient data on which to base well-specified CGE models and related
problems of inadequate or improper model specification. New economic
historians over the past two decades have proved very adept in
developing new sources of data, so with further data advances and more
sophisticated models these should be only short-term rather than long-
term impediments to the implementation of CGE models in economic
history.

References

Capie, Forest (1978). The British Tariff and Industrial Protection in
          the 1930's. Economic History Review, 31, 399-409.
Chandler, Jr., Alfred D. (1977). The Visible Hand. Cambridge, Mass.:
          Harvard University Press.
Darity, Jr., William A. (1982). A General Equilibrium Model of the
          Eighteenth-Century Atlantic Slave Trade: A Least-Likely Test
          for the Caribbean School. In Research in Economic History,
          Volume 7, ed. Paul Uselding, pp. 287-326. Greenwich, Conn.:
          JAI Press.
David, Paul A. (1975). Technical Choice, Innovation, and Economic
          Growth. Cambridge: Cambridge University Press.
Dixon, Peter, Parmenter, B. R., Sutton, John, & Vincent, D. P. (1982).
          Orani: A Multisectoral Model of the Australian Economy.
          Amsterdam: North Holland.
Edelstein, Michael (1982). Overseas Investment in the Age of High
          Imperialism. New York: Columbia University Press.
Eichengreen, Barry J. (1981). A Dynamic Model of Tariffs, Output, and
          Employment under Flexible Exchange Rates. Journal of
          International Economics, 11, 341-360.
Fisher, Franklin M. & Temin, Peter (1970). Regional Specialization and
          the Supply of Wheat in the United States, 1867-1914. Review
          of Economics and Statistics, 52, 134-149.
Fishlow, Albert (1965). American Railroads and the Transformation of
          the Antebellum Economy. Cambridge, Mass.: Harvard
          University Press.
Fogel, Robert W. (1964). Railroads and American Economic Growth.
          Baltimore: Johns Hopkins Press.
Fogel, Robert W. (1967). The Specification Problem in Economic
          History. Journal of Economic History, 27, 283-308.
Fogel, Robert W. (1979). Notes on the Social Saving Controversy.
          Journal of Economic History, 39, 1-54.
Frankel, Jeffrey (1982). The 1807-1809 Embargo Against Great Britain.
          Journal of Economic History, 42, 291-308.
Habakkuk, H. J. (1962). American and British Technology in the
          Nineteenth Century. Cambridge: Cambridge University Press.
Haines, Michael (1979). Industrial Work and the Family Life Cycle,
          1889-1890. In Research in Economic History, Volume 4, ed.
          Paul Uselding, pp. 289-356. Greenwich, Conn.: JAI Press.
Hawke, G. R. (1975). The United States Tariff and Industrial Protection
          in the Late Nineteenth Century. Economic History Review,
          28, 84-99.
Hueckel, Glenn (1973). War and the British Economy, 1793-1815: A
          General Equilibrium Analysis. Explorations in Economic
          History, 10, 365-396.
James, John A. (1978a). Money and Capital Markets in Postbellum
          America. Princeton: Princeton University Press.
James, John A. (1978b). The Welfare Effects of the Antebellum Tariff: A
          General Equilibrium Analysis. Explorations in Economic
          History, 15, 231-256.
James, John A. (1981). The Optimal Tariff in the Antebellum United
          States. American Economic Review, 71, 726-734.
James, John A. & Skinner, Jonathan (1983). Labor Scarcity in the
          Nineteenth Century United States. Unpublished manuscript.

Johansen, L. (1960). A Multi-Sectoral Study of Economic Growth. Amsterdam: North Holland.

Jones, Ronald W. (1965). The Structure of Simple General Equilibrium Models. Journal of Political Economy, 73, 557-572.

Jones, Ronald W. (1971). A Three-Factor Model in Theory, Trade, and History. In Trade, Balance of Payments, and Growth, ed. Jagdish Bhagwati et al., pp. 3-21. Amsterdam: North Holland.

Kahn, Charles (1981). The Use of Complicated Models as Explanations: A Reexamination of Williamson's Late 19th Century America. Unpublished manuscript.

Kelley, Allen, & Williamson, Jeffrey (1974). Lessons from Japanese Development: An Analytical Economic History. Chicago: University of Chicago Press.

Kelley, Allen, Williamson, Jeffrey, & Cheetham, Russell (1972). Dualistic Economic Development. Chicago: University of Chicago Press.

Kennedy, William P. (1982). Economic Growth and Structural Change in the United Kingdom, 1870-1914. Journal of Economic History, 42, 105-114.

Lewis, Frank (1979). Explaining the Shift of Labor from Agriculture to Industry in the U.S. Journal of Economic History, 39, 681-698.

McCloskey, Donald N. (1970). Did Victorian Britain Fail? Economic History Review, 23, 446-459.

McCloskey, Donald N. (1980). Magnanimous Albion: Free Trade and British National Income, 1841-1881. Explorations in Economic History, 17, 303-320.

O'Brien, Patrick (1983). The Impact of the Revolutionary and Napoleonic Wars, 1793-1815, on the Long Run Growth of the British Economy. Unpublished manuscript.

Passell, Peter, & Schmundt, Maria (1971). Pre-Civil War Land Policy and the Growth of Manufacturing. Explorations in Economic History, 9, 35-48.

Pope, Clayne (1972). The Impact of the Ante-Bellum Tariff on Income Distribution. Explorations in Economic History, 9, 375-421.

Summers, L., & Clarke, R. (1980). The Labour Scarcity Controversy Reconsidered. Economic Journal, 90, 129-139.

Taylor, Lance, & Black, Stephen (1974). Practical General Equilibrium Estimation of Resource Pulls under Trade Liberalization. Journal of International Economics, 4, 37-58.

Temin, Peter (1966). Labour Scarcity and the Problem of American Industrial Efficiency in the 1850's. Journal of Economic History, 26, 277-298.

Temin, Peter (1971a). General Equilibrium Models in Economic History. Journal of Economic History, 31, 58-75.

Temin, Peter (1971b). Labor Scarcity in America. Journal of Interdisciplinary History, 1, 251-264.

Thomas, Mark (1983a). An Input-Output Approach to the British Economy, 1890-1914. Unpublished manuscript.

Thomas, Mark (1983b). The Liberal Welfare Reforms and the Distribution of Income, 1906-1910. Unpublished manuscript.

Thomas, Mark (1983c). Rearmament and Economic Recovery in the Late 1930's. Economic History Review, 36, 552-579.

Williamson, Jeffrey G. (1964). American Growth and the Balance of
        Payments, 1820-1913. Chapel Hill, N.C.: University of North
        Carolina Press.
Williamson, Jeffrey G. (1967). Consumer Behavior in the Nineteenth
        Century: Carroll D. Wright's Massachusetts Workers in
        1875. Explorations in Entrepreneurial History, 4, 98-135.
Williamson, Jeffrey G. (1974). Late Nineteenth-Century American
        Development. Cambridge: Cambridge University Press.
Williamson, Jeffrey G. (1979). Inequality, Accumulation, and
        Technological Imbalance: A Growth-Equity Conflict in
        American History? Economic Development and Cultural Change,
        27, 231-253.
Williamson, Jeffrey G. (1980). Greasing the Wheels of Sputtering Export
        Engines: Midwestern Grains and American Growth.
        Explorations in Economic History, 17, 189-217.
Williamson, Jeffrey G. (1983). Why Was British Growth So Slow During
        the Industrial Revolution? Unpublished manuscript.
Williamson, Jeffrey G., & Lindert, Peter (1980). American Inequality.
        New York: Academic Press.
Williamson, Oliver (1981). The Modern Corporation: Origins, Evolution,
        Attributes. Journal of Economic Literature, 19, 1537-1568.